Monsters

and Revolutionaries

Françoise Vergès

MONSTERS AND

REVOLUTIONARIES

Colonial Family Romance

and *Métissage*

Duke University Press   Durham and London   1999

© 1999 Duke University Press
All rights reserved
Printed in the United States of America on acid-free paper ∞
Typeset in Adobe Garamond with Frutiger display
by Keystone Typesetting, Inc.
Library of Congress Cataloging-in-Publication Data appear
on the last printed page of this book.

For my parents, Laurence and Paul Vergès

and for Laurent Vergès (1955–1988)

Contents

꙾꙾

Illustrations

🙷

Preface

Bitter Sugar's Island

"But we can't go in," Chacko explained, "because we've been locked out. And when we look in through the windows, all we see are shadows. And when we try and listen, all we hear is a whispering. And we cannot understand the whispering, because our minds have been invaded by a war. A war that we have won and lost. The very worst sort of war. A war that captures dreams and re-dreams them. A war that has made us adore our conquerors and despise ourselves.

"We're Prisoners of War," Chacko said. "Our dreams have been doctored. We belong nowhere. We sail unanchored on troubled seas. We may never be allowed ashore. Our sorrows will never be sad enough. Our joys never happy enough. Our dreams never big enough. Our lives never important enough. To matter."

Arundhati Roy, *The God of Small Things*

This book is about the political history of my country, Réunion Island, and about emancipatory discourses developed there, about their power to shape reality, the possibilities they offered to, and the limits they imposed on, the population of a small island in the Indian Ocean. As the island's political history has been, since the 1930s, intimately tied to the history of my family, this book is also about members of my family. I do not underestimate the difficulty of retrieving the history of present times, when memory and history are deeply entangled. I play with what a French historian has called "human flesh," and I recognize that the stakes are still high. There is always the temptation to offer an anachronistic or embellished representation of the events. On which testimonies, which documents, which archives, do I rest my argument? How do I choose among archival sources? What do the exclusions that I perform say about the text's archaeological selection? I could not entirely avoid being ideologically involved, because traces of colonialism remain and my country is still dependent on France. My sympathies are clear. I side with the anticolonialists in Réunion, with those who have tried for decades to transform a political and economic situation of dependence. There is a high risk of producing a text that ends up being a plea, an apology, or an accusation rather than an explanation. It is a risk that I have consciously taken.

In the last decade, re-visions of the colonial and imperial project have shown that the study of a micropolitical colonial phenomenon can shed light on the complex mechanisms of the colonial relation. On the one hand, such a study insists on the singularity of each colonial experience; on the other, it allows analogies, comparisons, contrasts with other colonial experiences. We who come from our planet's smallest countries, where people had "no Industrial Revolution, no revolution of any kind, no Age of Anything, no world wars, no decades of turbulence balanced by decades of calm,"[1] may be said to "suffer from the traumata of insignificance."[2] As the Mauritian thinker Françoise Lionnet put it, insular "minorities" can "never be tempted by the illusions of leadership, never be deluded into thinking that we can represent anyone but ourselves."[3] Our joys will never be happy enough. Our dreams never big enough. Our lives never important enough. *To matter.*

Studies of French colonialism have paid little attention to the small islands of the French first colonial empire. They do not seem to offer a site of historical and political investigations that would add to postcolonial theory.[4] Yet within postcolonial investigations, the "power of historical locality becomes particularly persuasive," Homi Bhabha has written, "as the problem of cultural identity is staged in the discourse of geographical complexity—migration, diaspora, postcoloniality."[5] The history of Réunion (a colony) is part of the history of France (the empire). Geographically distanced but politically integrated, Réunion Island offers a specific site of research: it is a constituted minority within the nation France but is situated at the periphery; a mercenary minority to its neighbors (independent states that have to confront the West and global capitalism), for it is France's watchdog; a European territory (as a French department, Réunion belongs to the European Economic Community) in an African-Asian environment. What does the political history of emancipation in Réunion bring to postcolonial studies?

My country, Réunion Island, is a small island, formerly a colony on the margins of the French empire and now a French overseas department, a status the island acquired in 1946 along with the French Antilles and French Guiana.[6] These islands of sugar, which used to be known as the Vieilles Colonies (Old Colonies),[7] have been the "repressed" of French colonialism, territories that had not been conquered militarily, where there had been slavery, and that did not belong to the great narrative of the *mission civilisatrice.* Their demand for political assimilation rather than independence has generally situated them outside of the great narrative of decolonization.[8] It is from this position of "irrelevance" that I speak.

The formation of Réunion's society was literally the creation of a colonial act.[9] In 1642 the Compagnie Française de l'Orient took possession of the islands of the Mascarene archipelago in the name of the king of France. There were *no* inhabitants on Réunion when it was colonized. *None.* No native population massacred, no military conquest, no heroic battles and defeats, but settlement, colonization, slavery, and colonialism.[10] In 1674 governor Jacob De La Haye wrote the first law that sought to prohibit *métissage,* which was perceived as leading to degeneration and lack of discipline.[11]

There was slavery on the island at the end of the seventeenth century.[12] In December 1723 the French state published the *Code Noir,* a series of prescriptions regulating the slave's life.[13] Slaves, who, in the first years of colonization, had been bought in India, were now bought in Madagascar and Africa.[14] Sugar deeply transformed the island's social and cultural order. The plantation became the crucible of "creolization," the process whereby individuals of different cultures, languages, and religions were thrown together and invented a new language, Creole, a new culture, and a new social organization. Sugar also affected the pattern of land ownership. Poor white farmers lost their lands to wealthier landowners and were pushed inland. The existence of an important group of poor whites affected the ways in which race[15] and class interacted.

Slavery was abolished in 1848. But the plantation system in Réunion expanded even more *after* the abolition of slavery, affecting the class and racial distribution of the society differently than it did in the French Antilles. In Réunion, the great demand for a cheap workforce *after* the emancipation of the slaves led the landowners to look to a large diversity of sources for their workforce.[16] Indentured workers were sought in India,[17] Malaysia, China, Madagascar, and Africa.[18] Different religious beliefs (Tamil, Muslim, Christian, Buddhist, animist), languages, cultures, and traditions were put into contact in a small space. In the 1930s, a coalition of workers and republicans demanded the end of Réunion's colonial status and the assimilation of the island into the French republic. Their discourse mixed republican ideals with working-class politics, articulating anticolonialism with workers' rights. The island became a French overseas department on March 19, 1946.

Sugar, bitter sugar, has shaped Réunion's class formation, and we live with its legacy.[19] Today members of the wealthy white Creole families, descendants of landowners and factory owners, hold important positions in banking and commerce. Among the descendants of Indians, Muslims, and Chinese workers, some families have reached middle-class status and entered political life. The development of the civil service in the 1960s has facilitated the emergence of an important petite bourgeoisie, who earn, thanks to a colonial law still in effect, greater salaries and pay fewer taxes than civil servants in the metropole. The majority of the population—sharecroppers, tenant farmers, unemployed, skilled and unskilled workers, domestics, employees in the private sector—live on the margins of the postcolonial society. They are the descendants of slaves and poor whites. In the last decades, Réunion has been transformed into a "window" of French capitalism. Consumer goods imported from the metropole and the European Economic Community, commercial malls, cellular phones, all the gadgets of postmodern life, have given to the island the look of a French suburb in the tropics. The artificial wealth exhibits the schizophrenic character of a peculiar postcoloniality: the recolonization of a postcolony.[20] It feeds a certain French colonial nostalgia. It supports the fantasy that somewhere colonization has succeeded, blending peoples from diverse cultures under the paternalistic control of French republicanism.

The paradox has been that the 1946 law brought more French people to the island than ever before. French civil servants have imported their ways of living and their idealization of European "modernization." They have conveyed with them the metropolitan conviction that colonialism ended with the Algerian War and that racism has not been intimately connected with the empire and French national identity. As French metropolitans hold the majority of higher-rank functions in the administration, the judicial system, and the university and schools, they have been intent on imposing their ideology. Réunion Island, which belongs to the Indian Ocean Rim, is thus in the paradoxical position of being an appendage of a European country in an African-Asian region, running the risk of becoming an obsolete archaism. Resistance to the recolonization of the island has taken new cultural and political forms: affirmation of Creole as a language, rejection of the ways of living of *zoreils* (the name given to French metropolitans), and the desire for a greater cultural, political, and economic integration with the countries of the Indian Ocean Rim.

To a certain extent, these facts about Réunion's history are, as Édouard Glissant has noted for Martinique, deceptive. I look at the processes through which the Réunionnais constituted, and are still in the process of constituting, their Creoleness. In Réunion, there is no lost community to retrieve. Our "imagined community" is still in formation.

There is another genesis to this research, which partly explains its orientation. It started in March 1986. The United States was celebrating the bicentennial of Ellis Island with a big party in the harbor of New York and the renovation of the Statue of Liberty and Ellis Island. Magazines such as *Newsweek* and *Time* were telling the saga of millions of European families who had come through Ellis Island to live the "American Dream." On the other side of the country, at the border between California and Mexico, between the First World and the Third World, there was another kind of "Ellis Island," the U.S. consulate at Tijuana, Baja California.

In Southern California, the border with Mexico was becoming the last "wall" against the "invasion of illegal aliens," the protective barrier of a wealthy, white, healthy, educated group against a poor, brown, unhealthy, uneducated group. The *frontera* was entering political rhetoric, foreshadowing the debate of the 1990s about the meaning of citizenship in the country. The U.S. consulate at Tijuana was one of the sites where the battle to contain the "invading hordes" was taking place. The collapse of the Mexican economy, the civil wars waged by governments against their own peoples in El Salvador and Guatemala led people toward Tijuana, toward El Norte.

That year, 1986, I lived in Rosarito, a Mexican village on the coast some miles south of Tijuana. I was waiting for my entry papers to be processed, to enter the United States of America as a "legal immigrant." Although I was protected by my European passport and by the knowledge that if I failed to obtain a visa, I would not have to return to a country devastated by war, my life threatened by death squads, without the hope of a job, I was, as any person waiting is, subjected to the small humiliations that go everywhere in the world with being allowed by a state to enter its territory.[21] These small humiliations are intimately part of the immigration process. They are not aberrations, consequences of the employees' moods or even racism (though these aspects play a role). They *constitute* the immigration process. They consist in letting one believe that *all* the papers are finally in hand and announcing at the end of the day that one must come back; of asking women candidates for immigrant status to undress during the medical visit and to wear flimsy paper dresses while waiting to be examined by a male doctor. One waits for hours, hoping, lying, dissimulating, sharing happy endings or crushing refusals to the demands. Families sleep outside the consulate to be the first in line. They have a look of enduring patience, the patience of the dispossessed.

Between visits at the consulate, I read. I read while watching the whales going back to the northern waters of America, watching Mexican families having big picnics on the Rosarito beach, watching every weekend the young *gringos* and *gringas* getting drunk on margaritas. And that year, as I waited for the next appointment at the U.S. consulate, among the many books I read was one by Michael Paul Rogin, *Fathers and Children: Andrew Jackson and the Subjugation of the American Indian.* I recognized in the book what I thought historical political analysis should be. The book remained to me a model of research. My days in Rosarito were shaped by my reading of Rogin's analysis of how "America clearly began not with primal innocence and consent but with acts of force and fraud." The words were echoes of the paranoid discourse about the border with Mexico, the patronizing attitude of the consulate officers, and the arrogance of the bicentennial celebration. But these words also spoke of resistance, the possibility of critique and radical politics. I entered the United States on Bastille Day of 1986. In 1989 I was accepted into the Ph.D. program of the Political Science Department at the University of California at Berkeley, and Professor Rogin agreed to be chair of my dissertation committee. From Réunion to Algiers to Paris to Rosarito and Berkeley, I finally found the distance and a sufficiently foreign language to speak of the political history of my country. I also found the intellectual environment that made it possible.

Acknowledgments

I want here to acknowledge the work of the poets, writers, and singers, among them Aimé Césaire, Maryse Condé, Firmin Viry, and Boris Gamaleya, who gave Creole culture, literature, and language its deserved place. I want to thank the friends and activists in Réunion who, with their political action, had a large impact on this book, and Djamila Bouhired, whose courage inspired my childhood.

Many of the people I have to thank will recognize parts of conversation in these pages. Others will probably be surprised to see the final form to which some ongoing exchanges have ultimately led.

I want to thank Professor Albert Memmi and Professor Hanna Fenichel Pitkin, who generously gave me their time, advice, and support. The Regional Council of Réunion Island, the University of California at Berkeley, and the Doreen B. Townsend Center for the Humanities gave me their financial support.

The evolution of my research owes a personal debt to a group of close friends and colleagues, who throughout the years listened to me and helped in any way they could, and who, with their comments and continual stimulation, made this project a worthy endeavor. They are so many that I am bound to forget some of them, but they must know that I remain deeply indebted to all of them. In Réunion, they are Rémi Boniface, Ghislène Caillière, Cécile

Catapoullé, Sonia Chane-Kune, Jean-Marcel Courteaud, Brigitte Croisier, Marina Dobaria, Prosper Éve, Elie Hoareau, Claude and Edmundo Lopez, Jean-Claude Carpanin Marimoutou, Ginette Ramassamy, Jean-François Reverzy, Pierre Vergès, and William Zitte. In France, Etel Adnan, Ida Aït-El-Hadj, Raymonde Coudert, Antoine and Sylvie De Baecque, Sylvie Durastanti, Thérèse Filippi, Nadia DuLuc-Legendre, Catherine Imbert, Marie-Pierre Macia, Pascale Pillet and Jean-Max Toubeau, whose summer house has always been a friendly refuge, and Jacques Vergès. In the United States, my friends Nancie Caraway and Kathleen B. Jones, Laura Lomas, Kate McCullough, and Lisa Wedeen, and my *companera* Jackie Orr. In London, Isaac Julien, Mark Nash, and Céline Surprenant. There are others, friends and intellectual companions: Parveen Adams, Ann Banfield, Victor Burgin, Maryse Condé, Assia Djebar, Mariane Ferme, Luca D'Isanto, Jacques Hassoun, Carla Hesse, Françoise Lionnet, David Lloyd, Achille Mbembe, Chantal Mouffe, Ernesto Laclau, Lydie Moudileno, Francette Pacteau, Stefania Pandolfo, Richard Philcox, Paul Rabinow, Michael Rogin, Ann Smock, Paul Thomas, the members of the Imperialism and Colonialism Study Group and of the Doreen B. Townsend Center for the Humanities; and François Flahault.

I want to thank the anonymous readers of my manuscript and my editor Ken Wissoker. Bill Henry and Paula Dragosh provided indispensable editorial assistance. This work is dedicated to my parents, Laurence and Paul Vergès, with respect, admiration, and gratitude for their constant courage, determination, and love, and to the memory of my brother Laurent, killed in October 1988.

1

The Family Romance of

French Colonialism and *Métissage*

❦

This research emerged out of a number of questions I have carried with me over the years as a child and adolescent in Réunion Island, as a woman, a postcolonial subject living in Algeria, France, and the United States: What is a decolonized subject? What are the historical conditions of formation of discourses of colonial emancipation? Growing up in a former colony that remains dependent on France, I was haunted by these questions. Why did my anticolonialist foremothers and forefathers choose greater integration with France rather than independence? What was the importance of the French republican ideal of liberty, equality, fraternity for the colonial movement of emancipation? The great narratives of emancipation weigh on us, imprisoning us, and yet they offer us the means to escape.

As a young woman, I shared with many the myth of a pure historical rupture, that moment through which the colonized would accede to a dis-alienated self. I then spoke with the vocabulary of historical rupture: only a clear, sharp break with the metropole would guarantee the possibility of constructing a decolonized culture and identity that would affirm its radical difference with the legacy of colonialism and give birth to a purified identity, cleansed from the alienating, shameful elements of colonization. For lack of conforming to this ideal model, for lack of accomplishing this psychological repudiation, any emancipatory attempt was doomed to failure, any action inscribed in morbid repetition. For many of us, the notion of rupture and the "myth of historical rupture"[1] played determining roles in our conception of colonial emancipation. We exchanged a great narrative for another one. Rejecting the universalizing Western narrative of the discourse of rights and its historical complicity with exploitation and colonization, we sought theoretical purity and espoused the great narrative of anti-Western emancipatory discourse. The redemptive message of identity legitimized our contempt for the complexity of human relations, supported our desire for a clear explanation of human contradictions, and offered us a dream of regeneration through the rejection of past ideals and theories. We often confused radicalism with brutality, processes of identification with a search for authentic identity, political emancipation with a struggle for "roots."

However, when in 1992 to 1993 I went to Réunion, thanks to a research fellowship, I realized that I could not fully explain why anticolonialists had, in this French colony, for centuries adopted the French republican ideal, why they had followed the path of political emancipation, why this island wanted to remain French. Neither could I explain the violence of political *and* social life, and the reasons why French civil servants tended to adopt a colonial attitude quite rapidly in their stay. Or rather, I did have explanations, but they appeared ideological rationalizations once brought face-to-face with the complex, ambiguous world of politics. My confrontation with the social and cultural reality of Algeria in the early seventies, with feminism and radical politics in France in the seventies, and with the politics of race, class, and gender in the United States in the eighties progressively helped me to reconsider the approaches of my study. I decided to research the history of the political movement for colonial emancipation in Réunion Island from the abolition of slavery to the present. This is therefore a study of politics in a French colony and postcolony, focusing on the political struggle for emancipation and the reactive strategies of discipline and control developed by the French state and its representatives on the island.

As France still controls Réunion, it is impossible to examine the political struggle without casting the state as a central character. There are other legitimate approaches, but to me working through this history appeared a necessity to untie the bonds of fantasized alienation and to reestablish a filiation. I wanted to confront a reality that deconstructed illusions, idealizations, and romantic images of struggle. I thought that it was important to work through the Western and Christian origins of these idealizations and romantic images. Years of militancy in anticolonialist movements and, above all, in a French women's group unfortunately removed me from any serious intellectual enterprise. They gave me, though, an experience that made me suspicious of any form of romanticism.[2] I learned that human relations could not be reduced to a battle of interests. Passions, malice, hate, vindictiveness, altruism, antipathy, and love play an important role in shaping human behavior. The desire for recognition and the aspiration for dignity have mobilized individuals and groups as much as the demand for rights.[3]

Two notions run through this study: "colonial family romance" and "*métissage.*"[4] Colonial family romance because French republican colonial rhetoric filled the tie between France and its colony with intimate meaning, creating what Freud has called a "family romance," the fiction developed by children about imagined parents. In the colonial relation, however, it was a fiction created by the *colonial power* that substituted a set of imaginary parents, La Mère-Patrie and her children the colonized, for the real parents of the colonized, who were slaves, colonists, and indentured workers. Lynn Hunt has eloquently shown, in *The Family Romance of the French Revolution,* why one must pay attention to the "collective, unconscious images of the familial order that underlie politics."[5] The "family romances" of the French Revolution "were metaphors for political life, metaphors that developed in response to changing events (and in response to long-term cultural trends), but also metaphors that drove the revolutionary process forward."[6]

Freud traces the source of the romance back to the child's "most intense and most momentous wish" to be like his parents, who are the source of all beliefs.[7] The child, however, comes to realize that his parents are not the powerful persons he imagined. Freud argues that this fantasy is stronger among boys than girls because a "boy is far more inclined to feel hostile impulses towards his father than towards his mother, and, hence, has a far more intense desire to get free from *him* than from *her.*" Humiliated, disappointed, the child starts to compare and observe, to "replace faith with examination, eternity with the troubling reality of time."[8] A "biographical fable" is invented, "expressly conceived to explain the inexplicable shame of being wrongly born, badly off, and badly loved and that fable still gives him the means to complain, to console and to avenge himself, in a single movement of the imagination."[9] The child imagines a new set of parents, who are replaced in his imagination by persons of better birth. By associating this notion and the metaphor of social and political organization, the family, Hunt presents "both a narrative and a mode of knowledge of the revolutionary event."[10]

The colonial family romance, I argue, derived its character from the French Revolution's family romance. The rhetoric of the French revolutionary community of brothers paradoxically justified the subjugation of peoples in the name of *fraternité, liberté, égalité.* The French republicans were convinced that France was bringing the republican ideal to peoples under the yoke of feudalism. In the prerevolutionary romance of colonialism, the relations between the colony and the metropole were not suffused with affective ties and metaphors of love and protection. Men went to the colony to find gold or bring the word of Christ. The "savage" occupied a complex site in the European imaginary, whether as a monster or an innocent, but there was no discourse about bringing a political ideal.[11] The monarchy had imposed patriarchal rule; the republic would propose a rule among equals, under the symbol of Marianne. The state would play the role of a benevolent mediator, protecting the children against patriarchal tyranny. The republic's protection would naturally extend to her colonies. Colonization was the expansion of republican brotherhood, and France was La Mère-Patrie, protecting her colonized children from the abuse of local tyrants. With this fable, the French state aspired to substitute an ideal model of filiation for the historical colonial filiation. Colonial family romance invented *one* parent, the Mère-Patrie, and consequently sought to impose a process of identification that rejected the reality that each human being has *two* parents. Colonial family romance established a founding myth, the myth of the "unique root" against which Édouard Glissant has argued.[12] The construction of an ideal parent associated with whiteness and Europe denied the dimension of race in the making of colonial identity. The fable gave France the means to console itself when colonized "children" would rebel and to repress the reasons for which they rejected her. It was their ingratitude, rather than her tyrannical "love," that explained their behavior.

The family romance is the invention of children. Yet in the case of the colony, it was the invention of men constructing France as the parents of the colonized. Colonial family romance is therefore a romance created by the colonial "parents" who invented a single parent (La Mère-Patrie), a character mixing the feminine and the masculine: the castrating *and* protective mother. This creation had social meaning. The displacement of parenthood from the colonized parents to an abstract figure denied the reality of sexual intercourse between individuals on the island and situated the colonized as perennial children. However, colonial family romance was also invented by *revolutionary* men who embraced the ideal of fraternity and liberty and aspired to expand a social bond based on this ideal. The fraternal bond dreamed by metropolitan brothers was affected by colonialism and its logic of racism. Colonized men might be their brothers, but they were their little brothers. In the empire, fraternity masked the continuity of primogeniture—the law whereby the firstborn son received the heritage to the detriment of the other brothers and of the sisters. Yet this fiction was adopted by Réunion's educated colored, intellectuals, workers, and peasants. They imagined themselves as the brothers of French citizens. And they appealed to France to protect them against the tyrannical power of the landowners. The latter defended an old regime in which they held the tyrannical power of the patriarch. Revolution had not happened in Réunion, the colonized said. The 1794 abolition of slavery had not been accomplished because of the colonial lobbies, the passivity of the metropolitan brothers, and then their defeat. An "ideological bond was imagined in place of a political project. . . . The French people, the Gallick Hercules claimed to be the *frère aîné* [the older brother] of the other peoples, which, while remaining in a minor position, exchanged their filial subjection to previous authorities against a probably more oppressive dependency, but which justified itself with the idea of progress invented by the revolutionary culture."[13]

Yet because the colonial family romance was the child of the French Revolution, because it wanted to be a republican romance, it both suffused the colonial relation with familial metaphors and

offered the grounds to challenge French colonialism. It brought
with it the republican ideal of liberty and fraternity, and the promise of equality among peoples. To that extent, though it limited
their demands for autonomy, colonized Creoles would remain attached to the notion that France was their protector against domestic tyrants well into the mid–twentieth century.[14] And the words
liberty, equality, and *fraternity* continued to carry with them the
utopian dream of a more just society. The colonial family romance
did not remain fixed throughout colonial history. Its representations, its tropes, its discourse changed, but the structure remained.
Its perpetuation was the result of the need to claim the inferiority of
colonized peoples and of the peculiarity of French imperial discourse that declared colonization a republican duty. It played a
greater role in the Vieilles Colonies than in the other parts of
the empire because there the battle between the Old Regime and
French Revolution continued late into the twentieth century. Even
1848, the year slavery was abolished in the French colonies, did not
abolish the feudal and racist world of the plantation.

The family romance of French colonialism created a highly idealized maternal space, France La Mère-Patrie.[15] Dependence and
debt were the operative elements of the colonial family's dynamics.
Its rhetoric displaced social relations determined by the symbolic
and economic organization of exchange between the colony and
the metropole and replaced them with the theme of continuous
debt of the colony to its metropole. Colonized "children" had
contracted a debt to France. My goal is to show that in the colonial
family romance, the colonial *don*[16] (gift) transformed the colonized
into children permanently indebted to La Mère-Patrie. The debt
was constituted by the ideals of the French Revolution, of the
French republic. In territories where feudalism, barbarism, or
backwardness reigned, maternal France had brought Enlightenment and progress. She would save her children and elevate them
toward full humanness. The children, once women and men,
would naturally want to pay their debt. The transformation of
revolutionary ideals into maternal *dons* sought to deprive individuals of their agency. In the colonial family romance, children remained children forever. It was "full payment, forever. Because the
rescuer wanted to hear his name, not mimicked but adored."[17] To
subvert the terms of the colonial family romance, the colonized

reconstructed the ideals for what they were: "A source of conflicts forever."[18]

The colonial family romance produced two *fixed* categories, the giving colonizers and the receiving colonized. Studying its idiom means distinguishing between what was given and what was not given, how the *don* of France was transformed and reinterpreted by the colonial romance. The "gift," Marcel Mauss has argued in his *Essai sur le don,* introduces an elaborate web of social relations known as the symbolic order. There is always the expectation of a return, accompanied by a certain security that derives from such expectations. In the colonial political romance, the *don* of France was presented as a selfless, generous gesture, a pure *don,* and yet there was a sentiment among the colonized that they were neglected *and* in constant debt. Deconstructing the colonial romance would thus mean determining what in the romance put the colonized in perpetual debt. Precious woods, sugar, minerals, bodies to fight her wars, none of this would be enough to repay France for what she had given. The debt was construed between two unequal groups, not between subjects who mutually recognized each other as subjects. The colonized, constructed as "receivers," were not recognized as equals, and thus their reciprocal *don* never satisfied the metropole. And the colonial *don* could never satisfy the colonized. To begin with, it could not be perceived as Mauss's *don* because the colonized knew that it was not inscribed in an intersubjective relation between equal subjects.[19] The colonized continued to be second-class citizens, and their countries remained under French colonial control. They *gave* to the French nation wealth, sexualities, sites to excite the European imaginary, and received slavery and colonialism. The debt that they recognized was what France *owed* them: access to the vocabulary of rights and the democratic ideal. Yet when the colonized wanted to act on this debt, demanding their inclusion in the community of equals, France refused.

I read the colonial family romance partly as the construction of colonial relations as a debt owed by the colonized to the metropole and partly as the fantasy of an ideal model of filiation in which there is only one parent, the republic.[20] Today, the language of debt has been rewritten as the "culture of dependence," the process whereby a minority wants more and more from the metropole, which would like to wean its dependents. Réunionnais who receive welfare are said to have lost the "desire to work" and to revel in dependency. Dependency, it is said, breeds laziness and criminality and encourages single female-headed families. Matrifocality and dependency reinforce each other, experts argue, to produce an infantilized population, under the power of the mother. The rhetoric about dependency as disease, infection, and degeneration hides a reality. Réunion Island *is* dependent, economically and politically, on France. The space of autonomy that the island has won has been the result of long years of struggle. The French state long resisted any project that would open an autonomous space in the relation between the metropole and the island. Even today, the final decision rests in the hands of the French state. By invoking a Creole pathological dependence, the terms of the colonial debt are still operating: France is giving, giving, giving but receives nothing in return. The questions that one must ask are: What use is Réunion's dependency for the French state? What functions does this dependency ensure? In what strategies of power is it integrated? How does dependence function? If French assimilation had failed, why shift the blame of the failure on the community that had been subjected to slavery and colonialism? The notion of colonial family romance offers an interpretative tool that allows a reading of colonial relations that takes into account the metaphors organizing these relations. It is about *reraconter* (telling again) different moments in which the metaphor of family relations leads to a new narrative of these moments.

In Réunion, the fable of the colonial family romance encountered the reality of métissage. To the European imaginary, métissage was a site of both fascination and repulsion. The poetics and politics of blood invaded European literature and sciences in the empire. To the colonized, *métissage* was a term that spoke of the cultural and social matrix of diversity born of colonization and assimilation into the colonial project. Métissage was a site of dispute, for the term contained at heart an ambiguity, an ambivalence that to some anticolonialists offered a radical challenge to the process of mono-identification and European racism, and to others meant the disappearance of differences and a lapse of memory.

The question is whether métissage was a subversive notion in Réunion or another form of assimilation. In her autobiographical novel *Métisse,* the Réunionnais writer Monique Boyer both acknowledged *and* disavowed the origins of the island's population. A fully accepted métissage, she has said, would be built only on the withering away of the memory of slavery: "Every Réunionnais knows about his or her *métissage* but all have a difficulty *forgetting slavery*."[21] The story of her parents was the story of the island, a story of exile, separation, violence, and forced silence, but the conflictual history has ended with her, the *métis* child.[22] Slavery has become a "tragic," traumatic event that it is better to forget for the sake of reconciliation than to remember as a *constitutive* reality. Slavery was *the secret de famille*. Amnesia was the operative word.

Postcolonial discourse has criticized the notion of métissage and preferred the notions of grafting,[23] hybridity, rhizome, creolization, *peuple banyan*.[24] Édouard Glissant, though he wrote that métissage, which opposes essentialism,[25] is a "proposition" in which the glorification of a "unique origin, race being its guardian," is inoperative, has favored the notion of "creolization."[26] Creolization describes the cultures and identities forged through the plantation economic system, insularity, the permanence of Africanness, orality, the role of sugarcane, corn, and chili.[27] To Antonio Benitez-Rojo, métissage is a "form of nationality that would resolve the deep racial and cultural conflicts by means of a reduction or synthesis."[28] In the empire, métissage was both a fact—biological mixing—and a value—the colonized's condemnation of pure blood ideology and the expression of colonial anxiety.[29] Soon associated with the discourse of racial harmony and reconciliation, métissage lost what had once been its radical dimension. It became synonymous with denial and compromise. It was about *two* elements (black/white, Asian/white), whereas hybridity, creolization, peuple banyan, insisted on multiplicity, temporalities, excesses, disruptions. The continuing contest about métissage, its unstable foundations and constant renegotiation, shows how the term remains fundamentally charged with ambivalence. I have nonetheless focused on the notion of métissage because of its history as a source of anxiety and a site of rhetorical subversion in the empire.[30]

My reasons for adopting métissage as a focal concept have to do with the fact that métissage was developed *in the colonial world* as a response to European racism and the discourse of mono-ethnicism, of blood and nation. Little or no attention has been given to the reasons why métissage awakened anxiety. The colonial anxiety that this term historically brought up, signified, I contend, more than just a desire to absorb differences, an appeal to symbiosis, the wish to erase differences. Reading colonial anxiety about métissage reveals the ways in which legal, medical, and political discourses manipulated the signification of sexual relations in the empire.[31] The fear of, and desire for, métissage is inscribed in the history of human societies.[32] Although what accounts for these variations has not yet been the object of a comprehensive study, it seems that what has remained constant has been a suspicion about the loyalty of the métis because of their "division." And it is this suspicion that, I think, makes the narrative of métissage as a poetics and politics of blood inseparable from the dominant narrative about identity, the narrative of authenticity, and inseparable from the colonial world and its narrative of segregation.

To compound the difficulty, it is clear that the "West" is now not really disturbed with the addition of the métis' voice to the choir of the postcolonial world. There is no reason to "share the white man's helplessly hypocritical attitudes towards the time-honoured and universal mingling."[33] Global capitalism can absorb métissage as another commodity.[34] Métissage has become a trope in European advertising, business, and the media to signify the new globalization of the world, its fundamental unity under the sign of capital. The social organization of slavery and colonialism produced métissage, that is, an intermixing of groups, new cultural forms, new languages, and an identity that remained indecisive. Now the discourse of global capitalism has adopted métissage as a new cultural commodity. People are forced to emigrate in search of jobs, to escape war and political persecution, and they come to the metropole, the megapoles of the North and the South. The new social formations can be called *métissées,* a challenge to the narrowness of the nation-state, a celebration of the migrant as the postmodern individual, between languages and cultures, capable of learning new skills, of moving freely in the "global village," as long as the division of labor is preserved, as long as the métis remains a consumer, a worker, or an intellectual, or even a capitalist—in other words, as long as the symbolic filiation, to the slave, the indentured worker, the migrant worker, is not affirmed politically and culturally. Hence the "regional diversity" of a tropical, exotic island would not threaten the national unity of France.[35] Réunion, represented as an Eden, could become a model society in which cultural and ethnic differences are harmoniously mixed, a "dreamt society, without class violence or revolt."[36]

Thinking métissage, I argue, requires accepting a genealogy and a heritage. In other words, the recognition of a past of rape, violence, slavery, and the recognition of our own complicity with the wicked ways of the world. No projection onto the Other, no denial of one's complicity. Projection—"this process whereby qualities, feelings, wishes or even objects which the subject refuses to recognize or rejects in herself or himself are expelled from the self and located in another person or thing"[37]—allows a denial but perpetuates the split and the denial of the primal scene. To recognize the split in oneself means to accept that one can have conflicting desires and wishes, that an object can be both desired and rejected, that love and hate, envy and jealousy, are part of the human condition. To acknowledge the primal scene is to accept that one was born of sexual intercourse between a man and a woman and in the colony between white and black parents, whether the sexual intercourse was violent or loving. It signifies the rejection of the colonial family romance.

In the 1950s, Octave Mannoni, Frantz Fanon, and Albert Memmi transformed the paradigm of colonial studies. Until then, the colonizer had been seen as a benevolent missionary whose task was to study, discipline, and educate the native. The couple colonizer/ colonized rested on the understanding that the colonizer had no other motives than the "development" of the native. Whether the native was conceptualized as backward (School of Algiers) or as Other (Hardy) did not make much difference. Starting with Mannoni, the couple colonizer/colonized was understood differently. Mannoni's more important contribution was to show the stake of colonial parents in the colonial family romance. His "Prospero" embodied "colonial paternalism with its pride, its neurotic impatience and its need of domination."[38] Fanon said that there was a dual narcissism at play in the colony, which sealed the white man in his whiteness and the black man in his blackness.[39] Memmi concurred and wrote that the colonial relation was one that "chained the colonizer and the colonized into an implacable dependence."[40] Advocates of colonization had argued that if colonization did not work, it was because "bad" administrators and "mediocre" colonists were sent to the colony. This argument was challenged. The colonial relation *demanded* such people, Mannoni, Fanon, and Memmi claimed. The "white colonial is motivated only by a desire to put an end to a feeling of unsatisfaction on the level of Adlerian overcompensation," Fanon remarked.[41] Going to a colony was "simply a voyage towards an easier life."[42] The violence of the natives was thus no longer an atavistic psychological trait, but the result of the colonial relation. With this epistemological shift, the gaze was turned on the dynamics of the colonial relation.

Exploring the narrative of métissage, I try to show how it justified policies of discipline and control in the colony. But I also show how it was a response *from the colonial world* against European racism, eugenics, and mono-ethnicism. In the tension provoked by the irruption of a name in the colonial space—métis, Creole—and in the debates that follow, a space emerged that was not entirely dominated or contaminated by colonialism. More interested in the colonized's creative response to the colonizing discourse than in the colonizer's representations of the Other, I have focused on the Réunion community. The Réunionnais are still constituting themselves through the experience of articulating their being-in-common, of living groups that are continuously transformed by the arrival of new groups.[43] When the cultural reference of a community is a métissage forged through slavery, *marronnage,* workers' struggles against capitalism and colonialism, and refusal to submit to racial regulations that forbade métissage, then the "people" are not defined by a founding myth but elaborated through a continuous social transformation, informed by resistance to incorporation.

Joan Scott has argued that "treating the emergence of a new identity as a discursive event is not to introduce a new form of linguistic determinism, nor to deprive subjects of agency. It is to refuse a separation between 'experience' and language and to insist instead on the *productive quality of discourse.*"[44] Discourses of emancipation, whether emancipation was said to be further autonomy from the metropole or more integration with the metropole, whether emancipation was connected to working-class politics or to bourgeois fraternity, produced an *ideal* of what the Creole was and must be. A genealogy of these discourses reveals both the "discursive space of the positions made available by hegemonic discourses and the 'space-off,' the elsewhere, of those discourses."[45] As the discursive strategies of the past continue "secretly to animate the present, the task of the genealogist is to identify recurring figures, reversals, errors, and false appraisals."[46] I read the texts of the colonial family romance *with* novels and iconography, with texts from different disciplines, law, medicine, psychology, and with contemporary debates. I followed what Antoine de Baecque has called "nonquantitative serial history," bringing together in a dialogue diverse sources that, though they "are not born free and equal, nonetheless enjoy a *right* to the same multicultural consideration, a *right* to be linked together within a heterogeneous but coherent whole, accessible to a single interpretative gaze."[47]

The point of departure was to gather "documents," defined by Michel Foucault as "not the fortunate tools of a history that is primarily and fundamentally *memory*," "inert material," but material that will provide "unities, totalities, series, relations."[48] The reading of colonial archives offered a body of texts, allegories, and tropes produced by discourses that both gave enunciative practices of emancipation to the inhabitants of Réunion Island *and* reinscribed them in a global economy of signs. As the identity of the Réunionnais was partly constructed within the French symbolic system, it was to a certain extent bound within that system. The tension between speaking a discourse and being held under the power of this discourse proved to be paradoxically a site of creativity. This approach has been challenged because, its critics have argued, it denied the possibility of entirely escaping the colonial system of signs, of creating a system of signs free of past influences. Such critics have preferred to follow a Fanonian approach. But Fanon and those influenced by him tried to disentangle the colonizer/colonized couple in an effort from which this research departs. Fanon thought that decolonization had to be a tabula rasa, that it was "quite simply the replacing of a certain 'species' of men by another 'species' of men," an "absolute substitution."[49] Hybridity and syncretism were impossible positions: "The intellectual who is Arab and French, or Nigerian and English, when he comes up against the need to take on two nationalities, chooses, if he wants to remain true to himself, the negation of one of these determinations." Any analysis that would read colonial history as a discontinuous chain of ambivalent and subversive moments, rather than as a series of decisive moments of rupture, would mask the reality that the colonial world was the "murderous and decisive struggle between two protagonists."[50]

The rejection of imperialism's signifying system proposed by

Fanon supposes that the possibility exists of creating an entirely new signifying system. Fanonian theory depends on a system that organizes history as a progressive development. It implies that women and men have the power to reinvent their symbolic and material world, to shed memories. It construes memory as a morbid legacy, a melancholic nostalgia for a past long gone, shackles that hinder the path to freedom. In this approach is a fantasy of self-engendering, of refusing a filiation that is experienced as impossible to receive and to transform.[51] Memory is a wounded memory, and the wound seems impossible to heal, to be integrated as history. This might have been what Fanon had in mind when he advocated a total reconstruction of the self if decolonization was the goal. We are reminded of Marx's remark that "the tradition of the dead generations weighs like a nightmare on the minds of the living. And just when they appear to be engaged in revolutionary transformation of themselves and their material surroundings, in the creation of something which does not yet exist, precisely in such epochs of revolutionary crisis they timidly conjure up the spirits of the past to help them."[52]

Fanon, who described with force and passion what colonialism had made of women and men, wanted revolution to be a creation, unfettered by the spirits of the past who would burden the living with past losses and defeats. Revolution would be a means to negate these defeats. Yet Fanon did not discuss what was the *foundation* of his own society, the Creole society of Martinique, what was the *defeat* that slavery had been. A past of slavery, Toni Morrison has said, "until you confront it, until you live through it, keeps coming back in other forms. The shapes redesign themselves in other constellations, until you get a chance to play it over again."[53] This moment, this "loss," is constitutive of the present, and Marx's warning about the process of "world-historical necromancy" notwithstanding, the recognition of this loss is part of the process of becoming other, an "other" whose subjectivity is not contained in the colonial representation but transformed by its experience of colonialism. In other words, rejecting the self of colonization, when one has been subjected to the humiliations of colonialism, rejecting the shame produced by that moment, might simply be reconstructing a phantasied innocence, once polluted by colonialism.[54] I am therefore working with, and away from, Fanon. I want to save the father in slavery and in the colony, whereas Fanon sought to kill the father and establish a brotherhood of the oppressed. I contend that in the colony, to have access to a metaphorical fraternity (the politics of equality), the symbolic function of the father, denied by the system of slavery and colonialism, must be restored.

The past weighs on the present, solidified in denial and disavowal.[55] It hides a secret. What is repressed in Réunion? A crime. What crime? Slavery. With what words can this crime be told? The repression of that crime through a narrative that claims that slavery was "not that bad" in Réunion denies the *reality* of slavery. The issue cannot be the "quality of treatment" but what was the symbolic and material economy of this system. Slavery was "undigestible and unabsorbable, completely. Something that has no precedent in the history of the world, in terms of length of time and the nature and specificity of its devastation."[56] The fear is that if the repression of this history were lifted, there would be more horror. Horror was but no longer is, the narrative says. Why would one insist in showing the wounds, in bringing back this "tragedy"? To awaken the nightmare? How to put this crime on trial, a crime whose *reality* weighs on the present?

What has been the function of this narrative if not to absolve a group from its complicity in an event?[57] Speaking of slavery as a "tragedy" transforms this event into something that went beyond human intention, an event in which all participants were "victims" of history. And why should people "pay" for crimes committed long ago? It has been argued that no human institution can try such a crime. Nicolas Abraham and Maria Torok have remarked that if the epistemological alternative is between suppressing the reality of the crime and refusing the judicial system because it is arbitrary and relative, there is no way out. The participants in the crime would remain incapable of recognizing their participation and accepting a historical reality in its complex and multifarious expressions. The island is then like a grave, inhabited by ghosts whose presence haunts the living. Opening the grave, freeing the ghosts, mourning the dead, would be a start in the processes of anamnesis. Anamnesis is a different process from tabula rasa or morbid melancholia. One can start from the assumption that the "past has the value of representing what is lacking [*ce qui fait défaut*]." A group can express "what is still lacking, still to come, only through a redistribution of its past." From the knowledge of the past, of the conditions that made it such, a group can decide that what was lacking—freedom, equality—is still to come. History is always ambivalent, for the "place it gives to the past is equally a means to open the way to the future."[58] De Certeau warns that because of this ambivalence, this significance of a lack, historical analysis may vacillate between conservatism and utopia, reactionary and revolutionary politics. Yet, as he concludes, one can understand both these limits and the potential of the ambivalence, a symbolization of the limit and the possibility of going beyond this limit.[59]

The tension between a discourse of political emancipation that tends to essentialize a community and the discourse of métissage that is a deviation from this strategy seems to suggest that they cannot exist concurrently. But a discourse of emancipation that altogether ignores a situation of métissage would imitate colonial discourse, producing a community as a fixed reality that can be entirely knowable and visible. In Réunion, the differential identity of the island's population was integrated within a universalistic discourse. When demands remained unsatisfied, they were reiterated but were still not "made in terms of difference; rather they [were] made on the basis of some universal principles that the minority shared with the rest of the community: the right to have access to good schools, to live a decent life, to participate in the public space of citizenship."[60] Discourses of emancipation in Réunion must be analyzed in their heterogeneity. The strategy of borrowing was predicated on the history of the island. The people of Réunion first appropriated the "French book of republicanism" and its motto of liberty, equality, fraternity. But it was not a gesture of pure mimesis, of alienated colonized who credulously endorsed the Enlightenment project. The discourses of emancipation were creolized, métissés, hybridized. Xiaomei Chen has called this borrowing "Occidentalism," the process whereby the "semi-colonized Self used the discourse of the colonialist Other for its own political agenda within its own cultural milieu."[61] Anticolonialists of Réunion admired the tradition of parliamentary democracy and the Declaration of Rights of Man and the Citizen, but as Jacques Derrida has said,

You can recognize an authentic inheritor in the one who conserves and reproduces, but also in the one who respects the logic of the legacy enough to turn it upon occasion against those who claim to be its guardians, enough to reveal, despite and against the usurpers, what has never yet been seen in the inheritance: enough to give birth, by the unheard-of act of reflection, to what had never seen the light of day.[62]

Within their discourses of emancipation, Réunionnais first challenged their exclusion from the community of the free and equal. Then they proposed an identification with the community of the excluded, and lastly they opened, as a new social group, a political space in which to act. These three moves affirmed the *heterological* position of the subject, and to the colonized, a position "in-between": citizen *and* colonized, worker *and* citizen, member of the colonized community *and* member of a subethnic group, *and* women. This heterology was inscribed in the social and cultural matrix of race, gender, class, and sexual difference. It was a discourse that situated itself between suspicion (*le soupçon*) that signifies rupture and doubt, and filiation, that is, debt and the law.[63] In the movement between suspicion toward the ideals brought by Europe and the Enlightenment and the recognition of a filiation toward these ideals, Réunion's anticolonialists expressed a heterological position. Hence the white *fraternité républicaine* of the Second Republic was a *métisse fraternité* in Réunion. Hence the *égalité* of the anticolonialist movement of 1946 was not only an *égalité* with the French citizens but also an *egalité* of the oppressed against the feudal world of the plantation.

In chapter 2, my analysis of the narrative of *fraternité* and of the contested family romances of 1848, the year of the abolition of slavery, introduces many of the issues that will be developed further in subsequent chapters, in particular the issue of political emancipation through greater assimilation with the colonial metropole. When slavery was abolished, when the white master was no longer the figure to whom total obedience and respect were due, republican France, La Mère-Patrie, became the figure to whom obedience and respect were due. The 1848 abolition of slavery and the rhetorics of freedom, brotherhood, and equality engendered ironically a new disciplinary power relation between France, La Mère-Patrie, and the small island. Through the literary analysis of the work of Réunion nineteenth-century novelist Louis-Timagène Houat, I present the limits and problems of the dream of a republican fraternity in which "race" would disappear as a marker of difference thanks to métissage.

Chapter 3, "Blood Politics and Political Assimilation," presents the narrative of political assimilation in order to incorporate it into the larger narrative of colonial emancipation. It was not simply the expression of alienation but an attempt to recover dignity and freedom. Anticolonialists sought to demonstrate the illogical position of the metropole: if France defended republican values and supported the right of the peoples to self-determination, how could it continue to retain its empire? The personal and public history of a political leader and anticolonialist intellectual from Réunion, my grandfather Raymond Vergès, presents the complexities, hopes, and limits of political assimilation. I follow Vergès from Réunion to China, Indochina, and then back to Réunion, from being a French consul in Indochina to being a leader of the Réunion working class and of the postwar anticolonialist movement. His struggle for political assimilation stands as a metaphor for the dilemma of movements for integration: placing on an oppressed group the moral burden of redeeming its oppressors.

Chapter 4 focuses on the Cold War period in the postcolony of Réunion. In the late 1950s, the demand for political autonomy triggered a violent response on the part of the conservatives on the island. Politically, autonomy implied a radical transformation of the colonial bond. It acknowledged the historical ties between Réunion and France but insisted on the need to transform these ties so that the people of Réunion would acquire political responsibility. In its psychological consequences, political autonomy signified breaking away from a relation defined in the terms of an infantilizing couple, Mère-Patrie/colonial children. A Frenchman, Michel Debré, led the countersubversive campaign. Arriving in 1963, Debré remained a legislative representative of the island for twenty-five years. A fervent Gaullist, Debré distinguished himself as a zealous defender of French imperial grandeur, a staunch anticommunist, and an opponent of women's rights. Cold War rhetoric was filled with predictions of panic, chaos, and loss of boundaries, which, in a small territory such as Réunion Island, found a resonant echo.

The last chapter tackles the role of the psychiatric discourse that in the 1980s gained an unforeseeable authority to describe Réunion's society. The nature and specificity of colonial psychiatry and its legacy have been largely ignored in postcolonial studies. But if psychiatry, as Octave Mannoni has written, "collaborates in the

enterprise of isolating and excluding from society those who cannot obey the historically defined norms of propriety,"[64] then the
study of this collaboration in the colonial context is relevant. Although we know about medical discourse, a full investigation of
the ways in which gender and race figured in the definition of the
"mad" remains to be done. Psychiatry's goal is to define a "utilitarian policy, whose intent is to protect the tranquility of the
majority, but also to inculcate in this majority a certain way of
being reasonable."[65] The role of French psychiatrists in Réunion
has been essentially to authenticate and certify the "illnesses" of the
Creole soul and to inculcate a "certain way of being reasonable."
Their goal has been to help track down the marginalized, the
"abnormal" Creoles. They have defined a pathology, designated the
culpable: matrifocality, indigence, alcoholism, social and intellectual poverty. The politics of integration developed by Debré failed
to transform Réunionnais into modern French, but rather than
analyzing the historical reasons for this failure, the blame was put
on the Réunionnais community.[66] The adoption of psychological
terms to explain behavior, the tyranny of the notion of the Self, the
idea that internal life contains a "truth," have now come to the
postcolony. The postcolonial subject lives under the psychiatric
gaze and has learned the psychological vocabulary.

I have been asked why women's voices are so marginal, why men
are the principal actors of my research.[67] Confronted with the
political history of my island, I thought that I needed first to work
through a narrative that, I contend, shaped the political discourse
of emancipation. To the question of why I presented the history of
the *men* of my family to illustrate the conditions of the formation
of emancipatory discourses, the answer is that I located them in
history; that is, I used their history, the ways in which they produced hatred and fascination, to show the central tensions of their
times. The colonial family romance had for its main characters the
imagined figure of La Mère-Patrie and colonized men. Colonized
women were the repressed figures of this romance, and they were
further marginalized as women qua women by the discourse of
political integration, which needs for strategic reasons to essentialize groups, the "oppressed" versus the "oppressors." I could certainly have brought back in women's voices, made more central the
figure of the *métisse* woman[68] (which I evoke); in short, I could
have shown the ways in which women supported or subverted the

French colonial family romance. My task is more humble: as a feminist, I have tried to retrieve the voices of men who in my country have fought for emancipation, equality, and freedom, voices that I had neglected through my association with French feminism.

I have formerly spent years in a French women's group collecting women's voices around the world for a feminist weekly and a series of publications.[69] However, this French group showed little patience with thinking about French colonialism and its aftermath. Its feminism was Eurocentric, largely indifferent to women's struggles in its former empire.[70] I became an accomplice (and a subject) of what Chandra Talpade Mohanty has called being "under Western eyes."[71] French women had been passive or active accomplices of the colonial project, and few feminists opposed it. Later, the feminist support of women's struggles in the Third World more than once took the form of "opposition to local patriarchy." Although justified, this opposition could not account for the common struggle against colonialism. "French feminism," as it became known outside France, has been remarkably silent about French colonialism and its relation with republicanism. If some feminist authors have voiced their criticisms about the situation of women in the world and about racism in France, they have in their majority practically never considered the complicity between French feminism and the empire. For the subaltern to speak, she had to work within her own history, away from the ideological discourse of European feminism about patriarchy and power relations. This is not to say that there is not a history to be told, the history of Réunion's women, of the daughters of the colonial family romance. For Graziella Leveneur, a leading feminist on the island, women must join the struggle for the reappropriation of the past, of historical memory, to resist the *altericide* (destruction of otherness) led by the French state.[72] My reading is thus neither definitive nor comprehensive. It is an effort to retrieve a filiation, to lay down some aspects of the colonial struggle.

On this small island, very diverse groups, which were thrown together by the yoke of history, have built a society and a culture that are both fragile. Class divisions are sharp, and racism latent. The politics of emancipation are the politics of the Self as an Other, its logic a heterology. The logic of the Other is "never the simple assertion of an identity, but always at the same time the denial of an identity given by an other; it is a demonstration, and a demonstration always supposes an other. . . . There is a polemical commonplace for the handling of the wrong and the demonstration of equality; finally, the logic of subjectivization always entails an impossible identification."[73] My starting point was, and remained, the island of Réunion and its population. My contribution to the theory of the colonial relation lies therefore less in the domain of speculative theory than in the domain of political history through a slow reconstitution of metaphors, images, and symbols that mobilized the Réunionnais imagination. To understand the "concrete procedures by which social actors simultaneously borrow from a range of discursive genres, intermix them,"[74] and as a result invent original discourses of emancipation was the important concern. History is determined by material conditions *and* the kind of discourse that is adopted and disseminated. As Jacques Rancière put it, "What determines the lives of human beings, as much if not more than the weight of labor and wages, is the weight of names, or of their absence, the weight of written and unwritten names, of read or heard names, a weight which is as material as the former."[75]

2

Contested Family Romances:

Slaves, Workers, Children

❧

Méfiez-vous des Blancs, habitants du rivage. Du temps de nos pères, des blancs descendirent dans cette île; on leur dit: Voilà des terres; que vos femmes les culti-vent. Soyez justes, soyez bons, et devenez nos frères. Les blancs promirent, et cependant ils faisaient des retranchements. . . . leurs prêtres voulurent nous donner un Dieu que nous ne connaissons pas; ils parlèrent enfin d'obéissance et d'es-clavage: plutôt la mort!

[Beware of whites, inhabitants of these shores. In our fathers' times, whites came to the island. We told them: Here is some land; your wives can cultivate it. Be just, be good and become our brothers. The whites promised, but meanwhile they built strongholds. Their priests wanted to give us a God that we did not know. Finally they talked of obedience and slavery: better be dead!][1]

On December 20, 1848, sixty-two thousand slaves acquired the status of citizens in Réunion Island. Slavery was finally abolished. French commissioner Sarda Garriga proclaimed on that day: "My friends, the decrees of the French Republic are now the law: you are free. Equals before the law, you are presently brothers."[2] A new family romance was born, the romance of brothers united by love for France, the moral obligation to work, and respect for private property. "Owners and workers constitute now *a single family* whose members have the duty to help one another. All are now free, brothers and equals, and their union will bring them happiness," Sarda wrote.[3] An analysis of Sarda's rhetoric and of colonial policies after 1848 tells another story, a story of discipline and repression, of division and coercion. Sarda's narrative was an attempt to repress another family romance, the *métis* republican family romance that told a story of race and class conflicts resolved by a fraternity that challenged unequal economic relations. Yet the republican names of fraternity and liberty carried with them promises that threatened the colonial order founded on feudal inequality, subjugation, and racism. Sarda's discourse was not foreclosed; its boundaries were not hermetic.

The formation of the postslavery society justified new laws, new regulations, and new forms of social organization. White landowners feared the consequences of the collapse of their social, economic, and symbolic order and sought guarantees from the French state. They suspected that freedwomen and freedmen would refuse to continue working for their former masters. They were right. Blacks resisted the offers of the new order. They remained indifferent to the invitations to stable residency, waged work, and the creation of "Christian" families. They occupied pieces of uncultivated land, refusing to bother with property rights; they drifted from one place to another; they continued to constitute families without the sanctification of priests or mayors. Blacks were constructing their own community after two centuries of bondage, rejecting the established boundaries of the white aristocracy, founding their own answers to the revolutionary change in their lives. In response, the new administration instituted a "passport," forced labor and convict labor, and sought to "moralize" blacks. Women and men arrested for vagrancy, lack of passport, or because they could not justify being unemployed were condemned to *macadam*.[4] This form of punishment gave to the colonial administration free access to bonded work even though slavery had been abolished. Roads, bridges, railways, and harbors were built by a convict force. Modern Réunion emerged through the work of former slaves who now served the republic. When the order of slavery was abolished, when the white master was no longer the figure to whom total obedience and respect were due, the colonial order emerged, and France, La Mère-Patrie, became the figure to whom obedience and respect were due. Two family romances were invented, reflecting the contest between two interests, the interests of the French state and slave owners and the interest of a small elite of educated colored seduced by republicanism. One was imagined in the pre-emancipation period by a young métis of Réunion, Louis-Timagène Houat; the second was brought to Réunion by the commissioner of the French republic, Sarda Garriga.[5]

Houat sought to make *métissage,* connected with liberty and fraternity, the basis of a social bond. He raised a question that has remained a political question in the Old Colonies: how does one define the ties of Réunion with France, which has been both the country from which ideas of liberty and fraternity have come and the state that has maintained slavery and oppression? In 1844 Houat published in Paris the first novel of Réunion literature, *Les Marrons,* in which an interracial couple is giving birth to a métis son. The métis son embodied the emergence of a society whose model of filiation belied the colonial family model based on blood purity. Houat's transgressive plot was a re-vision of sexual relations in a plantation society at a moment of crisis, the preabolition years. It was a creative effort to imagine a polity freed from the rigid sexual and social taboos of a racially segregated society. Houat's gesture, the representation of the métis as a redemptive group that would save people "from war, slavery, destruction and which would insure happiness, equality, love, unity and mutual help,"[6] inaugurated a problematic of métissage that has been inseparable from Réunion's project of emancipation.[7] The dream of a racial democracy was the response of the island's republicans to colonial racism. It made the métis the best-suited individual to build a society that would not rest on one "extreme," whether black or white.

The colonial family romance developed by Sarda Garriga took fraternal love as its model, and as its ideal, unfaltering obedience to the figure of the Mère-Patrie. The republican family romance of the French Revolution arrived later in the colony, and it arrived transmogrified. Colonial fraternity was different from, and similar to, the fraternal family romance of the French Revolution analyzed by Lynn Hunt and Jacques André. Different because fraternity in the colonies was not the result of a parricide and the creation of an assembly of brothers but contemporaneous with the abolition of slavery; republican fraternity had to be in agreement with racism and colonialism. Similar because it nonetheless brought to the colony a promise charged with radicalism. Fraternity aspired to transcend race and proposed a community in which membership was chosen rather than imposed. The nation was a mother, as it had been in the revolutionary family romance,[8] but its representation was remodeled: it was still a "masculine mother" (Mère-Patrie), but brothers were not equal under her protection, because colonized brothers were not sovereign subjects. Emancipated slaves have not left novels or accounts; but letters, petitions, and demands, found in the police and judicial archives, demonstrate that emancipated women and men did not fully embrace the fraternity offered by Sarda Garriga, the fraternity of a political and symbolic order that still practiced exclusion on the basis of race.

Liberty, Fraternity, and Colonial Emancipation

The abolition of slavery brought to the island the motto of the 1789 revolutionaries, "Liberty, Equality, Fraternity." The Second Republic (1848–1850) was fulfilling the promise of 1794 when the National Convention had proclaimed the emancipation of slaves and given them full rights as citizens.[9] The French envoy announced a new order, the order of fraternity and equality among brothers.[10] But the family romance of fraternity and liberty was complicated by colonial reality. The fraternal bond between metropolitan brothers and colonial brothers was affected by colonialism and its logic of racism. Fraternity masked the continuity of primogeniture—the law whereby the firstborn son received the inheritance to the detriment of the other brothers and of the sisters—for metropolitan brothers continued to benefit from primogeniture. It concealed the perpetuation of economic dominance—the plantation economy and the existence of the "colonial pact."[11] Yet this fiction was adopted by Réunion's educated colored, intellectuals, workers, and peasants. They imagined themselves as the brothers of French citizens. And they appealed to France to protect them against the tyrannical power of the landowners. The latter defended an old regime in which they held the tyrannical power of the patriarch.

The family romances of fraternity of the colonized and the colonizers disavowed women but ended up creating different spaces of struggle. Feminist critics have shown that if the fraternal order of liberal revolution unsettled patriarchalism as the foundation of the social bond, it nonetheless defended a masculinized conception of selfhood. "Political creativity belongs not to paternity but masculinity," Carole Pateman has written.[12] The fiction of contract was invented by "*white* men, and their fraternal contract [had] three aspects; the social contract, the sexual contract and the slave contract that legitimized the rule of white over black."[13] Juliet Flower MacCannell has called this moment the "regime of the brother,"[14] a regime predicated on male homosociality. "The construction of a political state around liberty, equality, and fraternity," MacCannell writes, "is the very essence, the real hope and glory of modernity, the heart of democracy."[15] But this essence and this hope were diverted by the brothers who, instead of inventing an inclusive law to replace the tyrannical patriarchal law, created a law as tyrannical as the old. The fraternal law "repressed not just the mother but the father for the benefit of the son. Or rather, the brother."[16] The sister was excluded from the fraternal romance because her existence, her desire, her sexuality, reminded the brother of his own dependency on her to forge his own gendered identity.[17] In other words, the little boy constructs his sexual identity on his sister's difference and yet denies this dependency because it calls into question his fantasy of autogenesis. The "family of man—modern 'humanity' excluded the sister's function as the constitutive or foundational part of its genre (and of its gender), as forcibly as Oedipal patriarchy ever excluded the matriarchal function."[18] To Pateman and MacCannell, the fraternal order's claim of being a society founded on justice and equality is vitiated by its exclusion of the sister.[19]

However, there is in the fraternal social bond a relation that has not been stressed by Pateman or MacCannell. It is the relation between the mother and the son and the particular importance that this relation took in the colonial family romance. The fraternal order was also the order of the mother and the son.[20] The central question of the colonized brothers was the relation to the mother, or rather to their two mothers: the native mother and the *metropole*, the "mother country." The 1848 colonial family romance replaced the authoritarian figure of prerevolutionary colonial romance with a more benevolent figure, La Mère-Patrie. Tutelage was maintained, but it wished to be a compassionate tutelage. Women and men were both subjected to colonial tutelage, all under the protection of La

Mère-Patrie. The exclusion of the sister was not as essential for the "brothers" of the colonial family romance as it had been for the brothers of the republican family romance: revolutionary brothers had represented themselves as sovereign *sujets,* free of tutelage, whereas colonial brothers were still subjected to the metropole, still under the power of the metropolitan brothers. In the metropole, "because of its notions of the autonomous individual, liberal political theory actually [had] made the exclusion of women much more problematic."[21] The exclusion of the metropolitan women from public space became an issue. Colonialism, in contrast, maintained the notion of a group (the colonized group subjected to the colonizing group) and did not open the same space for feminist struggle. The colonial couple mother/son ignored, rather than excluded, the sister. The latter sought alliance with the brother who wanted to challenge colonial tutelage.[22] The gendered identity of the brothers in the colony was less "defined" than that of the metropolitan brother. Colonial family romance maintained a pre-Oedipal identity: all children of France, all little brothers and sisters. Feminist critics of fraternity tend to ignore the radical dimension of the republican rhetoric in the colony, where people lived under slavery and imperial tutelage. The modern category of the individual, these critics argue, has been constructed in a "manner that postulates a universalist, homogeneous 'public' that relegates all particularity and difference to the 'private' and this has very negative consequences for women."[23] But as Chantal Mouffe says, a "democratic project is better served by a perspective that allows us to grasp the diversity of ways in which relations of power are constructed and helps us to reveal the forms of exclusion present in all pretensions to universalism."[24] *Métisse* fraternity in the colony revealed the forms of exclusion of French republican universalism.

Republican fraternity cannot be reduced to family ties. Revolutionary fraternity imagines a family whose members are united not by blood but by a political choice: to reject the tyranny of an all-powerful father. Lynn Hunt argues that fraternity is the model of modernity, intimately connected with the idea of an autonomous individual and with democracy.[25] Jacques Derrida has asked if we can invent a democracy that will not be an insult to friendship *(l'amitié)* and will be situated beyond a homo-fraternal and phallogocentric scheme.[26] Democracy as a model of affectivity, a model of obedience, is confronted by the following problem: What makes one obey a brother? What founds the authority of the brother? Brought to the colony, the question is: what founds the authority of the white brother over his black brother?

Abolitionists and Métis

Analyzing the 1840s colonial family romance requires attending to a central figure in this romance, the métis.[27] During the Restoration (1815–1830) and the July Monarchy (1830–1848), abolitionists in Réunion and in France agitated for the slaves' emancipation, and mulattoes were active in the movement.[28] To retrace the history of the terms *métis* and *métissage* is to retrace the history of a debate in philosophy and sciences in the eighteenth and nineteenth centuries around the unity of the human species, race, and degeneration.[29] The partisans of the unity of the human species saw métissage as the inevitable future of humanity; peoples would mix, this was bound to happen, and it would enrich humanity. To those who believed in a hierarchy among peoples, métissage was a threat, leading to degeneration, mediocrity, and decline, and such views had political implications in the colonial world.

The term *métis* appeared in the French language in the thirteenth century and meant that "which is made half from one thing and half from another."[30] In the sixteenth century, *métis* was used to describe an ambivalent position, a moral flaw. "De se tenir chancelant et *mestis*," Montaigne wrote, "et en une division publique, je ne le trouve ni beau, ni honneste" [To be faltering and *mestis*, in a divided position, I find it neither good nor honest].[31] Honoré de Balzac wrote in 1831: "En deux mots, c'est un *métis* en morale, ni tout a fait probe, ni complétement fripon" [In a word, he is morally a métis, neither entirely upright, nor totally rascal].[32] *Métis* entered the colonial vocabulary in the sixteenth century.[33] Philosophers of the Enlightenment debated the meaning and impact of métissage on the future of humanity. Voltaire believed in "different human races," whereas Buffon demonstrated in his study *De l'homme* that there was *one* human species, whose diversity could be explained by the effect of climate and mores on human beings.[34] Condorcet agreed with Buffon: "What we call humans must all be seen as belonging to the same species, because all the diverse types together produce métis, who are generally fecund." Diderot was convinced that "all beings circulate among each other. There is a continuous, perpetual flux."[35] In his article on *Espèce humaine* in the *Encyclopédie,* Diderot concluded: "Everything concurs to prove that the human species is not constituted of essentially different species. There was originally one human race, which, because it multiplied and spread throughout the earth, has produced the diversity that we mentioned." To philosophers such as Kant, métissage threatened to produce a general degradation of humankind.[36] Theories of monogenism—the doctrine that all human groups have a common ancestor[37]—and of polygenism—the doctrine that human groups have different ancestors—used the figure of the métis to support their respective theses. Polygenists argued that the métis was a sterile hybrid and that mixing the races would lead to the extinction of the human species, whereas monogenists contended that the métis was as fecund as any other human being.

To colonial Europe, the existence of métis posed a political and ideological problem. The objective of colonial discourse was to construe a typology of colonial populations that reflected political and racial concerns. The desire for, and fear of, métissage in colonial societies raised a semantic as well as a political question. What name and what place would the colonial order give the métis? What to do with their "white" filiation in a world that celebrated whiteness yet constructed any other filiation as degenerate? Naming these individuals *métis, mulâtres,* was a linguistic performance that indicated their mixed origins, but soon *métis* became a reference about one's position in the social colonial order.

In Réunion, the colonial administration and the Catholic Church first tried to forbid sexual relations between Europeans and women of color.[38] The *Code Noir* stated: "It is forbidden to our white subjects, male or female, to contract marriage with blacks. It is also forbidden to our white subjects, as well as to the free or born free blacks, to live with slaves." The children of such unions were illegitimate.[39] The *Code Noir*'s goal was to racially control and discipline the colonial society of Bourbon.[40] The taboo of métissage was based on a series of fantasies and fears: fantasy of sterility of the métis, fear of deviance, fear of transgression of the social colonial order, fear of the degeneration of the white race, of the loss of its "purity."[41] Male métis were seen as potential revolutionaries because colonialists feared that they would demand, because of their part of white blood, a specific place in the racial hierarchy of colonialism. Female métis were constructed as deviant, sexually loose, and perfidious. The mulattoes' participation in the French Revolution's political debate made métissage a trope of the politics of race and rights.[42]

As the concern for a segregated ranking of races grew, one problem was to find a place for the métis in racial taxonomy.[43] René Chateaubriand wrote that "biological métissage creates vicious, ambiguous, and depraved individuals" who concentrated the "vices of both races."[44] Métis troubled the European imaginary because they were the signifier of forbidden desire, of the attraction of the white for the black formulated only as perverted libertinage, and they were, of course, the living testimony of the rape of black women by their masters. Bourbon colonial administrators expressed a similar contempt for the métis and the "free coloreds."[45] A leader of the Catholic Church described them in 1827 as a "class that offers few consolations. Those who have the benefit of individual emancipation because they are the children of whites are the fruits of libertinage. These individuals have the vices of the slaves and their liberty encourages reprehensible behavior."[46]

A Métis on Trial in Bourbon

Métis were feared because they could constitute a political force. Many were educated, aware of the mobilization against slavery in Europe and the United States. In the 1830s and 1840s, they met in Paris, as métis had done during the French Revolution. They joined abolitionist associations and published reviews and books urging the end of bondage. One of these reviews was the *Revue des Colonies,* founded in July 1834 by an "association of men of color." Its goal was to report about the "politics, administration, justice, and mores in the colonies."[47] The opinions expressed in the *Revue des Colonies* were those of the republican opposition to the July Monarchy.[48] Its director was Charles-André Bissette, a mulatto from Martinique, who had been banned from his island in 1824 because he had published a brochure demanding civil rights for the free colored.[49] In the second issue, Bissette published a "Declaration of Principles," in which he clearly situated his struggle for emancipation within the heritage of the Déclaration des Droits de l'Homme and the Ideals of *liberté, égalité, fraternité:*

The *Revue des Colonies* wants to make clear the principles upon which it will judge men and events. For us, in 1789, the immortal Declaration of Rights proclaimed by the National Assembly set the foundations of all institutions that claim to be democratic; this is why we inscribe the declaration on our front page; it is our "Tables of Law." We, children of France, do not desire that a Bolivar come to deliver us from an alien yoke. France is dear to our hearts; her gifts are too precious and her protection is too necessary for us to have hostile feelings toward her. . . . What man of color could forget that it was a French assembly which for the first time proclaimed the Rights of Man and the great principle of equality? And, is not France our real fatherland, of which we are so proud?[50]

To Bissette, as Nelly Schmidt has remarked, the inclusion of the free colored in the French family and the abolition of slavery were both implicit in the heritage of the French Revolution and logical with its principles.[51] Bissette's ambitions were to encourage education in the colonies, help the election of men of color to the National Assembly, and bring an end to slavery. On the review's cover, below the title, there was a sketch of a black man, in tropical surroundings, his right knee on the soil, his hands joined as in prayer, his feet and hands chained, his face turned to the sky, saying: "Am I not a man and your brother?"[52] In March 1836, the *Revue des Colonies* reported that a "conspiracy by men of color" had been uncovered in Bourbon.[53] The conspirators' goal was, Bourbon newspapers said, to abolish slavery by "massacring the whites and having the French garrison poisoned."[54] The editors of the *Revue* suspected the white landowners of having entirely invented the affair. The whites, they wrote, were seeking to break up a foreseeable alliance among poor whites, mulattoes, and blacks.[55] The trial was scheduled for July 1836.

Sixteen men were indicted for conspiracy against the state: Houat, artist; Jean-Pierre de Catherine, cobbler; Joseph Chryseuil, cobbler; Abel Salez, blacksmith; Louis-Pierre Bonhomme, blacksmith; Villiers, settler; Antoine, interpreter; Chery Florentin, tailor; Elie, carpenter; Floricourt Longvilliers, carpenter; Jean-Marie Lamour, cobbler; Jean-Baptiste Marcelin, settler; Nolbas Bachelier, settler; Amédée de Zéline, settler; Jean-François, slave; and Fomboisy Wilmann, no profession.[56] Four others were tried for "failure to denounce the conspiracy": Joson, slave; Théodose, slave; Alphonse, slave; and Montrose, slave.[57]

In France, the trial mobilized both sides of the abolitionist debate. The *Moniteur du Commerce* and the *Journal du Commerce,* supporters of the colonial order, denounced the conspirators. In Paris, the club Massia, which in the French Revolution had been the voice of the colonial landlords, used the trial to decry the role of mulattoes in the colonies. In the *Revue des Colonies,* the accused found an ardent advocate of their cause. The *Revue* had often been banned in the colonies because it had "consistently denounced the arbitrary power of the colonial administration and its contempt for the principles of law." That the review had repeatedly been confiscated in Réunion was proof that the colonial power feared the idea of liberty more than anything.[58] Bissette remarked that it was the first *political* trial on the island, and that it was important for the colonial power to make it a "trial of *color and caste.*"[59] Bourbon's whites, though they were themselves métis because all families that "claim a white origin descend on their mother's side from Madagascans or from Indians who are black,"[60] were transforming themselves into whites by symbolically and concretely expelling métis and blacks from their community and making them enemies of society. The *Revue* asked France to be an arbiter in the colonial affair: "Nothing can be done in the colonies without the high and intelligent intervention of France."[61] The editors anticipated the republican ideal that would be fully developed under the Third Republic: it was France's duty to bring *liberté, égalité, fraternité* to its empire. Colonialist crimes and abuses were the doings not of France but of the colonial white aristocracy. Seven months after first reporting the indictment, the *Revue des Colonies* published a letter written by one of the accused, Louis-Timagène Houat. Houat, who was twenty-four years old, was charged with being the leader and instigator of the conspiracy. A friend who had visited Houat in prison had smuggled out the letter and brought it to Bissette. The letter, evading colonial censorship, brought to the French public the first nonofficial account of the affair.

Born in August 1809 in Saint-Denis, the capital of Réunion, Houat was the son of an emancipated black woman of Réunion and of a white Creole from Ile de France (Mauritius). In the early 1830s, he started a correspondence with the association of Libres de Couleur in the Antilles and with French republicans. Together with a group of poor whites, métis, indentured Indians, and free colored, he organized an association that debated the abolition of slavery and the establishment of democracy in Bourbon. Houat, who had been arrested on December 13, 1835, and imprisoned since, wrote to the editor: "You know that if one wants to eliminate one or more mulattos or slaves, it is not difficult. One has merely to accuse them of conspiracy with intent to murder the whites." He explained his position thus:

I have not feared, come what may, to work for a just and legitimate cause. I have said that I will receive the *Revue des Colonies,* that I will always subscribe to it because no justice in the world could reasonably forbid it. I have said that I wanted emancipation. If France was ordering emancipation and if, in the colony, some group would resist the decision of La Mère-Patrie with arms, I have said that I would side with the government and that I would not abandon the party of the oppressed. Houat is a mulatto, they say, who must be deported or killed, or even better, left to rot in jail.[62]

Houat refused to be judged by his peers in Réunion and concluded: "Your role is to stigmatize this persecution, your role is to avenge the innocents who have been cruelly condemned by the colonial tribunals."[63]

The prosecutor was Charles Ogé-Barbaroux, who had been sent to the colony by the July Monarchy.[64] Barbaroux had been named Ogé by his father, a Girondin leader, in honor of a métis from Saint Domingue.[65] Barbaroux *père* had explained his choice: "I have wanted my son to have the name of this brave man who knew where his dignity was and defended it. I hope that, one day, having looked at the reasons for my choice, my son will bemoan the conquest of America, the greatest of human calamities; and that he will think that there are still slaves to set free."[66] Arriving in July 1831, Barbaroux *fils* occupied as state prosecutor one of the most powerful administrative offices in the colony.[67] He chose to disavow his father's legacy.

Barbaroux *fils* defended the colonial status quo. The conspirators' goal was to destroy established authority and the existing social order.[68] They had planned a gathering in which "the union between blacks and mulattos was to be sealed." Houat was without a doubt the leader of the conspiracy. He had declared, the prosecutor said, that authority in Bourbon should be in the hands of *la couleur brune* (the brown color) and that the time had come to put an end to the whip.[69] Barbaroux insisted on the danger that an alliance between métis and blacks would represent to the colonial order.[70] Houat had said, the prosecutor contended, that previous slave revolts had failed because mulattoes had not joined blacks. Houat's plot was different from slaves' plots, whose goal was emancipation, because this time the goal was also *material equality*.[71]

On the trial's opening day, Barbaroux read a long statement defending "peace and order" in which he presented the aims of his political crusade: "Conservation and amelioration."[72] In the spirit of the July Monarchy, the prosecutor advocated moderation and patience in the matter of emancipation. Only bitterness, resentment, wounded pride, and feelings of impotence could explain the behavior of Houat and his companions.[73] Houat was singled out because he read books that were "beyond his reach" and therefore "embraced ideas that he could not comprehend."[74] His motto was "Equality of all classes! Absolute equality between whites and men of color!"[75] Barbaroux related an anecdote that allegedly shed light on Houat's psychology. The young métis had applied for a post in the judicial administration that had been opened to free coloreds. There was no vacancy in Saint-Denis where Houat resided. When Houat was told that his demand could not be satisfied, he had replied that "he was entitled to this post because he was the member of a group whose rights and interests had been wronged for a long time."[76] This, Barbaroux said, explained the bitterness of Houat, a rebel driven by irrational passions, for a rational person would have understood that there was no job opening and accepted the logical explanation. What Barbaroux chose to ignore was Houat's indictment of a system that did not seek to redress the old inequalities based on racial and class discrimination, hiding discriminatory policies behind "rational" explanations.

The long and detailed act of accusation revealed more about the anxieties among whites than about the character, lives, and opinions of the accused. The fears were about a slaves' insurrection and about the possibility of a cross-racial and class alliance at the moment of emancipation. The 1835 bill of emancipation in Mauritius had given rise to considerable uneasiness among Réunion's plantation owners.[77] Some of them were already suggesting replacing slaves with contract workers.[78] Anticipating emancipation, wealthy landowners had started to organize, if only on a small scale, the importation of indentured workers from India and China.[79] They knew that reviews such as the *Revue des Colonies* were propagating pro-emancipation views, organizing a network of information and support among abolitionists on the island and abolitionists in the United States, France, and England. Novels such as Victor Hugo's *Bug-Jargal* (1832) were making the case for a peaceful termination of slavery. Slave owners in Bourbon followed the debate closely. They were aware that they would have to control the transition from slavery to wage labor if they wanted to secure their economic and symbolic power, hitherto founded on bondage.

The indictment against Houat and his companions rested on flimsy evidence given by a slave to whom freedom had been promised in return for his testimony. A conversation about emancipation held at Houat's house constituted the proof of the "crime." On August 3, 1836, the court pronounced its sentence: Houat, Jean-Pierre, Lamour, and Chryseuil were condemned to deportation; Bonhomme, Élie, and Jean-Baptiste Marcelin to five years of imprisonment; Abel Salez to two years; Alphonse and Théodore to a year. The slaves Montrose and Jean-François, guilty of the crime of nondenunciation, were condemned to flogging, six months in chains, and public exposure.[80] When the May 1837 law of amnesty for political prisoners was extended to the colonies, Houat and his coaccused should have been set free, but the colonial administration decided to convert the amnesty into a sentence of banishment from the colony for seven years.[81]

Houat arrived in Paris in 1838. He was twenty-nine. On his arrival, he published a collection of poems, *Un Proscrit de l'Île Bourbon à Paris*.[82] The poems situated Houat in a literary tradition in which poetry was the favored genre to denounce the dehumanizing effects of slavery and colonial society.[83] In his preface, Houat denounced the iniquity of his exile. The young métis demanded political equality, but his denunciation of the colonialist order did not entail breaking away from France. Houat believed in the superiority of the French, "our elders in civilization."[84] In a poem, he celebrated France:

> Oui, gloire à toi, gloire à toi! que maintenant l'on crie:
> "C'est un nègre, un mulâtre, il n'a point de patrie!"
> Moi, je brave ces cris!
> Car tout en m'arrachant mon maillot de misère
> M'adoptant pour un fruit de ton beau sein de mère,
> Tu réponds: "C'est mon fils!"

[Glory, glory to you! If now one says:
"He is a Negro, a mulatto, he has no fatherland!"
I defy these words!
Because extracting me from the swaddling of misery
Adopting me as one offspring in your beautiful maternal
    bosom,
You have answered: "He is my son!"][85]

France could not be the accomplice of the colonialist groups, and when informed of their deeds, she would welcome her sons who had "African skin" but "French blood."[86] Colonialist power was located in Bourbon white aristocracy. Houat set up not a conflictual dyadic political structure—whites/blacks—but a triadic one: Republican France/Bourbon white aristocracy/the free coloreds and slaves. In Houat's scheme, republican France was the Marianne of 1789, the opposition against the aristocracy, particularly because the island's name suggested a symbolic association with the *ancien régime,* the hated monarchy of the Bourbons. Réunionnais black intellectuals such as Houat or the poet Auguste Lacaussade saw themselves as sons of France whose legitimacy was denied by jealous brothers. France had delivered them from captivity in Africa, and France would deliver them from colonial chains. It was Bourbon that was guilty. "Hills of Bourbon, bow your haughty heads! Bend, bend," Houat wrote.[87] The colonial relationship was formulated thus: France, the good republican mother, and the colonies, where power was in the hands of bad men. France was the recourse against local landowners, vestiges of the Old Regime, and La Mère-Patrie was a protector against their abuses. Houat's appeal to France echoed revolutionary allegorical representations of the nation as a mother. He demanded equal access to the nourishing and loving motherly breast to which he was legitimately entitled as her son. He asked France to rest her protective hand on his head. But hateful white brothers in the colony were barring access to mother France.[88] He had to leave his native island. The black son had confidence in his metropolitan mother; it was she who had breast-fed him with "celestial thoughts."[89] She came now to his rescue and, "taming the lions, had taken [him] under the wing of [her] motherliness!"[90] Yet flying to her side in Paris, he had to leave a beloved sister and his native land, and he lamented over the separation.[91]

If Houat did not confront directly the regime that maintained slavery and unfair laws in the colonies, he showed his political opposition to the Old Regime by adopting the feminine representations of republican France.[92] Yet Houat resented his exile and wanted to vindicate himself and his companions. He published *Mémoire pour Louis Timagène Houat et pour ses compagnons d'infortune, tous hommes de couleur illégalement déportés de l'île Bourbon au mépris de l'amnistie royale de 1837,*[93] in which he pointed to the trial's numerous irregularities, analyzing them as the response of the colonial power to the demands of men of color for political equality. He protested the exclusion of mulattoes *libres* from public functions and the failure to apply in the colony the April 1833 law that had given them political rights.[94] He solicited for the exiles the right to return to their country and laid claims to indemnities for illegal detention. Houat wrote about his group's aspirations: "We know that emancipated slaves do not desire a separation from the metropole and that they appreciate the kindness of whites, their elders in civilization; we, who want the abolition of slavery, recognize the necessity of the institution of the family founded on marriage, morality and religion."[95] The political exile from Réunion reiterated the declaration he had made at the end of the trial: "Remember that one day we will be tried by the One who created in his own image whites, mulattos, and blacks."[96]

His novel, *Les Marrons,* published in Paris in 1844, imagined a postslavery Réunion.[97] The novel emulated a genre that was popular: the story of a slave who has leadership qualities and aspires to reconcile the divided colonial society but cannot succeed because of the irrational, stubborn, and racist resistance of colonial society. The slave has then no other choice than to rebel. Houat added to this script his own vision of a reconciliation based on métissage. He offered a utopian project of coexistence to compensate for the conflictual actual existence in Bourbon. Biological métissage, love, solidarity among the oppressed, and the ideals of equality and fraternity were the expressions of this utopia of racial harmony.[98]

Les Marrons

In *Les Marrons,* Louis-Timagène Houat struggled with the complexity of imagining a family romance that would establish the paternal function of the black man, a function denied by slavery and colonialism. This was an important issue, for the affirmation of the black paternal function would give the black man a place in the symbolic order. The symbolical (and during slavery, real) castration of the black man, Frantz Fanon later wrote, forbade him to construct his own Symbolic through the paternal function.[99] Even when Negroes were freed, Fanon argued, they remained prisoners of white racist stereotypes, their own images distorted by the images projected onto them by whites. The abolition of slavery would not necessarily guarantee the recovery of the paternal function by black men, for only a recovery achieved through violence and with the unconditional support of the black woman would reinstate a symbolized paternity. Houat's answer was to give Réunion's emancipated population a founding father who was black, but whose mother was white. Giving a black man the paternity of the island's population and making a white woman its mother set a genealogy contrary to the genealogy offered by colonialism.

French revolutionaries had sought to reduce the place of the father in the family romance. The displacement was necessary, Lynn Hunt argues, to establish the legitimacy of the romance of fraternity.[100] In the prerevolutionary days, the image of the "good father" gradually faded, and the father could only be a bad father, a tyrant. Through a series of legal regulations, the revolution sought to limit the power of the father and vested a large part of his power in the state. The state could now act as a protector of family members. The father had access to the paternal function but could not use this function to subjugate wife, sons, and daughters. The colonial system of slavery inscribed a structure of filiation in which the biological father had no access to the symbolic paternal function. The woman's maternal function was recognized insofar as her status determined the child's status: if she was free, the child was free; if she was a slave, the child was a slave. Slavery barred access to the double inscription that characterizes the paternal function: socially, the function is inscribed principally through the laws concerned with genealogy, filiation, and alliances.[101] Psychologically, the paternal function is inscribed in each individual by the means of the family structure. The father is the "representative of the Law." In other words, as Pierre Legendre puts it, "Each society fabricates some father [*du père*] for the child, and it is this operation that marks the child into a lineage and a genealogy."[102] Françoise Hurstel reminds us of the distinction between the social laws, which inscribe filiation, and the Law, which is the paternal function in which the Oedipus complex institutes the taboo of incest.[103] Social laws give an individual a place in a genealogy of names and a family structure: son of, daughter of, sister of. The law of the taboo of incest gives birth to culture and society, according to the Freudian scenario. Incest is an antisocial fact, Freud says, and to exist, civilization had to renounce incest. The paternal function institutes the Law by urging the child to renounce the incestuous love toward the mother.

Regardless of the debate about the universality of this law, what interests us here is that in a society in which the paternal function is recognized along the lines that have just been described, when a group of men is denied this function to reinforce the power of another group of men, this fact is not without meaning. Hurstel contends that every society offers *du père*. In other words, there is in every society a paternal function, and biological fathers, or individuals who are not the biological father, can assume that function. Subjective conditions—through the experience of the Oedipus complex—give the child access to the status of "subject" through the inscription of the father as the "representative of the law."[104] In other words, to become an individual, to reach subjectivity, to be detached from the maternal, the child must accept that the father represents the law, the authority. Psychoanalysis has confined the mother, the woman, to the realm of countercivilization.[105] Why then insist on the role of the paternal function in the colony if it means perpetuating the denial of the mother? It seems, though, that it is important to delimit the role of the paternal function in the colony insofar as its denial by slavery and colonialism has implied different constructions of the norms of masculinity and femininity. Or, rather, it is interesting to analyze how the norms about masculinity and femininity have been affected by race and colonialism.

In slavery, the symbolic paternal function was in the hands of the master. One was not the "son of" but the "slave of." Enslaved fathers could not assume the function of representing and imposing the law—the social regulations—because this power was vested in the master. That children inherited their status from their mother, and not from their father, further complicated the access of slave-fathers to the paternal function.[106] Scholars have argued that

slaves who were taken from matrilineal societies kept a system of
filiation through the mother, and this system constituted a coun-
terpower to the colonial law. The transmission of genealogy and
history was the function of the mother. Nevertheless, though one
must certainly recognize the transmission of genealogy through the
mother, one should not underestimate the extent to which the
paternal function was invested, in the colonies, in the white master.
Hortense Spillers has argued that "Fatherhood, at best a supreme
cultural courtesy, attenuates here into a monstrous accumulation of
power. One has been 'made' and 'bought' by disparate currencies,
linking back to a common origin of exchange and domination."[107]
From the fact that slave societies were often matrifocal, one cannot
infer that mothers had power. Again, to cite Spillers, "Such naming
[matrifocality, matrilinearity, matriarchy] is false because 'motherhood' is not perceived in the prevailing social climate as a legitimate procedure of cultural inheritance."[108] We have thus, Spillers
concludes, a "dual fatherhood comprised of the African father's
banished name and body and the captor father's mocking presence."[109] Houat, a *son,* wanted to inscribe the *paternal* function so
as to inscribe himself into a paternal genealogy. Metropolitan men
had proclaimed a metaphorical fraternity and challenged a patriarchal law that extended to the realm of politics. Republican
fraternity did not forbid the paternal function. Revolutionary men
were fathers, socially and symbolically, and brothers, politically.
Under the regime of slavery, the access to metaphorical fraternity
for republican men went through the establishment of the paternal
function. To become brothers, black men sought to be recognized
as fathers. It was not possible to be free of an essential feature of
slavery—the denial of the paternal function—simply by formulat-
ing a fraternity.

The narrative of *Les Marrons* opens with a secret meeting of four
slaves, at which they express their desire to end their servitude. The
year is 1833. The slaves are plotting an escape.[110] The conspirators
are three Madagascans and a Creole. All are "under the same yoke,
equal in misery and friends cursing the same oppression."[111] They
were forced to witness the murders of their mothers; they were
taken away from their homes and families; slavery is now compel-
ling them to be the witnesses of its abuses and crimes: rape, hunger,
and unfair punishments. They deplore the complicity of their
brothers and sisters who agree to carry out the sentences imposed

by the masters. The slaves ponder their options. Câpre says that he has read that "in France, in England, there are men, children of God, who think about us, pray for us, and claim that despite our black skin we are white like them. They are asking the King and the Queen to give us freedom."[112] Câpre encourages his companions to be patient, to wait for "this good thing called emancipation."[113] Meanwhile they can become maroons to escape bad treatments on the plantation. His grandfather is a maroon, and Câpre promises his friends that they will find a paradise in the interior of the island: milk, syrup, honey, birds, everything in abundance. But the other slaves are not convinced. They want to steal a small boat and return to their native land, Madagascar. The four conspirators decide to go their separate ways; Câpre will go to the mountains, and the three Madagascans will return to the plantation and escape by boat the following night. Câpre goes to the Salazes Mountains, known to be a hideout for the maroons.[114] Spotted by slave hunters, he is hunted down and cornered by their dogs, and he falls into a canyon. Saved from a deathly fall by a vine, he sees the entry of a cave carved in the cliff, in which he meets a "young white woman, who, seated in a corner, is holding a young mulatto child whom she is breastfeeding."[115] She presents herself: her name is Marie, and she has taken refuge in the cave with Frême, a young black man whom she has married.

Frême arrives and tells Câpre his story. He is the son of an African warrior; his African name was Coudjoupa, which means lion or panther.[116] He was taken too young to remember his people. Although he has no memory of his mother, he remembers his courageous father, who died resisting the capture of his son. First sold to Portuguese slave traders, the child was later sold to French slave traders and taken to be sold in the colonies of the Indian Ocean. But the British and the French navies were roaming the seas to enforce the ban on the slave trade.[117] The French navy intercepted the slave ship, and Coudjoupa became the property of the French state. "He could not have had a better master."[118] Baptized with the name of Frême,[119] the child, who was now six, was given to the children of the Atelier Colonial's warden to amuse them. The young slave learned to write and read by observing the children.[120] He even became their tutor and grew attached to the youngest girl, Marie. "He would have given everything for the right to remain at her feet all his life, like a slave!"[121] But as they grew up, they were separated. She lived in the master's house, and he lived in a slave cabin. One night (the young slave was now twenty), as a fire was destroying the master's house, Frême saved Marie and brought her to his cabin. On recovering, Marie, who was now an orphan, discovered that she had always loved Frême. Frême and Marie married. But their union was an insult to the racist colonies. Harassed, insulted, their house attacked, Frême beaten by resentful whites, the couple decided to flee to the mountains.

After being fed by Marie and Frême, Câpre decides to go in search of his grandfather. Frême shows him the way out of the cave. They are spotted by slave hunters, who shoot Frême and capture Câpre. He is brought back to his master, who throws him in jail. There, exhausted, Câpre falls asleep and has a dream:

He saw Frême appear on the top of one of the Salazes. Frême was of superhuman height, and, instead of one wound, he showed many wounds on the left and right sides of his chest. From these wounds, a flow of blood gushed forth falling over the island. And the scared inhabitants hid themselves in vain. As his blood was submerging the island, one could see Frême becoming taller and taller. . . . Soon, the island was a lake of blood where men were struggling for their life. . . . Frême disappeared like a rainbow. In his place, a beautiful, magnificent white woman who looked like Marie appeared with a child at her breast. The woman raised the child above her head, as the priest does with the host, and at once those who were struggling in the lake of blood took on the color of the child, which was a mixture of black, white, yellow and red. . . . A voice was heard which said things about a change, about the unity of colors, about the future of the colonial races. Then the woman disappeared like Frême. As she left, a drop of milk fell from her breast. And this drop of milk covered the lake of blood which became a land covered with trees and animals, a land rich and fertile, a land where there was a difference neither of color nor of condition among the inhabitants, where all were free.[122]

Mothers, Fathers, and Filiation

The character of Marie, the white mother, can be interpreted as a disavowal of Madagascan and Indian mothers, who were historically the mothers of the first children on the island.[123] Why this foreclosure of the black mother? If disavowal is the denial of external reality,[124] and foreclosure consists in "not symbolizing what ought to be symbolized,"[125] then Houat operates in a symbolic realm that demands the foreclosure and disavowal of the black mother. The black female slave is barred from the maternal function. I will argue that this foreclosure allows Houat to save France from an indictment for crimes of slavery and colonialism and to acknowledge the role of white Europeans in the making of the Réunionnais.

Houat imagined a new family for the island's population. Not only did Frême and Marie give birth to a new generation, but they also found a black grandfather in their *marronnage*. When the couple first arrived in the mountains, neither Frême nor Marie had the skills to survive as maroons. Unbeknownst to them, an old man had been following them, observing the couple and trying to decide whether they were maroons like himself. He finally introduced himself. His name was Jean, and he had been a maroon for the last fifteen years.[126] He was a soldier, a "French citizen" who fought for France. Yet when he returned to the island, whites wanted to reenslave him. He could not appeal to the courts because justice on the island was controlled by the whites and the wealthy.[127]

Surprised to hear Marie identifying herself as a maroon, Jean becomes even more interested in Frême and Marie's fate. He adopts the young couple and teaches them the life of *marrons:* "Do not be afraid, my children; you will be safe. Neither hunger, nor hunters, neither the whites nor bad weather, nothing will torment you. You can be sure of that. And I am calling you my children because I will keep you safe, I will take care of you until the end like a good father."[128] The filiation dreamed by Houat set up a black grandfather, a slave who had served France and was now maroon, his black adopted son, his white adopted daughter-in-law, and a métis grandson whom the old black man would hold on his knee and baptize.[129] With this rhetorical strategy, Houat imagined a genealogy that subverted the white patriarchal genealogy. Black men could marry and recognize their sons. Frême, himself an orphan, reinvented his history, emancipated himself from state slavery, and instituted himself as the founder of a people.

Frême gave himself two fathers, a father-warrior in Africa and a father on the island who was literate and entitled to the status of French citizen. Yet both fathers ultimately failed: they were unable to protect their child from slavery. The courage of Frême's father had not been able to stop slave traders from capturing his son. Jean had been a guide, but he could not lead the slaves in the struggle against the island's white aristocracy. He did not exhibit the qualities of a leader, as his adopted son would. Frême would save Câpre and the Madagascans from death and slavery, whereas his father had failed to save him from bondage. He would lead a band of "disciplined, resolute and indomitable maroons, which constitutes an army that is belying the theory of black servitude and recruiting new members every day under its valiant leader."[130] Frême understood the politics of colonialism and explained to Câpre the foundations of the white colonists' power: "The whites support each other, they are strong, they are rich, they maintain our enslavement with the money earned from our servitude. . . . They will make laws to protect plants, fish, horses, dogs, and birds but not for us, not to secure our liberty."[131] Frême does not believe that whites in faraway countries are mobilizing for the freedom of the slaves. He says to Câpre: "A large ocean separates us from them and they have so many other things to think about. They do not see us, they do not know us. They will take care of what is close to them, and we will be forgotten because we are far away."[132]

Jean-François Sam-Long's remark—that Frême was not born a leader but became one after an experience patiently acquired in a long period of solitude—could be modified. Frême's story contained the elements of the mythical hero's narrative.[133] The hero is the child of eminent parents. His birth is surrounded by threats and dangers. He is saved from tragic circumstances. Like the mythical hero, Frême is a rebel and an innovator, a revolutionary.[134] Frême was a born leader according to the conventions of the birth and solitary making of the hero; heroes are shaped and tested through long hardships. What this tale of a loving and protecting father said was that a black man could experience genuine love and that sexual intercourse between a black man and a white woman did not have to be rape. This strategy of representation allowed Houat to question racist assumptions about black masculinity, love, and sexuality. Frême was presented as a gentle father and husband, both functions that had been denied to the black man by slavery.

Câpre's dream symbolizes the primal scene. Câpre is a Creole slave, born on the island. He has no other native land. How will Câpre inscribe his origins in a land that denies his individuality?

The fantasy of origins in the dream is a response to this question. Câpre witnesses the engendering by Frême and Marie of a métis child and a new people. The fantasy of origins "translates, through the mediation of an imaginary scenario which pretends to recapture [the origins], the insertion of the symbolic in the real of the body. [The primal scene figures] the conjunction between the biological fact of conception (and birth) and the symbolical fact of filiation, between the 'savage act' of coitus and the existence of a triad mother-child-father."[135] In the scenario imagined by Câpre, the two events occur together. Father and mother preside over the birth of the child and of the future humanity. The father gives birth to the mother, who, in turn, gives birth to the child. These births are metaphorically enacted. The body of Frême fades into the body of Marie, who holds the child. The birth is both a biological and a historical act: the métis child and the free, nonracial and equal society are born together. The novel ends in ambivalence: "Frême, after appeasing the rebels, invited those who were not too compromised—and they were the majority—to return to their masters, giving them the hope of a future deliverance."[136] It is not clear whether the deliverance will come from France, as Câpre had said, or from Frême and his army of maroons. The last sentence of the novel suddenly subverts the narrative by introducing the present, whereas the narrative has been in the past tense. The last sentence, "Frême is still the valiant chief of this army today,"[137] leaves the reader with the sense that the struggle goes on. Houat saw colonial society as dying. Whites were symbolically represented by Câpre's master, Zézé Delinpotant. As Jean-François Sam-Long has remarked, Z is the last letter of the alphabet, and Delinpotant can be read *de l'impotent* (the impotent).[138]

In Houat's family romance, it was paradoxically the father who was *certissimus*, who could claim his paternity without doubt. In contrast, the mother function was uncertain. If it was clear that Marie was the biological mother of the métis child, I suggested earlier that the maternal function was distributed among three characters: Marie, the sexual partner of Frême and biological mother of his child; France, La Mère-Patrie; and the island's interior, the maternal native space. The interior of the island was shown as a maternal space, the native mother of the enslaved children of Réunion. Câpre was saved from a certain death when he fell off the precipice by a vine that brought him into the cave where

Frême and Marie lived. The cave suggested a uterine space, and the vine the umbilical cord. Câpre returned to the womb, the interior of the interior of the island, where the maternal island hides her children. The interior of the island was the heart of the island's body. Ranges of mountains encircle spaces opened by rivers that flow toward the coast. Between the high mountains and the vast expanse of the ocean lies a narrow strip, the dying world of the whites.

The novel was a pastoral that constructed a political geography that had aesthetic consequences.[139] The island was a garden, but a divided garden: on the one hand, the tame, cultivated garden of a cruel world; on the other, a wild, generous nature, feeding her maroon children.[140] On the coast, the plantations' beautiful gardens and magnificent mansions masked the ugliness of slavery. "Look now, in the middle of this wealth and abundance, these poor Negroes who are naked, emaciated, who are dying of hunger and are forced to work like animals!" Inland, nature and beauty reigned, albeit already invaded and threatened by slave hunters and their dogs. It was the duty of maroons to protect their world from the incursions of the whites. The narrative presented the two worlds—the coast and the interior—as antithetical and suggested that there could not be any exchange between them. This political geography suggested a specific reading of the political history of the island: rebellion was not possible in the plantation. There was no outside native land to return to; the Madagascan slaves had tried and failed in their attempt to reach Madagascar, the country of their ancestors. What had to be done was to transform the center of the island into a fortress. To defend the maternal space of the island's interior against the world of slavery was the duty of her legitimate sons.

France was the third mother, whom Houat saved from the accusation of complicity in colonial crimes by presenting France as a mother who would protect her colonized children against colonial masculine brutality.[141] The decaying world of colonialism and slavery lay in a narrow space between the mountains inhabited by rebellious brothers and the ocean from which France's messengers would arrive with orders contesting the white aristocrats' power. Houat's poem *Une action de grâce* set up the scene of rescue.[142] The poem ended each of its stanzas with "Glory to the Lord! It is French!—See, at her rear / The noble banner is shining / The three-colored banner! / From Le Havre, See its emblem! / It is a French ship that is coming, and coming from France! / Glory to the Lord!" The ship was bringing deliverance, love: "Yes, the glorious ship is full of love / It is like a lover who sees the smile / Of the virgin of his heart!"[143] But if the ship was bringing love and deliverance from France, she was also taking the son away from his native motherland. Sons were divided in their love for their mother-island and for La Mère-Patrie. The urban Houat invested the interior of the island with the native maternal function. The maroon was the legitimate son of the native mother. Zézé Delinpotant was the illegitimate son who had acquired his status through cruelty and abuse. The legitimate son turned to his mother-France and asked her to unmask the impostor. Houat challenged the white aristocracy of Réunion but saved the center of power because France offered the language of republicanism, a vocabulary through which the claims for emancipation could be expressed. The terms of the republican doctrine, *liberté, égalité, fraternité,* could be opposed to the terms of the colonial doctrine: enslavement, inequality, division. Houat gave to the characters of his drama a native birth, but he borrowed the language of French republicanism to make their claims.

Neither parricide nor matricide preceded the constitution of the fraternal social bond in *Les Marrons.* Instead, there was a displacement. The peripheral patriarchal white world was left to its decay. There was no bad mother in the world of the "bad" father; he was alone, impotent, no longer a father, barely a man. Slave women were not active characters in the novel. When they were named, it was as victims, to denounce the abuses and the crimes of slavery. The characters of Kaïla and Ravana appeared only to indicate that slave women were subjected to rape by the masters. A mother was evoked to speak the horror of being separated from loved ones.[144]

The Ideal of Métissage

With his dream, Câpre was giving birth to himself. In the cave (a womb), he had met the white mother breast-feeding the son. It is his *passage* through a vision of the white mother—coming into the womb, witnessing the scene of the mother feeding the child, as in a walking dream, then leaving the womb—that supplies Câpre with the symbols of his dream. Marie is the name of Christ's mother, and the dream has obvious Christian referents: the bleeding chest of Frême, the name of Marie, the son in which the humanity to come can recognize itself, the voice that is heard, the deluge that drowns a sinful world, the rainbow.[145] Marie is also Marianne, the symbol of the republic.[146] Marie holding the métis child claims to the colonial society that she, the republic, is the mother of Câpre. And the father of her son is black. The black father has inseminated France, the republic. The progress represented by métissage and equality is made possible only because the white mother has given birth to it. The mother "stands for law and necessity: of time, Death, *difference.*"[147] There is further the Fanonian interpretation of the choice of a white woman as Frême's lover. It is the effect of black man's alienation, namely, of his desire for the white woman.[148]

Houat's narrative presents a series of reversals of the stereotypes of métissage. He gives to a black man the role of the father, and the union between Marie and Frême is fecund. Yet what Frême ejaculates is blood, and what Marie ejaculates is milk or sperm. Blood is ambivalent: it fertilizes and it defiles.[149] The legend says that the blood that came out of Medusa's head "had magical properties: blood flowing from the left vein was a mortal poison, while blood flowing from the right vein was a remedy capable of resuscitating the dead."[150] Frême has wounds on both sides of his breast. His blood destroys the colonial society. Blood is the blood of the slaves from which colonial riches have been made. Blood gushing out of the black man's body washes out the violence of slavery. Blood is the sign of the unspeakable, the martyred bodies of the slaves. How to say the pain and suffering of being taken from one's land, one's parents, thrown in ships, taken to foreign lands, working under the whip, being dehumanized? Blood says it. It destroys and purifies.[151] Frême's blood reenacts the Flood: it drowns the colonial society; then comes the rainbow, the sign of reconciliation; nature is again plentiful, the world is peaceful, a new humanity cleansed of the sins and vices of the old world appears. Biblical allegories are invoked to express the condemnation of colonialism's immorality and wickedness. Then the milk of the white woman fertilizes the land and restores the island to the state of precolonial days: a beautiful and fertile Garden of Eden. If Houat has given Frême a fertility that was refused to blacks by literature, in the metaphoric dream, it is Marie's milk or sperm—milk and sperm are both of "milky" aspect—that fertilizes. This milk or sperm falls from her breast, whereas Frême's contribution to the birth falls from wounds on his chest. The ejaculation of blood is red like a tumescent penis: "These wounds were large and deep, as canyons in the sea, and from them, with the same strength as a whale's when it spouts water from its mouth, columns of blood rose in the air, like immense red rockets, and fell back on all parts of the island."[152] The blood of Frême is the blood that covers the newborn child, the blood of the mother's uterus. The African provides the womb in which the métis takes form: Mother-Africa, black mother-island. Houat blurs the boundaries between man and woman, black and white, sperm and milk: each element had a role in the making of a new race. Two essential elements of life, blood and milk, purify the land of its sinful origin: slavery and rape are followed by loving fecundity.

The métis child is the fiction on which new identifications are built. He is the mirror in which the island's population can identify itself. Lacan defined the mirror-stage as *identification,* "namely, the transformation that takes place in the subject when the subject assumes an image." The mirror-stage is "a symbolic matrix in which the *I* is precipitated in a primordial form, before it is objectified in the dialectic of identification."[153] In other words, the mirror-stage is the stage in the process of identification whereby the individual finds the image that would sustain a primordial identity. The métis is the site of primordial identification, the *imago,* a fictional but necessary stage in the construction of one's identity. Marie holds up a mirror to the population in which they find their symbolic ego ideal. A social pact is made through the identification with the métis child, a pact that overcomes the impasse of aggressive relations, of the murderous racial relation constructed by slavery. But, in Lacan, the *I* needs also to meet the *Other,* so that the illusion of autonomy given by the first imago is challenged. The primordial "I" of the mirror-stage thinks of itself as autonomous; it is a fiction constructed on a illusory autonomy, an autonomy that excludes the other. This illusion finds its limits when the individual understands the necessary connection with the other. The métis in Houat appears to fulfill both functions, of the *I* and of the *Other,* because the child bears the marks of plural origins and, from these foundations, may escape the fiction of the undivided "I" that informs most discourses about identity. But the fusion of all colors defeats the construction of a heterogeneous subject, because fusion is the foreclosure of the distinctive qualities of the different components. The métis's color is now a "mixing of black, white, yellow, and red, similar to the color of some Orientals or mulattos."[154] Color disappears as a marker of difference rather than becoming a difference among others. The mirror in which the population recognizes itself, the fiction that supports the process of identification, is specifically gendered: it is a boy that Marie holds.

Houat's idealization of métissage has been contested for its views of race and class reconciliation and the disavowal of the feminine. Rose-May Nicole argues that Houat was still obeying "white aesthetics." The character of Marie still posits an absolute superiority of the whites, Nicole writes.[155] Africa is totally forgotten, and Marie monopolizes the place of the feminine. Nicole further points to the historical role of métis slaves as mediators between the masters and black slaves: "Creole slaves were presented as social models by the masters. Enslavement was mixed with affectivity, [because Creole slaves often worked in the houses as domestics or nannies]. It was through the Creole slaves that contacts between the white and the non-white culture took place, facilitating acculturation."[156] Métis were not the harbingers of change but those who promoted the integration of nonwhites into white culture. Mary Louise Pratt has argued that the "lesson to be learned from the colonial love stories" is that "cultural harmony through romance always breaks down."[157] Romantic love was a device for "embracing groups like the mulattos into the political and social imaginary as these groups gained new political importance."[158] In the late nineteenth century, métis became positive characters in stories of romantic love with white partners. Abolitionists encouraged such novels. To Vera M. Kutzinski, "*mestizaje* becomes legitimated as an exclusively male project or achievement in which interracial, heterosexual rape can be refigured as a fraternal embrace across color lines and, significantly, across a female body absented by rape."[159]

Houat's choice of a white mother and of a métis child as the image of a future humanity entailed a disavowal and an exclusion. It contained the dilemma that would haunt anticolonialists in Réunion: How to construe the relation to France? How to think politically the contribution of France in the making of the island's population and culture, of the alterity French people had brought, of the Other that they were? Houat wanted a love story between

France and her colony in the Indian Ocean. He offered a romantic love solution to a political, sexual, and cultural problem. He recognized that filiation could not be thought through the foreclosure of one element, but he resolved this question by operating the foreclosure of the native woman: no girl child was born, no Madagascan, African, Hindu, or Chinese mother existed. Houat's novel imagined a new polity, but it remained ensnared in patriarchy and fidelity to France, that is, to La Mère-Patrie, both being elements that would long haunt emancipatory politics on the island.

The novel pledged a healing of class and race divisions through fraternity and equality and the erasure of differences.[160] Houat's utopia promised regeneration. Truth and the Good were embodied in Beauty, the beauty of an island in which the sins of illegitimate fathers were washed by a flood. Houat spoke like a prophet, and through his messianic tone, he invented himself as a messenger of men and progress.[161] Frême was the *réprouvé,* the outcast, and the savior of a dying society. Houat's doctrine was a mix of beliefs anchored in Christian spirituality and humanism. The family romance dreamed by Houat was a means to "interject a forbidden alterity"[162] into the colonial imagination, the encounter between a black man and a white woman. Houat introduced in literature a historical character, *le marron* (the maroon), that had until then figured only in judicial condemnations or in texts that expressed fear and hatred for this character. And this historical agent would take on a mythical dimension in Réunion's imaginary.[163]

Houat was right to include France in the island's genealogy, but he looked to France to redeem a dignity threatened in his native land by the whites. The more his dignity was threatened, the more he clung to France. He made no assault on the bonds that kept people of the island in dependence to France. Colonial "children" protested against parental abuse, but the agents of the abuse were local agents, not the mother country. Studying another example of colonial children rejecting parental abuse, Edgar Burrows and Michael Wallace have argued that in the American Revolution, "the key lay in the realization that children grow up, and as they grow acquire increasing rights."[164] The repeated violation of the rights of the free coloreds and the slaves in Réunion did not lead them to sever the bonds with France. It was the white colonists who had threatened, during the French Revolution, to break those bonds with France.[165] To the oppressed, fraternity and equality were still the promise. Houat's discourse of racial democracy masked and showed that the logic of métissage produces an unassimilable *reste*—something that resists or escapes incorporation.[166] The vagrants, Creole culture and language, escaped the logic of Houat's métissage. To disown and to found are the two intertwined operations that structure the family romance, Monique Schneider has said.[167] Houat's family romance was both a foundation and a disavowal. Four years after the publication of *Les Marrons,* the Second Republic abolished slavery.

"In the Name of the French People . . ."

In the name of the French people,
The Provisional Government,
Considering that slavery is a violation of human dignity
That by denying man's free will, slavery suppresses the natural principle of right and duty
That it is a flagrant violation of the republican dogma:
Liberty, Equality, Fraternity,

Orders
Article 1—That slavery be abolished in all French colonies and possessions two months after the promulgation of this decree March 4, 1848.[168]

Nine months after the decree, sixty-two thousand individuals, six out of every ten inhabitants, became free citizens in Réunion.[169] Conservation was the principle of colonial society, Barbaroux had said, and that meant liberty and equality for all *with* colonialist exploitation and the perpetuation of colonial culture, racism, and politics. Emancipation was incontestably a radical change, and yet it enforced, as Marx has written, the "separation of man [*Mensch*] from his community, from himself and from other men."[170] They had been the slaves and "children" of the masters, and now they were workers; now they became children of the state.

The act of emancipation was preceded by both a series of disciplinary measures and a campaign of "moral" indoctrination led by the Catholic Church. Houat's choice of ending his novel with a maroons' revolt that was supposed to take place in 1833 ignored or disguised the new social forces that were emerging.[171] By 1815 the sugarcane industry had imposed its monopoly on the island's economy. Growing sugarcane demanded a larger workforce than growing coffee, and the workforce was in majority male.[172] However, access to slave labor had become more difficult and expensive because of the ban on the slave trade. Expansion of the sugarcane industry between 1830 and 1848 meant more work for the slaves and a worsening of work conditions. A series of regulations issued in July 1845 allowed the masters to extend the workday and to demand night work between July 1 and January 31 every year.[173] If these laws made provisions for breaks and holidays, they were barely respected, and the administrative authorities had neither the will nor the means to enforce the laws. The white aristocracy was preparing for the transition from slavery to wage work.[174] In a February 1843 issue of the *Feuille Hebdomadaire de Bourbon,* an article advocated contract work, this "eminently philanthropic oeuvre: seeking enslaved men to make them free."[175] The immigration of foreign workers would promote the public good and serve the "interest of the metropole, which needs colonial goods."[176] It would be an enterprise that would help the populations of Africa and Asia, "populations that are so poor that they would agree to work for 10 or 15 francs a month."[177]

Indentured work would replace slavery. Contract workers were brought to the island as soon as the restrictions of the Treaty of Paris began to threaten the slave trade. In the early years of the July Monarchy, workers were recruited from Africa, Malaysia, Madagascar, and India.[178] A series of measures were taken to define the rights, duties, and responsibilities of these workers, since they were not subjected to the laws of the *Code Noir.*[179] However, they were often treated like slaves. They protested their conditions of work and living, petitioning the colonial authorities. "On many occasions, we have had the honor to address to you pleas denouncing the conditions of work and living of the Indians, our fellows, whom we represent. Until this day, we have received no answer and yet our situation is worsening," the Indians Sarapa, Soubasaidou, Natchiary, and Vincalois wrote to the governor in February 1838.[180] Chinese workers, coming after 1843, acquired the reputation of being extremely "difficult." A planter, De K/Veguen, said that despite an initial apparent submission, they showed a stubborn determination to disobey orders and that they were a bad example for the slaves.

Revolts, refusals to go to work, protests, and marronnage were the forms of resistance that indentured workers adopted.[181] Their form of marronnage was different from Frême's. The social deviants who haunted the 1830s were no longer the maroons who hid and settled in the mountains but vagrant maroons feared by the bourgeoisie and the landowners. The vagrant-maroon entered the colonial psyche as a threatening figure, disrupting the social and sexual order. Poor whites and métis were often vagrant-maroons as well.[182] Even though vagrancy was not yet a major social phenomenon in the 1830s, it already menaced the forms of social control on which the plantation economy rested: absolute regimentation of movements and strict regulation of relationships among people. In 1843 local authorities ordered free workers to carry a work pass; if they were found without the pass, they would be punished for vagrancy.[183] In the same year, the governor created a colonial institute whose "principal goal was to offer to the poor an education that would enhance their industrial and moral progress."[184] An 1844 article in *La Feuille Hebdomadaire de Bourbon* summarized the whites' racist beliefs:

The Black is dissolute, lazy, lacking foresight. In more than one way, he is more like a depraved child than a man. How will we civilize these unrefined creatures, how will we elevate their ideas, ennoble their instincts, cleanse their mores, inspire in them love of cleanliness, need for order, taste for marriage, and desire for family? Finally, how will we give them the moral habits that support society? . . . Emancipation will be in our colonies the most profound revolution that a society can experience because it will affect private propriety, laws, classes, social conditions, work, all the institutions. . . . Yes, we must find ways to maintain order in a society where the proletarian class will be much more numerous than the class of owners.[185]

Slave owners pondered where to find new workers. Should they be taken from Africa? Madagascar? India? China? The "qualities and defects" of each group were carefully weighed.[186] Colonial authorities regretted that there were not enough women imported as contract workers because women served to root men in a country. Women could furthermore serve as domestics.[187] The class of landowners lobbied for the opening of markets to recruit indentured workers *and* for the colonization of these markets. "The destiny of the island of Bourbon is to give the first and greatest impulsion for the colonization of Madagascar," a newspaper wrote in 1845. Landowners feared the alliance between poor whites and the emancipated population. Sending poor whites to Madagascar would accomplish three goals: getting rid of a threatening social group, having a cheap army, and supplying colonists.[188] Poor and despised in Bourbon, they would experience racial superiority in Madagascar.[189]

The 1848 Romance of Fraternité

On February 24, 1848, the French provisional republican government published its first declaration,[190] which delimited the dual preoccupation of the government: order and unity. Violence in the streets had to stop, and the fraternal unity of the people had to prevail over proletarian fraternity.[191] The 1848 revolution affirmed the discourse of fraternity with even more strength than the 1789 revolution had.[192] Mona Ozouf has outlined the difficult history of fraternité in the republican motto.[193] She has shown that during the French Revolution, the terms of the motto were not stable. The favorite pair was liberty and equality. Fraternity did not appear in the 1789 declaration and occupied a very secondary position in the Constitution of 1791 and the Declaration of Rights of 1793. Although there were festivals to celebrate liberty or equality, none celebrated fraternity. The difficult history of fraternity could be attributed, Ozouf has argued, to its symbolic implications, which were of a different order than those of liberty and equality. Fraternity of the French Revolution was rebellious; it was a "revolutionary and not contract, community and not individuality."[194] The fraternity of the French revolution was rebellious; it was a "revolutionary fraternity," which consisted in "helping the unfortunate, defending patriots who are oppressed, pursuing corrupting aristocrats, denouncing counter-revolutionaries."[195] After the long interval of the empire and the July Monarchy, the republican triad reappeared. And it was the 1848 revolution that gave fraternity its place. "Of the three terms, fraternity is the highest, the most accomplished: the one which resumes, contains and goes beyond the two others, for it is able to weave together the partial truths inherited from the Revolution and to construct a common religion," Ozouf has written of the 1848 fraternité.[196] Crémieux, the 1848 minister of justice, defined fraternity in these terms: "All class distinctions are erased, all antagonisms disappear when confronted with this sacred fraternity that makes the children of one fatherland the children of one family."[197] Lamartine claimed that what had defined the 1792 social bond could no longer define the 1848 social bond. "Today, there are no distinct and unequal classes. Liberty has emancipated the people. Equality has leveled everything. Fraternity has united us."[198] To the French historian Marcel David, Lamartine's insistence on fraternity indicated not an indifference to liberty and equality, whose inscription had been consolidated in the 1791 Constitution, but rather a desire to transcend social classes. "Fraternity [to Lamartine] was more absolute, more sacred, and also more conservative"[199] and could be opposed to the aspirations to equality that led to the June insurrection.[200] David has called this moment *la fraternité officialisée* (the officialized fraternity). Although Karl Marx's opinion on this kind of fraternity is known, it deserves to be fully quoted:

The phrase which corresponded to this imaginary abolition of class relations was *fraternité*, general fraternization and brotherhood. This pleasant abstraction from class antagonisms, this sentimental reconciliation of contradictory class interests, this fantastic transcendence of the class struggle, this *fraternité* was the actual slogan of the February revolution. The classes had been divided by a mere *misunderstanding* and Lamartine christened the Provisional Government of 24 February "*un gouvernement qui suspend ce malentendu terrible qui existe entre les différentes classes.*"[201]

Marx seemed to deny a revolutionary dimension to fraternity. He did not see that in the case of colonialism and slavery, the principle of fraternity could be a genuinely radical doctrine. Yet already in January 1844—the year of the publication of *Les Marrons*—a thousand Parisian workers had signed a petition in favor of abolishing slavery. They wrote that slavery was a plague: "It is in obedience to the great principle of human fraternity that we come to you in the name of our poor brothers, the slaves. In the name of the working class, we want to protest vigorously against those who support slavery. . . . The worker belongs to himself: nobody has the right to whip him, to sell him, to separate him violently from his wife, his children, his friends."[202] Workers in Lyon followed the Parisian workers' example and petitioned the government.

In 1848 Victor Schoelcher alluded to the workers' petitions in his speeches in favor of emancipation. He concluded the report of the commission constituted in March 1848 to prepare the decree of emancipation with these words: "[The republic] repairs the crime that took these unfortunate people from their parents, their native country, by giving them France for their *patrie* and, as their heritage, by giving them all the rights of the French citizen; and with this decision, France testifies that she does not exclude anyone from her immortal motto: *Liberté, égalité, fraternité.*"[203] The argument was different from that of the 1844 workers' petition that had demanded the end of slavery in the name of the worker's inalienable right to own his body. Schoelcher argued that slaves were ready to be freed because they were already "good workers," respected private property and social order, and were good Christians.[204] 1848 fraternity had without a doubt a religious dimension, and the representations of fraternity were full of Christian referents. The engraving *Aux Peuples* showed Fraternity carrying a cross.[205] Equality and Fraternity have the visages of saints. At their feet, women and men, workers and bourgeois, blacks and whites are on their knees, unchained. The link of republican fraternity with Christian and Freemasonry fraternity mitigated revolutionary fraternity (the union of the oppressed).

One can clearly see the differences between the emancipations of 1789 and 1848 in their allegorical representations. *L'abolition de l'esclavage proclamée à la Convention le 16 pluviôse an II* (February 4, 1794) shows the president of the convention announcing the abolition of slavery to the assembly.[206] He is opening his arms to a young black man. On his left, a black woman is seated, and another one is standing. In the public, whites and blacks are embracing. On the right corner hangs the Declaration of Rights. There is a burst of enthusiasm, an élan. In contrast, Auguste François Biard's 1848 painting *Abolition de l'esclavage* shows a French official announcing their liberation to a crowd of grateful blacks.[207] He is no longer opening his arms to a black man. Black women are on their knees. One is in prayer in front of an idol; another bows in front of two young white women. The republican flag has replaced the Declaration of Rights. In the first representation, blacks are present in the assembly that decides their fate. In the *Abolition de l'esclavage,* the decision has been made without them, and a white man is bringing them the news.

The Republican Petit Bourgeois in the Colony

In Réunion, slave owners protested when they learned that abolition was near. They claimed that "the colonists have not invented
slavery, they were subjected to it. . . . They were, and still are,
governed by men that they have not chosen, subjected to laws that
they have not made, often treated with contempt, even though
they were always devoted to France."[208] They demanded to be
consulted and insisted that they did not oppose emancipation but
wanted the harvest to be completed, disciplining workplaces instituted, and asylums for older slaves created. They were entitled to
compensation and indemnities, they wrote, because slaves were
their property, having been bought and paid for. Slaves on the
island were aware of their impending freedom. They were restive
and already walking off the plantation in many places. News of
the proclamation of the republic had arrived in May. There was
a climate of expectation mixed with fears, apprehensions, and
trepidations.

    Joseph-Napoléon Sarda Garriga arrived in Réunion on Octo-
ber 14, 1848, bringing the decree of emancipation.[209] In Paris, he
had been the secretary of Benjamin Constant, a writer and an important thinker of liberal democracy, who was a member of a small
but very active group that advocated the end of slavery. Under
Constant's influence, Sarda joined republican circles.[210] He was arrested and jailed for three months in July 1833 with other members
of the Sociéte des Droits de l'Homme.[211] He was at the Hôtel de
Ville of Paris when the Second Republic was proclaimed. Sarda
Garriga embraced the slogan of moderate republicans, "L'Ordre
dans la Liberté" (Order with Liberty). He feared the proletariat
and was said to have recoiled at the sight of workers demonstrating
with the red flag.[212] Three days after his arrival in Réunion, Sarda
Garriga made his first declaration. He had come, he wrote, to
"bring unity, fraternity," along with "order, prosperity and development."[213] Slaves should not forget that they "had a great debt
toward the society they were entering. Liberty is the first need of
humankind, but this supreme blessing imposes important duties;
liberty elevates work to a duty. Being free does not mean deserting
the fields and the factories. Being free entails the obligation to
employ one's time usefully. . . . If, once free, you remain at work, I

will love you; France will protect you. If you desert work, I will
withdraw my affection; France will abandon you like bad children."[214] The first declaration subsumed the principles of a disciplining project: enfranchised women and men as the children
of France, work as duty and the true form of emancipation, religion
as life's foundation, marriage as social salvation, debt toward France
as the truth. Édouard Glissant has seen in the decree of emancipation an act that dispossessed the colonial population of its political agency, for it "introduced a vocabulary of affectivity in sociopolitical relations; it stated that it was in France that things must
change; it implied that decisions always come from elsewhere
(Paris is making the law); it asserted that liberty was not a right but
a duty, the duty to work for the masters; it declared that marriage
was the social stabilizing element; it constructed the understanding
Negro; the grateful Negro; the Negro as dancer and musician."[215]
Sarda's performance carried out a similar act of dispossession. Sarda
spelled out the three terms on which the future colonial society
would rest: order, liberty, and work.[216] Colonial fraternity was, as
Ozouf has implied, about duties, not rights; ties, not statutes; harmony, not contract.

   Two authoritative figures legitimated Sarda's performative act:
the republic (the representative of the people) and God. Sarda
authorized himself in the people's name and told sixty-two thousand persons that they would "soon receive from *his hand,* like a *gift*
from regenerated France, the liberty that they rightly deserve."[217]
Presenting emancipation as a gift, Sarda transformed an event that
had become economically and politically inevitable into an event
charged with patronizing affect. Sarda was an organ of the republic,
the carrier of its will, the agent of its power. Behind the republic,
greater than the people, another "subjectivity guaranteed his signature," God.[218] God, creator and supreme judge, presided over
emancipation. Work would not only pay the debt owed by the
slaves to the republic that accepted them in its bosom but was "the
mission imposed on man by God: work elevates man in God's
eyes; it makes him a citizen; it calls him to found a family."[219]
God's representatives on earth, the "Ministers of Christ," were
called on to help the republican envoy in the endeavor of "moralization and civilization."[220] A common purpose united political and
religious authorities: disciplining the workers. When Sarda campaigned throughout the island in the two months preceding the act

of emancipation, he attended mass everywhere and held meetings in front of the churches. Bishop Maupoint wrote: "He [Sarda] always started by telling [the slaves] that it was God who was sending them freedom. . . . He never forgot to add that he had a paternal affection for the blacks who remained faithful. Those who would desert work and trouble the social order would be sent back to Madagascar without hesitation."[221] Sarda Garriga ordered a religious ceremony to be held in all counties to consecrate the December act of emancipation. Liberty for slaves was predicated under the sign of the cross; in the colony, "Liberty was proclaimed at the altar."[222] A mid-nineteenth-century historian declared: "Religion is not freedom but it is the mother and the first teacher of freedom. How does the slave raise himself to the condition of freedom? With religion, family, and property."[223] Whereas in earlier times the efforts of the church had been hindered by slave owners who feared the Catholic credo of equality under God, the French republic encouraged the Catholic Church in its campaign of conversion of the newly freed population. The state increased the public funds for the Catholic Church to educate new priests and build churches and religious schools.[224] The image of a society in which masters and former slaves were reconciled at the altar was far from reflecting the reality, however. Whites did not want to share the churches with the colored. Special separate masses were organized for the emancipated.[225]

Work and Discipline

To ensure the availability of a cheap workforce, Sarda issued a decree on October 24 that imposed an obligation to work: "Work is mandatory and society must make sure that no individual escapes this providential law."[226] Vagrancy became a serious offense. In April of the same year, disciplining workhouses had been created in which coloreds condemned for vagrancy and begging were held.[227] The October decree stated that slaves must have a work contract before the day of emancipation; married women whose husbands were contracted would not be subjected to these regulations. A free slave unable to present his work pass would be considered a vagrant and prosecuted to the full extent of the law against vagrancy.[228] The vagrant served to define a community within which peace and order had to prevail. Work was the condition of liberty. "Fortunately I am here to reward the hardworking and to punish the lazy. My children, believe me, work is order," Sarda declared.

> In the name of the French people
> To the workers
> My friends
> The decrees of the French Republic have been enacted: you are free. All equal under the law, you now have only brothers. . . . You will prove that you love me by respecting the duties that society imposes upon free men.
> These duties are virtuous and simple. Give back to God what belongs to Him; work as good workers like your French brothers to raise your families: this is what, through me, the Republic is asking you. . . .
> I have found you honest and obedient. I trust you. I hope that you will give me few occasions to exercise my severity; I reserve it to the mean, the lazy, the vagrants, and to those who, after listening to my words, would still let themselves be seduced by bad advice. . . .
>
> *Owners and workers are now one family.* . . .
> You have called me your father and I love you like my children; you will listen to my advice.
> Eternal recognition to the French Republic that made you free!
>
> *And may your motto be: God, France, and Work!*
> Sarda Garriga, December 20, 1848.[229]

Emancipation was declared under a new sacred trilogy. The republican motto, *liberté, égalité, fraternité,* was replaced by the unambiguous terms *Dieu, la France, et le travail.* It was no small irony that this displacement occurred on December 20, for on that same day, Louis-Napoleon Bonaparte became the president of the Second Republic. The 1848 revolution had ended. Emancipation in Réunion was proclaimed on the day the revolution was buried in France. Republican colonialism, embodied in Sarda Garriga, the petit bourgeois, the servant of the state, the ally of slave owners, the friend of the bishop, laid out its program: discipline, control, economic exploitation, political disfranchisement. Opponents of the new order were warned: "Last Sunday, three miserable free coloreds talking to slaves at the Club de la Régénération violently attacked the principle of the work-pass. It is absolutely vital to stop the odious propaganda of the communists. The institution of the work-pass has not been well understood by blacks. They have been surprised and unhappy, and they have seen this measure as an attempt to abridge their freedom."[230] The proclamation of emancipation was carefully controlled, announced in churches where the *Te Deum* was sung. Authorities, fearful of the slaves' joy, ordered a series of measures whose goal was to contain the enthusiasm of the emancipated. In some instances, slaves had to report to work immediately after the mass celebrating emancipation.[231] The authorities forbade the sale of rum and other alcoholic beverages.[232]

The family romance of post-emancipation displaced patriarchal authority from the master to the state, embodied in Sarda. "Since that day [of proclaiming the abolition of slavery], the black population has had faith in my love for them," Sarda said, adding: "In every village, without exception, my word has been heard with religious reverence and true filial obedience."[233] When Sarda talked of fraternity, he meant what Lamartine had called "the magical word borrowed from the Gospel."[234] Fraternity, according to the poet, represented "the religion of humanity toward God."[235] In the colony, men who had been denied their rights as men because they were enslaved became children of the state. Women who had been enslaved were given an identity in the family, as wives. The 1848 colonial political romance imagined a world of children. The hills of Bourbon were bending, as Houat had dreamed, but not to freedom. Rather, they bent to the colonial state. The authority of the white brother over the black brother was legitimated by racism. If emancipation was a gift, if freedom was constructed as a debt, colonial authority perdured, masked as a benevolent gesture. Liberty was a rhetorical figure.

The Name of the Father

The abolition of slavery put an end to a series of interdictions such as forbidding the slaves to have a last name, to wear a hat, to wear shoes, to wear bright colors, and for women to wear jewelry.[236] Social status and racial status were doubly marked: by skin color and by clothing. Slaves were forbidden to adorn themselves. The desire to embellish oneself, tolerated among the wealthy, remained a sin for the slaves. Slaves received a last name according to an arbitrary pattern.[237] The name of the slave became her or his first name, and the patronymic name was left to the whims of the officers of the civil registry. Last names were often anagrams or puns on the first name of the slave's owner: from Suilman, the officer invented Sumanli, Limanus, Mansuil, Mansuli, Linamus, Laminus. Wordplay on the slave's first name was also popular: Lamour Cupidon, Dufumier Police, Desservant Docile, Reluque Luc. The slave master had named slaves, given them a first name; the state added a second name. Rather than displacing a sign of slavery, this gesture reinforced it.

Scholars of societies that have experienced slavery have argued that this perverted access to the Name of the Father has hindered the society's access to the Symbolic.[238] The (slave) father's absence has produced a lack that impedes the access of the child to the Law. Spillers has offered an eloquent counterinterpretation of this phenomenon peculiar to slave society. She shows that "legal enslavement removed the African-American man not so much from sight as from *mimetic* view as a partner in the prevailing social fiction of the Father's name, the Father's law."[239] The law of the father's name is a social fiction, and because of slavery, black men could not participate in this fiction, not even through mimesis. There is therefore, Spillers proposes, the possibility of constructing a different symbolic order, one in which African American men, because they "had had the specific occasion to learn who the female is within itself,"[240] would be able to recognize the heritage of the mother. Their conditions made them share certain experiences culturally linked to women's: being deprived of autonomy, unable to choose one's name, being dependent on a legally and culturally more powerful person. Entering the symbolic order would not mean entering a law that has been marked by race and class but mean entering one that integrates history and memory. In the colonial situation, the master had the right to name and to kill the child, combining and exceeding the power of the father and the mother. With emancipation, the state took that power away and named the slave. Yet, the demasculinization of black men has weighed on postslavery societies. Redefining masculinity has become a site of contest.[241] Spillers's argument has opened the way to a reconfiguration of masculinity that would not try to mirror the signs of virilism. However, the wound has not healed, and the effects of this denial can still be witnessed.

The Deviant in the Late Nineteenth Century

The rhetoric of infantilization and discipline was supported by legal decisions and by a meticulous organization of the mechanisms of control. The goal of the disciplinary institutions was to catalog, train, penalize, and reward people, and even to determine their identities.[242] "But not everyone was successfully disciplined. Many drifted from the norm. For the deviants, society erected asylums, prisons, hospitals. During slavery, in the ceremonies that displayed power and justice, the physical suffering of the offender figured prominently. Punishments of slaves were public, and many bore openly the marks of their sentences: iron necklaces, the lily flower (mark of the king) branded on their shoulders, a damaged limb.[243] In February 1709, a maroon male slave had his right foot cut off as punishment because "burning them with the *fleur de lys* is not enough anymore because Blacks do not feel it." In September 1709, at Saint-Paul, five slaves were punished for plotting their escape in a small boat. The slaves of their quarter were ordered to whip the condemned, and the leader was branded with the fleur-de-lis. In December 1709, two slaves were punished for stealing a boat, with the intent to return to Madagascar. They were whipped by the other slaves of the plantation and received the fleur-de-lis. In June 1706, another slave plot was discovered, and its leader was publicly strangled and hung. The owners of small boats were warned to tie them solidly, or they themselves would be punished if slaves succeeded in escaping. The slave Marie was condemned to have her right hand cut off, then to be hung and strangled for having attacked her master. The beaten, tortured bodies of the slaves were exposed. Such display was necessary, colonialists argued, because slaves had an irrational disregard for the consequences of their crimes and did not experience physical suffering like other human beings. Under slavery, the exposed severed head of the slave had represented restoration of order. In the new order of fraternity and work, justice had to be demonstrated differently.

Vagrancy threatened Sarda's trilogy of God, France, and work. The vagrant was the maroon of postslavery society. Emancipated slaves wandered throughout the island like nomads.[244] They migrated to the interior of the island.[245] They occupied state land or spaces on plantations that were not cultivated. If driven out, they moved on to another piece of land or came back. "They constantly move from one point of the colony to another, leaving one miserable place for another," a newspaper noted in 1852.[246] And they kept moving.[247] Authorities complained that it was not possible to "control this mobile and vagrant population that has no roots."[248] The vagrants were surviving by selling wood and coal. The island's interior had been the land of the maroons, the refuge of slaves escaping bondage. It was now the refuge of the social deviants, the maroons escaping wage slavery. A social geography, inherited from the eighteenth century, was drawn. Mountains, cirques, and margins of cities were the spaces occupied by the emancipated, the deviants, the vagrants.

In 1848, to protect the large plantations against the vagrants' pilfering, the Colonial Council authorized the creation of groups of wardens.[249] In February 1849, Sarda Garriga ordered new disciplinary measures. He denounced the ways by which women and men escaped social control. People were entering into fictional contracts. "In return for some domestic services or even a small amount of money given by the emancipated," an "employer" signed the contract while leaving total freedom to the worker. Sarda first wrote a "Proclamation to the Workers," which opened with these words: "I am not pleased with you."[250] The disciplinary father expressed his discontent with his unruly children: "Fortunately, I am here to reward the workers and punish the lazy. A child of La Mère-Patrie, I came in her name to give you liberty; inspired by her solicitude for your beautiful country, in her name, I will strike against those who disturb the public order by refusing to work."[251] He warned the workers that they could not hide: "I will know about your behavior sooner or later and I will punish you." Sarda was omnipotent. And there was always God and his justice, threatening the "dangerous" individuals who continually wandered. "My heart and my protection to the workers; disciplinary work to the lazy!"[252] Fear of punishment, exclusion, and imprisonment served as a pedagogical tool, but it was not the same fear that had been used during slavery.[253] Now Sarda sought to instill anguish and anxiety among the freed population so that they would integrate the new order and its laws.

The containment of the vagrants became an obsession. Authorities turned now to women who were accused of supporting men's vagrancy. In June 1849 the regulation concerning emancipated women was modified. The declaration of October 24, 1848, had exempted married women from contract work. Now married women had to be indentured workers as well. Women and men protested, but the authorities insisted. "Who knows what emancipated women have become, married or not?" a newspaper wrote. "Where are they? We certainly do not find them working as domestics. No, it is around the centers of prostitution, around factories that they bring their shameless vagrancy."[254] The female deviant was a prostitute. Colonial authorities were caught between their desire to make women economically dependent on their husbands, defining women as mothers and housewives, and the need for order and a disciplined workforce. The 1848 republicans encouraged marriages between emancipated slaves to distinguish republican morality from the immorality of monarchy, which had tolerated "free" unions between slaves. The republicans complained that women, no longer servants or laundresses, had become "vampires" living off men, who were their victims.[255] In December 1849, Sarda Garriga issued a decree, remarking that the October decree had not achieved its goal of "moralizing the family of former slaves." He claimed that marriages were arranged just to save women from work, that "marriage is a means, idleness a goal."[256] Forcing women to work would have a double purpose, Sarda wrote. It would teach their children the love of work, and it would supply a cheap workforce to the colonists. Women had to work in the same geographical area as their husbands.

From the 1850s to the early years of the twentieth century, discursive strategies, legal decisions, and an apparatus of discipline and punishment were established to create what Foucault has called "the first moment of production of modern sexuality."[257] The necessity to provide a workforce and to guarantee its reproduction (through the regulation of sexuality and conjugality) defined this moment. Colonial authorities emulated the strategies of control that were being developed against the French workers.[258] *Ateliers de discipline* (disciplining workhouses), the requirement that the worker carry a *livret de travail* (work pass), the moralization of family life, punishment to promote an internalization of the law,[259] and construction of asylums and prisons were the strategies deployed to transform slaves into obedient workers. Indentured workers became the object of the anthropological gaze as slaves had been. A series of photographs taken fifteen years after the abolition of slavery showed naked indentured workers. Under the categories "Mozambique," "Métis Arab Indian," "Chinese," "Annamite," "Malbar," "Black Creole," female and male, young and adult, workers were photographed, in profile and front-face, some with chains at their ankles. The white Creole elite was fascinated by the new human "types."[260] The Society of Sciences and Arts of Réunion published studies of writers and scientists who described the "soul" and the physiology of blacks and Asians. The "African is awkward, naive, apathetic"; the "Annamite has a bad odor"; the "Chinese have brought to the colony the vices of their race. They are violent and short-tempered, received stolen goods and are the accomplices of the majority of thefts."[261] The color of the skin, the shape of the skull, of the legs, eyes, breasts, and hair, were the signs of a difference with the white race. The images of the indentured workers expressed a metaphor, a fantasized vision of the Other. The imaginary of the white Creoles, who were themselves colonized, was shaped by the racist assumptions of European science. They sought "to intensify their own sense of themselves by dramatizing the distance and difference between what [was] closer and what [was] far away."[262] They helped build a hierarchy of colors in the colony, with them at the top—even though the hierarchy they had borrowed situated them below the white Europeans. A new thematics of blood emerged. European science provided white Creoles with a metaphorics of blood and a typology of race.

The development of the sugar industry justified the program of postslavery economy. To a certain extent, the new disciplinary practices and techniques were successful. Between 1850 and 1860, the sugarcane industry prospered,[263] and access to an unpaid workforce, thanks to the measures against vagrancy, favored this prosperity. Macadam had two functions: depriving the vagrants of their liberty and supplying an abundant and unpaid workforce to the colony.[264] In 1849 colonial authorities had to confront another danger. An article of the Constitution of the Second Republic, voted on November 4, 1848, had given the populations of the Old Colonies the right to be represented in the National Assembly.

Sarda was entrusted with the task of containing and diverting the political aspirations of the emancipated population.

Freedom and Rights

Colonial authorities, landowners, and the bourgeoisie resisted the political emancipation of the vagrants who yesterday had been slaves. They might now be free, but they lacked the ability to understand power, the authorities claimed. They needed guidance, and Sarda Garriga would be their benevolent and fatherly shepherd: "It is my duty, as your father, to teach you your rights and your duties."[265] He knew better than the vagrants themselves what they needed: "You have been free for a short time, you were born yesterday. How would you know how to distinguish in this world, so new for you, who are your best representatives? Ask your boss or any other authority. . . . If you do not know anybody, then abstain from voting; stay at work."[266] Newspapers had racial arguments against universal manhood suffrage: "Are they French, these *cafres* [name given to the descendants of Africans], these Madagascans, these Asians, slaves in their countries, brought to the colonies as slaves?" and "Blacks must spare France the humiliation of accepting African suffrage."[267] The first elections were marred by intimidation and fraud.[268] Barbaroux, the prosecutor at Houat's trial, was a candidate for the colonial party, and Houat was a candidate for the republicans. Houat was defeated, and Barbaroux elected.[269] The Second Empire abolished universal manhood suffrage in the colonies; new laws forbade the creation of clubs and associations, and the press would be censored. White Creoles celebrated the end of "democratic negrophilism."[270]

In Réunion, the abolition of slavery was not the result of a popular insurrection. However, this formidable social transformation was not as peaceful as many historians have claimed. André Scherer's remark that it was an "abolition accomplished with intelligence and without social disorder" has been widely shared,[271] but this view does not take into account the deployment of disciplinary measures that preceded and followed the act of emancipation. Slaves were deprived of liberty when they were set free. W. E. B. Du-Bois's remarks about the post-emancipation order in the United States echoed Réunion's: "Not a single Southern legislature stood ready to admit a Negro, under any conditions, to the polls; not a single Southern legislature believed free Negro labor was possible without a system of restrictions that took all its freedom away; there was scarcely a white man in the South who did not honestly regard Emancipation as a crime, and its practical nullification as a duty."[272]

Vagrancy was a plague, and macadam did not cure it. Indentured workers and emancipated slaves were still leaving jobs and refusing to settle under the conditions imposed by colonial law. Judge Coulon noted in 1852 that macadam was disorganized, that "Indian women were insolent and that the slogan 'No more macadam' was "heard everywhere."[273] Coulon wrote that "neither the native nor the immigrant is governed by a sense of dignity like the free men of Europe. . . . He is not impressed by punishment, nor by imprisonment. The only thing that affects him is work." Therefore, Coulon concluded: "We must keep *forced work* to maintain *free work.*"[274] Women and men continued to eschew the new bourgeois colonial order and pursued their nomadic life throughout the island. Authorities increased the repressive measures. Thousands of people were arrested throughout the 1850s for "vagrancy" and condemned to disciplinary work. Under the repressive regime of Napoleon III, the governor took harsher measures to enforce work. All workers, women and men, whatever their age, had to carry a work pass. Emancipated people no longer had the freedom to move around the island except with the authorization of their bosses. The worker could not stay for more than twenty-four hours in a place that was not her or his residence without reporting to the police.[275] In 1859 every county had a police force whose mission was to go through forests, mountains, and other remote places to hunt vagrants. Six years later, four brigades, each with thirty-six agents, who were fed, housed, and paid by the colony, were established to arrest vagrants,[276] just as armed groups had once hunted maroons.

"Of all the dangers that threaten public order and the future of production in the colony, vagrancy is certainly the most serious one," the director of the interior for the "Research and the Repression of Vagrancy" wrote thirteen years after emancipation.[277] A juvenile penitentiary for boys was opened, with priests as its wardens. The children built their own prison and then constituted a free workforce for the priests, with the complicity of the judges and the police. Complaints of mothers, fathers, and sisters against abusive arrest and detention in the penitentiary were sent to the administration. Furcy Orcely protested to the prosecutor that her son, Joseph, age eight, had been unjustly arrested and detained.[278] The repression touched all the workers, since indentured workers, immigrants, and emancipated slaves had to be contracted.

Women were often arrested for prostitution. Reports claimed that there had been "an excessive increase of prostitutes since 1848."[279] Colonized women were said to have no "awareness of their ignominy." Prostitution had its "roots in the total absence of modesty, of any moral and religious principles among the natives."[280] The control of prostitutes was organized. A clinic was opened. Women were taken to jail just because they lacked the appearance of the respectable woman of colonial society. Marie Eugénie wrote to protest against a summons to the clinic. She said she had always worked; she had a shop and had paid her license. Testimony from her former master supported Marie Eugénie's claim, but the police charged that Marie Eugénie was known to receive loose women in her home.[281]

Rituals were organized to produce assent to the new order. Colonial authorities used the date of December 20 as an opportunity to celebrate not the new order but the old. A decree instituted a Fête du Travail. Emancipated slaves were rewarded for their good behavior. In 1849, December 20 had been marked by masses. But in 1850, and from then on every year, the Fête du Travail was observed. On May 4, 1850, *Te Deum,* games, fairs, and balls were organized, and Jean-Marie Bruno was the laureate of the day.[282] Bruno was an emancipated slave who had raised the orphaned children of his master. The good worker was the emancipated slave who had not forgotten his duties toward his former master, serving him even after his death.

The vagrant, the woman, those who worked only enough to survive, contested the principles on which capitalism was based: work, discipline, and private property. Vagrants and loose women were "primitive rebels" whose existence and ways of living were reminders of the failure of hegemonic social control. The end of slavery was pregnant with radical ideas. Sarda Garriga's rhetoric, with all its prudence, compliance to the colonial order, and petit bourgeois ideology, carried with it a potential radicalization.[283] No power could contain the names of liberty and equality within the narrow limits of obedience to the new social order.

The vagrants went underground, creating a métisse culture, language, and symbolic system. They did not forget the promise of equality. And *fraternité,* the aspiration to an equality with the metropolitan brothers, continued to challenge the fiction of republican universal brotherhood. Divided between their love of France and of their native island, their two mothers, the sons of Réunion had looked for a family romance that would keep the constellation in place: two mothers and their beloved sons. No sisters and no fathers. In the pre-emancipation period, the colonized saw themselves as abandoned by France to the arbitrary and tyrannical power of white masters. They envisioned emancipation as a reworking of these relations and the institution of a republican community that would remove geographical, cultural, and social barriers.

Emancipation proved to bring unexpected consequences that had altogether escaped the imagination of metropolitan and colonial republicans. Capitalists did not care about reconciliation or the creation of a new community. The new economic order meant the exclusion of groups—poor whites, emancipated slaves—who refused to play by the new rules. To the French republic, these citizens remained in the domain of the unthinkable, of the inconceivable. The republican dream of universal fraternity was enmeshed with French imperial hegemony and ethnocentrism.[284] Fraternity was neither a given nor an effect of reciprocity but the sign of inequality between a dominating and a dominated nation.[285]

3

Blood Politics

and Political Assimilation

❧

A century after the abolition of slavery, Réunion Island became a Département Français d'Outre-Mer. The law of March 19, 1946, meant that metropolitan laws and decrees would now be applied to Guadeloupe, Martinique, Réunion, and French Guiana. To the Old Colonies' anticolonialists,[1] the 1946 law was the successful outcome of a long struggle for the integration of their populations into the French nation. "After fraternity and liberty," the Guianese leader Gaston Monnerville said, the populations would accede to the "equality of rights and equality before the law." To become a French department signified defeating the colonialist lobbies. Raymond Vergès, a representative of Réunion Island at the French Parliament, declared: "To be a colony is by definition to be an exploited country. Ten families control the wealth on the island. The administration, the armed forces, justice, in a word the whole state apparatus, is in their hands while the majority of the population, kept in ignorance and fear, has only one right: to shut up and work itself to death."[2]

Political assimilation is usually seen by postcolonial intellectuals as the result of middle-class alienation, the delusion of an educated

elite credulous enough to believe that colonized people could accede to equality through compromise and integration. Yet historical research shows that anticolonialist movements often turned to
assimilation. World War II deeply changed the political debate in
the empire. The victory of the Allies had affirmed democratic
values and condemned all forms of political subjugation. Anticolonialists justified the end of colonial oppression with principles
that had been articulated by the colonial powers themselves. The
August 1941 Atlantic Charter asserted the right of peoples to self-
determination, and this right was reiterated in the 1945 Charter of
the United Nations.[3] France, though it had signed the charters,
resisted the demands of equality and self-determination in its empire. Armed struggle soon appeared inevitable because of the stubborn deafness of the French colonial administration and the continuing violation of human rights by French colonialists.[4] In many
instances, armed struggle proved unavoidable and necessary to
break the colonial bond.

To be sure, the narrative of compromise in which the main
characters try to convince, to reason with, the enemy is not as
attractive and romantic as a story of heroes. Heroic struggles of
decolonization, where dignity is recovered on the ruins of defeated
colonialism, offer a more captivating narrative than discussions,
compromises, and negotiations. Heroes of the decolonization narrative are those who bore arms and stood erect against the colonialists rather than men who sat at a table and debated with the enemy.
This conception of emancipation is enmeshed in a conception of
virile masculinity and what constitutes dis-alienation. The masculinity of colonized men had been wounded by colonialism,
which projected onto them the image of inadequate, emasculated,
incapable men, unable to defend their land and their mothers,
their wives and their sisters, their sons and their daughters. Defeating the enemy in a battle offered a psychological satisfaction that
cannot be underestimated. The fighters of the Algerian war of
liberation became the heroes of the most famous version of this
epic.[5] Frantz Fanon gave a theory of dis-alienation that constructed
an ideal of social, cultural, and psychological emancipation.[6] His
call for "la libération totale qui concerne *tous* les secteurs de la
personnalité" [the total liberation of all sectors of the personality]
meant that "l'homme nouveau n'est pas une production a posteriori de cette nation mais coexiste avec elle, se développe avec elle,

triomphe avec elle" [the new man is not a production *a posteriori* of
the nation, but coexists with it, develops with it, triumphs with it].
Colonial dis-alienation now had a script. Political assimilation did
not belong to that script.

In the French overseas departments, 1946 inaugurated an economic, social, cultural, and political transformation. However, the
choice of political assimilation already appeared in the 1940s as an
inaccessible goal and, more importantly, one that was out of date.[7]
The successive French governments had repeatedly proved that
they were not ready to accept equality for the populations of their
empire. The postwar period was a time of reassessment, in which
the old demand for integration was abandoned and replaced by the
demand for national independence. The leaders of the Old Colonies appeared timid, still credulously relying on a promise that
events had shown to be outdated: the promise of inclusion in
French citizenry on a basis of equality. To be sure, 1946 was *not* a
decolonization. In the second half of our century, decolonization
has signified rupture with the *metropole,* construction of a nation-
state, access to sovereignty. There was no rupture, no construction
of a nation-state, no access to sovereignty in the Old Colonies. The
majority of their populations called for a greater integration within
French democracy. Their demand focused on social equality between the inhabitants of the Old Colonies and those of metropolitan France. The logic of political integration led the anticolonialists to eschew a series of questions pertaining to the specificity of
their colonial situation: racism, the past of slavery, the perpetuation
of the colonial pact. Yet the 1946 demand also represented a question addressed to the French democratic state and formulated by
groups that it had until then maintained in subjugation: what
equality is possible between descendants of slaves, indentured
workers, and colonists and French citizens? Democracy could not
be reduced to the access to material comfort; it should include the
extension of the democratic process. But could a liberal democracy
integrate groups that it had enslaved, colonized, taken from their
native lands, and that had been the scorned, despised members of
its empire? In France, democracy and national identity were built
on the subjection and the exclusion of certain groups (women,
slaves, colonized people). The French Revolution[8] ended up excluding women and slaves from the community that it had engendered. The rhetoric about equality appeared a pretense. But in the

colonies where there had been slavery, the conceptualization of emancipation, of the entrance into the community of the equals, followed the model of integration. These "unthinkable citizens"[9] came up against the limits set up by a nation that had nonetheless affirmed the universalism of rights. The ideals of equality and fraternity, which the revolutionary discourse had affirmed, collided with the will to redefine the separation between the members of the community and the aliens to the community. Nevertheless, the descendants of slaves and indentured workers would continue to turn to revolutionary ideals to reintegrate the community of humans from which they had been excluded. Political assimilation was the reintegration in the community of the equals. The colonial white aristocracy and its allies in France had always resisted the integration of minorities within the republican nation. Vichy opposed assimilation on racist grounds.[10] The opposition to colonialism in a society created in the prerevolutionary empire took the form of assimilation into the community created by the revolution.

To the post-1946 generation, anticolonialist leaders have failed their sons. Their legacy has been paternalism, more acculturation, and, paradoxically, a greater French presence than during colonialism. "Fraternal colonization," Glissant has said, has been as "uprooting as paternal colonization."[11] Betrayed by its fathers, the post-1946 generation would see in this event a shameful compromise, a culpable desertion. Sons want their fathers to be heroic. Raphaël Confiant, in his biography of Aimé Césaire, speaks of assimilation as "the original sin,"[12] "legitimized" by Césaire. Assimilation "has accomplished its mortiferous work," Confiant writes, "Jacobin France had its revenge. . . . Little by little, we have regressed to the infantile stage." It is time, Confiant argues, to "break a taboo" and denounce the 1946 generation that brought "abjection" and misery on its peoples. I agree with Confiant that a critical approach to the actions and ideology of the 1946 generation is necessary, but I want to investigate the 1946 generation's demand from a different position than Confiant's. Confiant presents his essay as "the sincere cry of a *son* who thinks that he has been betrayed by his *fathers* and, to begin with, by the first among them, Aimé Césaire."[13] The son is betrayed by the father, who, the son has hoped, should have saved him from centuries of humiliation. Confiant's analysis transforms 1946 into a narrative of family relations, and, among those, about one charged with ambivalence, conflict, and guilt, the relation between father and son. The narrative of 1946 is about a boy's relation to his father, the boy's expectations, his sense of betrayal when these expectations are not met, and consequently his judgment about his father.

Confiant's and Fanon's reproach against the 1946 generation goes further than saying that it made a political mistake. It charges betrayal, an intimate betrayal: our fathers led us to our downfall. We cannot admire them; we might have to reject them and put them on trial so that we can free ourselves of the memory of their existence. Postcolonial sons despise their assimilationist fathers. Freud analyzes the complex relationship of the son to the father by looking at his relationship to his own father. Freud, who writes that "we know that in the mass of mankind there is a powerful need for an authority who can be admired,"[14] recalls in *The Interpretation of Dreams* an incident involving his father:

I may have been ten or twelve years old, when my father began to take me with him on his walks and reveal to me in his talk his views upon things in the world we live in. Thus it was, on one such occasion, that he told me the story to show me how much better things were now than they had been in his days. "When I was a young man," he said, "I went for a walk one Saturday in the streets of your birthplace; I was well dressed, and had a new fur cap on my head. A Christian came up to me and with a single blow knocked off my cap into the mud and shouted: 'Jew! get off the pavement!' " "And what did you do?" I asked. "I went into the roadway and picked up my cap," was his calm reply. This struck me as unheroic conduct on the part of the big, strong man who was holding the little boy by the hand. I contrasted this situation with an another which fitted my feelings better: the scene in which Hannibal's father, Hamilcar Barcas, made his boy swear before the household altar to take vengeance on the Romans.[15]

For little Sigmund, the story of Hannibal is a source of greater satisfaction than the story of Jacob. Freud remarks on the ambivalence of the boy who wants to admire his father but is disappointed by the father's behavior. Because of this ambivalence, the adult will experience a sense of guilt that has "something to do with the child's criticism of his father, with the underevaluation which took place over the overevaluation of the earlier childhood."[16] Freud, as Marianne Krüll shows, thinks that "the authority wielded by the father provokes criticism from his child at an early age, and the severity of the demand he makes upon the child leads him, for his own relief, to watch keenly for any weakness of his father's; *but the filial piety called up in our minds by the figure of a father, particularly after his death, tightens the censorship which keeps such criticism from becoming conscious.*"[17] If the father has been set on a pedestal and is later shown in a manner that does not fulfill the expectations of the son, the son has two choices: to close his eyes to the father's weakness—as Freud did, according to Krüll—or to destroy the image of the father—as postcolonial sons do with assimilationist fathers. Yet there might be another choice, one that accounts for the father's weakness but does not seek his destruction.

The narrative of betrayal bespeaks a longing for a political judgment that can foresee all the consequences of a choice. It does not take into account the weight of words, the accidents of history, the role of human pride, weakness, naïveté, and trust in politics. Hannah Arendt has argued that "political thought is representative."[18] To think politically, she said, "I" must enter the issue to be analyzed from different viewpoints, "by making present to my mind the standpoints of those who are absent."[19] This process means, however, neither blindly embracing the actual views of others nor empathizing with them, but thinking as if I, myself, were in their position. Forming an opinion about the 1946 anti-colonialists entails looking at the genealogy of their thinking so that a complex image emerges of the historical and cultural context in which they made their decision. In other words, to follow Arendt's suggestion, I have to situate myself in their (imagined) multiple positions. To retrace the history of the ideas and mentalities that led the 1946 generation to defend assimilation, I must look at the relationship between the determined sites in which they lived—the colonial world, the French education system, the culture and literature of the times—and the discourses that produced these worlds.[20] I read the acts of the fathers of decolonization in the Old Colonies neither closing my eyes to their weakness nor condemning their actions as "unheroic." To confront the "weakness" of the colonized father and to accept his inheritance opens, for the postcolonial critic, a different way to think about emancipation. This chapter adapts its approach from the feminist and postcolonial critics who, through revisionist history, have sought forms of resistance and struggle by the subaltern that escaped notice in the heroic narrative about resistance. As Freud said, quoting Goethe,

"What you inherited from your father, acquire it to possess it." The postcolonial is confronted with two temptations. One is to jump over the generations and to seek in the past glorious heroes with whom to identify.[21] The other is to maintain the illusion of a history without a past, of a life beginning here and now, carefully avoiding any examination of what could be very revealing events in this past. In both temptations, the individual is the first of a dynasty, the heir neither to a name nor to a culture or a history; the individual invents herself or himself.[22]

Citizenship, anticolonialists argued, should be extended to the populations whose lives had been dependent on the decisions of the French state for three centuries. They set their demands in the idiom of the Declaration of the Rights of Man and the Citizen, the vocabulary of democratic rights, citizenship, justice, and equality. They framed their discourse about the wrongs to which their peoples had been subjected within the grammar of French law and the universal principles of liberal democracy.

Anticolonialist leaders revealed the principle of inequality hidden behind the myth of shared membership in the French citizenry. They demanded passage from subordination to effective citizenship. But they also introduced into the parliamentary debate on the status of the colonies the term *capitalism,* thereby exceeding the liberal terms that framed the discussion of citizenship. They were citizens *and* workers. Besides national loyalty, they used the metaphor of class solidarity between metropolitan and colonized workers. The populations of the colonies, Aimé Césaire said, were "abandoned without any recourse to the avidity of a capitalism without conscience and of an uncontrolled local administration."[23] Leaders of the four colonies opposed the "reactionary doctrine of discrimination to the republican doctrine of integration."[24] And Raymond Vergès saw assimilation as "the strongest guarantee for a withering of the colonialist spirit and behavior. We must destroy once and for all a spirit and behavior that has notably served the capitalist trusts but has brought what we called the empire to the verge of the abyss."[25]

Jacques Rancière has remarked that "the kind of ideological compromise first (schooling for all), then political compromise (the different forms of sacred union and of contractual policies) that [the bourgeoisie] has sought to give the working class since the turn of the century, prevents the bourgeoisie from producing [positive]

images and even from offering positive historical images of reconciliation."[26] Colonial crimes were denounced. Anticolonialist leaders had accepted the ideological compromise that was republican
education. Now they accepted the political compromise proposed
by the French state: the French Union.[27] The sacred union between
the metropole and the colonized hindered, if we follow Rancière,
the possibility of producing positive images of reconciliation. So
did the memory of slavery and of the abuses of colonialism. The
ghosts of slaves, maroons, and vagrants, the excluded of the colonial order, loomed over the 1946 assembly. But their exclusion from
the 1946 representatives' speeches facilitated the production of
a dominant fiction: the possibility of reconciliation when past
wrongs have not yet been expressed.

The doctrine of assimilation was contained within two great
narratives: the narrative of the French revolution and its triptych,
liberté, égalité, fraternité, and the socialist narrative of the universal
brotherhood of workers. The narrative of the republic was a narrative of emancipation whose function was to legitimize a myth.
However, "in contrast to myths, it [did] not base its legitimacy in
any originary founding acts, but in a future to be brought about, in
an *Idea* to be realized."[28] The idea was equality. The scene of
Liberty, the abolition of slavery, had been played in Saint-Denis
with, as the messenger, a French envoy. The decision came from
Paris. The drama of Equality was enacted in Paris, at the heart of
France, in the symbolic theater of the republican people: the National Assembly.[29] The anticolonialists were Creole men, messengers of their peoples. They had finally joined the assembly of
brothers.[30]

Anticolonialist representatives pointed to the interesting turn
that the republican triptych had taken in the Old Colonies. In
France, the triptych was liberty, equality, fraternity. In the Old
Colonies, the order was different: fraternity, liberty, equality. Fraternity in 1789 with the French Revolution; liberty in 1848 with the
abolition of slavery; and now, in 1946, equality should be extended
to the brothers in the colonies.[31] Equality, the "set of practices
guided by the supposition that everyone is equal and by the attempt to verify this supposition,"[32] meant the recognition of the
humanity of the colonized. There has been a wrong, anticolonialists said, and this wrong should now be condemned by the French
Assembly. The wrong was colonialism, which had left the popu-

lations of the colonized territories at the mercy of pro-slavery capitalists.

Socialism provided the other theoretical foundation for the demand of assimilation. Three traditions, non-Marxist French socialism, Marxism, and Soviet communism, supplied the 1946 generation with arguments and justifications. Non-Marxist socialism had always claimed that colonized populations had to be included in the nation. Republican doctrine demanded it, as did the principles of working-class solidarity. Poverty brought by colonial exploitation was denounced as forcefully as poverty brought by capitalist exploitation. Republican socialism advocated the personal promotion of the individual protected by the principles of the French Revolution. The universality of its principles took precedence over the particularism of colonial revolution. Socialists supported colonization because it would bring together workers throughout the world against capitalism and nationalism, both seen as the enemies of workers' emancipation. The socialist doctrine rejected "indigenous nationalism," because, socialist activists contended, it would have "the same consequences as imperialism, that is the subjugation of the workers."[33] The empire was another site of the struggle against capitalism and the bourgeoisie.

Colonization would unite peoples of different religions, customs, and races against a common enemy: capitalism. "Socialist colonization" should be promoted because it would free the natives from feudalism and tribalism and make them the equals of the European workers.[34] Joachim Durel, a socialist activist, declared in 1928 that "We [socialists] want unity, not the absorption of one race by another or by extermination, but through the fusion of the different ethnic groups, of natives and Europeans."[35] Political *métissage* led to political assimilation. The Second International promoted assimilation throughout the colonial empire and claimed that the emancipation of the workers would be realized through the "fraternity of the races" and not through national divisions.[36] Colonization, socialists said, was an inevitable component of human life. People had always sought to expand their territory. If they were guided by principles other than self-interest and greed, their expansion would bring not subjugation but republican and socialist ideas; it would be a "human, just, and fraternal colonization." The Union Intercoloniale, created in 1920 and grouping the anticolonialist colonized, endorsed a discourse that would prevail in the next thirty years: "Oppressed brothers of the metropole, duped by your own bourgeoisie, you became the instruments of our conquest. . . . Confronted with capitalism and imperialism, our interests are common."[37] Nguyen That Thanh, the future Ho Chi Minh, wrote in 1922: "We will not stop calling for the unity of native workers so that, in agreement with their metropolitan brothers, they fight for a regime where justice reigns, a regime that will free them all."[38] The idea that there were "two" Frances gained popularity among the anticolonialists. "We can say without dispute that colonial France is in deep and profound opposition to France."[39] There was the France represented in the colonies by "decadent civil servants, crooks and corrupted individuals," and republican France, the propagator of liberty, equality, and fraternity. The intimate relationship between the French republican ideal and the imperial project, between republican ideology and colonialist ideology, was not an issue.

After World War II, Soviet socialism, whose ideology was disseminated by the French Communist Party, brought new justifications for the demand of assimilation. A 1948 document of the French Communist Party entitled *Les problèmes des Antilles et de La Réunion,* addressed to Raymond Vergès and annotated by him, explained assimilation as the "logical and natural outcome" for these territories and a "historical necessity" for their populations.[40] The communists divided the world in two camps: the "imperialist and anti-democratic" world and the "anti-imperialist and democratic" world. The incorporation of the Old Colonies into the French nation would set an obstacle to American imperialist expansionism.[41] Furthermore, to the French communists, the history, culture, and identity of the islands belonged to French history, culture, and identity:

The populations of these territories have lived through three centuries of French history. They have adopted the language, mores, and traditions of this powerful nation with which a large part of their commerce was done. Therefore, when they became conscious of their historical situation, when they united and stood up, searching for their own road to progress, justice and democracy, they expressed this consciousness, *necessarily and naturally,* through the demand for assimilation.[42]

The French communists rewrote the history of these territories and situated it within the great Jacobin narrative of the unity of the

French nation and in a Marxist narrative marked by the Soviet vision of the world. Their Marxism offered a rational explanation of the "alienation" of the masses. It explained history in terms of logical steps toward the full realization of the happiness of human-kind. It told colonized populations that they had allies in the metropole, oppressed like them, their brothers. French commu-nism adopted the colonialist rhetoric of "adoption" by colonized populations of the culture of the colonial metropole. Economic relations defined by the colonial pact were rebaptized "commerce." Socialism gave to the colonized an idiom that transcended race, the notion that had justified differential treatment. There were two enemies, capitalism and imperialism, supporting each other. If socialism supplied the leaders of the Old Colonies with a social claim, republican doctrine provided them with a moral claim. Its motto of *liberté, égalité, fraternité* meant crushing all forms of op-pression. Demanding assimilation meant paying homage to France and to the republic.[43]

The Creoles of 1946 saw themselves as subjects emerging through the experience of class. The 1946 leaders took seriously the demo-cratic promise of the republic, reaffirmed after the defeat of Nazism. They asked: If democratic ideals such as equality and justice are again governing the making of a community, why should some French citizens be excluded from this democratic community? What marks them as different?

The 1946 anticolonialists argued that the populations of the Old Colonies had been "made" by France; hence their specific connec-tion to the metropole. Yet they were also Creoles, whose ancestors were African and European, Madagascan and Asian. If this marked them as different from the metropolitan French, this difference did not constitute an obstacle to their integration into the French citizenry. Their demand for inclusion was consistent with the long quest of Creoles to be accepted within the French family. But for the sovereign, for the state, this quest for inclusion carried with it a demand for recognition as equal subjects that the state refused to accommodate. The *métis,* the Creoles, came into the Parliament, the space created by the brothers to enact a metaphorical fraternity, an assembly of peers, equal and free, to bring their message: "We are your brothers." But the enactment of the métis' demand dis-rupted the norms on which the bourgeois family was constructed in the empire. If they asked for recognition, they brought into the open the father's secret: his violation of sexual bourgeois norms and propriety. What was the secret of the métis? None other than the secret of the white father: that he has had sexual intercourse with a woman of color. The métis would reveal this secret. He could denounce the hypocrisy of the white father, the complicity of his white wife, the jealousy of his white brother, and the rape of his mother. The métis came to claim his part of the inheritance and was feared for it. He brought to the assembly of brothers the sign of forbidden sexuality. For if the metropolitan brothers had perfected their fiction of fatherless individuals,[44] the presence of the métis, the colonized brother, broke apart this fiction.

The debate about equality was affected by the debate about métissage. The advocates of assimilation claimed that métissage was the fertile ground between European and non-European cultures.[45] Partisans of blood purity advocated a strict control of métissage, for they were fearful of "race degeneration." Colonized intellectuals were divided. To some, the assimilationist version of métissage occluded the unequal relation between European and non-European cultures. Its aim was nothing more than the extinction of local and native cultural practices. *Métissage* had become a term rather too closely connected with the colonial project to be fully embraced by the colonized. If métissage acknowledged the distinctive cultural productions of non-European territories, its use by European assimilationists aimed at subsuming these productions into European culture. To others, métissage was the answer of the colonial world to European racism. Class, dignity, and incorporation in the French citizenry constituted the foundations of 1946 anticolonialist rhetoric. The anticolonialist leaders avoided the question of race because they wanted to stress class discrimination over race discrimination.

This chapter investigates these questions by following the life of an anticolonialist Creole of Réunion, Raymond Vergès. Vergès was a white Creole whose life put him in places and times intimately connected with the sexual, cultural, and social politics of the empire. His journey outside his native island took place between 1905 and 1932 and took him from Réunion to France, from France to China and Indochina, and from Indochina back to Réunion. Vergès witnessed the slaughter of World War I and the racism of

European imperialism in China and of French colonialism in Indochina. Yet he defended the goals of the Third Republic's colonialism, namely, to bring to peoples throughout the world the ideals of French republicanism: faith in progress and science, secular education, the superiority of French civilization, and liberty, equality, and fraternity. He was an engineer in China, a doctor and a consul in Indochina, a union leader and anticolonialist political leader in Réunion. He studied medicine at a time when medical culture and discourse were highly racialized.[46] His marriage in 1928 to a young Vietnamese, Pham Thi Khang, and the legal recognition of their twin sons cost him his post as consul of France at Oubone, Siam. The years spanned by Raymond Vergès's life were years of social and political upheaval: World War I and World War II, the Popular Front, the Spanish Republic and its defeat, the expansion of the French colonial empire and the struggles against colonialism, the emergence of the "colonial novel" and the display by the French state of its colonial wealth at the colonial exhibitions in Paris (1931, 1937), the birth of a modern Left in Réunion and of a strong union movement, and finally decolonization and the struggle for national liberation in the Third World. Vergès encountered the different discourses of the Third Republic: medical, imperial, cultural, republican, and socialist.

To investigate the terms of the political romance that emerged in Réunion in the 1930s and the 1940s, I have looked at a variety of discourses. I examine the medical colonial discourse and the medical construction of the métis, the ways in which the Third Republic shaped the representation of colonization as a civilizing mission framed within republican principles, and the different rhetorical strategies that defined the Creole specificity of Réunion and the nature of its attachment to France. One rhetorical strategy was represented by writers such as Marius and Ary Leblond and Raphaël Barquissau, who constructed a Creole myth that posited a white, Celtic dominant part in Creole culture, thereby erasing its African and Madagascan components. The other, developed by union leaders and leaders of the Left, insisted on the Creole as social subject, as the exploited worker of a capitalist system. A close reading of the anticolonialist rhetoric and tropes is essential if we want to understand the transformations, limits, and multiple meanings brought by the discourse of assimilation.

From Réunion Island to Indochina

Raymond Vergès was born on August 15, 1882, at Saint-Denis, Réunion, the second son of Charles and Marie Noémie Vergès.[47] Vergès's family belonged to a small group of landless urban whites. His mother was from a family established in Réunion in the early years of colonization. His father's family emigrated from Catalonia to the Indian Ocean in the 1830s.[48] His paternal grandfather, Adolphe Vergès, settled in Réunion after the death of his father, Raimond Vergès, a low-ranking officer in a French battalion that fought in India in 1831. Adolphe's son, Charles Vergès, became a pharmacist at Saint-Denis. He left the island with his wife and two sons in 1883 and went to Madagascar in search of a better life. His wife, Marie-Noémie, died that year. Two years later, Raymond lost his older brother, and Charles sent Raymond back to Réunion, where he was raised by his paternal grandmother, Hermelinde Vergès, and his young aunt, Marie Vergès.

Raymond, who was baptized, was sent to public school at Saint-Denis and to the Lycée Leconte de Lisle. A very good student, he received a fellowship to study in France, given to poor but promising students by the Réunion General Council. In Paris, he attended the Lycée Saint-Louis to prepare for admission to the École Polytechnique. After receiving his bachelor's degree in sciences, Raymond applied for a fellowship for his doctoral work. His request was rejected by the Réunion General Council, which proposed to help him financially on the condition that he entered an engineering school. He was accepted at the Ecole Supérieure d'Agronomie Tropicale and graduated first in his class in 1907.

Raymond Vergès, who married Jeanne Daniel in 1908, accepted an offer by the Société pour la Construction et l'Exploitation des Chemins de Fer en Chine for a three-year contract as a draftsman. Vergès's position was at Shih-Chia-Chuong—the capital of the province of Hopeh.[49] Vergès was a collaborator in the review *La Vie,* founded by the Leblonds, two Creoles of Réunion. In an article describing the 1911 Chinese Revolution, Vergès revealed his profound republicanism and admiration for European science and progress: "Revolutionaries want to take back China from those who have debased their country so that they can regenerate it. They want to erase the trace of monarchy and built the republic."[50] The regeneration of China would be accomplished through the "free adoption of European technology, the end of famines and industrial progress. The millions of *sujets* [subjects] are becoming *men*. China is resuscitated; China is moving."[51] Vergès made a distinction, popular among the proponents of republican colonialism, between the *project* of colonization and the *individuals* who carried out this project. The project was inherently good. "The colonies," Vergès wrote in 1912, "are not what too many Europeans would like to believe: an outlet for the worst vices. We must defend the colonies against harmful invasion; we must send there our best and brightest so that we can do worthwhile work and bring civilization."[52] Through the encounter between the colonists and the natives, a new community would emerge that would overcome the division of the races and feelings of hatred between individuals. Colonization would add to the wealth of the fatherland while developing the economy of the colonies.[53] Vergès shared with republican colonizers and the anticolonial Left the belief that there were two Frances, the France of corrupted functionaries in the colonies, and a generous republican France.[54]

At the end of his contract, Raymond and Jeanne Vergès left China and went back to Paris, where he entered the Faculty of Medicine. A son, Jean, was born in January 1913. At the outset of World War I, Raymond was drafted into the infantry and was wounded on September 11, 1914. A year later, he was sent back to the front as an auxiliary physician. A daughter, Simone, was born in 1916. Raymond was wounded again in 1918. After recovering his sight, he went back to his studies, joined the School of Medicine at Rennes, and was awarded his diploma by the Faculty of Medicine at Toulouse.

In 1920 Raymond Vergès was offered the appointment of professor of sciences at the Institut Technique Franco-Chinois in Shanghai.[55] Deeply frustrated by the working and teaching conditions and by his low salary, Vergès petitioned to negotiate a new contract. Unsatisfied with the terms of the new contract, Vergès left the institute and accepted a post as chief doctor in the Assistance Médicale, the medical health service in Indochina. The post was at the hospital of Savannakhet, a city on the left bank of the Mekong in the southern part of Laos. Raymond Vergès and his family arrived in Savannakhet on January 18, 1922. Vergès was an employee of the Colonial Medical Service. The "colonial doctor" was, in Vergès's own words, "long before the creation of the term, a 'social doctor' with a concern for the human value of his patients, for whom he was, on occasion, an educator."[56] Going to Indochina meant, he said, participating in the French project of "constructing and reinforcing with a sustained energy the vital link that unites the Metropole with its possessions in the four corners of the world."[57] Vergès adopted the rhetoric of colonization as a republican project.

The Doctrine of Republican Colonialism

The student:
Does the Republic have duties toward other peoples?

The Schoolteacher:
Yes, the Republic must be just toward all the nations and assist
those which are oppressed. It must practice fraternity beyond
the limits of its empire, because whoever oppresses a people
is the enemy of all peoples.

This imaginary dialogue from the *Manuel Républicain de l'Homme et du Citoyen* summarizes the colonial doctrine of the French republic.[58] The republic had the duty of bringing its ideals to other nations, and there was no doubt that its imperial enterprise was fed with the spirit of the Good. Colonization was a component of the larger republican project. At home and abroad, the French republic was engaged in redefining citizenship. *Colony* was a trope of this project. The term had been used to describe the integration of provinces that had a culture and a language that were not French, such as Brittany or Alsace, into the French nation. *Colony* also referred to the project of "discipline and punish" described by Michel Foucault, as in the expression "penal colony."[59] Through the colonization of provinces and colonial expansion abroad, the French republican state refabulated its identity. It also reconstructed norms about masculinity and femininity.[60] Progress and science provided the scientific foundations of republicanism. An army of colonizing and republican soldiers was created; schoolteachers, nurses, doctors, scientists, and soldiers were sent to the provinces of France and the colonies to propagate the ideals of

French republicanism. In the 1880s, Jules Ferry defined the colonial project thus: France "is bringing to the world *sa langue, ses moeurs, son drapeau, ses armes et son génie* [her language, her mores, her flag, her weapons, and her genius]." The preface of a 1887 schoolbook rephrased Ferry's claim for the children of the Tonkin through a series of maxims:

> Love the French people. They came from the distant land of the West to chase the pirates who were ravaging the Tonkin, killing the men, stealing the buffaloes, and selling women and children. They came to protect you, your families, and your belongings against the villains and the thieves. They shed their blood for your country. They spent a lot of money to construct beautiful cities and roads in the Tonkin, to build schools so that you would become educated men like your brothers of Saigon. Be thankful for all these good deeds. Love France that protects you.[61]

Arthur Girault, who was the architect of the assimilation doctrine, expounded in his classic *Principes de colonisation et de legislation coloniale* (1894) a systematic exposition of the ideas of assimilation, "the constantly more intimate union between the colonial territory and the metropolitan territory."[62] Colonial assimilation was the direct heir of the French Revolution's project, because the Constitution of Year III (1795) had declared the colonies to be "integral parts of the Republic."[63] Assimilation was contained, Girault wrote, in "the principles of 1789, the equal access of all citizens to public functions and to jury duty, freedom of the press, and universal suffrage."[64] Men such as Jules Harmand and Albert Sarraut, who perceived the contradictions of the founding myth of colonial domination, developed the doctrine of "association." Association rejected the doctrine of colonization predicated on the superiority of the white race and on its destiny of colonizing "inferior races."[65] Marshall Gallieni, who had led the colonial conquest of Madagascar, said that the goal of association was "to interest the natives in the administration of their country and to associate them to the development of our new possessions."[66] The doctrine of association echoed the economist Paul Leroy-Beaulieu's famous position. He wrote in *De la colonisation chez les peuples modernes* (1874) that colonization was a "permanent exchange of influences, a reciprocity of services, a continuity of relations, in a word a mutual dependency, between a society that is still in infancy and an adult society."[67] Sarraut finally synthesized the two doctrines and published in 1923 *La Mise en valeur des colonies françaises,* in which the politics of the neocolonial state was already announced.[68] Health and education were the pillars of this politics. Sarraut affirmed the moral superiority of France, which "does not oppress, she liberates. She does not exhaust, she fertilizes. She does not exploit, she shares. Out of the shapeless clay of primitive multitudes, she shapes the face of a new humanity."[69] Paul Bert, who was the first residing governor of Indochina, declared on his arrival in Saigon: "When a people has set its foot on the territory of another people, the former has three choices: to exterminate the defeated people, to subjugate it into shameful servitude, or to associate it to its own destiny. . . . We have only one choice, the third choice, which is the politics of interest and honesty. We must bring peoples to a superior civilization through association. Yes, we must associate peoples to our destiny and interest."[70] The historian Jean Fremigacci has shown how the concept of assimilation was an ambiguous and extremely contradictory concept that led to misunderstanding and discontent.[71] In its "political and economic aspects, assimilation meant oppression and was therefore in total contradiction with the social and progressive meaning suggested by the term."[72] When the colonized demanded the full realization of assimilation in the realm of civil law, the colonial power refused.[73] On the one hand, a strategy of assimilation was advocated whose goal was to homogenize all individuals, to erase particularisms. On the other hand, a "strategy of differentiation and of segregation was deployed founded on the premise that there were differences between the colonized and the metropolitans."[74]

Raphaël Barquissau, a Creole of Réunion who worked in Indochina and wrote extensively on this colony, claimed that the "real conquerors are the conquerors of the soul: apostles, doctors, magistrates, professors."[75] Through the figure of the doctor, French colonialism was able to represent its colonial policies as part of a civilizing project, whose goals were the end of obscurantism and the dissemination of hygiene.[76] Vergès could be said to be a true "disciple of Paul Bert."[77] He talked of the "gentle and maternal face" of France reflected in "countries situated at the end of the world."[78] In the "vast territories of our splendid and multiform Empire," he said, "metropolitan France with its glorious mission has always given, with total generosity, the best of herself."[79] He shared with many of his contemporaries a faith in progress and science and believed that France would end feudalism and other oppressive structures in the colonies. Vergès's themes and style emulated his compatriot Leconte de Lisle's republicanism. A poet and an ardent republican, Leconte de Lisle published the *Catéchisme populaire républicain* in 1870, whose purpose was to counter Christian catechism by using its form and style to enforce an anticlerical and republican message. Reason, moral liberty, and intelligence were opposed to fanaticism, ignorance, and false beliefs.[80] Vergès embraced the ideology of anticlericalism and secular progress largely disseminated by the institutions of the Third Republic. Serge Halimi has said that "never before the Third Republic, and never since, has the State been so effective in terms of spreading throughout society an ideology that would legitimate its rule."[81] *Republicain* referred to a series of ideals and directions that were said to be the heritage of the French Revolution: the intellectual ideal of the Enlightenment; the patriotic ideal of the *sans-culottes;* the moral ideal of *fraternité,* emblematic of the 1848 republic; an anticlerical direction; and a revolutionary direction whose aim was the extension and completion of the political republic into the social republic. Vergès proved to be the republican described by Halimi: an anticlerical, a great admirer of the French Revolution and of the principles of the Enlightenment, a moral and revolutionary republican, a partisan of the French empire.

The "Good Foreigner"

"Of all the deeds done by France in Indochina, we can affirm that medical assistance was one of the most beautiful, the most fecund, and the most proper to gain the trust of the natives and to develop our influence in the country," Albert de Pourvouville wrote in 1942.[82] Created in 1905, the service of medical assistance in Indochina sought to convince the native of the beneficial effects of French civilization.[83] Vergès took seriously his mission as doctor. His description of the role of the colonial doctor entirely fitted the model of the humanistic, scientific agent of European science who "goes to deliver the native populations from the threat of infectious diseases, infant mortality, and from sorcerers and famine."[84] In a 1928 conference about his work in Laos, he declared, harking back to Ferry's doctrine, that it was "thanks to us [the colonial civil servants] that peace reigns in these regions, that the pirates, looters, bandits of all stripes have ceased their operations."[85] It was necessary, Vergès said, that civil servants respect local traditions and customs that did not threaten the work of the scientific colonizer. Saving lives, curing diseases, and caring for the children transformed the natives' view of the foreigner, who became "the good foreigner."[86] Because of his work, the doctor had access, more than any other European, to the core of native society. "With respect to his results, the dignity of his behavior, and his tireless disinterest, a trusting intimacy and an affectionate deference are established between the doctor and the inhabitant; the doctor is adopted by the native population."[87] The doctor "knows what other Europeans will never know: the home, the family, the woman."[88] In a 1941 lecture,[89] Vergès related the multiple activities of the colonial health service: creation of indigenous clinics; vaccination programs against epidemics and venereal diseases; prenatal and postnatal care.

The beneficial effects of medical assistance in the colonies constituted an important part of the rhetoric of colonization as a civilizing process. Through the medium of photography, one that developed parallel to colonization, the French public was exposed to the image of the doctor as a benevolent, caring, and disinterested person in the colonies. Shots of Raymond Vergès at the hospital of Savannakhet belonged to this genre.[90] The photographs were carefully constructed scenes in which the European doctor occupied a central place.[91] The series of pictures constructed a universe of care, cleanliness, and trust supervised by the European doctor, whose presence guaranteed a scientific approach to disease.

Vergès learned Laotian and Vietnamese to communicate with his patients. He reorganized and expanded the hospital of Savannakhet.[92] To him, science was undoubtedly beneficial to the natives, previously subjected to epidemics and the power of native healers who exploited their patients' "credulity and beliefs in supernatural forces." His dream was to eradicate malaria and leprosy, and to teach the principles of hygiene that had already become, in France, the foundations of republican life.[93] There were results to his enterprise: infant mortality was reduced; children were vaccinated; epidemic diseases were contained. But the actions of the colonial health service also meant the control and disciplining of populations and indifference to, if not repression of, traditional ways of healing. In the colonies, the campaign against infant mortality had to do as much with protecting the reproduction of a workforce as with stopping infant mortality. "The demographic increase of the native population became the *sine qua non* of the development of the territories," Yvonne Knibiehler and Régine Goutalier have written.[94] Collaboration with local midwives or healers was avoided, because Western education in prenatal and postnatal care were thought to be the best. European feminists supported the project. At the 1931 États Généraux du Féminisme, the French Federation of Women Doctors proposed that "1—In the colonies, women doctors will be entrusted with the care of native women and children; 2—that maternity hospitals with women doctors as directors will be opened; 3—competent native nurses will be trained to help women doctors in their consultations and the penetration into the families."[95]

Vergès directed the Savannakhet hospital until 1925. His wife, Jeanne, died in 1923. In 1925 the General Government of Indochina appointed him to the post of consul of France at Oubone, in the kingdom of Siam. Vergès became consul on February 25, 1925.[96] The new consul wanted to develop the commercial relations between France and this part of the world, and to serve this goal, he opened a commercial delegation that promoted French products to the population. Learning French was part of a "good" education, and the consul opened a school for young natives. Vergès never publicly denounced French colonialism in Indochina, although during his stay there movements that challenged French rule had started to make their struggle public.[97] Vergès should have noticed, despite his defense of the progress brought by French colonialism, that poverty, disease, and exploitation were the rule rather than the exception.[98]

By 1927 reports were sent to the General Government of Indochina that criticized Raymond Vergès's actions as doctor and consul. In an extremely critical report of July 11, 1927, Vergès was denounced for having no medical activity whatsoever and for leaving the hospital in a neglected state.[99] However, the event that seemed to have triggered the campaign against him was that he lived in the consulate with his Vietnamese companion, Pham Thi Khang, and their *métis* sons. Vergès had met Pham Thi Khang in Savannakhet. She was a twenty-two-year-old elementary school teacher, the oldest daughter of Pham Van-Phuc, an entrepreneur, and of Tran Thi Long, a housewife. Pham joined Vergès at Oubone in late February 1925, and twin sons, Jacques and Paul, were born on March 5, 1925. The French colonial society of Oubone, particularly the priest, was extremely shocked that the consul was openly living with his Asian companion and their children. Many colonial administrators, civil servants, and soldiers had native concubines, but according to an unspoken and unwritten—yet carefully observed—rule, native concubines were not supposed to live with their companions, more so if they were colonial administrators. The colonial administration and the Catholic Church strongly discouraged unions between French men and native women; the army forbade them.[100] Native female companions were called *congaïe*—a Vietnamese term that means "young woman."[101] The term was adopted by French colonists and writers to designate women who were prostitutes, spouses, or concubines of French men. Congaïe became the trope of the Oriental woman: submissive and cunning; charming, graceful, and capricious.[102]

The reaction of the Oubone colonial society to the cohabitation of Vergès with Pham Thi Khang and their children was the expression of racial beliefs and colonial fears about relationships between native women and European men. Raymond Vergès's gesture was not only a gesture of defiance against colonial racism. He was also defying the social norms of French bourgeois society. Before World War I, it was quite rare for a man of his social position to live with a woman to whom he was not married. Unions between men and women had to be sanctioned by the bonds of marriage. The bourgeois ideology that marked the Third Republic reproved concubinage, and one could only guess that concubinage was even more scandalous for the small, narrow colonial society of Oubone. Raymond Vergès, who was the representative of the French state at Oubone, the enforcer of its laws, transgressed a social law and exhibited his transgression by bringing to the consulate his mistress and their children. He could justify his gesture only by appealing to a "higher" law, a law that mocked or ignored social laws. Vergès was making his own law based on beliefs that were not shared by the colonial society. Even if the reaction of the colonial society had not reflected racism and hypocrisy, Vergès certainly knew that his gesture would entail reprobation and punishment. But that knowledge did not stop him. The double gesture—on the one hand, of defiance of social laws, and on the other hand, appeal to reason and obedience to the republican law—marked Vergès's life.

Raymond Vergès married Pham Thi Khang on March 6, 1928, and recognized Jacques and Paul as his sons on the same day. The marriage precipitated a series of reports that led to the dismissal of Vergès. Administrative reports about Vergès made a distinction between his white children, pitied for what they had to endure, and his métis children.[103] These reports contained examples of what constituted French colonial mores, anxieties, and concerns in Indochina: the standing of colonial administrators, the flag as the sign of France's presence, the fear of métissage, racial fears, and contempt for native women. The anxiety that the union between Vergès and Pham provoked was congruent with the racial ideology of French colonialism and the fear of métissage. Louis Rougni, the colonial civil servant who acted as officer of the state at Vergès and Pham's marriage, protested in a letter to the governor of Indochina that:

Dr. Vergès has forced me to marry him with the Annamite with whom he has been living since his first wife's death. He has two charming children from this first marriage whom we can pity, particularly a cute little twelve year blond girl, and two métis children who are the subject of all his solicitude. I do not want to insist on the "prestige" that he has earned here because of this union; neither do I want to imagine what the Consulate would be when, upon his return, *Madame Française* would be the host at parties and dinners.[104]

Gossip and rumors became denunciations. Doctor Trancière described a visit to Vergès and his family in a letter dated March 18, 1928:

I arrived at the French Consulate February 26 [1928] at eleven P.M. Doctor Vergès is an amiable scientist singularly transformed by four years of concubinage with an Annamite woman. I want to let you know that we lived like gypsies until our departure on March 7. Doctor Vergès has two children. One is an adorable eleven year old girl from a first marriage with a European who died of sunstroke five years ago at Savannakhet. Since then, he has been living with a native [*indigène*] with whom he has had twins. I was told that he was living in a less dignified manner than a Laotian and I can confirm this. . . . [A detailed report on the living conditions follows.]

In a word: ruins, poverty, disgusting filth, and absolutely no sign of the prestige one would expect of a French consulate; since the departure of Mr. Simon [the preceding consul] the tricolor flag has never flapped over the Consulate. . . . [The report goes on insisting on the decay of the consulate, then turns to the activities of Vergès.]

About the tours that he must conduct as Consul, this is what I was told by Mr. Chatenet: Doctor Vergès had gone to the river Simoun with his *congaïe,* his *métis* children, and his other two children. At Pakmoun, perhaps because he was concerned to use the boats of the *Messageries Fluviales* with his *congaïe* and *métis,* or because of stinginess, it is said that he asked for pirogues and went on the Mekong to Naphong and Savannakhet. At Savannakhet, he left his *congaïe* and *métis* with her Annamite parents and went to Khou Panom. [The report goes on to argue that Vergès's trip did not constitute an administrative tour. It says: "In fact, Vergès has traveled as a tourist through French Laos." Proof of this is "his report where he has written extensively on the difference of French Laos from Siam," rather than on administrative matters.][105]

The politics of blood in the empire spoke of the fear of degeneration, a powerful trope in imperial discourse. Yet the European anxiety about métis could not be explained simply by their number, because métis remained a minority in colonies, with the exception of Réunion. Neither could such anxiety be explained by the role métis played in revolutionary politics, for if some joined anti-colonialist movements, many served in the colonial army and administration. The sources of the anxiety that mobilized the imagination of writers and politicians must be sought elsewhere. The "Eurasian métis" responded to a variety of cultural and psychological anxieties. In the larger reconfiguration of otherness that was taking place in France to situate a coherent national bourgeois identity, the métis did not quite occupy the role of the Other, whether Asian or African.[106] The métis' position as an "in-between," a "not-quite" white, reactivated old anxieties about mixed blood in the age of eugenics and nationalism.

Blood Politics in the Colonial Empire

The discourses of nationalism and colonialism worked together to reconstruct a sense of the specific destiny of France. Both were "regarded as a means of moral and national regeneration."[107] Degeneration became central in French political rhetoric at home and abroad. The regeneration of France entailed a careful approach to the mixing of classes and races. It was Benedict Augustin Morel (1809–1873) who originated the concept of degeneration.[108] Morel was deeply concerned with the decline of the white race produced by lower education and morals and advocated a campaign of remoralization.[109] Morel took as his reference of a nondegenerated group the Petits Blancs of Réunion Island, poor whites pushed to the mountains by the expansion of the capitalist exploitation of the sugarcane industry.[110] Their mores were "simple and peaceful," and they were content with their life. "Despite their poverty, they never associated with the mulattos; nothing would make them alter their race with a drop of mixed blood."[111] Daniel Pick has shown how Morel's treatise "spoke to, and displaced, deep concerns about the genealogy of history," whose "problems were displaced into the problem of inheritance."[112]

Race, as Leon Poliakov has remarked, became the "motor of history."[113] Arthur de Gobineau, a contemporary of Morel, introduced in his *Essai sur l'inégalité des races* (1853) the discourse about degeneration because of métissage. Each nation, Gobineau contended, has been subjected to métissage and consequently to degeneration. There was no longer a pure race.[114] Gobineau warned European nations that their decline was inevitable unless they controlled métissage: "Degenerated man will definitively die, and civilization with him."[115] Métissage led to decadence, to the inescapable descent toward mediocrity and the decline of the race. It brought to life unstable and disharmonious individuals. It threatened the survival of humankind because the métis was sterile.[116] But decline could be avoided. There was a choice: to conquer or to be conquered.[117] Saving the white race dictated that European nations conquer peoples who threatened their racial purity.[118] In the words of Pierre-André Taguieff, "the condemnation of *métissage* entered the political and ideological domain at the very moment when nationalist doctrines with a racist base emerged."[119] In the 1920s, French psychologists and scientists espousing Gobineau's ideas developed a discourse that informed immigration and colonial policies.[120] The dominant view was that the métis was impure and inferior. In 1927 the *Revue de Psychologie Appliquée* published a study of métissage and its role in the production of abnormal

children. A psychotherapist, Doctor Bérillon, argued that métissage was one of the most frequent causes of mental and physical
degeneration.[121] Doctor René Martial, who was the chair of the
Department of "Anthropo-biology of the Races" at the University
of Paris, published a series of very popular books and articles on
métissage and its dangers.[122] In his *Race, Hérédité, Folie: Étude
d'anthroposociologie appliquée à l'immigration,* Martial argued that
immigration was inevitable and constituted a form of "massive
métissage."[123]

Yet within this métissage, it was necessary to determine the qualities of a "good métis," and psychology would help to select these
good individuals. The "French race could still be saved" because
there were enough good elements within the French nation, but it
was "necessary to eliminate not only the gangrenous parts but all
those suspected of being impure."[124] Bad métissage was métissage
in which the bloods of the two parents were "mixed in equal quantity," and it led to madness. The blood belonging to the "inferior
races," when in equal quantity with the "good blood" of the superior race, would win out over "good blood" and therefore bring
decline.[125] In *Les Métis,* Martial singled out the Jews as the first
group to have brought degeneration to the French race.[126] "Vul-
garity extending to bestiality, psychological instability, perversity,
morbidity, asymmetry of facial traits, ugliness, of the hybrids,"
Martial wrote, "provoked horror and repulsion in the well-born
[*aux âmes bien nées*]."[127] Anti-Semitism and fear of métissage were
related. Martial's paranoia—displayed in his manic list of defects of
the métis, his mad calculations of percentage of various bloods in
the métis—prefigured the trope of the métis as an object of abjection in the racial ideology of the 1930s and 1940s. Medical discourse
justified legal decisions.[128] The psychological discourse about the
duality of bloods marked the métis with a indelible defect. The
biological framework of racial ideology determined that (1) métissage had to be controlled because it threatened the purity of the
race; (2) the métis could be saved at the price of renouncing what
was not white in her or him, and this was generally a renunciation
of the mother; (3) when racial ideology was pursued to its logical
conclusion, the métis had to be exterminated. The "symbolics of
blood" and its preoccupation with legitimacy, madness, and pure
blood was, as Laura Ann Stoler has shown, worked and reworked
on colonial ground.

The anxiety provoked by the "invisible" difference of the Jews echoed the anxiety provoked by the métis. Both could "pass."[129] And a recurrent theme of fictions about the métis was about passing. The smallest difference was tracked down: the form of an eye; a tendency to hide, to lie; a gesture suddenly charged with meaning. In Indochina, where boundaries between genders were not visible to a European eye, the anxiety produced by this opacity was intensified by the anxiety about race boundaries.[130] Gender, race, and blood had to remain expressive markers of difference. On métis' bodies and souls whom they accused of menacing duality, white colonizers projected their own duality: their discourse about *fraternité* and equality of human beings *and* their desire to annihilate, to destroy the differences that they confronted.

The debate about métissage and its political and cultural consequences agitated colonial administrators and writers. In contrast to Martial's discourse, there existed a discourse in which the notions of "métissage," "cultural graft," and "Eurafrican culture" were opposed to the notions of "cultural and racial purity," "racial hierarchy," and "racial shame."[131] Colonial education had to be adapted to local needs and culture, and an integration of "African culture" in the colonial curriculum was promoted.[132] Colonial rhetoric was divided. French republican imperialism tended to promote "cultural métissage" while maintaining political subjugation. Racial French nationalism defended a separation of the races. Racial theories of French nationalism and the ideology of National Socialism, whose theses were disseminated in France around 1933, strongly opposed any notion of métissage. To National Socialists, racial métissage, *Rassenmischung,* was a threat to racial purity, because the qualities of superior races would be polluted by "mediocre blood." There was nothing unique in the National Socialist fear of métissage; it echoed the European imperial fear. What Hitler wrote in 1928 about the *Mischlinge* was similar to what could be found in many colonialist texts: "It is there [with the métis] that a discord against nature emerges. It is known that spirit and mind are strong only when they are anchored in the totality of the being, when body and mind are one. But as soon as there is conflict in this unity, then these men [the métis] experience being pulled apart; body and mind are no longer united. It becomes a source of constant torment, of eternal pain and discontent." The 1937 Nazi plan of the colonization of Africa included specific articles about the regulation of métissage. Gunther Hecht, the author of the racial policies in the future *Kolonialreich,* wrote:

Biologically, the mixing of races is the fusion of the hereditary cells of many races. A pool of cells represents an optimum, the most favorable result of physical, intellectual, and spiritual factors that are inherited. Any *mischling* [métissage] is a threat to, if not the destruction of, the highest values of both original races. The *Mischlinger* loses social referents, scruples, which for us are obvious. It is known that a majority of serious crimes are committed by *métis.*[133]

Among the anticolonialist colonized, the debate was organized around two themes: métissage as the future of humanity, as a challenge to European mono-ethnicism (and its association with National Socialism), and métissage as erasure of differences, unity under the sign of the empire. The Senegalese writer Ousmane Socé defended métissage, arguing that it represented a challenge to European racism. In his novel *Mirages de Paris,* Socé had his hero, Fara, arguing: "I will even say that, if the intermixing of races continues at its actual rhythm, the *métis* will be the man of the future."[134] But to Léopold Sedar Senghor, métissage had the political and ideological function in the empire of absorbing, swallowing difference.[135] At the 1937 Congrès International de l'Évolution Culturelle des Peuples Coloniaux, Fily Dabo Sissoko, a writer and future representative of Mali at the French National Assembly, mocked the African métis and declared: "The Black man must remain Black, in life and education."[136]

In colonial literature, the métis was an object of both pity and contempt.[137] Robert Randau, a popular writer of colonial literature, contended that "our race will become degenerate with *métissage.*"[138] Métis women were highly sexualized characters, supporting Gilman's argument that "no realm of human experience is as closely tied to the concept of degeneration as that of sexuality."[139] Métissage was at the center of a matrix of anxieties about sexuality, genetic inheritance, race, and environment.

The "Métis Race"

Albert de Pourvouville warned that the "*métis* race, that we helped to develop, has always been the curse of the territories where it prevailed."[140] In Asia, slowing down the "creation" of métis became a colonial duty. But if colonial rhetoric wanted to dictate an order based on the segregation of races, it could not impose a hegemonic control on sexual and social intercourse, and forbidden unions continued to occur.[141] Colonial administrators who believed that métissage was inevitable in the colonies sought to devise a policy that stressed the assimilation of the métis and found ways to give them a particular and important role in the colonies.[142] Métis would become "intermediaries," a function for which they were "naturally" prepared because of the "duality of their origins."[143] Men such as Marcel Sambuc, Ernest Babut, Jacques Mazet, and Colonel Bonifacy believed, along with racial scientists such as Martial, that the métis was morally weak, a potential rebel, a resentful and bitter person. "The history of colonizing nations shows that everywhere it was among the mixed-blood men that the malcontents and the rebels emerged. The *métis* is dangerous because he has his feet in both worlds and often possesses qualities of intelligence and flexibility that he uses for bad purposes."[144] But these men also believed that through education, the biologically determined defect could be disciplined and contained.[145] Hence they encouraged the opening of orphanages, the separation of métis children from their mothers, and the training of these children as auxiliaries of colonial expansion.[146]

French women's organizations added a feminist dimension to that project. At the 1931 General Assemblies of Feminism at the Colonial Exhibition, the "great champions of feminism . . . solicited the presence of colonial women—spouses of colonial administrators, nuns, nurses, doctors, teachers."[147] The feminists embraced the colonial project. They looked at women's conditions in each colony and protested against practices that they felt oppressed women. They were indignant that the right to vote had been given to the Kabyles, who "rape little girls." But the feminists also demanded that women workers in the colonies be protected by the same laws as in France. It was a colonial and humanist feminism, and in that respect, they were not different from many of their male peers. They wanted colonized women to enter progress and civilization as they defined it. The case of métis children was the theme of a special session. The feminist rapporteur claimed that "this primordial problem concerns the entire future of our colonies and even our civilization."[148] Feminists wanted to put an end to what, along with most colonialists, they saw as the destiny of the métis, revolution for the male and prostitution for the female. They called for "the establishment of centers in which abandoned young girls or those in moral danger could be transformed into worthy women."[149] The rapporteur concluded her appeal with these words: "We do not have enough mothers overseas. *Métis* women would be perfect for that role: married to native men, they would create homes where our civilization would reign; married to French men, they would accept to live in places where young women from the metropole would fear to go; married to *métis* like themselves, they would create a bourgeoisie which will be attached both to its native country and to France."[150]

Those who wanted to incorporate the métis talked nonetheless of their "vanity and pride," of their propensity to rebellion,[151] of their ability to mimic,[152] and of their touchy character.[153] Administrators emphasized the deficient paternal function in métissage. "Many French fathers fail to recognize their métis children," Babut wrote. "It is therefore from the paternal side that they experience abandonment."[154] Bonifacy also deplored the laxity of men, reinforced by the French metropolitan law about paternity that was applied in the colonies and absolved fathers of their legal responsibility. After much lobbying from colonial administrators, a decree was adopted in 1928 providing that "any individual born in Indochina of parents one of whom is presumed to be French would be able to obtain the status of French nationality." "Eurasianity," Ida Simon-Barouh has argued, "was an impossible condition, lived with ambivalence, ambiguity, and division." Eurasians were mostly found in the cities, working for the colonial administration, the army, or the police. Very few had manual jobs. To the Vietnamese, the métis often remained strangers, even though, Simon-Barouh argued, the Vietnamese were more tolerant toward them than the French colonists. But the colonial society remained distrustful of Eurasians, who, they said, "because of their abnormal heredity, could not embrace the notions of family, fatherland, honor, work, prosperity, all what constitute the normal social order. Deprived of the faculties of judgment and control, they are the toys of their passions and the tools of their impulses."[155]

The fear of rebellion touched a nerve, but none of these documents presented an account of why the métis should be particularly susceptible to rebellion. Sambuc turned to fiction to support the argument that the deficient paternal function was the source of the métis' nature, and consequently of their potential for hatred and rebellion. Literature provided the argument that sustained colonial policies and explained the colonists' anxiety: white male colonists feared the revenge of their abandoned métis son. The sins of the fathers would come back to haunt them through their illegitimate métis children. Albert de Pourvouville's novel *Le Mal d'argent* offered Sambuc a case of métis' imbalance.

Le Mal d'argent opens with the trial of the young Nguyen Thuc, accused of having killed a French officer.[156] Nguyen Thuc answers his judges that his patronymic, Nguyen, is the patronymic of the majority of the Annamites—he could be any of them; he has no "real name," he says—and *Thuc* means "the pirate." His father threw him out of his house, and his mother died of grief and shame. He is acquitted. When the judgment is given, he looks at the officer's widow, who "recognizes with terror the features of her husband's face." The métis was the son of the officer. He had killed his father. He was a parricide. In a fictional work, an argument was made that linked métissage, lack of the father's patronymic, and parricide. There was a solution to the apparently inevitable outcome: since French fathers could not be expected to fulfill their functions (neither should they be asked to), the state had to intervene and occupy the place of the deficient father. By taking the paternal function, the state would ground the métis in the patriarchal and colonial law. The métis were made unstable not so much by mixed blood but because they lacked a father who could legitimate them through their inscription in the colonial/paternal law and control their tendencies toward revolution, disorder, and parricide. The son killed his father not to possess his mother but to protect and avenge her. The world of the métis's mother was dangerous because it kept the child outside the law and the symbolic order of the colonial world. The state, acting as a surrogate father, would separate the child from the mother, thereby facilitating the child's entrance into the patriarchal world and the colonial law. Authors agreed that métis children had first to be taken away from their mothers and then educated by the state. Mothers were connected to disorder. Even if they wanted for their children a "white education," they would not be able, assimilationists argued, to counter the atavism of Asian blood. Children staying with their mothers would remain rooted in native society, but the white part of their blood would build resentment and hatred in them, particularly if they had been in contact with the white father's world.[157]

The narrative of the métis as monster and revolutionary was about the fear of the French father dreading, as in a nightmare, the return of an avenging son whom the father might not even recognize at the moment of being struck. It was about the father's guilt at having abandoned the son and broken the sexual and racial taboos of the colonial society. The métis daughter was rarely an avenging figure. Her destiny was usually prostitution. Incestuous relation with the white brother could then occur. The father's guilt over having abandoned his son was projected onto the native mother, who was seen as the source of aggression, inciting her son to parricide. The state would act as a disciplining father: sons would be tamed into good soldiers of the colonial army under the authority of white officers, their fathers.[158]

Anxiety was about disclosure of the family secret, about discovering a half sister or half brother whose existence brought out into the open the father's infidelity. "To talk would mean the ruin of this family which is whole without me. To talk? Their peace, their happiness would be irremediably destroyed. To talk? Is my happiness worth the destruction of this happiness? I am the bastard, the child of sin. Bastard . . . I do not have the right to talk," said the hero of the novel *François Phuoc, Métis.*[159] It was a secret that was striking for its banality. After all, the norms of bourgeois life were seldom respected, and illegitimate children were not a rare occurrence. Yet the efforts to maintain this fiction were relentless. Pictures destroyed, names concealed, papers burnt, denials and dissimulation wove a cloth of lies to conceal the secret. There was a deeper forbidden drama behind the apparent scandal of the child's origins, and this drama was the primal scene. On the bourgeois scene of sexless relations between women and men, the métis child was the sign of the sexual encounter between the father and the native woman. The métis, apparently "a tormenting stranger in the home, [was] ultimately no stranger at all—the uncanny [was] but the disguised return of something already familiar."[160] The métis signified the double, a slightly deformed double, of the white brother.[161] The paranoid theme of intrusion in the bourgeois family bespoke not only fraternal jealousy but also the fear of incest between brother and sister.[162] François, the métis, has left his native country and gone to study in France. No longer confined to his native mother's home or to the state orphanage, the métis entered the metropolitan home. François befriends Pierre, who soon imagines that his friend will marry his sister, Geneviève. But François, the Eurasian, is his half brother. There is no escape from the métis's fate.

In metropolitan France, the sisters were entering public space, demanding equal rights.[163] Women were participating in the socialist mobilization against capitalism; they demanded equal access to education and professions and sexual freedom. But women were also supporting the project of the Third Republic and its domestic feminism. To these feminists, rebellious women were victims, like the Communardes whose wanton sexuality and defiant spirit had been abused by revolutionary men. Native women were abused by native men and by European men who could not control their sexuality. The respectable bourgeois wife had shed sexuality at home, so that the "relations of husband to wife" were "spiritualized" and modeled on the relation of brother and sister.[164] The European man fled the bourgeois wife and the rebellious female worker and sought an adventurous life in the colony. Far from home, away from the condemnation of the bourgeois ideology, the European man entered into a sexual relationship with the native woman. But his escape was marked by the betrayal of his society's norms. He would not pay, though, for his transgression. As in the biblical narrative, there would be visitation of the sins of the fathers on the heads of their children.

In colonial literature, a constellation of characters constructed the ideal family: a white mother, innocent and at home, a white father, and their children. But lurking in the background, the native woman and her son threatened to explode the bourgeois myth. They were the couple that triggered anxiety about revolution and disorder. Men had gone to the colonies and had sexual intercourse with native women whom they had abandoned. They felt guilty about having desired these women. They did not want their mothers to know that they had been sexually active in the colonies. They both desired their sisters and feared that those sisters could be seduced by native males. Hence they devised a fiction that situated the métis at the nexus of these anxieties. They wished to contain, discipline, and tame the métis by taking them away from their mothers and giving them to the state, which would remake them into servants of the colonial project.

It was in this context that Raymond Vergès married Pham Thi Khang and recognized his métis sons, Paul and Jacques. Vergès's gesture of defiance could be read as the indirect denunciation by a French citizen, yet still a colonized Creole, of the hypocrisy of the colonial doctrine of association. Racism belied the tale of mutual respect and exchange. A Vietnamese woman remained a congaïe, and her children were bastards. Through the legitimization of marriage and the father's recognition of his children, Raymond Vergès marked the inscription of his métis sons into the paternal law and recognized their native Vietnamese mother as his wife. The recognition was achieved through the bonds of marriage, and the children's inscription into the European law was achieved through their official inclusion in the father's genealogy. He grounded Paul and Jacques into a paternal filiation and integrated them in a world that had denied their own mother the status of citizen because she was a colonized subject. By legitimating his sons, Vergès gave them the opportunity to contest the colonial law not from a position of resentment but from a position of respectability. Le Huu Khoa has spoken of the "singular history of colonial Eurasianity: that is the absence of recognition by both parental communities."[165] Paul and Jacques Vergès enjoyed the recognition of both parental communities: they lived with their mother, the legitimate wife of their father. Vergès gave his sons a name and a genealogy that had its roots in colonized Vietnam, colonial Réunion, and French republican law.

In 1928 Raymond Vergès left Indochina for Réunion with Pham Thi Khang and his four children. His father had died in the preceding year on the island. Pham Thi Khang died in Réunion in 1928. Vergès left Paul and Jacques in the care of his aunt, Marie Vergès, and returned to Indochina with Jean and Simone. In a letter that he sent to the governor on June 24, 1929, Vergès protested the abrupt and unjustified termination of his contract at the Oubone consulate.[166] He bitterly resented the accusations against him and demanded to be heard. "After five months, I remain in the eyes of many, in a country where I am well-known, a suspect against whom the worst accusations have been made."[167] In April, the administration offered him the post of doctor at the hospital of Ventiane. In December, he was transferred to the hospital of Faïfo, in the province of Quang Tri. The following year, he published in Saigon, under the pseudonym Jean-Paul Sker, a novel *Boscot, sous-*

off. et . . . assassin?[168] Sker began the book with an epigraph that read: "Those who provoke a hatred of authority because they abuse it, who corrupt men with their behavior, should be condemned to public vengeance."

The novel is the story of Boscot, a low-ranking officer married to a Vietnamese, Thithành. One day, his superior officer sends Boscot on a mission and, while he is away, rapes Thithành. Boscot, suspicious of his superior, returns early from his mission and surprises them in bed. He kills the officer, forgives his wife, and flees to China, where he joins a friend, Véron. They plan to get to Shanghai and to find a ship that will take them to San Francisco, but a wound on Boscot's leg becomes gangrenous, and he can no longer run. When French troops find them, rather than surrender, Boscot and Véron kill themselves. Thithành, who has been imprisoned after Boscot's escape, takes her own life by swallowing poison on learning of Boscot's death.

Thithành is petite, timid, like a child, adoring her "master."[169] Boscot is a simple, honest man who has chosen to marry her to "signify his desire to embrace the ways of living and customs of the indigenous, to use his situation to serve the just interests of France rather than guilty fantasies, and to signify the serious character of their union."[170] Boscot is the representative of "our great France, our glory and our safeguard."[171] The officer, Alexis Duflor de Labratte, is the quintessential aristocrat, a military man, holding "absolute power."[172] Instead of earning the love and esteem of his men, de Labratte abuses them. The French and Vietnamese peoples are gendered: France is an honest republican Frenchman, and Vietnam is a gentle woman defiled and raped by the colonial aristocrat. Both are presented as victims of unprincipled colonization. Both can go beyond ethnic, religious, and cultural differences and love each other.

Vergès's novel was atypical, considering the conventions of colonial literature. Advocates of "colonial literature" insisted on their opposition to the school of exoticism that had been, in the early years of colonial expansion, the dominant form of literature taking Africa or the Orient as its object. Eugène Pujarniscle, who wrote a manifesto in defense of the colonial novel, denounced the lack of complexity and the stereotypical views of the exotic novel.[173] The aim of colonial literature was to "represent" the colonial reality. "Exotic is opposed to national, colonial, and metropolitan," Pujarniscle wrote; "But colonies are not alien to us. A French colony is still France, the France of Asia, Africa, America, or Oceania."[174] In colonial literature, the colonial writer and the native informant collaborated: the "native providing material and the French transforming this material in a form accessible and agreeable to the European reader."[175] Colonial writers, who knew better than the metropolitan writers the "secrets of the Asian soul," would go beyond the "dogma of the yellow enigma, of impenetrable and hidden Asia."[176] The colonial writer had the task of rendering the colony transparent to the European public so that it could become a province of European learning.[177] Yet, as Lisa Lowe has shown in her study of French and British Orientalisms, Orientalism was never a monolithic discourse.[178] It was heterogeneous and contradictory. To the Réunionnais writer Marius Leblond, the colonial novel was able to "show intimately man in his racial diversity" and would thus give back to French literature and culture a "fecundity which has been exhausted."[179] France had lost many of her sons in World War I, and the colonized males would provide the masculinity that she was lacking.

Vergès's novel is more "a-colonial" than colonial or anticolonial, Carpanin Marimoutou has argued.[180] There is no revelation about the "Asian soul," nor a psychologization of the natives' behavior or picturesque scenes, but rather long descriptions of the scenery, short scenes, and short dialogues. Although the novel is filled with stereotypical descriptions of Asians, which shock the contemporary reader, a careful reading reveals less a moral doubt about colonization than a general disillusion about human beings. As Marimoutou has shown, the stark presence of the landscape and the severe weather conditions signified the "reign of the a-human" and the limits of human possibility. They spoke of the difficulty for a man to encounter other men.[181] Vergès's novel was a novel about disenchantment, "about that 'thing,' that *rien:* the colonial man." It was about the "absurdity of a political project, of an adventure which had been planned for nothing, for that *rien.*"[182] With *Boscot,* Vergès wrote a paradigmatic story: the story of a hero, a rebel alone against the world. It showed Vergès's conception of republicanism, its connection with individualism, and of the fate of republicanism in the colony: the republican was a man who had to fight against greater forces and whose colonial destiny was death. The presence of death and murder, betrayal and disillusion, gave the narrative a melancholic dimension. There was no relief, no refuge for Boscot as he was chased through Indochina and China, but his own death. The fate of the Vietnamese woman was suicide.

Boscot's story evokes Vergès's own story. Both had gone to the colony with an ideal of fraternal love; both loved a Vietnamese woman; both were state employees; both were subjected to the arbitrary power of colonial authorities; both defied social and colonial norms; both defended republican ideals. However, the conclusions of the novel and of Vergès's life were different. Vergès married his Vietnamese lover and legitimized their children. He defied the colonial condemnation of his union. The métis sons did not kill the father and avenge the mother. The Vietnamese mother, beyond her early death, remained an important figure in the Vergès family romance. She would tie up, in the family imaginary, Réunion to Vietnam, a Creole world to an Asian world and to an anticolonialist and anti-imperialist struggle. And we will see later how, because of her racial origin, she would become a character in the 1960s political demonology in Réunion.

Return to the Native Island

Vergès, afflicted with chronic malaria, received permission to leave Indochina in September 1930. He left on October 21, 1930, never to return to Asia. In 1931 he was offered the post of doctor at Hell-Bourg, a village in the mountains of the Salazes in Réunion. The island to which Vergès returned after thirty-two years was extremely poor; the majority of its population was living in dire conditions.[183] In 1933 Vergès settled in the city of Saint-André, where he opened a training center for nurses and, in 1940, a training school for midwives. He joined the League of the Rights of Man and Citizen, the Academy of Réunion, and the Freemasons, institutions historically tied to the spread of republican ideas on the island. He became the mayor of Salazie in 1935 and, in 1936, the president of the Federation of Réunion Workers.

Vergès's discourse about justice and progress revealed a deep respect for the virtues of rectitude and honesty and an idealization of the poor and dispossessed. In a lecture celebrating Robespierre, Vergès insisted on the virtues of the "incorruptible": Robespierre scorned money, that corrupting force, and despised the rewards of pleasures and profit.[184] "Comrades," Vergès said, "the incorruptible is the social contract embodied; he is Democracy marching on; he is the revolutionary epic."[185] Vergès concluded: "Let us hope that Robespierre will guide us and our sons toward the realization of the republican ideal, toward the city of liberty, equality, fraternity, still enveloped in clouds but for which he fought and for which he was killed." Words such as "probity," "honesty," "altruism," "uprightness," "incorruptible," "sacrifice," and "devotion" resounded through the text. Serving the people was the highest goal to which one could aspire. The republic would exist with the construction of the ideal city. Vergès's rhetoric belonged to a long tradition of republican discourse, emphatic and moralist, decisively separating the righteous from the corrupt. His imagined community was the child of the most demanding revolutionary dream, in which the virtuous punished the lazy and the corruptible.

The imagined community of the anticolonialists was the community of the workers and the republicans. It was not the community concurrently imagined by a group defending a "white Creole myth," defending and reworking French civilization on the remote island of Réunion. Both groups were republicans and looked up to France as the protector of their rights as citizens, but the Creole myth's advocates rejected the notion of class.[186] Their leaders were Marius and Ary Leblond, prolific writers extremely active in the defense of the French colonial empire.[187] The linkage of "Bourbon and Leblond" (the Leblonds often used the island's prerepublican name of Bourbon, even though Réunion had been the island's definitive name since 1848) made manifest their political agenda: to rewrite Réunion's history, making it white and a part of France. On the island, different races harmonized by the French genius would create the vanguard of the French glory, generous and fraternal. The Leblonds constructed the Creoles as ahistorical and abstract subjects, entirely separated from the economic, social, and psychological conditions of their formation. They had nonetheless to explain how the whiteness of Creoleness had been preserved despite métissage. To do so, the Leblonds invented the concept of "impregnation": Réunion had been inhabited by the descendants of Celts, the true Aryan people, and their creolization was the result of "Creole impregnation." The white Celtic child born on the island was "impregnated," and thus creolized, by the island and by the milk and care of people of color such as the *nénènes,* female domestics attached to the care of the children of Réunion's bourgeoisie. The semantic difference between "impregnation" and "métissage" was the result of a desperate move to maintain that no sexual contact had occurred between whites and blacks, or if there was physical contact, that it was contained in the domain of innocent childhood. Milk, instead of semen or the uterine liquid, had "impregnated" the whites. The term *impregnation,* itself a sexual term, reintroduced sexuality in an apparently desexualized explanation. It situated the Creole man as a passive, feminized object impregnated by the breast of the black nanny, as if her breast were a penis and the man a woman.

Imprégnation had produced colonial harmony in Réunion Island. Because it was uninhabited, the island offered a site for a fantasized harmony, innocence, and primitivism.[188] "It is important," the Leblonds wrote, "to destroy a legend that some travelers have spread: the legend about a *métissage* which is at the origins of the island's population."[189] The project of the Creole myth was to elaborate a discourse in which the island was more French than France because its Frenchness had developed in a contained space, protected from foreign invasions and influences by its isolation in the ocean. This paradox—to construe an island as remote and different from France as Réunion was as the site of an unpolluted French culture—was consistent with the desire to discover a virgin land, untouched by "foreign" influence, in which to rebuild a regenerated French state and culture. In this fantasized space, a new aesthetic was possible. In Réunion, the Leblonds said, one could experience the "*supreme form,* which is the result of the most refined and fecund mixtures and alliances."[190] The island was a "cosmos," a "global museum."[191] Nature had provided the white man with an island in which the universe was contained, where a new humanity could develop. Réunion was construed as the scene of primal narcissism, where man could be powerful, autonomous, and free to shape the land in his own image. The white man was doubly blessed: he had found nature untouched by man, in its primal form, and he already had culture. The white man did not have to meet the noble savage. He was both the noble savage *and* the civilized man. To the Leblonds, rewriting the history of the island was essential, because colonization had to be separated from colonialism to construct an abstract and ahistorical subject, the Creole, whose history was forged on the erasure of the social and economic conditions of its formation. The Creole of the Leblonds was a subject who could totalize all particularisms because, in the Creole, the fusion of particularisms was finally achieved. The product of this fusion carried the best of each element, but one element, the Celtic, could claim superiority. Because of this Celtic element, the Creole could epitomize the qualities of Catholicism, charity, hospitality, and, of course, whiteness.

The geography of the island presented, though, the racial division that was repressed in the narrative about the population. The island had inscribed the repressed on its landscapes. The Leblonds' garden was the reverse of Houat's. Alongside the "white Eden," there was a "Black Eden," or rather, a "*maroon* Eden."[192] Names on the island constructed a double circle: "at the top, a crown of names, strange and barbarous, at the bottom, a protective belt of names of Catholic saints to ward off the evils of color."[193] The Creole myth racialized the culture and history of the island. It presented Réunion as the cradle of Western culture, of Greek and Indian culture— both Aryan cultures to the Leblonds. Creole identity and culture were French identity and culture in the tropics. The Creole myth, which was characterized by self-glorification, pervaded not only Réunion's intellectual and literary life but also the island's ideological institutions. A schoolbook published in 1910 in France for the island's pupils defined the Creoles in these terms:

The Creoles of Réunion have gentle and peaceful mores. Affable, hospitable, generous, they bring to their relations a refinement which, along with an artistic sense, constitutes the precious inheritance passed on by their ancestors, these men without fortune of Louis XIV's and Louis XV's times, the *émigrés* of the Revolution escaping popular revolt, the persons condemned for political reasons by a monarchic and despotic government. During their times of leisure, some are poets or writers, others draw or paint; the greatest number are musicians. One may say that the Creole is a born musician. Everywhere they sing and the citizen composes in the streets the songs which animate any dance, the other favorite leisure activity of the Creole.[194]

Although its creators were republicans, the Creole myth's republic was a "colonial republic." Réunion embodied republican colonialism. Yet in the Leblonds' writings, there was a recurrent complaint against the French. Their plea had a plaintive tone, and their fantasy became all the more megalomaniac as the island be-

came more impoverished. The Leblonds wanted Réunion to become a province of France, because they wanted "colonialism to
become the greatest province of [French] regionalism."[195] They
articulated the duties and responsibilities of La Mère-Patrie to her
child but had difficulty articulating what the rights of the child
were. Hence their self-aggrandizement, their blown-up rhetoric
that masked a narcissistic failure. They saw the island as a maritime
fortress in the Indian Ocean,[196] as the "vanguard of the expansionist
and civilizing mission of France."[197] Standing for France against the
hostile forces coming from the ocean was their sacrifice to Mother
France. But they did not understand that if French colonialism was
using the metaphor of motherhood, it was not because it understood its relation with the colonies as one of benevolence, care,
and concern for the development and autonomy of the colonized
"child." Rather, this metaphor was there to fix the Réunionnais
under the gaze of a phallic mother. Or, in Frantz Fanon's words:

Colonialism therefore sought to be considered by the native not as a
gentle, loving mother who protects her child from a hostile environment,
but rather as a mother who unceasingly restrains her fundamentally perverse offspring from managing to commit suicide and from giving free
rein to its evil instincts. The colonial mother protects her child from itself,
from its ego, and from its physiology, its biology, and its own unhappi-
ness, which is its very essence.[198]

Bound by a symbolic link to a metropole that frustrated their
desire for autonomy, dependent economically on the same metropole, Réunionnais intellectuals such as the Leblonds were like children demanding attention from a mother who was indifferent to
them, who had not recognized them as her children, and who had
constantly shown that she preferred the children of the metropole.
Unwillingly weaned from a love that they expected to last, these
intellectuals produced texts revealing a subtext of aggression, hidden under claims of eternal love.

Workers' Rights and Emancipation

1936 marked a turning point for working-class organization in
Réunion.[199] In the 1930s, the Left in Réunion progressively unified,
and in August 1936, the Parti Réunionnais d'Action Démocratique

et Sociale was founded.[200] Its members claimed to support democracy and the republic. They asked for the extension of fundamental liberties, the creation of workers' associations to promote welfare and public hygiene, secular and public education. Léon de Lépervanche established the first Marxist circle on the island, in the working-class city of Le Port. Organizing the working class had at first been difficult. The high rate of illiteracy, the work conditions close to slavery, and the chronic epidemics that affected the workers explain why it was not before 1912 that workers as such entered the public space.[201] The first to organize were the workers in the sugarcane industry and the railroad. The two groups had been in contact with each other for years, since trains were used to carry the sugar from the factories to the island's harbor, Le Port. They developed a sense of shared identity and exchanged information about work conditions and struggles around the world. In 1936 the working class emerged as a new organized and militant force, with the slogan: "Réunion, French Department." Through strikes and demonstrations, the workers intervened publicly. The unions were predominantly male, yet women played a role in the public performances. During the general strike of January 1937, women led the demonstrations in Le Port.

During World War II, the working-class movement experienced a setback. The governor and the colonial administration supported the Vichy government. Leftist organizations were banned, and the associations of Freemasons were closed and their archives destroyed. Vergès remained in Réunion during the war and remained the director of the Health Service. As a mayor, he participated in demonstrations organized by the governor and took the oath requested from civil servants by the Vichy regime.[202] But Vergès refused to sign a letter supporting the Vichy regime, or to enroll his sons in the Pétain League, two gestures that were required of civil servants. He later explained that he had remained at his post during the Vichy period because he felt that he would be more able to accomplish something for an abandoned population by staying than by leaving. Vergès did not leave extended explanations about his attitude during the war. The British-enforced embargo on the island isolated Réunion from the outside world even more so than usual. The landlords supported the Vichy government, but their role in French politics remained marginal. To the population, the war was a period of hardships, shortages, increased poverty, and isolation. The Free French Forces liberated the colony on November 28, 1942. Paul and Jacques Vergès joined the Free French Army soon after and served in Europe.

After the war, Raymond Vergès participated in the foundation of the Comité Républicain d'Action Démocratique et Sociale (CRADS, the Republican Committee for Democratic and Social Action), a united front of the Left and the Center-Left, workers and peasants, civil servants and entrepreneurs. In the 1945 elections, the candidates of CRADS won control of the majority in city councils and in the General Council and sent two representatives to the National Assembly: Raymond Vergès and Léon de Lépervanche.

The principles of the French colonial policy were the same in 1944 as they had been in the 1920s: economic and political superiority of France over her overseas territories, with some space allocated for the emergence of a class of *évolués,* the natives who had adopted French culture. Within this context, the Old Colonies' anticolonialists asked for equality. Was French democracy ready and willing to live by its words? The eulogist of *négritude,* the Martinican Aimé Césaire, presented in 1945, in the name of all the representatives of the Old Colonies, the demand for political and social assimilation.[203] Césaire had been a partisan of assimilation as early as the 1920s.[204]

The anticolonialist leaders of Réunion carried to the French Parliament the demands of the colonized and the workers. Equality was the mobilizing concept. By taking the workers' demands to the Parliament, Vergès and Lépervanche gave to this body the authority and status of a people's tribunal, before which they could lament the wrongs suffered by the peoples of the Old Colonies. Within this forum, they spoke the language of rights, claiming to be the voice of the oppressed: the workers and peasants of Réunion.

At the assembly, Vergès declared that he was there to speak for those about whom "one never speaks."[205] His role was to bring the voices of the voiceless to the assembly of the French people, those exploited by capitalism and colonialism. The workers' first concern was the "amelioration of the living conditions of our comrades, the peasants, who are the majority of the oppressed." "Incorporation" into the "French family" was fundamental for the extension of the social laws that protected the workers and for the political rights until then reserved to the privileged. Assimilation would mean economic development and government of the island *with* the people. In a speech given in March 1946, Vergès recounted the genesis of the demand for integration.[206] If Réunion was geographically far from France, its population had nevertheless forged solid bonds with the metropole. The first inhabitants had been French sailors.[207] Vergès repeated the dominant fiction about slavery in Réunion: it was a "crime" but softened by the "good treatment" accorded to slaves by the island's slave owners.[208] The population of the island, the result of "racial fusion, had shown their loyalty to France, and their patriotism deserved the reward of the status as a department."[209]

According departmental status to the Old Colonies would be a symbolic act that would erase the "abhorred terms of colony and colonialism."[210] Aimé Césaire talked of assimilation as the "normal outcome of a historical process and the logical conclusion of a doctrine."[211] Vergès described the Old Colonies' demand as an offer of the colonized to strengthen France in a moment of need. "France needs the union and the efforts of all her children. We say to you: 'Everything we are, everything we have is yours. Welcome us! We have been waiting for you for three hundred years!' "[212] The language was that of incorporation. The addressee was the French Assembly, and behind this assembly, the people of France. Anticolonialists joined the assembly of brothers to fulfill the promise of the French Revolution, the promise of fraternity and equality. To justify their demand, the anticolonialist leaders erased their differences and proclaimed their membership in the French community. But at the very moment that they put forward their demand, "We are French too," they indicated their difference: for if it had not been for that difference, how could inequality be explained? They adopted the Enlightenment vision of a generic individual. They appealed to reason and objectivity. The inhabitants of the Old Colonies, they argued, had proven that they shared with the Europeans a common humanness. Slavery had been an insult to the notion of common humanness. Colonialism was a denial of full humanness. Would the French people, who had liberated themselves from racist Nazism, deny full humanness to other peoples? 1946 anticolonialist leaders said: "We, the populations of the Old Colonies, have to be included with the French community because we have proved that we belong to this community." Yet was it possible to formulate such a demand within the language of republican rights when this language had been used to exclude certain groups—women, colonized, workers? The people of Réunion were colonized subjects of the French state; they had been denied the same social and political rights as French citizens. The majority of the population had been enslaved. Jean-François Lyotard has expressed the dilemma faced by a plaintiff trying to express a grievance in an idiom that rejects the possibility of the complaint.[213]

"There are no more victims." No, to say that the Jews are no longer victims is one thing, but to say that there are no more victims at all is another. A universal cannot be concluded from a particular. . . . For example, the referent labor-power is the object of a concept, but to speak like Kant, it does not give rise to an intuition nor consequently to controversy and to a verdict before the tribunal of knowledge. Its concept is an Idea. Here is another example: a Martinican is a French citizen; he or she can bring a complaint against whatever impinges upon his or her rights as a French citizen. But the wrong he or she deems to suffer from the fact of being a French citizen is not a matter of litigation under French law. It might be under private or public international law, but for that to be the case it would be necessary that the Martinican were no longer a French citizen. But he or she is. Consequently, the assertion according to which he or she suffers a wrong on account of his or her citizenship is not verifiable by explicit or effective procedures. These are examples presented in the phrase universes of Ideas (in the Kantian sense): the Idea of nation, the Idea of the creation of value.[214]

The anticolonialists of the Old Colonies brought to the assembly of representatives, which they saw as the legitimate tribunal of the French people, their complaints as French citizens. But they lacked an idiom in which they could fully testify to the wrong they had suffered. The vocabulary of assimilation did not offer words to denounce France as the perpetuator of the offenses suffered by the populations of the Old Colonies. Slavery and the abuses of colonialism had to be the deeds of groups that were not members of the French republican family so that the incorporation of the descendants of slaves and colonized into the French family appeared a subversive gesture. If republican France was found guilty of slavery and colonialism, how could a demand for assimilation by its victims be justified? Hence slavery was nowhere mentioned in the speeches of Césaire and Vergès. They marginalized their past as slaves and colonized by situating themselves first as workers and brothers of the French workers.

I would like to make the following hypothesis: Does the exclusion from the community of equals of a minority that does not have a precolonial past on its territory (Réunion's population was entirely the product of colonization) inevitably lead the minority to demand its integration into the community of equals? Because they were blacks, because they were slaves, because they were colonized, the members of the minority were rejected from the revolutionary community. The demand of equality and fraternity fundamentally represented an *integration* into the human and fraternal community. The moment of integration had to be inscribed symbolically and in the law. When those who were excluded appealed to the laws that the master abode by (the laws of the republic), they symbolically summoned the master to a court in which he, who violated the laws he had himself established would be judged by those who were under his subjection. But this hypothesis could not be applied to all societies with colonial slavery. British colonies, and of course Haiti, became independent territories.[215] One should therefore insist on the attractive strength of the republican ideal and the fascination with the French Revolution. The names *equality* and *fraternity* played a *material* role. Women and men were not only mobilized by economic and political interests but also by the suggestive power of the names of liberty, equality, fraternity. With these words, they dreamed of a just society, breaking the prison of the colonial vocabulary—inequality, bondage, humiliation. Whereas the whites rejected the republican vocabulary, the oppressed and the poor adopted it. The demand of equality proved to be a threat not only to the economic interests of the white bourgeoisie but also to their symbolic power.

Réunion anticolonialists' speeches constructed an image of social and political reality in which the proletarian played the principal role. The goal of their newspaper, *Témoignages,* was clearly expressed in the editorial of May 12, 1944: the newspaper would be the "echo of the Réunion proletariat's voice" and would denounce the "policy of social regression which has until now served the interests and privileges of the landowners, multinationals, and factory owners." A reading of the articles in *Témoignages* should be articulated around the specific contexts of the end of World War II, the defeat of Nazism and its racial ideology, the fascination with the Soviet Union, and the role in Réunion of a "primitive" communism that aspired to defend those without defense (*défendre les sans défense* was the motto of *Témoignages*). The division between "us" and "them" was social: "We are wage-earners, which means that we live off OUR WORK: THEY live off the WORK OF OTHERS" (22 December 1944, emphasis in original). The duty of the "members of the city" was to engage in public life to serve the "republican IDEAL " (27 July 1945). The ideal city was a fraternal and republican city in which the work of the proletarians was recognized, in which abuses and injustice were condemned; it was not, however, the Soviet city, because it was still part of the French republic. In 1946 the candidate Vergès appealed to the "Republicans, Workers, Honest people, French men and women of Réunion. For the defense of their rights, For Liberty, Equality of the citizens, for the Fraternity of all the French people without distinction of race. Long Live Réunion French Department, Long Live France, Long Live the Republic." The end of the colonial status signified a greater integration, the realization of republican principles.[216] Equality would erase class and race differences. "Colonialism" became associated with economic exploitation, not cultural, racialized, sexual exploitation. "Colonialist" became the name of the small group of landowners who controlled the island's economy. France appeared in the plaintiff's testimony not as one of the villains in the violent drama of colonialism but as the authority to which the testimony was addressed.

Anticolonialists embraced the politics of representation, disciplining thereby the radical effect of the appearance of the colonized qua colonized on the public scene. What would a radical intrusion have been? The figure that embodied their claim was the figure of the proletariat. What they asked for the proletariat was not the transformation of the relations of production. Rather, they asked the state to protect the workers against capitalists. In doing so, they subscribed to the reformism of the French Communist Party, to which they were affiliated in the Parliament, and gave the French state full legitimacy. But as Karl Marx wrote: "The constitutional state is that form of the state in which the state-interest, i.e. the real interest of the people, is present only *formally*. . . . The *Estates* are the *lie, legally sanctioned* in constitutional states, that the *state* is the *interest of the people* or that the *people* is the *interest of the state*."[217] Oudin-Bastide has argued that the Left in the Old Colonies was prisoner of the dilemma created by France, between the regime of exception and the regime of assimilation.[218] Within this framework, the choice, she said, appeared logical, for only assimilation would offer the expansion of the rights of the colonized. Assimilation was experienced as a conquest, not as another form of subjugation. The collapse between the interest of the people of Réunion and the interest of the French state, believed to represent the workers, proved to have ideologically charged consequences for the people of Réunion. Again the sons of Réunion claimed their attachment to France. And again they expressed this attachment by denying wrongs committed by the French state.

Yet even their demand for integration proved to be too radical. As early as 1948, the anticolonialist leaders expressed their discontent in the French Parliament. In Réunion, landowners and the white bourgeoisie had created an organization opposed to departmental status and lobbied to prevent the full application of social laws in the island. In 1948 they founded the Association des Droits et des Intérêts de La Réunion (ADIR) to organize the attack on the 1946 law. Its president was Gabriel Macé, who had been a supporter of the Vichy regime. Assimilation was viewed as part of a larger communist conspiracy whose purpose was "selling" Réunion to Russia.[219] "Assimilation is a criminal heresy that will lead us to spiritual collapse and ruin," leaders of ADIR declared.[220] Vergès protested. Nothing has changed, he declared at the National Assembly on July 9, 1948. Political repression was the answer given to the workers. "Our populations," Vergès said, "think that you are mocking them. . . . When we speak of the sabotage of assimilation, you protest vehemently. But is there any other word for what is happening?"[221] And the leader of the Réunion Left continued to denounce the perpetuation of inequality between metropolitan and overseas French citizens.[222]

To the extent that they forced the state to articulate its argument about their exclusion, the republican anticolonialists revealed the limits of the democratic discourse and disrupted the illusion of its universalism. Vergès declared in 1949: "We are against any form of mechanical assimilation, against any illusory form of assimilation."[223] They forced the community of republican France to name itself as such. Republican France existed on the exclusion of certain populations that nonetheless were forced to remain within the French state. What had been the hidden clause that had designated the community as such appeared: purity was the name of that hidden clause, purity of blood.

Assimilation as the project of social fraternity, however false its theoretical roots, brought into the open the complicity of the French republican state with economic and political groups that wanted to maintain their control of the island's economies. To the conservatives, assimilation would only bring trouble. As Gustave Le Bon had said in 1889, European-style education in the colonies was dangerous because it "only showed the natives the distance we put between them and ourselves."[224] Now the conservatives realized that assimilation could serve their interests. They could promote a "conservative assimilation."

I have suggested that 1946, despite all its limitations, was an attempt to break away from the mother-and-children framework of colonialism, and for the anticolonialist leaders, an attempt to become the fathers of a Réunion free of colonial infantile relations. To the anticolonialists, France was the France of 1789, of the Declaration of the Rights of Man and the Citizen, of the Popular Front, not the France of colonialism. They demanded, in Fanon's words, the "right to multiply the emancipated and the opportunity to organize a genuine class of emancipated citizens."[225] As Aimé Césaire said in 1945, assimilation was the way "to escape the social chaos that threatened [our islands]."

The Left in Réunion affirmed the specificity of a population born on the island but did not want to deny the place of the French among the African, Madagascan, and Asian parents of the Réunionnais. It confronted the French republic: either we are citizens and we must be granted political emancipation, or the French republic must renounce its motto of equality. Yet if they affirmed, as Vergès declared at the French Parliament, the existence of a "Réunionnais race" that is the "result of the intimate fusion" of the groups that have constituted the population of Réunion, they believed that parity with France would entail the recognition of their difference. Vergès acknowledged métissage, creolization, but his political goal was solidarity with the workers of France. With Lépervanche, he saw Réunion society divided into two worlds: the poor and the rich. And to them, the poor had a moral claim. The suffering of the poor was proof that the existing social system was intolerable. In that, they were similar to the 1848 French revolutionaries. However, if their goal was social justice, it was not fulfilled. The status of department, once achieved, still maintained the island's cultural and economic dependency on France. France did not confront its colonialism and racism.

In 1947 Raymond Vergès launched the Fédération Communiste de l'Océan Indien. He supported the Madagascan representatives at the French Parliament who were accused in May 1947 of conspiracy against the state, and he denounced the colonial war in Indochina. Until 1953, the end of his mandate as a representative of Réunion, Vergès protested against the nonapplication of the law of March 19, 1946. To him, the Creole was a worker, a figure emblematic of the oppressed; and for the workers of Réunion, assimilation meant an alliance with the workers of France, who "are themselves exploited by capitalists."[226] He did not speak of a Réunion *nation,* although he spoke of a "Creole people." But class remained the determining factor. "With the Creole people, with the people of France, we will pursue here and everywhere, our struggle against oppression and for freedom," he declared in 1951. Raymond Vergès died in July 1957. He left a widow, Joséphine Savigny, whom he had married in 1945.

A postcolonial reading of assimilation gives back to the 1946 generation its political agency while underscoring the limits of its "imagined community."[227] Such a reading asks why anticolonialists seized the idiom of assimilation that had been the founding myth of colonial policy. It attempts to read their demand beyond the wish of alienated brothers crying for admission into the republican family. The appeal to those modern universals that appear to transcend race—equality, fraternity—was the means through which the 1946 anticolonialist Creoles invented forms of political relations that contained a dimension of universality beyond capital and race. Nation was not yet one of these universals.

One limit of the demand of assimilation was that transcending a racialized process of identification did not get rid of the race question. It reproduced the repression of conflicts born out of slavery. By insisting on the identity "workers," the anticolonialists did not "meditate on the history of economic and sexual enslavement" that produced the category of the Creole.[228] To be sure, 1946 anticolonialists remained faithful to republican fraternal universalism. Yet what Kwame Anthony Appiah has said about Pan-Africanism could be said also about 1946 Réunion. Each was "the project of a continental fraternity and sorority, not the project of a racialized

Negro nationalism [and each could] be a progressive force."[229] 1946 was a project of workers' solidarity against capital. It was a promise informed by the October Revolution,[230] Republican Spain, the Popular Front, and the role of the Soviet Union in defeating the Nazis. It imagined a community under the auspices of liberty, equality, fraternity, and justice. It called for an anticolonialist and antifascist union.[231]

The promise of social equality within assimilation was full of contradictions and limits: "On the one hand, a trust in the notion of progress, on the other hand the determination of a revolutionary subject (the proletariat) and of its meta-subject (the party)."[232] The 1950s brought more disenchantment and discontent among the anticolonialists of the Old Colonies. The economic interests of the landowners were protected. Creole language and culture were repressed. Political repression increased. The demand for assimilation proved to be unrealizable, not because it was inherently illogical, but because colonialism could not be defeated through assimilation. As Albert Memmi said: "Under the contemporary conditions of colonization, assimilation and colonization are contradictory."[233] Its failure was a demonstration that the French state had chosen to protect the interests of the capitalists. In 1946 the image of France as La Mère-Patrie suffered. But 1946 had also put a burden on the colonized, the burden of the moral redemption of the metropole.[234] Assimilation was justified because it was a *moral* act against unjustified poverty.

4

"Oté Debré, rouver la port lenfer,

Diab kominis i sa rentré":

Cold War Demonology in the Postcolony

❧

On May 17 and 18, 1959, in the working-class city of Le Port, 150 delegates of the Fédération de La Réunion du Parti Communiste Français met and discussed organizing a Réunion communist party, independent of the French Communist Party. On the walls, banners proclaimed, "Long live the struggle of the working-class! Long live the struggle of the people of Réunion for its liberation from the colonial yoke!" "We will build a strong Communist Party, the guide and organizing force of our struggles for emancipation!"[1] The worldwide movement for decolonization and the anti-imperialist struggle justified the creation of a separate communist party, Paul Vergès, Raymond Vergès's son, declared. Vergès, who presented the argument for a local communist party, celebrated the struggle of the Algerian people for their independence: "The only solution is national independence and negotiations with the Algerian people's legitimate representatives." He greeted the spirit of Bandung,[2] the anti-imperialist struggle in Latin America and Africa, the antiapartheid struggle in South Africa, the emergence of China as a new communist power, and the organization of the Third World against European capitalism and imperialism. The

connection that Vergès built with Third World anti-imperialism
situated Réunion's political identity squarely within socialist internationalism. The 1946 anticolonialists had defended *métissage*
and the principles of republican France. Now Réunion's communists declared solidarity with the Third World's anti-imperialism
and working-class struggle. However, neither French republicanism nor socialist internationalism could help define a Réunionnais
identity. Vergès devoted much of his speech to the island's unique
history. Despite French claims to the contrary, there existed, he
affirmed, a Creole language and a Creole culture, both at the core
of Réunionnais identity.[3] To this end, the communists demanded a
reform of the education system so that it would include instruction
about the island's history and culture. The new party claimed that
it would fight for "democratic and popular autonomy." More than
any other demand of the 1959 communists, the demand for *political autonomy* mobilized the anticolonialist forces in Réunion. The
term became popular and was written on banners and walls. The
idea captured the imagination of an important part of the population. Political autonomy was explained thus:

The Réunionnais must first obtain the right to manage democratically
their affairs in order to free themselves from the colonial yoke.

Autonomy, the right to decide about local affairs, will be exercised
through: 1—a local assembly with legislative power over local affairs, 2—an
executive power elected by the assembly and responsible to the assembly.

The demand for autonomy cannot be confused with the demand for
independence, which would suit neither the actual aspirations of our
people, nor the historical conditions in which we live.

The demand for autonomy is compatible with the possibilities laid out
in article 72 of the French Constitution.[4]

The history of the island justified an anti-imperialist stance. The
evocation of the maroons—Anchaing, Cimendef, Mafat, Cilaos,
Dimitile, Diampare—stressed the historical resistance of the people of Réunion.

In the early days of colonization, two contradictions emerged: one was
between the slaves and the masters; the other, between the masters and the
tyrannical Company of the Indies. Poor whites and slaves, both victims of
a dual exploitation, found a common ground of struggle.

At the end of the Second Empire, the "bloody day" of December 2,

1868, at Saint-Denis, when people demonstrated for their rights, showed the profound aspiration of our people for universal suffrage and for the creation of a democratically elected local assembly.[5] Under the Third Republic, the ownership of land and of sugar mills was systematically concentrated in the hands of a minority. This operation accelerated in the following decades, and resulted in the division of land and industrial capital between local capitalists and French capitalist societies. The latter extended their control over Réunion's economy. Our situation fits the Marxist-Leninist definition of a colony in the era of imperialism: a country whose economy is subordinated to the needs of metropolitan monopolies.

The island's economy was still governed by the rules of the "colonial pact."[6] Two worlds coexisted on the island: one living in luxury, and one in misery, despair, and humiliation. Demanding autonomy was a political project, but with psychological consequences. Réunion communists aspired to break the relation of dependence between the *metropole* and its colony, a dependence that expressed itself politically and psychologically. Politically, autonomy implied a radical transformation of the colonial bond. It acknowledged the historical ties between Réunion and France but insisted on the need to transform those ties so that the people of Réunion would acquire political responsibility. In its psychological consequences, political autonomy signified breaking away from a relation defined in terms of the couple Mère-Patrie/colony. The communist program defined a political relation, without recourse to family metaphors, in which two communities would discuss their political and economic exchanges. The 1959 political movement tried to break away from the form of republicanism that had previously characterized anticolonialist forces.

The communists explained their choice of political autonomy over political independence with a historical and social argument. They said that there was a Réunionnais *people* that had a common language, culture, and history, but which did not constitute a *nation*. There was a Réunionnais cultural and linguistic identity forged through a common history, but not a national identity. The communists thought that the majority of the Réunionnais were not ready to affirm their existence as a nation against France. Among the communists themselves, few thought of Réunion as a nation.

The tone of 1959 was different from that of 1946. A critique about the nonapplication of the 1946 law had been made as early as 1947. In 1952, Raymond Vergès still insisted on the "urgency" of extending to the territories social laws that existed in the metropole.[7] It was, the representative said, up to the National Assembly to "decide whether it was for or against equal rights, for, or against, racial discrimination."[8] In 1945, Léon de Lépervanche and Raymond Vergès joined the communist group in the French Parliament.[9] In the late 1940s, the French Communist Party sent instructors to Réunion to teach Marxism to the Réunionnais. To the French communists, the relation was of the master to the pupil. Nationalism was suspect because it threatened the alliance of the working class worldwide. 1946 had been a social struggle. 1959 sought to announce a political struggle, Vergès said. "In Réunion, class consciousness preceded anti-colonial consciousness," he later explained.[10] The 1946 law, the communist argued, "signified a step forward in the conquest of social rights," but an "analysis of the last thirteen years has proved that assimilation had not brought any fundamental change in our situation. On the contrary, assimilation has been used to worsen the living conditions of our population."[11] The leaders of 1946 had adopted the rhetoric of "the French philosophy of Rights. The Popular Front and its program of social progress had found a deep echo among them. It was, one can say, a pre-Marxist period in Réunion."[12] Now the idiom was Marxist-Leninist and Third Worldist. There were no longer two entities, republican France and local colonialists. France was now a colonial power, squarely in the camp of local capitalists and world imperialists. The allies of Réunion's population were the French workers and the oppressed peoples of the Third World. Réunion's anticolonialist struggle was now associated with communist ideology and goals, and the association positioned the island's communism in the larger context of the Cold War. Réunion's political life became shaped by the terms of the conflict between the "free world" and "totalitarianism." Communism, despite its own blown-up rhetoric and the ideological poverty of the discourse propagated by the Soviet Union, brought to anticolonialist movements in the Third World a vocabulary of emancipation different from republicanism. It connected local organizations to a larger movement, opening their world, ending their sense of isolation.[13] It said that there were people elsewhere fighting for the same goals.

Léon de Lépervanche, who, with Raymond Vergès, had fought

for assimilation, opposed the condemnation of 1946. He thought that assimilation should be given more chance. Lépervanche feared that autonomy would lead to the suppression of state funds at a time when the island was still suffering from severe poverty and a lack of economic development. The island, he said, had no material resources. French state funds were still needed. The solution, Lépervanche concluded, was to continue to fight for the full application of the 1946 law. He announced that he would vote against the creation of an independent communist party and against its theses. On Monday, March 18, 1959, the majority of the delegates adopted the program presented by Paul Vergès and voted for the creation of the Parti Communiste de la Réunion.[14] Vergès, at the age of thirty-four, was elected general secretary of the new party.

The demand for autonomy triggered a violent response from the conservatives. There were historical and ideological reasons for their response. Although they had at first been violently opposed to the 1946 law, they now captured the discourse of assimilation to defend an emotional, cultural, and economic attachment to France. Conservatives came to see assimilation as a rampart to protect their interests. Réunion's bourgeoisie, which had invested its capital not in local industry but in trade, understood that it could benefit from the French policy of integration. They could draw substantial benefits from becoming middlemen. Conservatives preferred social and economic power to political power. France, they soon noticed, had no intention of fulfilling the 1946 promise. Their interests were in fact protected, and the Left was marginalized by the socialist metropolitan governments. Assimilation could be on their side, whereas autonomy threatened their hold on society. In the hands of the conservatives, the 1946 law was emptied of its republican dimension and reduced to a version of colonial dependence. The goal of 1946, which had been equality, became a justification for inequality. Réunion needed France and, in its needy state, was not in a position to demand equal treatment. The assimilation sought in 1946 was a "republican assimilation." The kind of assimilation defended by the conservatives was a "conservative assimilation," the organization of dependence and cultural assimilation. The defense of conservative assimilation was played on a larger scene. The French colonial empire was crumbling, and communism was emerging as the enemy of democracy and freedom. Cold War rhetoric provided Réunion's conservatives with the idiom of anticommunism. Communism infiltrated the world, hiding behind the discourse of national liberation and pretending to have a concern for the wretched of the world. Communists were a difficult enemy because their soldiers were everywhere, indistinguishable from one's next-door neighbors. The demand for autonomy also brought to the forefront of Réunion's politics an anxiety that had informed the island's history, the anxiety of being separated from the metropole. Conservatives exploited the population's fear of being abandoned on a little island. France provided and guaranteed a connection to the "free world."

A Frenchman, Michel Debré, led the countersubversive campaign. He arrived on the island in 1963 as a conservative candidate in the parliamentary elections and remained a legislative representative of the island for twenty-five years. A prime minister in the first government of the Fifth Republic, Debré was a zealous defender of French imperial grandeur, a staunch anticommunist, and an opponent of women's rights. He was famous for his uncompromising stand against the Algerian nationalists. During a 1959 trip in Algeria, Debré declared: "The authority of France in Algeria is required by history, nature, and morality."[15] To the French prime minister, the end of Algeria's dependency would signify a return to "wretchedness, barbarism, and bloody destruction." Debré's remarks foreshadowed the view that he would later defend in Réunion: either dependence on France or chaos.[16] Yet in 1959 de Gaulle proclaimed the right of the Algerians to self-determination. The war lasted four more years. Debré resigned in April 1962 when a majority of voters, in France and Algeria, approved the referendum on the Evian negotiations. Debré's program, described by Frantz Fanon as a program "to wage war, to deny the existence of the Algerian nation, to extend the subjugation of our country," was defeated.[17]

Going to Réunion and leading the campaign against autonomy gave Debré the opportunity to fight the war he had lost in Algeria. It also gave him an explanation for, and an alternative to, a blocked political career: he had lost his official functions in France, as minister, general councilman, and mayor. Debré went to Réunion because he wanted to "defend faraway France."[18] "I am the candidate of the Nation, the candidate of France," he wrote in 1963. To go to Réunion was a crusade because Réunion was the "France of the Indian Ocean," the "parcel of land that was the most French among all the possessions of France."[19] With Debré, the conservative forces in Réunion acquired a determined, active, and committed ally in their struggle against anticolonialist forces. Debré gave to political demonology in Réunion its grammar, its vocabulary, its nationalistic approach, and its virulent, paranoid, patriarchalist, racist tone. Debré overestimated the role of France in the world and in Réunion. The French colonial empire had been defeated in Indochina, Africa, and Algeria, but there were places where it could still be victorious, territories throughout the world that could still testify in favor of France's grandeur. Réunion Island would be one of these territories. Debré would be the last general of imperial France.

Conservatives answered the demand for autonomy with a violence—political repression, ban of the communist newspaper, electoral fraud, intimidation—that pointed to an anxiety deeper than they could themselves acknowledge. Indeed, the Communist Party, even though it became one of the best-organized and most influential political movements on the island, was limited by an equally strong traditionalist and legitimist movement. Its audience was important, but never large enough to even suggest the possibility of hegemonic control.[20] Conservatives nonetheless named the communists as the enemy with a vigor suggesting more than ideological difference. At the heart of their anticommunism lay anxieties about their own autonomy and identity. Communists stressed the equality of women and men, the brotherhood of the oppressed, the merit of self-government. Assimilationists lacked the strength to sustain this autonomy. Fears about the subversion of gender identities, about the irruption of the poor, the dispossessed in their world, and about autonomous behavior informed the conservatives' apprehensions. Assimilation became a ground in which to root an identity that asserted its full dependence on France, an identity predicated on obedience to an idealized Mère-Patrie. Autonomy was linked, in their minds, to rejection and hatred, rather than to the thoughtful distance needed between individuals and groups.

Between 1963 and the mid-1970s, a predominantly rural and poor society was modernized, and a "post-industrial society without industry or economic development was created."[21] Supermarkets, cars, and television arrived on the island together with the Cold War, modernization together with political demonology.

Conservatives controlled means of dissemination previously un-
available, such as radio, television, and the education system. They
reinforced the island's economic and political dependence in ways
that are still framing the island's society. Their Cold War rhetoric,
filled with predictions of panic, chaos, and loss of boundaries,
found a resonant echo among the population. Conservatives uni-
formly employed a language of familial dependence to justify their
rhetoric of assimilation. Historians and political scientists have
usually been deaf to this language and its metaphors. But the
conservatives' words should be taken seriously. Gender and racial
tropes carried the conservative message of demonization. The narrative and the rituals that sustained it throughout the last thirty
years, as conservative propaganda transformed anticommunism
into a principle of self-definition, would affect the political and
cultural debate for years to come.

Radio became a central medium of propaganda, and the French
state made ample use of its monopoly on radio programs. Communist events were never announced. Nonconservatives were never
invited to comment on local news. *Autonomy* was a forbidden
term; newspapers were seized for using it. It disappeared from the
French vocabulary. Political demonology used the techniques of
mass demagogy to collapse Réunion's political identity into the
conservative agenda. Being a true Réunionnais—that is, a true
French person—meant being anticommunist. Programs and debates were subsumed under two names that together occupied the
entire semantic field: *nationals* (those supporting the conservatives)
and *separatists* (those supporting the communists). The political
choice became simply "YES or NO to *France.*"[22] France became
the ideal object of love, and the Réunionnais had to love France as
their ideal. In Debré's words: "To the women and men of Réunion,
France is a distant and tutelary goddess, presently governed by de
Gaulle, a legendary therefore immortal man!"[23] The island lost its
history and memory. It was now merely a French province, populated by French men and women.

Masculinity and femininity were reconfigured. The French administration enlisted women to stop the autonomist forces. It
would protect them against native men. Réunion's women, who
were the main recipients of welfare, were asked to combat autonomy, which would, they were told, take away welfare benefits.
Women were set up as the allies of the antiautonomist forces.

Women needed the French state and its representatives, they were told, to protect them against Creole men, who would bring misery to Réunion if they won autonomy. "Vote for Réunion French Department for Peace, for your Children, for the peace of your homes!" a conservative electoral poster claimed in 1963. The 1946 generation had demanded *equality* with the social allowances that French workers received. The conservatives transformed this demand into *welfare* dependence.

Politics became an arena of violent battles. The delusion of a worldwide communist conspiracy and the fantasy of Réunion as the "fortress of France, democracy, Catholicism, and the free world in the Indian Ocean," with the Réunionnais its heroic soldiers, combined to preclude fruitful conflict, compromise, and reasoned debate. The conservatives psychologized politics, transforming a political demand into a family drama, using a psychological vocabulary to mobilize images of dependence. They split the world of Réunion between bad and good objects. Internal persecutory elements were projected onto the communists. Yet France's image was also split. France was an object of both love and hate. To have France both as a protective power and as a scapegoat for what went wrong offered psychological rewards to the Réunionnais but kept them from becoming responsible political adults. Persecution and conflictual feelings were ascribed to external objects: either the communists or, to a lesser extent, the bad mother, the metropole. The monsters created by the conservatives' discourse—the communist, the rebellious worker—and the fears—of autonomy, of independence—became familiar figures and fears in Réunion political discourse.

Political Autonomy

Autonomy, Hanna Fenichel Pitkin has written, "concerns borderlines, found or made; it concerns the question of how and to what extent I (or we) have become or can become a separate self (or community)."[24] Pitkin reminds us that the word *autonomy* "derives from the Greek *auto,* meaning 'self' or 'own,' and *nomos,* meaning 'law, rule, binding custom, way of life.' "[25] Martin Oswald, in his study of the genesis and history of the term in Greek politics, argues that "*autonomia* came into being as part of an attempt to find sanctions against the arbitrary use of force by a major state against minor states moving in its orbit."[26]

To Réunion's communists, autonomy answered a historical contradiction, "to remain French citizens *and* to be ourselves."[27] They sought to reconcile the apparently antagonistic wish of "responsibility—through self-government—and participation in the national community—through French citizenship."[28] The time had come to redefine boundaries. The communists demonstrated the inadequacy of the status of department to resolve the island's problems. They showed the inevitable failure of a status that entailed policies made in France, "13,000 km away, applied by metropolitan civil servants nominated by ministries in Paris, and in which local officials have been reduced to a consultative role." The decisions made in Paris could indeed lead to absurdity. There was the story about the sunless terrace of the sanitarium for tuberculosis, because the Parisian architect, forgetting that the island was in the Southern Hemisphere, had wrongly oriented the terrace.[29] There was the story of the low-income houses that had so few windows that they were acutely uncomfortable in the tropical summer, because architects had designed them with French suburbs in mind. So long as decisions were made in Paris, regardless of the island's needs and the population's aspirations, the island would not emerge from its dependency. The French state could lament the "pathology of dependency" of the Creoles, but why should the Creoles take responsibility for a situation over which they had no control? In Réunion's political debate, autonomy meant *interdependence*, not independence. Duties and responsibilities would have been shared between France and the island. The communist's autonomy was not national sovereignty but local control of the island's economy, culture, public education, housing, and health. Communist autonomy sought to reintegrate the island in its region, to increase the relations between the island and the countries of the southwest Indian Ocean.

In April 1975, the communists held an "Extraordinary Conference" in which they observed: "We are no longer a colony of production but only a market for colonialist societies. French colonialism is no longer interested in our exports.[30] Its major goal is now to extract the greatest financial benefits from a market which it artificially created."[31] They explained that the "foundations of the actual crisis and of the system's failure were built between 1946 and 1963."[32] Their document, "An Immediate Plan for Survival," looked at economic, social, and cultural sectors. It claimed that there "was no freedom in a country in which 60,000 people are unemployed, 88,000 or 40 percent of the adults illiterate, and the majority of working people does not receive the minimum wage."[33] It accused the public education system of selecting students according to social status.[34] The only economic sector that had experienced growth was the tertiary sector—service industries and the civil service; consequently, a significant portion of state funds went to pay salaries in the public sector.[35] The hypertrophy of the tertiary sector led to a social disequilibrium, because a nonproductive sector was absorbing most of the state funds that could have been directed toward local economic development. In 1981 the communists reiterated their analysis: thirty-five years after the 1946 law, the island was still a colony. Culturally, the status of department had denied the "existence of a Réunionnais people, with its own identity, traditions, language, and history."[36] Economically, the "big companies are in the hands of European capitalists. Local banks are subsidiaries of metropolitan banks. The sugarcane industry is financially dominated by a French company."

Communists challenged the conservatives' claims that Réunion's population had derived important benefits from its status. The conservatives' claim that Réunion's peasants were guaranteed preferred prices for their products overstated the reality.[37] Conservatives claimed that France was buying Réunion sugar at a preferential price. Yet the price of sugar, the principal product of Réunion, did not obey the laws of the free market: the prices of 91.1 percent of the world production were decided by the regulations of preferential markets.[38] Réunionnais did not draw advantages from trading chiefly with the metropole: France imposed its prices and inflated costs for its manufactured goods.[39] Academic studies and government reports supported this analysis. John Ostheimer remarked in 1975 that "one impact of the colonial economy is that France's inflation automatically becomes Réunion's—the more so as one must add in the inflationary effects on costs that intervene between production in France and consumption in Réunion."[40] The president of Réunion's Economical and Social Committee, a conservative politician, was compelled to declare in 1977 that the "Overseas Departments have remained minor departments with a colonial type administrative structure." To Marc Oraison, a univer-

sity professor, the "problem of the island is one of dependency, because the island's economy has remained on the periphery, geared
to the satisfaction of the European core."[41] Philippe de Baleine, a
conservative journalist, denounced in 1979 the "scandalous fact"
that French taxes served to finance an "aristocratic class of state
employees," living in luxury unlike their counterparts in France.[42]
The sociologist Jean Benoist, in a 1983 study, argued that the economic organization specific to the plantation still existed in Réunion.[43] Benoist showed that Réunion's society was fundamentally
bipolar, with socioeconomic and ethnic bipolarities coinciding, the
rich white Creoles pitted against the poor *métis* Creoles. He observed that though the new status had deeply transformed the
island by bringing the structures of a modernized society, the transformation was full of antagonistic contradictions. The gap between
the rich and the poor had increased. Although Réunion had all the
appearances of a postindustrial society, there was no local industry.[44] Most goods and supplies came from the metropole.[45] France
remained the main supplier and client of the department's agricultural product, sugar.[46] The world was organized around two poles:
the island and France. News on the television was partly local and
partly about France. Even the weather in the metropole was reported daily.[47] The economic policies of conservative assimilation
produced a large group that became dependent on state welfare,
and a petite bourgeoisie of state employees whose job security also
depended on the state. The state encouraged young, unskilled
Réunionnais to emigrate to France, creating a specific institution to
carry out the policy.[48] The disparity between classes increased.[49]

To be sure, the island was modernized during the late 1960s.
Schools, roads, hospitals, and housing projects were built.[50] Free
medical care significantly ameliorated the general health of a population suffering from endemic and parasitic diseases.[51] Yet when it
came to drawing conclusions about modernization, reviews were
mixed. Conservatives pointed to the undeniable progress, contrast-
ing it to the situation in neighboring countries. But according to a
1984 official report, "three families out of five in Réunion had poor
lodgings."[52] In 1989 the majority of the population was still suffering from parasitism.[53] Despite undeniable progress in health
infrastructure, Réunion's population was still suffering from "serious vitamin deficiency, generally poor health, and serious alcoholism."[54] Nor did the important effort made in public education

yield the expected results. One success was a reduction of the rate of illiteracy. In other areas of education, however, the failures appeared greater than the successes. Few students received the high school diploma that gives access to college.[55] The denial of the Creole language in schools explained the high rate of students' failure.[56] Sonia Chane-Kune's conclusion, based on thorough research about the island's conditions since the 1960s, is shared by most observers: "The status of department brought significant cultural, social, and political transformations to Réunion's society. Yet, the results are mixed, and economically, it has not been a success."[57]

Conservative assimilation signified "putting One and the Other under the sign of the Same."[58] It meant mastering the difference between the Réunionnais and the French not through physical extermination but rather through a "symbolic extermination, a mastering of the difference, a forced assimilation, perceived as the final Truth."[59] The identity that conservative assimilation proposed was the dissolution of Creole identity into French identity. But it was not "French" as the product of history, as the product of a multiplicity, a diversity of class, languages, cultures. The "French" identity advanced by Réunion's conservatives was their own construction of a pure Frenchness identified with the idea of La Mère-Patrie. It was, to a certain extent, the heir of the Leblonds' Creoleness, a Creoleness that was not the product of métissage but the pure essence of France, kept unpolluted, untainted, on an Indian Ocean island. The other, the Creole who was the descendant of slaves, of indentured workers and European colonists, represented a "maximal difference" from Frenchness, which had to be erased so that a Frenchwoman or Frenchman could emerge. Conservative rhetoric rested on the denial of slavery and colonialism, because they disturbed the conservative vision of harmony. The fiction that the unity of the population was due to its identification with Frenchness and opposition to autonomy rested on the denial of social division and of the cultural formation of Creoleness. The colonial metropole was the sole guarantor of harmony. Conservatives argued that "the very fact that Réunion was poly-ethnic made France's presence necessary."[60]

The theory and language that conservatives employed cemented the historical ties between France and Réunion with intimate symbolic meaning. France had, throughout three centuries, constituted the main pole of reference for the island's population. The Creole educated elite had explored the meaning of the bonds between the colony and its metropole. It had tried to specify the content of the ties between France and its island, with Houat and his utopia of a *métisse* republic, the Leblonds and their dream of a creolized France as the purest France, the 1946 anticolonialist leaders and their aspiration for equality.[61] What the communists of 1959 aspired to do was to reduce the emotional aspect that had suffused the discourse about the relationship between France and Réunion, to transform the sentimental narrative of a colonial family romance into a political relation. White Creoles had constructed Réunion as the dutiful, good daughter of France.[62] This fiction brought a certain satisfaction, the illusion of being loved. Now the Communist Party questioned this fiction and declared that it was time to reconsider the ties that bound the Réunionnais to their metropole.

The Radicalization of Anticolonialists

The young leader of the island's communists, Paul Vergès, had gone to Europe in 1944 to join the Allied forces, and he returned to Réunion in May 1946. On May 15, 1946, he was arrested, together with another communist, Roger Bourdageau, and charged with the murder of a conservative, Alexis de Villeneuve. Anticolonialist groups campaigned for the transfer of the trial to France because they distrusted the independence of Réunion's courts. The trial of the two Réunionnais mobilized the anticolonialist forces in France; they saw it as an opportunity, in these years of renewed attack against all forms of subjugation, to denounce French colonialism.[63] French conservatives understood the challenge, and their newspapers, *Le Figaro* and *L'Aurore,* claimed that the murder of Alexis de Villeneuve was the result of a communist conspiracy. The prisoners were transferred to the prison of Lyon in April 1947. Raymond Vergès went to France to lead the campaign of solidarity with the prisoners. He described Réunion as an island where the "colonialist system existed in its full horror."[64] The trial ended in August 1947 with the release of the indicted.

Paul Vergès then went to Paris, the center of anticolonialism in the French empire. After World War II, a new generation of anticolonialists, inspired by the Vietnamese national struggle, emerged, adopting a Third World approach to politics. It challenged the idea that Europe had a historical right to lead or subjugate peoples. The French government responded with repression to colonial protests. In Vietnam, it ordered the bombing of Haiphong in November 1946 and the attack on Da Nang in December. In Madagascar, the repression against the 1947 national rebellion left thousands of dead. That same year, strikes and demonstrations in Tunisia ended with dozens of Tunisians killed by the French forces. In 1949 nationalists in the Ivory Coast were arrested. When they realized that France would not yield, nationalist forces launched wars of national liberation. Anticolonialism had been reactivated by the defeat of Nazism, in which so many of the colonized had participated, and anticolonialists felt vindicated by the condemnation of racist doctrines.[65]

Paul joined his twin brother, Jacques, in a hotel that had been rented, in 1948, by the General Council of Réunion for the island's students. The two brothers were communists. Jacques Vergès, with a team of African, Vietnamese, and North African students, launched the newspaper *Étudiants Anticolonialistes*. On the front page was the picture of a dove, with the words: "For Peace and the immediate end of the war in Vietnam. For national independence and the liberation of the colonial peoples. For a democratic education."[66] In the first issue, Daniel Lallemand, a young Réunionnais who would later join the Parti Communiste Réunionnais (PCR), defined the goal and purposes of the Front Uni des Étudiants Anticolonialistes: to denounce French colonialist repression and "U.S. imperialism." The sixth issue took up the situation of Réunion. Max Rivière condemned the colonialism that gave sugar trusts full control over the island's economy. He called for fraternization between African and North Africans soldiers (sent to Réunion for repressive purposes) and their "Creole brothers."[67] Jacques Vergès insisted on a "Creole specific identity forged through three centuries of struggle."[68] He made a distinction between a "pro-slavery tradition," represented by the Leblonds, whose "name would bring shame to any Réunionnais student," and the "Creole tradition" shaped by the first colonists, the maroons, and the people. The latter tradition had given birth to a "Creole fraternity which unifies the different ethnic groups in a common struggle." Paul Vergès participated in the activities of the Front Uni des Étudiants and worked at the Section Coloniale of the French Communist Party, a special office that coordinated communist activities in the French colonies.[69] Paul Vergès remained in France until 1953. He married a Parisian woman, Laurence Deroin, who was also a communist activist.

On his return to Réunion in 1954, Paul Vergès joined the communist organization led by his father. In January 1956, the Fédération Communiste de La Réunion presented a list of three candidates to the National Assembly: Paul Vergès, Raymond Mondon, and a woman, Isnelle Amelin. The conservatives' list was led by Raphaël Babet and Marcel de Villeneuve (the brother of Alexis, killed in 1946). The communists' list received 53 percent of the vote, sending Vergès and Mondon to the National Assembly. The conservatives' list had one representative, Babet. For the first time in Réunion, a majority of small farmers had voted for the communists.

The colonial war in Algeria was two years old, and Réunion's anticolonialists expressed their solidarity with the Algerian nationalists.[70] In its issue of November 19, 1954, a couple of weeks after the war began, *Témoignages* denounced the "war operations in Algeria, where repression has touched the civil population." France was conducting the war, Réunion communists said, because "in the eyes of the colonialists, Algeria is guilty of wanting more freedom and less poverty." They decried the arbitrary arrests and house searches and concluded:

We are witnessing another provocation from the French government, whose goal is to drown in blood the legitimate demands of the Algerian people, as they did in 1945.

Under the false pretext that Algeria is France, the French government wants to maintain a people in subjugation and poverty, in order to let the colonialist companies realize their profits. The Réunionnais workers, who are also experiencing the weight of the colonial yoke, protest against the armed repression in Algeria. Together with those who are committed to progress and freedom, they will stop the arms of the murderers of the Algerian people.

The French government feared the increasing influence of the communists in Réunion and their move toward Third World politics. In 1956 a new prefect, Jean Perreau-Pradier, arrived in Réunion. His task was, as he said later, to "get rid of the Communists." Perreau-Pradier immediately launched a campaign to take over the city councils held by the communists (twelve out of the island's twenty-three). His first target was Saint-André. Elections

for a new mayor were scheduled in November 1957, after the death
in July 1957 of Saint-André's mayor, Raymond Vergès. Fraud and
violence marred the elections.[71] A conservative was elected. The
measures obtained by the communists to make the elections more
democratic—colored ballot papers so that the illiterate population
would be able to distinguish between the candidates, as well as the
presence of a representative of each candidate and a representative
of the prefect at each polling place—were repealed by the new
prefect. The methods inaugurated at Saint-André—stuffing the
ballot boxes, making the dead vote, voting many times with false
identities—were extended to the whole island.

The Fourth Republic collapsed in 1958. De Gaulle came to power
as the leader of a new government and a new republic, the Fifth
Republic.[72] In March 1959, at the municipal elections in Saint-
Denis, Réunion's capital, massive fraud ensured the victory of the
conservative candidate. The communist candidate, Paul Vergès,
who was denouncing police brutality at the polling place, was
surrounded by French gendarmes and beaten until he lost consciousness. He was saved by Laurence Vergès from being killed.
Éliard Laude, a young communist, was assassinated on the same
day. On his visit to the island on July 9 and 10, 1959, de Gaulle
talked of Réunion as the "southern vanguard of France."[73] "Yes,
you are French, you are French *par excellence,* you are French with
passion," he said. De Gaulle developed the theme that would feed
political demonology on the island: "There is at present in the
world a great menace that looms over free men; one must be firm,
strong, united to stop it, to defeat it. One needs the vigilant power
of France. . . . The struggle implies the love of each woman and
man for the fatherland." At the meeting, hundreds of communists
demonstrated, carrying banners denouncing electoral fraud. Debré
claimed later that the president cried: "*Arrière!* You, carrying banners, *Arrière!* Get back!"[74] The prime minister was so traumatized
by the scene that he recalled it thirty years later with these words:
"There were France and anti-France."[75]

Civil servants active in unions and supporting the communist
demand for autonomy became a target of political repression. In
October 1960, they were the victims of a decree that became known
as l'Ordonnance Debré.[76] The ordinance gave the prefects of the
overseas territories the exceptional power to "suspend state employees from their functions and to expel them to the metro-

pole."[77] The prefect was under no obligation to justify his decision. There was no possibility of appeal. Legal scholars and the commission on constitutional law at the National Assembly condemned the decree for its violation of constitutional law. Despite these condemnations, the government applied the law in the overseas departments, and twenty-six state employees in the overseas departments were its victims. Thirteen of them were from Réunion, and they were forced in August 1961 to leave the island with their families.[78] It was a traumatic event for the families, and it served as a warning to any civil servant who would dare to challenge the state. Its effect should not be underestimated, as it instilled fear among a group with an important social position whose members would then tend to resist political and cultural commitment.

1962 was a year marked by peasants' revolts and communist mobilization against electoral fraud. Peasants revolted because the price of a ton of sugarcane had been lowered by the state under pressure from the metropolitan sugar industry. In February 1962 peasants and sharecroppers rebelled in the city of Saint-Louis. Gendarmes and Compagnies Républicaines Sécurité (CRS) were sent to crush the revolt and left, after two days of battle, one demonstrator dead, many wounded, and dozens arrested. The March 1962 elections in Le Port were the scene of violence. Police forces chased the communists out of the polling places. The city was under siege for two days. Union workers were arrested and jailed without trial.

1962 was also the year the Algerian War ended. In 1961 Réunion's communists abstained from voting at the referendum of January 8, which de Gaulle had organized to decide the fate of Algeria. Paul Vergès explained the decision of his party: "The Réunionnais refuse to decide what must be decided by the Algerians themselves: the future of their country." On July 5, 1962, date of the independence of Algeria, *Témoignages* proclaimed: "A new defeat of colonialism, a new victory of the peoples! Long Live the Independence of Algeria! Long Live the Heroic People of Algeria!" The victory of the Algerian people was "our victory," the communist newspaper declared, "because the defeat of colonialism in Algeria is the defeat of colonialism; it is a new setback for imperialism." Jacques Vergès, now an attorney, had been very active on behalf of the Algerian nationalists. With other lawyers, he developed a "strategy of rupture" to defend the Algerian nationalists. The lawyers challenged the authority and legitimacy of French colonial tribunals to judge nationalist soldiers.[79] They denounced the widespread practice of torture by the French special forces.[80] Réunion's conservatives argued that Jacques's activities proved Paul's association with terrorism and the enemies of France.

The French Imperialist Jacobin in the Colony

In 1963, the modernization of the island and political demonology were accelerated. The elections of November 1962, won by conservatives, had been marred by such violence and fraud that the majority of the Réunionnais expected them to be nullified. The newspaper *Le Progrès* wrote in its January 21, 1963, issue: "We have heard that a new prefect will be named and that General de Gaulle has showed his intention of putting an end to the scandal of electoral fraud. We may now hope that we will soon witness a loyal and free competition."[81] The French government, however, seemed reluctant to enforce de Gaulle's wish. On January 31, Paul Vergès, who was boarding a plane to Réunion at the Paris airport, was notified by the French police that a decision of the Ministry of the Interior forbade him to return to his country.[82] On February 22, 1963, the Conseil d'État, the French institution that reviews the complaints about the legality of an election, nullified the elections of November 1962. New elections were scheduled for May 5, 1963. The prefect Perreau-Pradier was replaced by Alfred Diefenbacher. Vergès was allowed to return to Réunion on February 28.

The metropolitan allies of local conservatives were wary. French public opinion was informed of the political violence on the island, and it was becoming increasingly difficult to justify colonial forms of repression in a French department. Michel Debré declared in April 1963: "The local administration was afraid. It organized electoral fraud on a large scale and in the crudest fashion. Voters were forbidden to enter polling places in which votes had already been cast in their names!"[83] Communists were winning the sympathy of democratic forces in France, who were scandalized by methods reminiscent of the worst days of colonization. They had a strong moral stance congruent with the claims associated with modern democracy: the inalienable rights of free opinion, association, and speech. They were successfully presenting themselves as the defenders of democratic rights, and the conservatives as opposed to these rights.

The conservatives wanted a strong, and apparently legal, electoral victory, but they feared that none of their leaders could legitimately defeat the communist candidates. The conservatives turned to Michel Debré and asked him to lead their campaign. Debré was a good choice. He had firmly expressed his opposition to demands for autonomy and independence in the colonial empire. He had also shown with his 1960 ordinance that he did not hesitate to resort to anticonstitutional measures against political foes. The program of the conservatives was ideology and force, but they were not well versed in the ideological vocabulary of countersubversive rhetoric. The late-1940s anticommunist rhetoric had been formulated in religious terms: to be communist was atheistic, anti-Christian. But by now the appeal to religion had lost its impact, and priests were no longer exercising a hegemonic power on the population. New formulas, new images, new fictions, and modern means to disseminate them were necessary. Debré was the man for the mission.

Debré had long been interested in the splendor of France. The son of a prominent pediatrician, who "taught [him] tolerance, respect for life, a taste for science and literature, and the desire to lead a full life,"[84] Debré learned early the love of the republic: "To him [Debré's father], and to us, the republic reunited Péguy and Jaurès, the struggle for social laws and the French expansion in the world, public education and the return of Alsace and Lorraine to the nation."[85] His mother, the daughter of a rabbi, was among the first women to enter medical school.[86] But Debré reserved his greatest admiration for de Gaulle. Their first encounter occurred in August 1944: "The events of the preceding years had hardened me. I did not show any emotion. And yet, I was touched deep down in my heart."[87] Debré hoped with all his "soul" that this man, who personified "revenge," the "liberty and unity of the fatherland," would be the one who would "re-build France."[88] "My dream which, for so long, has seemed impossible to attain, was now reality." Debré decided, then and there, to dedicate his life to the service of Gaullism. "My destiny was sealed there."[89] Debré would be the "faithful among the faithful," and his fidelity would earn him de Gaulle's full and undying support. "No one ever prevailed over him with me," Debré claimed.[90] He became a soldier of de Gaulle.

Debré expressed a similar love for France. France was, to him, a pure, unpolluted, fiercely loved object. The duty of her sons was to prevent her rape by alien men. In the opening of the first volume of his memoirs, Debré chose three moments to illustrate the threats against the body of France. The first event occurred in November 1918, at the end of World War I: "La France est de nouveau la France" [France is France again, or, France has found its essence again], Debré wrote. Debré, who was then six years old, made a French flag with the help of his sister to praise the return of the "lost provinces," Alsace and Lorraine, to the nation's body. The second event was in July 1940. With other officers and thousands of soldiers, Debré was a prisoner of the German army. A German soldier came and asked Bretons and Alsatians to step forward because Germany had decided that these regions were now part of the "new Europe." "Nobody moved. Nobody uttered a single word," Debré remembered. "The translator repeated his vile words. One soldier, only one, stepped out of the ranks. The following day, we learned that he was the son of a German woman who had become French through her marriage with an Alsatian." It was a moment of "intense pain."[91] The last moment took place on August 25, 1944: "France was France again." Between the two events when France recovered its pure essence intervened the moment when the "nation was dismembered" and men's loyalty to France was tested. The only reason for which a man could betray the motherland was being the son of an alien mother. The body of the nation was threatened, not just by external enemies, but also internally, by infiltrating enemies, impure blood that could not guarantee loyalty.

France was an idealized object. It was *La France,* a country abstracted from its historical formation. It was not the France of the monarchy, of the French Revolution, of the 1871 Commune; of the working class, the bourgeoisie, the peasants; of the collaboration, of the Resistance; of the colonial wars, of imperialism. No, it was "La France," a name, a pure symbol, or more clearly, a blank screen on which a fantasy, a fiction, an illusion, could be projected. Illusion—the fantastic realization of the ego's aspiration to return to a moment of full satisfaction, before the reality principle—reinforced

Debré's narcissism. He was the true son of France, the fantastic realization of his ego. No conflict was experienced, only a state of blissful content. Debré, a strict Jacobin, an opponent of the division of the motherland, could not see the demand of Réunion's communists for autonomy as anything but an attack on the body of France. To ask for autonomy was a threat to an idealized object necessary to Debré's ego. To ask for autonomy was to attack Debré personally.

Debré feared that France would lose her imperial *grandeur,* her place as a leading world power. One means to preserve this grandeur was to encourage the birthrate of the population. Debré, an unflinching adversary of reproductive rights, led the battle against the liberalization of the laws on contraception and abortion. He advocated financial incentives to encourage women to bear children. "Women's right to work outside the home, their liberation are bad excuses to justify contraception: if society offers a choice between family life and work, a majority of couples would accept to expand their family."[92] Two concerns governed Debré's approach to politics: the glory and unity of France and the falling birthrate. He was a soldier of France and had a sense of personal duty. "Who still thinks primarily of *serving* the Motherland?" he asked.[93] And he answered: "I do." Debré remembered being concerned about his colleagues' lack of interest in France's future, and wondering: "Is it possible for me to transform this situation? I intend to do it and I think that I can."[94] Going to Réunion was a continuation of Debré's personal crusade for his motherland. He evoked de Gaulle's 1959 visit to explain his interest in a "small and faraway land." Algeria was then "our problem, our great problem."[95] In contrast to a land where the "hatred against France was causing agony," Réunion was a "land that had chosen fidelity to the motherland." He had been shocked to discover that the clauses of the 1946 law were not applied.[96] He would be the one to remedy the situation and consequently pushed for a series of projects: military service for all young men,[97] public works, the creation of an administrative agency to organize the migration of Réunionnais to France, a program to distribute milk in schools, the building of high schools.[98] Debré experienced his arrival in Réunion as a personal battle against Paul Vergès, the "communist leader who led the separatist demonstration in 1959 and sought to be elected in order to lead a movement of secession."[99] By contrast, Debré's own election would be an opportunity to affirm that France "is present in all the oceans, in all the seas that make up the universe."[100]

Political Demonology in the Postcolony

The convergence of the conservatives' fears, Debré's crusade, and the communists' demand for autonomy and rhetoric set the scene for political demonology. "Political demonology" is Michael Rogin's phrase for the "creation of monsters by the inflation, stigmatization, and dehumanization of political foes."[101] Although Rogin studies the form and content of political demonology in the United States, many of his insights can be applied to the study of political demonology in a postcolony. In the United States, Rogin argues, "the Soviet Union replaced the immigrant working class as the source of anxiety, and the combat between workers and capitalists, immigrants and natives, was replaced by one between Moscow's agents (intellectuals, government employees, students and middle-class activists) and a state national-security apparatus."[102] A similar displacement occurred in the Third World. As national movements of liberation were often supported by the Soviet Union, the Third World became a battleground of the Cold War, and the demand for national liberation was often associated with communist conspiracy.

Political demonology in Réunion developed first in response to the growing discontent among workers, sharecroppers, and peasants and to the expanding influence of the Communist Party; second, as a response to the organization of the anticolonialists of the French overseas departments—Réunion, Martinique, Guadeloupe, and Guiana—into a unified anticolonialist front;[103] and third, as an answer to the anxieties of French imperialists, who were witnessing the crumbling of their empire. Réunion Island entered the postcolonial era as a pawn in the Cold War game.[104] In the conservative imaginary, Réunion Island became an outpost in the war between the "free world" and totalitarianism. The Cold War provided Réunion's conservatives with images and words that spoke to to the fears of a population witnessing a rapid transformation of the world and wondering about its future. The countersubversive narrative was attractive. There was a villain (the communist), people to protect (women and children), and a well-defined site where the story was unfolding (an island in an ocean that had become important to the world powers—whoever controlled the ocean controlled the transportation of oil, the Middle East, and East Africa).

To construct a successful villain, the storyteller must attract the public with an uncanny character, make it want to know more about the character, and stimulate its curiosity about him. In Paul Vergès, the conservatives found a perfect villain. He was a communist, and communism was the embodiment of evil; as a communist, he had no fatherland, was at the orders of foreign powers, and negated God.[105] Assimilationist conservatives understood that to succeed, a demonological narrative must be accompanied by material rewards, and they used the clientelism that had long been part of Réunion's politics. People were rewarded for voting "for the right candidate" with welfare, protection, jobs, housing. Entertainment events were organized in every town and village: games, balls, ceremonies, beauty pageants in which young white women were encouraged to participate with promises of money and jobs.[106] Assimilation appeared more appealing than autonomy. It promised more goods, more games, more rewards. Autonomy, by contrast, promised work, effort, sacrifice, and dignity. Its advocates celebrated the struggles of Algerians, Vietnamese, South Africans. It seemed that with autonomy, the future was one of struggle and long-term rewards, whereas conservative assimilation offered the protection of a Western power and immediate rewards. Réunionnais could compare their situation with that of their neighbors, Mauritians or Madagascans, who had chosen independence and now suffered hardship.

Cold War discourse succeeded in Réunion because it was able to make use of a paranoid style and tendency to violence that had long characterized Réunion's politics. The themes of the 1960s countersubversive discourse had already been announced in the 1930s.[107] The electoral campaigns of 1910, 1914, 1932, and 1936 had been extremely violent.[108] The style of Réunion's politics has been explained by the history of the island and its geographical isolation. Commentators have suggested that the life on a small and isolated island encouraged a paranoid approach to anything coming from outside. From the outside have come hurricanes, pirates, the dangers from which one cannot escape, because the island is like a prison. The Réunionnais historian Prosper Eve has called Réunion an "island of fear,"[109] arguing that since its original colonization, at the heart of Réunion's imagination there had been fear, a fear created by slavery and colonialism—fear of punishments, of separation from loved ones, of death—and sustained by the colonial power, reinforced by patriarchy, and fed by religious beliefs:

Conservatives used to blackmail women, retirees, people on welfare. Application for a fellowship, a grant, financial aid at school, provoked an investigation by the gendarmes. Parents were afraid because they did not want to be an obstacle to their children's future.

People were afraid to go to the polls. They feared the violence of the thugs paid by the conservatives. By staying away from the polls, they hoped that they would avoid being associated with the communists. Some were even afraid of being expelled from Réunion under the 1960 Ordinance, even though their situation prevented them to be subjected to it.[110]

Conservatives had access to unprecedented resources for disseminating their message: ideological mobilization through schools, access to radio and television, and the use of public funds for the organization of spectacles and demonstrations. In 1963 Réunion's journalists declared that they supported Debré's candidacy and committed themselves to promoting his views in their newspapers. A declaration signed by their editors—except for *Témoignages,* the communist newspaper—read: "The following journalists, upon learning that a delegation has gone to Paris last Saturday to solicit Mr. Debré, approve unanimously this initiative and commit themselves to support his candidacy. The journalists who have signed this appeal have shown how the position of *Témoignages* is extremely ridiculous and isolated."[111] Réunion's conservatives understood the power of radio, which had been installed on the island in 1947. In a few years, thanks to welfare checks that guaranteed a regular income and to attractive credit from merchants, the radio appeared in a majority of homes. By 1979, 70 percent of the population had access to the radio.[112] Television, for which Debré had lobbied, appeared in 1967.[113]

Public administrators, elected officials, and religious leaders provided their help. The prefect, whose role is not to intervene in local politics but to protect public order, intervened clearly in favor of the conservative candidates. In 1963 the prefect Alfred Diefenbacher declared: "I am convinced that the population will see the good, the true, the unique path, which is offered by General de Gaulle. *Vote Debré!*"[114] Mayors offered the resources of their administration to the countersubversive campaign. They provided transportation of the population to the conservatives' meetings, opened the public schools, and volunteered the service of their employees for the campaign.[115] City services checked how people voted and withdrew welfare aid, which they controlled, from those who voted communist. The Catholic Church joined the conservative campaign. Bishop Guibert issued a declaration in 1963: "I want to remind you, in agreement with the teaching of the Church, that a Catholic cannot support the communist doctrine which rejects the existence of God and defends materialism."[116] Priests said masses on election day in which they stressed the antagonism between the Catholic faith and communism. Priests refused to baptize the children of communists, or to give communists absolution. They promised "hell" to those who voted against the conservatives.[117]

The messages of the countersubversive rhetoric were imperative: "You have a simple choice: Either You Vote Debré, *Or Tomorrow You Are Russian!*"[118] The messages simplified and reduced the issues. The emblematic figures of these messages could be found in the Cold War dictionary, whose vocabulary was evangelical, millenarian, and zealous. "Freedom, which is total assimilation with France, or slavery, which is autonomy."[119] Setting reality on its head, the conservatives called autonomy *from* France slavery, when in fact slavery had been imposed *by* France.

When Debré launched the countersubversive campaign, the island had 370,000 inhabitants. Today it has twice that number. Half of today's population were born during Debré's mandate from 1963 to 1989 and grew up in a world deeply divided between France and "evil." Conservatives constructed a Réunionnais identity by splitting off and demonizing the Other. "Countersubversive politics—in its Manichean division of the world; its war on local and partial loyalties; its attachment to secret, hierarchical orders; its invasiveness and fear of boundary invasion; its fascination with violence; and its desire to subordinate political variety to a dominant authority—imitates the subversion it attacks," Rogin has written.[120] Practices attributed to the communists actually depicted conservative aspirations. Debré accused the communists of fraud, even though reports showed that fraud and violence were sponsored by conservatives. Accusations of communist conspiracies with a local basis justified using the island as a military base against

African nations. The representation of the communist foe was needed; it was the reason for a politics of repression.

Fears of Autonomy

The communist demand for autonomy brought into the open the foundation of Réunion's political dilemma: what ties do we want with the metropole? It raised the question of the ability of Réunion to govern itself. This ability was not merely a political or economic question—the possibility of creating administrative structures and enforcing a viable economic program of development—but also a psychological question. Colonialism was not a bad psychological situation. It was a bad political situation that had disastrous psychological effects. The solution was not "psychological reconciliation," but an end to the colonial relation, one of whose worst aspects was the confusion of sociopolitical relations with familial, emotional ones. The sentimental narrative developed by Debré— "The island has a special place in de Gaulle's heart," "Réunion is *la terre fidèle,*" "Assimilation has *spiritual* benefit"—constructed a community entirely devoid of autonomy whose sole aspiration was a greater emotional connection with La Mère-Patrie.

The threat of being abandoned by France, the tutelary metropole, found an echo among Réunion's population, who wondered if the benefits of autonomy were really greater than those of dependence. Conservatives exploited the difficulties of neighboring independent countries: "Look at the situation in Asia and Africa and compare!" cried Debré in 1967. Autonomy meant that the responsibility for failure or success would rest mainly on the community. Autonomy did not always appear desirable. Notwithstanding the concrete difficulties of political autonomy, we need to turn to psychoanalytical theory to understand the foundations of the conservative discourse.

Winnicott has written that autonomy "puts a strain on the individual's whole personality."[121] The individual is left "with no relief from any ideas he may have of being persecuted. He is left with no logical excuse for angry or aggressive feelings except the insatiability of his own greed."[122] Individuals may find it more satisfactory to renounce responsibility and to maintain external objects onto which they can project their internal conflicts. Dependence provides a certain form of security for the individual, and threats to dependence produce a disequilibrium, which in turn may be transformed into anxiety. What does it mean to be autonomous? How does the individual reach autonomy? Autonomous from whom or what? In psychological theory, autonomy follows dependency. Dependence is the state of the infant, who is first entirely dependent on the mother or the prime caretaker. If the infant has received from the prime caretaker enough love and sense of protection, if the mother has been what Winnicott calls the "good enough mother," then the child can separate from her and reach a state of independence.[123] There is a developmental process from the dependence of the infant, to the independence of the older child, to, finally, the autonomy of the adult.[124] Autonomy is the moment when the individual accepts that there is an alternative to dependence and solitary independence. Autonomy is the moment after independence, or more clearly, to follow Winnicott, autonomy is about interdependency, mutuality. To Octave Mannoni, any form of self-government must be built on "those ideological and psychological foundations we call democratic."[125] The acquisition of a democratic outlook is "part and parcel of emancipation from psychological dependence and the attainment of an independent personality."[126] Political reform may speed up the psychological process, but Mannoni contends that it is, foremost, people's capacity for deciding for themselves and taking responsibility for their actions that facilitates the acquisition of the democratic outlook. Autonomy and democracy are related. By taking away a population's responsibility for its actions and arguing that it is unable to decide for itself what is good, a country holds the population "in bondage by innumerable ties of dependence."[127] Albert Memmi has also spoken of a form of autonomy that evokes mutuality, interdependency.[128]

Autonomy awakened anxiety among Réunion's conservatives, who employed a language that evoked strong primary fears of abandonment, solitude, and loss of love. They played on the historical ambivalence of the population, oscillating between demanding more care, more love from France, and more respect, more self-determination. The potential disruption of relations between France and its colony found the conservatives "reaching for the idea that the rights and duties of the mother country and her

overseas dependencies corresponded exactly to the rights and duties of parents and children."[129] But history has shown that "parents" (king, colonial metropole) abused their rights and forgot
their duties. Réunion's conservatives never protested against patriarchal abuse because their dependence was the very nexus of
their Creoleness. They were Creoles because they were dependent,
and their dependence was a proof that they were the best children
of France. The metaphor—that the Réunionnais were the children
of La Mère-Patrie—summed up all the perils of colonial existence
and the need for external imperial support.[130] Conservative assimilation wanted to maintain unnecessary dependencies. "Autonomy"—the recognition of limits, the acknowledgment of a "necessary interdependency: that human freedom lies not in eradicating
or escaping our necessary connections with others like ourselves,
but in acknowledging them and using them to liberate us from
other, unnecessary dependencies"[131]—became, in the conservative
vocabulary, synonymous with erasure, disappearance, and loss of
self.

Countersubversive discourse employed the phenomenon of psychological projection to expel internal doubts about the union of
Réunion with France. Striving to protect the illusion of being undivided, they projected onto the external other what was in fact an
internal division. Those who resisted and questioned the illusion
became the target of the individual's anger because they were the
daily reminders of the weakness, of the possible failure, of that illusion. Psychoanalysts have insisted on the defensive structure of projection, which, according to Freud, is especially at work in paranoia
and phobias.[132] Melanie Klein has talked of the "negation of psychic reality" in the process of projection.[133] The response of Réunion's conservatives connoted "both the action of defending—in
the sense of fighting to protect something—and of defending oneself."[134] Their group reacted against an incompatible idea, "which
provoked on the part of the ego a repelling force of which the
purpose was defense against this incompatible idea."[135] The incompatible idea was autonomy. The threatened psychic space was the
special love between France and Réunion. Led by Debré, conservatives defended the psychic space of this special love with the perpetuation of its fiction. They pounded out the message that Réunion
was "unable to live by its own means" and asked: "What would
become of us without the help of our Mère-Patrie, France?"[136]

Réunionnais were helpless, and conservatives appealed to their feeling of being isolated, living in a poor country with so few resources. Yet this poor country had yielded important benefits to local capitalists and constituted a nonnegligible market for French goods. What made the country and its population so helpless? The communists argued that France owed a debt to the Réunionnais after having exploited the island's population for three centuries. The conservatives affirmed that France would not help the island if its population chose to ask for a greater role in its own governance. The subtext of the conservatives' argument was clear: help would be given at the expense of self-determination; help and dependency were related. There were different motives in the resistance to autonomy, self-interested economic motives as well as unconscious motives. Short-term goals were chosen over long-term goals. Irrational unconscious motives triggered separation anxiety. Both were at work in the conservatives and their audience. They adopted the colonial discourse that had transformed colonization into debt to the metropole.

The dominant conservative fiction was that France loved her colonized children. France was idealized and transformed into a pure essence of love. For France to be innocent of the crimes of colonialism, imperialism, and racism, what was bad was projected on the communists. A concern of the colonial state had always been to transform France into an idealized and coveted figure. With the movement of decolonization and emancipation throughout the Third World, this concern changed into an obsession. To produce a colonial subject in love with France, it was necessary to construct an object to expel—the one who did not love France. For the love of France was an exclusive, absolute, undivided love. France was the "perfect object of love." The transformation of the colonial metropole into a "mother" for the Réunionnais brought forth the question of the power that this mother held. In the conservative family romance, France appeared as a mother in drag, or a phallic, all-powerful mother.[137] For behind La Mère-Patrie was a state, a capitalist, imperialist state. The image of France as a kind mother was an attempt to hide the violence of the French state in its colonies, its repression and exploitation. The idea that France was perfect could only produce anxiety, for the demands of perfection are tyrannical.[138]

Réunion's conservatives themselves had trouble with the perfect image of a maternal France. On the one hand, they expected undying protection and love from her. On the other hand, they resented her for the dependence their love entailed. Her perfection was a constant reminder of their own imperfections. Anger and resentment sometimes took over from their love. They could not, however, bring themselves to direct their anger at La Mère-Patrie, so they turned it against those sent by France to carry out her policies, the civil servants who came from the metropole to fill administrative functions, the *zoreys*.[139] The zoreys' arrival coincided with the development of conservative assimilation. They "developed a parallel society, turned in on itself, with its own neighborhoods, its own way of life."[140] Their impact on Réunion's society was effective. They became a cultural referent, envied and resented. The conservatives' Creoleness expressed itself through an animosity against the zoreys. They expressed their ambivalence toward the assimilation they had wanted by turning their resentment against the zoreys.[141] The good image of France was preserved by projecting onto the zoreys the other side of this love, resentment. The conservatives' principal enemy, however, remained the separatists, the natives who wanted autonomy. Debré rescued the people of Réunion *from* autonomy with France. He presented himself as a rescuing father. Debré brought the people of Réunion back to the colonial family. The relations of daily life were governed by fear and suspicion. The logic of conservative rhetoric imposed a "discriminatory way of thinking, in which only one way of thinking was innocent and inoffensive, and all the others culpable and dangerous."[142]

Réunion's conservatives, through demonization, defined the identity of the Réunionnais *individual*.[143] The terms of their discourse established social connections between individuals that mirrored the ties that preside over a relationship between a protector and a defenseless individual. This type of social connection was accompanied by social violence, to which the population responded in different ways. A part of the population entered a "state of alienation." This group "identified with the alienating force" and became "the combatant of a 'cause' to which it attributed the extraordinary power of guaranteeing the truth and supremacy."[144] Identification with the alienating forces reassured the members of the group, offering them certitude and allowing them to avoid commitment to political conflict. Another part of the population identified fully with the group in power and supported it without question. And a part of the population tried to resist. As those responsible for violence were protected by state power, individuals lost confidence in the desire of the state to protect them. A structure of "protected versus powerless" emerged, and individuals were faced with a binary choice: to ally with the protected or to be excluded. The atmosphere of social violence pushed the individuals, in a gesture of protection, to become passive accomplices of state violence. If political opponents of such political organization were harassed, there had to be some good reason. The norms, imposed by ideology and violence, demanded that the community adhere to a code of conduct based on avoiding reality and demonizing political foes. It was better not to dwell too deeply on the events and to trust the administration because the price of political disagreement, which is a feature of democratic debate, was exclusion, punishment, or demonization. This code of conduct had a rule: "Do not get involved in this," pushing individuals toward an indifference for the community and a withdrawal from politics. Within such a code of conduct, the image of the accomplice was countered by the image of the hero. Political identity resolved around dignity and heroism, opposed to submission and cowardice. The logic of political demonology reduced the political debate to heroic battle and passivity. The identity attributed to the Other—terrorist, communist, separatist—evoked, at once, either a potential or a real menace, or punishment or heroism. Such a codification of human behavior hindered the autonomy of the individual, who preferred to obey the laws of the order of social violence rather than risk punishment or exclusion.

Aliens and Revolutionaries

In Réunion, social violence and political demonology produced both passivity and heroic resistance but pushed aside debate and constructive disagreement. The social rupture was not 1946, according to the conservatives, but 1959, when the communists called themselves "Réunionnais." Conservatives wanted to break the trust between the communists and the population, which was largely a legacy of the generation of 1946. Conservatives claimed that Raymond Vergès's son, Paul Vergès, had betrayed his father. They removed issues from the level of interests, principles, and economic and political realities to that of family dynamics. They construed the difference between the 1946 and 1959 communists not in terms of their respective programs—which have yet to be examined—but in terms of legitimate paternal filiation. If the focus could be kept on the father's inheritance, it seemed possible to charge betrayal by the son. The inheritance was said to be French identity, and this identity was associated with blood purity. Paul Vergès was born in an alien land, of an alien mother. He could not be the legitimate heir of a Frenchman. Heritage, whiteness, purity of origins, and politics were linked.

The betrayal of the son could be traced to the alien blood he carried, the blood of his Asian mother. Even though her name was never evoked, Pham Thi Khang, Paul Vergès's Vietnamese mother, haunted the conservatives' rhetoric. The betrayal was programmed in the blood she had given her son. "Of Asian blood . . . Jacques and Paul were born in Oubone (Siam) on March 5, 1925, and owed their nationality to their father, the Doctor Vergès, who was unanimously respected even by those who fought against his Marxist ideas."[145] Raymond Vergès became the "sole authentically French reference" of the communists. Conservatives reminded people that it was the son who had wanted a *Réunionnais* Communist Party. The father may have been a communist, but at least he was a French one. Like the soldier who, in Debré's anecdote, had betrayed France because his blood had been polluted by his German mother, Vergès was under the power of a barbarian mother, an Asian woman. The mother of the communist leader had infected French blood with an anti-French virus. Paul Vergès was a "son of Siam," and this explained why he opposed the Vietnam War.

Vergès's Vietnamese mother had made him "yellow"; he had his "race's mysterious smile," and his "race's patience and cruelty."[146] The "yellow race" was a "race" of people who kept their feelings hidden, whose faces were deceitful. Their history was a history of barbarian conquests. The "yellow race" evoked the hordes of Genghis Khan, stories and myths that had been taught to schoolchildren. This trope was used at a precise historical moment: after the defeat of the French army by the Vietminh and during the U.S.

war in Vietnam. Hence evocations of the past mingled with contemporary images of the "little yellow men in black." "Vergès
Yellow! We are not racist. We are only talking about Vergès' voting
ballot bulletin. Vergès YELLOW!"[147] Conservative newspapers published fake job demands that stressed Vergès's Asian origin: "Personal: Unemployed. I am looking for a job as political agitator,
preference Southeast Asian sector, my native region. Write to P.V."
(What followed was the address of the communist's newspaper).[148]
Vergès was called "Paul' Ho," and his nationality was "Pro-Viet."[149]
Vergès, the "child of Siam" who tried to hide his "yellow smile,"[150]
embodied the stereotypes of the cruel, hypocritical Asian who has
no concern for human life. The "Orientalization" of the communist leader confirmed the fears of the Réunionnais readers. They
could read, along with denunciations of the "child of Siam," articles about the Vietcong, their support by the Soviet Union and
China, their communist ideology. Communism and the East were
intimately related, and cruelty and hypocrisy characterized the
communists. By orientalizing communism conservatives sought to
expel its vocabulary from its European origins and to racialize an
ideology. Métissage and communism were connected. Vergès was a
métis and a communist, and the combination, conservatives argued, took away Vergès's right to be a legitimate son of Réunion.
Conservatives implied that the Réunionnais could not be métis,
because otherwise they would be aliens.

Vergès had, the propaganda contended, a "secret plan to construct, with his friends in Madagascar and Mauritius, the first
communist empire of the Indian Ocean."[151] Behind Vergès, one
could see the "hand of Moscow or East Berlin," where the communist of Réunion had gone to "promise his masters an autonomous
Réunion converted to bolshevism."[152] Paul Vergès may have had a
Réunionnais father and masqueraded as a Réunionnais himself,
with the island's interests at heart, but countersubversive propaganda claimed to have unveiled the truth: Paul Vergès was an agent
of totalitarian forces, their henchman, their slave. If Paul Vergès
demanded autonomy, it was because he did not love La Mère-
Patrie, and only his métissage could explain this rejection. His alien
mother, his adoption of an alien ideology, and his ties with the
"enemies" of France in Algeria and Vietnam marked Vergès as an
illegitimate son. In the conservatives' narrative, Paul Vergès had
squandered his father's inheritance. The narrative opposed his dis-

loyalty to Debré's unalterable loyalty to his "father" de Gaulle and to his motherland, France.

The two following lists about Paul Vergès and Michel Debré illustrate the ways in which the conservative narrative construed the figure of Debré as a "good son," and Vergès as his dark twin:

Appeal for Michel Debré, Conservative Candidate,
Elections to the French Parliament, Réunion Island. April 19, 1963:
Behind Debré: FRANCE

Behind Vergès: MOSCOW
Vergès = No Fatherland
        = At the orders of FOREIGN POWERS
        = Separation from France to install Russia in Réunion
        = Moral Fraud, Lie, Calumny
        = Negation of GOD.

Debré = A Good Frenchman
       = Réunion = France of the Indian Ocean
       = Prime Minister
       = Perfectly Honest
       = Catholic, like all of Us.[153]

Debré	Vergès
Has de Gaulle behind him	Has Khrushchev behind him
Loyal son of the Professor Debré	Betrays his Father
Builder, Reformer	Exploiter of the Poor
Humanist	
Untainted Past	Murderer[154]
Serves France	Serves the Enemies of France
	No National Loyalty
National Interest	Under Alien Powers' Control
French	Asian, Chinese
	Brother who defends Fellagha, is Muslim, is Chinese.[155]
	Parisian[156]
	Popaul[157]
France	Moscow, Beijing
Loves Youth	Seduces Youth
Catholic	Anti-Christ.[158]

Each column draws a moral picture and alludes to morals, systems of belief, and principles that guide each man's actions. The character of Debré is solidly grounded. One can immediately trust him because he has served, and will serve, France. He has held important positions in the government. In contrast, Vergès is connected to disloyalty, betrayal, duplicity. He is a manipulator, a liar, a mercenary. One does not even know what he really is: Asian, Chinese, Parisian? The narrative opposes "France-loyalty-Debré" to "autonomy-disloyalty-Vergès." Debré presents himself as the most loyal, the preferred son of de Gaulle, hence the true son of France. The insistence of Debré throughout the 1960s on being the repository of France's authority and de Gaulle's favorite son suggests a fragile sense of legitimacy. One of Debré's 1963 electoral posters showed his profile superimposed on de Gaulle's, with these words: "For France, For Réunion, With de Gaulle, Michel Debré."

The conservative campaign was clever. It invented scenarios that appealed to the Réunionnais' imagination.

> SENSATIONAL!
> Three weeks of suspense worthy of Hitchcock with the Soviet
> super-stars who speak French: Paulef Vergeskoff and
> Raymondeï Mondonovitch, in a super-production signed by
> the Communist Party. A Play, poignant with truth:
> THE RENEGADES.
> *Scene 2:* We are in the Communist Party Headquarters. A
> discussion opposed the communists who want independence to
> those who want to remain French.
> A communist:
> "Komrad Vergeskoff,[159] in a word, you are repudiating your
> own father, who, since 1936 and until his death, actively fought
> so that our territory would become a department. Remember!
> As soon as he was elected to the Parliament, he signed the law of
> 1946 creating the Overseas Departments."
> A heated debate follows. One of the communists opposed to
> independence calls Vergeskoff a renegade. The latter leaps up, a
> revolver in his hand, and shouts: "One more word and I shoot
> you!"
> "Beware, Komrads, he is capable of it."
> "Yes, he is used to it. He proved it before . . ."[160]

It is at this moment that, as in *Don Juan,* the portrait of
Komrad Vergeskoff *père* speaks, uttering these simple words:
"They are right: RENEGADES."
Liberté, April 19, 1963.

Conservatives found "friends" of Raymond Vergès who testified
that the father was wary of his son's politics. According to these testimonies, Vergès *père* "suffered when he witnessed the direction taken
by his sons, who wanted to separate Réunion from France."[161] He
confided to his friends that "one is the master of one's life but not of
one's children."[162] When the communist newspaper *Témoignages*
appeared by mistake with its title spelled *Témoignage,* that is, without the *s,* the *Journal de l'Île de La Réunion* declared:

"Doctor Raymond Vergès died the day before yesterday for the second
time." The new masters of the communist party wish to erase the only
authentic French mention that was on the red local newspaper. Indeed,
Doctor Raymond Vergès—with whom we did not agree but whom we
respected as an honest man—was the champion of departmental status. . . . It is a second death that Doctor Vergès experienced, the man
whom so many people called *Papa* Vergès. One knows that, respectful of
the memory and the French ideas of her husband, Mme. Vergès has taken
the side of Michel Debré, shouting to the world her indignation at seeing
her own step-son defend separatism.[163]

One of the conservatives' greatest coups was to enroll, in their
1963 electoral campaign, the widow of Raymond Vergès, Joséphine
Vergès. Debré showed up with her at meetings and photo sessions.
Joséphine Vergès was photographed receiving flowers from the
conservative candidate. She spoke at electoral meetings and gave
interviews in which she explained why she supported Debré: "If I
vote Michel Debré, it is because I want to remain FRENCH. Faithful to the wish of my husband, I have joined those who fight
against autonomy."[164] To the question "Your son [*sic*] Paul Vergès
is exalting autonomy. Is his opinion reconcilable with his father's?"
she answered: "My stepson is a henchman of the Communists. He
is repudiating his father. I contest his right to speak in the name of
his father."[165] The widow was endowed with the true inheritance.
She could transmit the words uttered by the patriarch and testify
that he would have disowned his son had he lived. She spoke in the

name of the father. Vergès's Vietnamese wife was erased and replaced by a true servant of France.

Masculinity and Race

The trope of the good son in Réunion's conservative rhetoric was enmeshed with a certain understanding of virility. It was a triumphant, racially defined virility: the virility of the Frenchman versus the virility of the métis, always a faltering virility. The good son, whose legitimacy had been established by La Mère-Patrie, by the widow of the native leader, and by the chief of the nation, exhibited a masculinity that was supposed to be reassuring. Réunion's population needed a courageous and virile soldier to lead the campaign against the separatists.

A caricature that appeared in a conservative newspaper in February 1963 illustrates the way in which tropes of masculinity and race were played on by countersubversive propaganda.[166] The caricature was entitled *The Chinese Cock and the Gallic Cock: A Fable.* The context of this caricature was a 1963 local election: Debré had expected Vergès to be the communist candidate opposing him, hoping for a showdown between the "son of de Gaulle" and the "Chinese." But the Communist Party presented Vergès in another district, the second district. Debré was deprived of a face-to-face confrontation. The caricature is about this frustration. The mountain represents a range of mountains that separates the north of the island from its western coast, where the second district was. On the right of the mountain, a Gallic cock is shown, triumphant and singing. On the left, a cock with Vergès's head falls down the mountain. He has lost some of his feathers and looks more like a hen than like a cock.

Since the Roman conquest of Gaul, the cock has been the emblem of France.[167] The image of the cock, which was adopted by the monarchy, the Revolution, and the republic, represents the "country and the nation," as well as "the people in arms and the State." As such, it has been a unifying emblem, one about which there have been few disagreements.[168] As the king of the farmyard, the cock is an emblem of virility.[169] The Gallic cock of the caricature embodies France, Christianity, and virility. The Chinese cock refers to Vergès, the "Chinese," and to Creole men. In Réunion,

1. *The Chinese Cock and the Gallic Cock: A Fable.*
Political Cartoon, 1963.

cockfighting is a very popular form of entertainment, and an all-
male affair. Men gamble, drink, and talk around the arena where
cocks are fighting. Bets can be high. Men attend to their cocks with
tenderness, carefully training them. Among the cocks, "Chinese
cocks" are prized, cherished for their combativeness and fierceness.
The caricature is a parable on masculinity and race. The cock of
France has defeated the cock of Réunion. France has defeated Asia.
The Gallic cock has all its features erect: its body, its tail, its head;
under its chin hang two balls, like two testicles. In contrast, the
Chinese cock has practically no tail, no wings. It seems deprived of
all virile attributes. Its body is plump like a hen's. The Gallic cock
has knocked the Chinese cock over, head over heels. The Chinese
cock, emblematic of traditional Réunion's masculinity, is defeated,
without a fight, by the Gallic cock, the emblem of French virility.
Yet the Gallic cock is also a devalorizing emblem of masculinity.
People throughout history, Michel Pastoureau has shown, have
made fun of the relation between the Gallic cock and the virility of
the Frenchman. The cock's vanity and stupidity makes it an easy
target of humor. Its most common representation—erect—seems

to hide an anxiety about its ability to perform virile exploits. The "victory" of the Gallic cock, that is, of the conservative candidate, might be the celebration about avoiding the confrontation with the Chinese cock, the communist candidate. There is a relief in this easy victory.

Masculinity, for the conservatives, was about physical force, about beating one's adversary to the ground. This vision of masculinity found an echo among Réunion's men, who also tended to regard the use of physical force as a sign of true manhood. French virility tried to seduce Réunion virility. Yet in that cartoon, a representation of Réunion's masculinity, the Chinese cock, was beaten by French masculinity. It was the kind of masculinity exhibited by the Frenchman that was truly powerful. French masculinity took as its accomplice a colonial masculinity that did not question the assumptions on which it was founded—force, brutality, the denial of sexual difference. It was a masculinity founded on the denial of the historical victimization of men's bodies: men taken as slaves, sold, their bodies marked by the whips and the red-hot iron, separated from their lovers and children, deprived of the paternal function, deprived of their dignity, exploited, treated as inferior beings because of their skin, their class. The masculinity endorsed by Cold War rhetoric used some of the constitutive elements of that history—violence, physical force—to enforce its message but repressed other aspects of Réunion masculinity: physical resistance to slavery, endurance. The masculinity expected from Creole men was a display of blind aggression. The bodies of the communists were legitimate targets of physical violence, with the communist leader a favorite target. The thugs, themselves métis of Réunion, were encouraged to project their aggression onto him. Led by white men, local bourgeois, or a French prime minister, métis Creole men turned their wrath against the communists.

Legitimate Fathers and *Papa*

Good sons made good fathers. Debré, who had dutifully served his father and proved his masculinity, could fulfill the role of a father. The trope of fatherhood has been evocative in politics. It has referred to the benevolent role a man assumes for the community. In Réunion, "Papa" was a familiar term for leaders. Historians used to say that Sarda Garriga was called "Papa Sarda" by the thankful slaves. Raymond Vergès was called "Papa Vergès" during his life.[170] Paul Vergès himself was called "Papa," even by people older than he was.[171] Commentators have read this as essentially a submissive relation to power.[172] There has been, to be sure, a strong tradition of paternalism in Réunion reinforced by rural patriarchy, the power of priests and of landlords, and by the clientelism of elected officials. But not every elected official, every political leader, was called "Papa." Calling a leader "Papa" signified a demand for protection, a demand for love, a desire to emulate, as well as gratitude and affection. Réunionnais projected onto Raymond and Paul Vergès their desire to find someone who would lead them in their fight against the arbitrary colonial power. Conservatives were aware of this relation between protection, affection, and the role of the political father. They wanted now to associate the term "Papa" with Debré. Using a narrative about fathers and sons and inheritance, conservatives fabricated the story of "Papa Debré."

In 1963 a story in Debré's official newspaper introduced the tale of "Papa Debré." The Réunion public was told that "in the past, Professor Debré investigated the diet of the island's children. He found that Réunion children had a poor diet, lacking in fundamental nutrients. Upon his return to France, he went to see his son, Michel Debré, then Prime Minister of the government. The latter, convinced by his father, decided that the metropole would regularly and freely send milk every year to the children of Réunion. . . . These distributions are now known as: the milk of PAPA DEBRÉ."[173] Since the end of World War II, social workers, doctors, and political activists had denounced the poor diet of the majority of Réunionnais. In 1949 Raymond Vergès had told the French Parliament that the health situation in the island was scandalous. As a doctor, he had seen the consequences of poor diet and poor living conditions on the population. The island had the greatest infant mortality rate of overseas departments.[174] In 1954 an investigation showed that the daily diet of the adult averaged 1,800 calories, when the needed daily average is 2,700 calories. The majority of Réunionnais experienced a lack of vitamins and the symptoms of a poor diet.[175] Ten years later, Rachel Varondin, a social worker, said that "sixty to seventy percent of the population are suffering from a lack of vitamins, and are therefore exhibiting numerous symptoms that a good diet would eliminate."[176] The

2. "Goûte ça, c'est un fortifiant de mon invention!"
(Taste this, it is a tonic that I have invented!)
Political Cartoon, 1967.

situation Debré claimed his father had discovered had long before been denounced by Réunionnais. "My father opened my eyes," he wrote, to the real causes of the problem: poor and insufficient diet. The knowledge about Réunion came from Debré's father. The French doctor had assessed the situation better than the Réunionnais doctor.

Through the performance of a maternal function, giving milk, Debré named himself the "Papa" of Réunion. "Papa Debré" was a good son, who had listened to his father's medical advice. The resonance of "Papa Debré" harked back to a contest between the father of Paul Vergès and the father of Michel Debré. Which of these fathers had really had at heart the welfare of Réunion's children? Who had triggered the action for a better diet? Who was the "Papa" of Réunion? Debré, by pointing to his father's determining role, displaced Raymond Vergès's role. Doctor Debré's diagnosis had been heard by the son, and the right medicine had been brought to the children of Réunion. Debré and Vergès were both sons of doctors. Yet whereas Debré had followed his father's pediatric concern for children, Vergès had transformed the doctor's duty of saving children's lives into threatening their lives. Paul Vergès gave poison to Réunion's children. A 1967 cartoon showed Vergès giving a spoon of poison to a black man who looks like a child. Vergès, whose gesture evokes a mother giving syrup to her sick child, is smiling and saying: "Taste this, it is a tonic that I have invented!" The bottle's brand is "Autonomy" and displays the skull and bones symbolic of death.[177] The Réunionnais were fed poison instead of milk by the bad father. So perhaps Doctor Vergès's diagnosis was also wrong. If his son was offering poison disguised as medicine, then Doctor Vergès's concern with the welfare of Réunion's children might have been faked.

The French Soldiers of the (Post)colony

Réunionnais were French, the conservative propaganda asserted. One of their posters said: "Français Votez La France" [French men and women, Vote France].[178] Marianne, the symbol of the French republic, was shown walking on the image of the island, sowing. She was inseminating the island, represented as a flat, blank space with no name, populated by a French people who voted for France. Those who wanted to "separate La Mère-Patrie from the France of the Indian Ocean" had "no future."[179] The election of 1963, conservatives warned, was a "vital event when the fidelity of Réunion to La Mère-Patrie was challenged."[180]

Workers had fought for republican assimilation. Conservatives sought to gain their support and organized a demonstration on May 1, 1963, on Labor Day, at Saint-Denis, Place Sarda Garriga.[181] It was a symbolic response to the workers' demonstration of May 1, 1946, in which they celebrated their victory, the end of colonial status, through the streets of Saint-Denis. Now conservatives told them that it was "essential that they testify to their unfailing attachment to France under the double sign of departmentalization and Workers Day."[182] In 1963, the stakes were high: "Workers! The whole world is watching. Come to the Place Sarda Garriga on May 1 to show to the world that we are FRENCH."[183] On May 1, schools and public administrations were closed, and free transportation for the demonstrators was organized. Workers were given banners that read "Les Communistes à Moscou," "Les Moujiks à Moscou," "Independance Non," "Nous sommes Français car la

France est la lumière du monde," "Du Lait grace à Papa Debré."
Some workers later testified that they had been forced to join the
demonstration under the threat of losing their jobs.[184]

To the conservatives, the Réunionnais' ancestors were the white
Europeans. To the communists, the Réunionnais should not have
to choose among their diverse ancestors. In a 1963 meeting, Paul
Vergès said:

Our people will win autonomy as a part of the general movement of
decolonization that has mobilized peoples throughout the world.

We, Réunionnais, are the descendants of Africans, of Indians, of Madagascans, of Chinese, and French. We do not choose among our ancestors. We are Réunionnais. We are in our country. We are proud of being
Réunionnais.[185]

The communists wanted the Réunionnais to be aware of their
difference from the French people. Their culture, history, and language were not French. As a people, they had the right to self-
determination. The conservatives' reasoning was that since the
people of Réunion were French, there was no foundation for a
demand of self-determination. Self-determination was a principle
that made sense only for a people with a specific culture, language, and history. The prefect Alfred Diefenbacher declared in
his first address to Réunion's people: "The island has been destined
to be a piece of France. It is an island where a patriotism so pure
is expressed that it reminds me of the feelings of Alsatians and
Lorrainers."[186]

As the May 1963 elections approached, the conservatives' messages became more direct. They warned the Réunionnais about the
consequences of a communist victory: "France pays your family allowances—Autonomy will suppress them." The elections attracted
the attention of the French media. French opinion was interested in
Debré's results, since he was a national figure, and in local answers
to accusations of electoral fraud. Debré reaffirmed his pledge to
enforce free and democratic elections. In an April 20, 1963, interview with *Le Monde,* he said: "When the mayors of Réunion asked
me to be their candidate, I told them that these practices had to
stop. I believe that we can have honest elections. The administration has received very precise instructions to avoid any form of
fraud."[187] Despite Debré's pledge that his election would be democratic, a journalist from *Le Monde* later wrote that "the incidents

that occurred in the majority of the polling places are too numerous to be reported in detail. Many of my colleagues witnessed ballot papers for conservatives being stuffed in poll boxes."[188] Debré won more than 80 percent of the vote, and in the second district, the conservative candidate won against Paul Vergès.

After 1963, Réunion's elections continued to be marred by fraud, and conservative thugs, the equivalent of *tonton-macoutes,* continued to terrorize the voters. The communists asked their supporters, after March 1965, to abstain from voting as long as the administration was not taking necessary measures to ensure the fairness of the elections. Réunion's newspapers, which were not sympathetic to the communists, started to express their disapproval. In December 1965, the Catholic daily *Croix-Sud* sent an open letter to the prefect, wondering if the administration really wanted honest elections. Yet fraud remained the main conservative tactic for winning elections.[189] Debré shifted the blame to the communists. "After World War II, the communists systematized fraudulent practices," he wrote. "One of their tactics is to accuse their adversary before election day! Every defeat of a separatist is said to be caused by fraud. A considerable effort was made to counter these practices and I was instrumental in enforcing the anti-fraud regulations. The separatists never participated in this effort. In fact, they have continued to engage in fraudulent practices."[190]

Public opinion in Réunion seemed to distrust Debré's declarations, and in 1969 an association was created, the Association pour le Déroulement Normal des Élections, in which some conservatives, together with communists and Réunionnais from other political groups, vowed to enforce free and democratic elections. Under the pressure of public opinion in France and on the island, the minister of the overseas departments asked the prefect of Réunion in 1971 to take all necessary measures to ensure that the March city elections would be held "with scrupulous respect for the law." On March 21, 1971, for the first time since 1957, the communist lists won majorities in three cities.[191]

Debré remained the "conservative champion against the Left."[192] The 1964 elections offered a new opportunity to attack the demand for autonomy. A series of cartoons that appeared in one of the most widely distributed newspapers, the *Journal de l'Île de La Réunion,* showed autonomy as a seductive trap for credulous Réunionnais.[193] Réunionnais were represented as donkeys, a stupid

3. & 4. Political Cartoons, 1964.

animal in French popular culture, attracted by the communists' carrot. Communists were seducers. The task of the conservatives was a parental task: to warn the trusting Creole children of what awaited them if they were not more cautious. The cartoons were clever. Although appealing to a population by calling it stupid as a

5. Political Cartoon, 1964.

donkey might appear strange, talking of seduction proved that the conservatives had understood the attraction of autonomy.

By 1964, conservatives looked for reasons to indict the communists, arrest them, and deprive them of their civil rights. The criminalization of politics became a tactic that reduced the conflictual nature of politics to criminal activity. Bruny Payet, the secretary of the Communist Party, was deprived of his identity card and passport for ten years. Paul Vergès, in his function as the editor of the communist newspaper *Témoignages,* was charged with endangering the security of the state. *Témoignages* had published articles that condemned the violent repression of Algerians by the French police during the October 1961 demonstrations in Paris.[194] In 1964, Réunion's Court of Justice, using the articles as proof, sentenced Paul Vergès to three months of prison for having "threatened the security of the state" and posing a "threat to the safety of the state." The sentence deprived Vergès of his civil rights for life. Vergès challenged the sentence and declared that he refused to comply with the tribunal's decision as long as the thugs of the conservatives' electoral machine were not tried for their crimes. Vergès went underground in March 1964 to contest the judgment. He also wanted to prove that there was more sympathy for the communists' struggle among the population than the conservatives' victories suggested.

Vergès remained underground until July 1966. During these two years, his name could not be printed in newspapers; houses were searched; people were arrested. His family was under constant police surveillance and was subjected to petty harassment and house searches and was forbidden to travel. His wife, Laurence Vergès, received death threats. The repression had mixed results. On the one hand, it confirmed people's belief that it was dangerous to show any interest in politics. On the other hand, it gave some Réunionnais pride in a common resistance to the police, the state, and the island's authorities. During the 1960s, more than two hundred communist activists were arrested and thrown in jail for their activities. Vergès surrendered on July 29, 1966, and was imprisoned that same day. He went on a hunger strike, seeking to be transferred as soon as possible to a French court, the Cour de Sûreté de l'État, that would judge him, and he obtained satisfaction. The French court concluded that there was no basis for the charges. Vergès returned to Réunion on December 24, 1966.[195]

Political repression was not limited to the communists. When in the late 1960s priests preaching liberation theology tried to disseminate its teaching in Réunion's churches, they encountered strong resistance from the Catholic Church hierarchy. Liberation theology spoke of poverty and justice to a population that was deeply Catholic. Liberation theology's respect for popular religious beliefs that had been sternly condemned by the local church hierarchy, and its openness to syncretism, reinforced its appeal among Réunionnais. But sermons by liberation theologians were disrupted, and priests who supported a revolutionary reading of the gospel were expelled or forbidden by the diocese to exercise their ministry.[196]

Conservatives organized pageants to celebrate the attachment of Réunion to France. The apotheosis of this form of ideological campaign was the celebration of the tricentennial of the colonization of the island in October 1965.[197] The project received generous funding from the French state and the support of its representatives. Debré lobbied for the celebration, and as early as 1963 he created a committee to organize the festivities. The choice of 1965 spoke of racism, because it took as the population's moment of birth 1665, when French settlers sent by the Company of the Indies had landed on the island. It ignored 1663, when French *and* Madagascans had settled on the island. In the official brochure, the conservatives stated the goal of the celebration: "To reaffirm the permanence of the French presence in Bourbon."[198] The monarchic name of Bourbon, instead of Réunion, harked back to the Leblonds' desire for a return to the prerevolutionary days and evoked nostalgia for the days of the plantation. The tricentennial was an occasion to reaffirm "three hundred years of filial love of the fatherland.[199]

It is important to celebrate this date with the greatest splendor. The tricentennial is an extraordinary occasion to remind France that there has been, for the last three centuries, a French land in the Indian Ocean, a land that was French even before the provinces of Lorraine and Savoie became part of the French nation.[200]

In the first script of the tricentennial celebration, there had been no Madagascans. When the communists denounced the racism of the inaccurate official account, and the director of the Archives had to confirm their assertion, a second script introduced the Madagascans, but only by promulgating a new fiction. Now Madagascans were on the island, but not as maroons—which was the historical fact—but as servants. The French presence was inscribed through geographical signs and monuments. A cave near the Bay of Saint-Paul was said to be the "Cave of the First Frenchmen," though there was no archival proof that the cave had been inhabited by the first Frenchmen. Another marker was a monument with the inscription "Petite île de Bourbon sans cesse tendue vers la Mère Patrie et si éprise de l'amour d'elle qu'elle enivre tous ses enfants de cet amour" [Small island of Bourbon, always stretched toward La Mère-Patrie and so enamored by the love of her that it has intoxicated the island's children]. The "passion" of the Réunionnais for France was expressed through hyperbolic speeches with spurious claims. It "is an incredible good fortune to be French when elsewhere there is cannibalism and slavery. It is well known that there is the civilization of bread eaters and the civilization of rice eaters. We are a country of rice eaters but we have been accepted by the civilization of bread eaters," the mayor of Saint-Paul, a black, a descendant of slaves, declared.

Réunionnais were called to swear publicly their allegiance to France. A ninety-two-year-old woman testified: "I was born French on May 1, 1871. I have learned to love France, our *Mère Patrie*. As I reach the end of my life, I have come to tell you: *Vive la France!*"[201] Former communists repented in the newspapers, reenacting the acts of repentance demanded by the Catholic Church in the early 1950s. "For fifteen years I was a red. During this period, I was exalted, as if I had been hypnotized and brainwashed," a communist testified.[202] Another told of his despair when after being forced to learn Russian, he received new party directives requiring him to learn Chinese.[203] An anonymous "disgusted communist" published a letter in which he warned the communists of the workers' wrath.[204] An atmosphere of colonial mediocrity pervaded the society. Political demonology diminished the vocabulary of public debate. Insults and mockeries peppered political speeches. Academic research was not encouraged and always suspected of obedience to an ideological camp. The island became a refuge for the nostalgics of the empire. French metropolitans arrived by hundreds to find a financial and psychological heaven.

Political Demonology in the 1990s

In 1981 the socialist candidate was elected to the French presidency, and a Left majority was elected to the National Assembly. Two communist candidates from Réunion were elected to the French Parliament. The Réunion Communist Party declared that it was putting aside its struggle for political autonomy. It was a bet on François Mitterrand's promise of full social equality between the overseas departments and France. Réunion's communists warned that the socialist project would run into difficulties and "would end up showing the impossibility of applying a policy of integration in Réunion." Vergès declared that it was time to "expose the illusion of treating Réunion like it is an integral part of the French economy."[205] Nonetheless, communists participated in the new institutions created by the socialist government, such as the Regional Council. Their strategy was one of "critical participation," they argued, and of alliances with the groups interested in Réunion's development. Their decision astonished some of the party's followers, particularly intellectuals whose political identity had been formed through the struggle for autonomy. They felt betrayed. To renounce the battle for autonomy had consequences.

Although on the one hand it opened the political debate that had been frozen around the question of status, on the other hand, it deprived the population of a powerful and mobilizing concept to resist French assimilation. The political and cultural question of autonomy was soon transformed into a demand for the recognition of cultural and ethnic difference.

Under the socialist government, violence subsided. Yet conservatives continued to speak with the vocabulary of political demonology. Although their arbitrary power was curtailed, they still dreamed of a world without opponents. They warned, in 1992, that the communist party was "preparing its revenge" after having "placed the island under a reign of terror for many years."[206] They argued that the "suppression of the communist party," its "elimination from the political scene,"[207] must remain the principal goal of Réunion's political organizations.[208] The habit of blaming communist conspiracy for social troubles endured. In February 1991, violent riots erupted in a ghetto of Saint-Denis, aptly named Cité Debré. It was a huge housing complex on the outskirts of Saint-Denis, built under Debré's administration. Three days of riots resulted in twelve deaths, and the city suffered millions of francs worth of property damages. Conservative representative Jean-Paul Virapoullé talked of the "communists' responsibility" and asserted that "members of the Communist Party had gone to Madagascar and other countries to train in terrorist activities."[209] He had proofs, he said, that the riots were the result of a long-planned communist attack. The 1991 accusations of manipulation of the young were similar to Debré's accusations in the 1960s.

In 1992 conservatives launched another campaign against the communists, in which the terms of political demonology—conspiracy, manipulation, threat to the healthy social body—were reiterated. The similarities with the rhetoric of the 1960s were eerie. It was as if conservatives could not imagine another world than one rigidly divided between the two abstract notions of "good" and "evil." Again there were speeches about expulsion, destruction, annihilation. Conservatives refused to consider that there might be problems at home that were the result not of a communist conspiracy but of unemployment, of nondevelopment, of a population with no future but dependence. They denied that the problems of the relationship between the metropole and its overseas department were the logical outcome of dependence, and of multinational capitalist interests indifferent to local interests, and insisted that they resulted from a communist conspiracy.

Paul Vergès remained the principal target of the countersubversive rhetoric. He was still "Popaul,"[210] a "komander," whose goal was to strengthen his hegemony.[211] An alliance of political forces was more than ever necessary to "bar the road to Paul Vergès."[212] Vergès was *l'antéchrist,* whose sincerity was always in doubt.[213] He was "responsible for everything bad that has happened to us!"[214] Vergès's very existence was a "handicap to Réunion."[215] Communists still repented publicly in the columns of the conservative press, accusing Vergès of selfish goals: "Paulo, you fooled us, the communists. You have given your relatives good jobs and you have put money away, on the side, in the name of your wife," an anonymous and "disgusted communist" wrote in 1992.[216]

"In the name of the father," a newspaper claimed in March 1993, Jean Louis Debré, the son of Michel Debré, came to the rescue of the conservatives during the campaign for the National Assembly. On February 28, 1993, Jean-Louis Debré said at a meeting:

We should put the old communists in a park at the Plaine des Palmistes and we will open it to tourists. It would attract tourists. Everywhere, communism is falling. It exists only in Réunion. We will organize visits to the park, and watch the communists graze on weeds. We will put up a sign: "Do not feed them, they bite. When they are happy, they wag their tails."[217]

In April 1993, the gendarmes went to Pierre Vergès's house to deliver a summons to appear at a judge's office. Pierre, the son of Paul Vergès, the mayor of Le Port and a member of the General Council, was suspected of having accepted a bribe to favor a company in a bid for a huge contract.[218] The conservative media immediately launched a campaign in which they denied to Pierre Vergès the presumption of innocence. He went underground, because, he declared, the judge clearly had the intention of arresting him rather than interrogating him. At the end of April, a warrant for the arrest of Pierre Vergès was issued. His house and the house of his parents were put under surveillance. His wife and children, members of his family, and friends were followed, and their phones tapped.[219] This affair gave the conservatives the opportunity to connect the communists to corruption, a problem that had plagued the island since the 1960s. In a repetition of the script they favored, a script about family ties rather than political struggle, conservatives indicted the father through the son. They also compared the son to the father, giving the latter the better role, as they had done with Raymond and Paul Vergès. Paul's going underground from 1964 to 1966 was now justified: "The republic then employed the methods of hoodlums. Fraud was prevalent and freedom of speech was muzzled by the conservatives and the media. Nowadays, things have changed, and *Petit Pierre* [220] does not fool anyone, except the hystericals of his sect (the PCR) who have replaced the cops and the wolves of the past. His father took to the maquis, as was done during World War II; Pierre is on the run like a vulgar delinquent." [221] The father was once a vulgar criminal; now it was the son. Now Paul Vergès was a hero, and the conservatives of the sixties were compared to the Nazis! The tone of the conservative politicians and media was hyperbolic, and they made wild declarations. The conservatives of Réunion demonstrated their difficulty with confronting the complexity of historical experience. It gave their narrative a compulsive, repetitive tone. Their story was one of family dynamics, in which the son is subjected to the rigid law of patriarchy, a law in which the rebellion of the son shows that he cannot free himself from the shackles of his servitude. Political vocabulary gave way to a vocabulary of betrayal, bloodlines, father and son. Pierre Vergès was the subject of cartoons in which he was portrayed as a child. Conservatives wrote the history of Réunionnais communists as the story of a family. They argued that Paul Vergès, the "old semi-god," had secured a dynastic direction of the organization. [222]

Women and Daughters

Cold War narrative was a narrative about men, about father and son. Yet lurking behind father and son were mothers and wives. As Michael Rogin and Cynthia Enloe have argued, Cold War discourse rested on a rigid division of gender roles. [223] The Cold War depended on a "deeply militarized understanding of identity and security, and militarization relies on distinct notions about masculinity legitimized by women as well as by men." [224] In the United States, where Cold War rhetoric had been powerful and had infected private life, the "fundamental division" was between motherhood and Communism.[225] In the postcolony, a similar division was enacted. In the drama conservatives invented, the monsters, Creole men who had embraced communism, threatened the welfare of women and children of Réunion. Countersubversive propaganda exploited the images of women and children as potential victims of an autonomous future.

The Creole society of Réunion was a society governed by machismo, by a form of aggressive masculinity. Monique Payet, a feminist activist, has shown how in *séga,* the popular music of the island, women have usually been depicted in stereotypical ways that express the anxiety of men toward the autonomy of women.[226] Women were expected to marry and be obedient. Young girls were not supposed to have lovers before marriage. The Catholic Church enforced the image of a woman devoted to her children and her husband, and who did not engage in public affairs. Race and class played a role in the construction of the categories "good" and "bad" woman. The good woman was white, a good Catholic, with no apparent sexual desire and needs. The bad woman was black, her sexuality was undisciplined, and she resisted the bonds of marriage. Relations between genders were affected by laws in the mid-1970s that facilitated divorce and liberalized welfare, abortion, and contraception. These laws gave the women of Réunion important resources for escaping repressive social norms and masculine oppression.[227]

The masculinization of Réunion's politics—*batay kok* (cockfighting)[228]—situated women outside of the political arena. Yet conservatives assigned women an important role: to act in the home as a counterforce against the Creole men, and outside the home as supporters of conservative assimilation. Countersubversive propaganda targeted women and children not only as the result of patriarchal ideology but also as a response to the militancy of Réunion's women. Women had been among those who fought for the 1946 law. Women, encouraged by CRADS to join the anticolonialist movement, were among its candidates in local elections. Many served in the communist city councils until 1957, when electoral fraud deprived the communists of representation until 1971.[229]

The first women's association, a local section of the Union des Femmes Françaises, the French communist women's organization, became the Union des Femmes de La Réunion in 1958, with Isnelle Amelin as its president. Amelin, a young Creole from a white lower-middle-class family, remembered that growing up in a Catholic family, she learned to fear the "reds."[230] "Anti-communism was the rule," she said. Her family would never have received a black person because "racism was everywhere."[231] A meeting with Raymond Vergès transformed, she would say, a young Catholic woman into a feminist, an anticolonialist activist, and a union organizer. Amelin joined the anticolonialist movement after World War II and was elected to the city council of Saint-Denis. She credited CRADS with leading the condemnation of racism on the island. "Until the war, a white person would not have shaken hands with a black person," Amelin said. "Raymond Vergès encouraged blacks, like Recherchant of Saint-Pierre, and Muslims like Afeedjee of Saint-André, and others, to join the movement."[232] The Union of Women mobilized for day care centers, free school meals, the application of social laws, the freedom to vote, better salaries, and better working conditions for women. It denounced the inequality between women in France and women in Réunion and supported the demand for autonomy.[233] Their feminism was a response to the needs of the poorest women: women working in the fields, as domestics, in the markets. French feminists often chose to ignore their struggle because they did not appear "radical" enough. Réunion feminists denounced the violence of Réunion men and the sexism of their society, but they always sided with Réunion men against French colonialism.

To counter the feminism of Réunion's women, conservatives championed the "mother"—every year, on Mother's Day, a mother was celebrated for having given birth to more than ten children—or the beautiful white Creole woman, elected in a beauty pageant. The communist woman, the woman worker, the single mother, represented bad womanhood. They were wanton women, with no morality and no maternal instinct. Communist women were vilified by the conservatives. By joining the communist movement, they had lost their femininity, and they had even fewer excuses than men because, as mothers, they should have "naturally" rejected communism and autonomy.

Debré aimed his speeches at the women of Réunion. He sought to transform the politicized woman into a soldier of conservative assimilation, through depoliticization and co-optation. Debré told the women of Réunion what their role was: to confront the communists and to help the power unmask the sympathy of their husbands for communism. He often addressed them directly in his speeches. In a 1967 electoral meeting, Debré turned to the women who were present and told them:

The issue is very clear. You just have to ask a communist: When the ties between the metropole and Réunion are severed, who will pay the family allowances? Who will assure aid and social security? Who will build schools, hospitals, houses, roads? Who will pay the civil servants? Who will buy sugar at a good price? In a word, who will pursue the development of the island?[234]

An episode of a serial story, *L'auto nomie,* illustrates the countersubversive theme of the political opposition between Creole women and men. The title plays on the homonymy between *auto* (self) and the French term for car. The play on the name of the husband, *Nomie,* points to the complicity between men and dangerous politics. Nomie, the father, is driving his new car, with his wife Bordette, and their son, Sello. Nomie runs the car off the road. Bordette says: "Nomie, Nomie, you are a pain. Do you see where your car led us? I told you so! This car would only bring us calamity, but you wanted your auto Nomie!" A French gendarme arrives, but he is nice and lets them go. Bordette again turns to Nomie: "So you found your auto Nomie! You saw where it took you! Do you still want to ride in this hearse that would lead us to death? Tell me!" Nomie answers: "Bordette, you are right. I have understood. It is better that we remain without an auto [a car]." Bordette concludes: "Yes, auto Nomie, the day you arrive in every house happiness will be gone."[235] The woman was reasonable; autonomy threatened her home and her family. She had tried to warn her husband and was now vindicated. Her husband could only agree with her. The attempt of a Creole man to drive a car, his car, to be autonomous, endangers his family. The gendered narrative emasculated the Creole man and made the woman an accomplice of his emasculation.

Women received substantial benefits from the state in return for accepting their political subordination. Welfare, which became the main source of income for a large number of families, was given to *mothers.* The greater number of jobs created in the 1960s and the 1970s were in the service industries, which tend to favor a female workforce.[236] The social laws of the mid-1970s helped women to free themselves from Réunion's rural patriarchy. Women's dependence, however, was not eliminated but shifted from the patriarch to the state. As most social welfare benefits were delivered by cities, and control over women's access to these benefits was exercised by social workers, women were subjected to social control and the power of the administration. Since mothers were the recipients of welfare, women appeared "better off" than men. The perception that women enter situations that would guarantee access to welfare, that they "prefer" to stay poor and pregnant, resonated with men deprived of agency in their own country.[237] However, as for other groups in Réunion, the conclusions about the amelioration of the women's situation were mixed.[238] Their representation in political institutions such as city councils and local councils remained extremely low; fewer women than men went to college; women constituted the majority of the unemployed.[239] Women's emancipation was hindered by "a strong religious and social conformism" and "socio-cultural obstacles" such as rigid norms about gender roles.[240]

Réunion feminists had demanded the application of social laws favoring women as mothers in the name of equality with French women. The programs of aid to families with insufficient resources to support their children had been worked out by French feminists and supported by the French communists.[241] They were not unlike the program of Aid to Families with Dependent Children in the United States.[242] In both countries, progressive women sympathetic to the plight of mothers and children fashioned programs that were characterized by a maternalist sentiment. The protection of mothers and children was the main goal of these programs, rather than facilitating the access of women to work. Linda Gordon, writing about the U.S. experience, argued that the pioneers of welfare policy established a "needs-based program instead of a guarantee of support—an entitlement program—for single mothers who were either in the labor force or caring for children at home."[243] In Réunion, the high rate of unemployment transformed welfare into the single source of income for many families.[244] Communist and feminist women on the island continued to support these programs because they said—and data confirmed their argument—that withdrawing welfare would mean condemning women and children to greater poverty. Furthermore, the Union of Women of Réunion always insisted on the necessity of developing the economy of the island and of challenging men's sexism. It connected the demand for welfare—as a guarantee against utter poverty—with the struggle for an autonomous Réunion and women's emancipation.[245]

Mothers and children were the favorite couple of political demonology's iconography and discourse. The Creole man, as a father and an adult man, barely appeared in the pictures with Debré. Debré was with women and children, and when Creole men appeared, they served as the enthusiastic bearers of the *bon zorey* (good Frenchman). The pictures of Debré with women and children constructed a gentle and attentive man. Debré took the place of the father of Réunion's children, or of the Réunionnais *as* children. In a brochure celebrating Debré's accomplishments, *La Réunion, notre fierté*, all the pictures presented Debré with either women or children. This iconography of couples—Debré and women, or Debré and children—presented Debré as a man benevolent to women and children, as a lover, a husband, a father.

Debré, who had stubbornly opposed the liberalization of contraception and abortion in France,[246] saw the problem differently in Réunion. He wrote: "Since the first days of colonization, women of Réunion have heedlessly given birth. It was necessary. The island was empty, and the mortality rate high: masters and servants had to reproduce. There existed also the tradition of the provinces of France of encouraging large families, a tradition maintained by a vigilant clergy. And we shall not forget the natural lack of concern of Creoles in sexual matters."[247] However, the solution was not to give women free access to contraception. "For the future of the fatherland, a generation of men and women must leave behind a more numerous generation. A well balanced family is a family with many children."[248] Debré laid out the three aspects of his alternative plan for Réunion. The first was to develop contraception, as long as it was understood that contraception was acceptable only for a married couple. The second aspect was to develop better housing conditions because, Debré argued, "overpopulated homes have created among boys and girls the desire to escape the paternal roof. Finally, the hot tropical nights encourage a lack of concern for the consequences of sexual intercourse."[249] The third solution was to encourage emigration. Since the "door to Madagascar was closed," the metropole, which needed workers, was the logical destination. Women of Réunion were encouraged to give birth so that their children could serve as workers of France.

Debré, who had sworn that he would protect mothers from Creole men, claimed that he would also protect little girls against the communist seducer. On April 29, 1963, the newspaper *La Nation* published on its front page the picture of a little black girl with the legend: "This little girl, when she grows up, you want her to remain a woman of France. Then say: YES to France! YES to de Gaulle! YES to Debré! And reject the autonomy of Paul Vergès."[250] The little black girl was looking directly and very seriously at the reader. With her hat, she looked like a country girl, and she did not smile. There were no indications when and where the picture was taken. The little girl stood for all the little girls of Réunion.

What the picture said was that what was at stake in the forthcoming elections was the future of this generic little girl, as a citizen, but above all as a woman. Out of love for this child, this little girl, the epitome of what must be protected, the Réunionnais must make their choice. And the choice was simple: France, de Gaulle, and Debré,[251] or Vergès. On one side, a country, a nation, and two men. They did not have first names; their names were sacred, like the name of France, invested with a transcendent symbolical power. On the other side, the name of a man, Paul Vergès, linked to the term of autonomy. Vergès must be defeated so that this young girl, who would become a woman, would remain a "woman of France." The legend could be read thus: if Vergès is elected, this girl will never be a "woman of France." The expression "woman of France" signified "spouse of" (legal identity) as well as "French" (cultural and political identity). Yet the newspaper did not simply say "French." It was not so much the national identity of the little girl that was at stake but her incorporation into the masculine and patriarchal law. Her incorporation in the world as "woman"—that is, as "spouse," because her future was understood only within the patriarchal space of marriage and family—was dependent on the husband that Réunion voters would choose for her. It was understood that a woman could not make her own choice. The text said: "You want."

If the little girl did not remain a "woman of France," what kind of man would have her? The answer could be found in another conservative newspaper, *La Voix des Mascareignes*. The entire front page of the newspaper was taken up by two pictures. The picture at the top of the page showed Paul Vergès facing Khrushchev, then the general secretary of the Communist Party of the Soviet

Union, during an international congress of communist parties. The legend said: "THE CHOICE is ours. It is CLEAR. EITHER VERGES-KRUSHCHEV. That is ANTI-FRANCE and SLAVERY." The other picture showed Debré with de Gaulle, who was giving a military salute. The legend was: "OR Debré-De Gaulle that is LA FRANCE. Integration with LIBERTY. Women and men of Réunion! French we are, French we will remain." The choice that women and men of Réunion would make about the little girl was clear. If they voted Vergès, they condemned her to be a slave in the world of anti-France. Her future was grim: rape, abandonment, slavery. "Anti-France" was Russia, Asia, Moscow, and Beijing.

The body of the silent little girl was a hostage of sexual politics. Her innocent and virgin body was used to write a sexualized text. Who would mark her, the legend implied, make her a woman? Who would inscribe on her female body the masculine law? If she escaped the law that incorporated her into the world of patriarchal servitude, she could choose to be autonomous. The patriarchal and masculine order would be disrupted. An autonomous woman would make decisions about her own sexuality and her future. She could refuse to let political and sexual choices be made for her. The reinscription of sexual metaphors in the political debate revealed a deep anxiety among conservatives. They did not want to promote conjugality because they did not trust Creole men, yet they did not want women to be independent. Women were asked to live according to bourgeois norms while refusing sexual intercourse with men.

Through the configuration of a Réunionnais femininity protected by the Frenchman, the norms of masculinity were reconfigured as well. They were reconstructed along lines that stressed the contrast between Frenchmen and Creole men. The Frenchman was a good worker, a gentle man, a good and attentive lover, whereas the Creole man was violent, lazy, and inconstant.[252] The conservative discourse promoted a "modern," urban masculinity opposed to a backward, rural masculinity. Fanon has powerfully described how the colonized male body has been constituted as passive, as the target of white paranoia. Although Fanon's theory is deeply masculinist, it reminds us not to forget the ways in which colonialism used gender constructions to reinforce its hegemony. The discourse on women's rights "given" to Creole women (another debt)[253]—as emancipation had been "given" to the slaves—masked the new forms of repression and oppression exercised against women. The norms of femininity offered by the counter-subversive narrative made Creole women sexually available to Frenchmen. Naturalized as the exotic object of desire, the Creole woman turned to the Frenchman as her object of desire. Frenchmen in Réunion occupied a pivotal role in defining modes of behavior. The desirable family was modeled after the French family, represented by the zoreys, a father, a mother, two children, and domestic servants, rather than after the traditionally extended Réunionnais family. A discourse about the "pathology of the Creoles" emerged, defining a psychotic, violent, incestuous man and a victimized woman.

Poor, unemployed female and male Creoles were particularly targeted by countersubversive ideology in the 1960s and 1970s. They constituted a dangerous group. They were often sympathetic to the communists and their program of autonomy. Political and church repression, social control, and exploitation of fears and of traditional themes of Réunionnais culture intervened to re-discipline this dangerous class. Conservatives wanted a compliant poor, and then they decried the "welfare mentality" of the Creoles, the irresponsibility of Creole women who bore children even though they had no resources. This rhetoric was not imposed solely through repression. Its themes were adopted by an important part of the population. It fitted their vision of the world. This was a population that took pride in belonging to the "colony that colonizes," a population that had participated in the military "pacification" and colonization of Madagascar. It was a population sensitive to imperialist rhetoric who looked with racist contempt at Mauritians and Madagascans, who might be independent but were poor. Réunionnais were also poor, but compared to their neighbors, they felt that they belonged to the First World.[254]

Political demonology in Réunion produced an idiom of fear, a sense of insecurity, and reconfigured the dependence of the post-colony in terms of Cold War rhetoric. It was able to play on old fears and create new ones. It encouraged mediocrity and a lack of civil courage. Anonymity of attacks in newspapers and on radio became a rule. Conservatives refused the history of the island, its multiethnic, multicultural origin, and defended the ideal of a community defined by a French identity. When the hysteria of the Cold War started to wane, some terms were taken out of the conservatives' dictionary. France was now called *la métropole* rather than *La Mère-Patrie,* the new name suggesting a peaceful integration of peripheral regions yet harking back to a colonial vocabulary.

The strategies of discipline through ideology and force that informed the policies in the 1960s and 1970s opened the way for strategies of control. There were overlaps between these strategies. The 1970s brought new agents of integration: social workers, psychologists, and psychiatrists. The gendarme made room for the social worker and the psychiatrist. Two displacements occurred in the discourse about the Creoles. The familial metaphors of the Cold War family romance shifted. The meaningful ties were no longer between La Mère-Patrie and her colonized children, but among the members of the Creole family. The domestic family was now the focal unit, observed by the French psychiatrist, and the native mother became henceforth responsible for the pathological problems of the Creoles. The maternal and generous figure of La Mère-Patrie faded away, replaced by the Creole mother, who, psychiatrists would say, castrated her men—husbands and sons—and smothered her daughters. The second displacement was that the political analysis of dependence, which had been made by Réunionnais activists, gave way to a psychological analysis of dependence made by French psychiatrists.

5

Single Mothers, Missing Fathers, and

French Psychiatrists

On the evening of November 25, 1992, at the criminal court
of Saint-Denis, Réunion, Yves-Joseph Olivier was condemned to
eight years of imprisonment.[1] When the president of the tribunal
asked him if he wished to add something to his lawyer's defense,
Olivier said: "What?"[2] He did not seem to understand the question. The president repeated his question, and Olivier now answered: "No." In the morning, when the president gave the indictment, Yves O. had seemed as indifferent as he was when the jury
retired to decide his fate. He did not look at the president, nor at
his lawyer, but absently at the public. He had been in jail for a year,
and nobody had visited him.

Yves O. had killed his father, a crime that, legal and psychiatric
experts contend, happens more in Réunion than in any other metropolitan or overseas French department. The president narrated
the facts: On January 9, 1991, at 7:00 A.M., Yves's ninety-one-year-
old father had been found dead by his daughter. His death was the
result of head wounds inflicted by a rock. Yves was suspected at
once, because he was known to have fights with his father. Yves
later said that he had gone to his father to ask for some rum. The

father had refused, had threatened him with his cane, and insulted Yves's mother. Yves took the cane from his father, beat him with it, then picked up a rock and threw it with all his strength at the old man, who was lying on his bed. Once he realized his father was dead, Yves laid him on the floor, put a red cushion under his head, left the house, put the cane against the entrance door, and nailed the door shut.

The president drew a portrait of the couple of father and son in which the "normality" of the patriarch was set against the "abnormality" of the son. The family lived in a very small and remote village in the mountains of Salazes, La Mare à Citrons. The father, an illiterate poor *métis* Creole—part Indian, part white, part Madagascan—had started to work the land as an agricultural worker when he was twelve years old. Working hard, he had become a sharecropper, then a tenant farmer, and at the end of his life, he was finally able to buy a small piece of land. According to the president, the father was "hardworking, peaceful, and in good health. He provided his two daughters with a good dowry." If he was drinking, it was because he "needed some pleasure." Yves was born in 1954, the youngest of eight children. His parents entrusted him to his godmother's care when he was six months old. His mother died when he was three, and he suffered from meningitis when he was six. He was, according to the court report, "lazy, indulging in idleness, and alcoholic." He never had a sexual relationship, never lived with a woman. He used to burn the clothes that his sisters gave him. In 1988 he had been condemned to thirteen months for attacking his father with a knife. After presenting the act of accusation, the president turned to Yves and told him: "The society demands redress. You must tell us who you are, so we can judge you."

The interrogation did not shed much light on Yves O.'s action, because the defendant scarcely participated in his own trial. His answers often were inaudible, the result of a malformation of his mouth and a lack of teeth, as well as his use of a poor rural Creole. The president said: "You were doing nothing every day. Did you go dancing?" "No," answered Yves. "You were not clean, you were even repulsive to others. You sometimes wore a dress. Why was that? You burned the clothes that your sister gave you. Why? Were you jealous of your brothers and sisters?" "No." "What were you doing? Were you bored?" "No." "Was your father a bad father?" "No." "Was your father beating you?" "No." "Did he insult you?"

"No." "But the accusation says otherwise." "Sometimes yes, sometimes no." "What interests you in life?" "Soccer." "Your father, who was hardworking, who worked all his life, was he happy to see his son being so lazy?" "Sometimes yes, sometimes no." "You were supposed to follow psychotherapy after you tried to kill your father in 1988. Why did you not seize this chance?" "Well, no." "Do you think that you are weak?" "No." "Did you ever try to work the land?" "Sometimes yes." "Why did you not take your medicine?" "I do not know." "Why did you fight with your father?" "la têt té y block" [I was not thinking].

The psychiatric expert Jacques Denizot noted that Yves O., who had a "poor but coherent discourse, suffered from social rejection." His relation to his father was a "mixture of admiration and distrust." To the president's inquiry about the meaning of Yves O.'s response "la têt y block," Denizot answered: "This is because acting-out takes the place of reflection." The defendant "has no vocabulary to speak of his feelings, of his internal life, of his psychology. He speaks through metaphors, using the notions of Devil or Hell to speak of violence." Yves O. has experienced his "sense of being" essentially from "the others' gaze. He is unable to define himself by himself." Another psychologist declared that even though Yves had gone to school until age sixteen, he was illiterate. His life consisted in cooking for his father and drinking at the *boutik sinwa* (Chinese grocery store).[3] When he was at his father's home, he slept on the ground. He never expressed resentment against his life. Yves O. had an "infantile way of thinking, in which magic had great importance." He had a weak intellectual level, partly, the psychologist said, because Yves O.'s sociocultural origin was not stimulating. He had difficulties with "grasping reality," and when he felt "unprotected, he felt lost because his sense of inner security was very fragile." Aggression was not a fundamental element of his character. According to the psychologist, Yves O. had no desire to kill his father but wanted to intimidate him so that he would stop insulting his son. Yves O. was not loved, the psychologist concluded, either by his siblings or by the inhabitants of his village.

Once the experts had given their opinions, the president again asked Olivier to explain his act. The president asked: "What happened?" Silence from Yves O. "Why did you go to see your father?" "I was afraid." "Of what?" Silence. "Why did you beat him?"

Silence. "Did he insult you?" "Yes." "This angered you?" "Yes." "How many blows did you give?" Silence. "How many?" "I do not know, man." Yves O. barely acknowledged the questions; he often shrugged. His only explanation for his act was that he wanted to stop the voices that he heard in his head, and, among them, the reproaching voice of his father. His sister and brother, called as witnesses, answered in monosyllabic sentences, or more often with "I do not know." The district attorney, a Réunionnais, challenging the psychologist's and the psychiatrist's expertise, opened his statement with the sentence: "*Who* is Yves-Joseph Olivier?" He affirmed that Yves O. had no excuses for his crime and asked for a sentence of twelve years in jail. Article 64 of the Penal Code could not be applied to Yves O.[4] The defendant was hiding his criminal intent behind a fake mental illness. "Idleness is the root of all evils," the district attorney said. He stressed that "Yves Olivier had clearly expressed his resistance to reform." He had a "choice: to drink or not to drink; to work or not to work." The district attorney concluded that Olivier "is not mad. If he wants, he can refute what I say. He must learn to *control* himself because he knows that he is dangerous. Society is like an orchestra, in which everyone must play his part." The jury decided that Yves O. was responsible for the murder of his father, but they followed the district attorney's recommendation about the defendant's extenuating circumstances. "The island's history explains the extenuating circumstances of his crime. A part of the population, which did not wish to work for another group, went to live in the mountains. There was consanguinity among them and these people lived in terrible conditions for many years, without schools or any other social institutions."

Journalists, psychiatrists, and lawyers have remarked that criminal defendants often seem absent, indifferent, or resigned to their fate, unaware of the court's ceremonial. This behavior is intensified by the fact that most of them do not understand French, much less French legal vocabulary, and attend the debate passively. Yves O. was no exception, and throughout his trial he exhibited a "distraught look, smiling for no reason."[5] He spent his time chewing on pieces of paper that he had first put into his ears.

Yves O.'s trial was not merely the absurd scene of acting out the law in a French department where the majority of the population does not speak French and the judges do not speak or understand Creole. What made the trial even more remarkable was that it presented a matrix of discourses, legal, medical, cultural, and social, that took psychology as their principal reference. It was emblematic of a trend that emerged with the development of policies of social control on the island. The case of Yves Olivier displayed the features of the Creole drama, according to the medico-psychiatric experts: a pathology born of poverty, illiteracy, marginality, the inability to conceptualize, to express one's inner life in abstract terms, and a crime, said to be a common crime, parricide.

Michel Foucault has shown how, in France, with the advent of the psychiatric expert, "another truth penetrated the truth that was required by the legal machinery."[6] The question, Foucault said, was "no longer simply: 'Has the act been established and is it punishable?' But also: 'What is this act, what is this act of violence or this murder? To what level or to what field of reality does it belong? Is it a fantasy, a psychotic reaction, a delusional episode, a perverse action?' " The goal was no longer to "explain the action but to define the individual behind the action and to make the individual accept his or her punishment." Or, as the judge and the prosecutor implied at Yves O.'s trial, We must know you in order to judge you. You must participate in your own trial and knowingly accept your punishment, because otherwise our decision would lack legitimacy and the edifice of social order would be questioned.

Throughout Yves O.'s trial, the interventions of the president, the district attorney, the defense lawyer, the psychiatric expert, and the psychologist were a mixture of psychology and concern, of contempt and colonial assumptions about the defendant. They never were openly contemptuous and racist. These men, whose professions had made them part of Yves O.'s life, who were trying him, took their roles seriously. The president patiently and paternally tried to extract from Yves O. an explanation of his behavior. The psychiatrist and the psychologist translated the discourse of Yves O. into scientific terms. Yet there was a sense of absurdity. The formality of the legal scene could not totally hide the fact that, to a large extent, Yves O. was tried in absentia.

If I recount the essentially pathetic and sorrowful life of Yves O., it is not to make an apology for the criminal or to transform the criminal into the "true" Réunionnais. Rather, it is to look at the ways in which the lives of the poor métis of Réunion appear in psychiatric discourse. Their lives emerge in police and psychiatric reports, when they riot, or during the biannual session of the criminal court. Appalled by a "violence for no reason," by the "primary instincts" exhibited by this population,[7] judges, prosecutors, and Réunion's petite bourgeoisie suddenly make a note of their existence and condemn them in the name of morality and propriety. I do not seek to romanticize the crimes or the social violence of the poor Creoles, but I want to "understand the structure and discourse of a power that constructed its foundations upon their negation, while creating a network of institutions that has invaded their lives."[8]

The psychiatric order has occupied a special place in the social and political order of the postcolony of Réunion. Psychiatry, Octave Mannoni has written, "collaborates in the enterprise of isolating and excluding from society those who cannot obey the historically defined norms of propriety."[9] Its goal is to define a "utilitarian policy, whose intent is to protect the tranquillity of the majority, but also to inculcate in this majority a certain way of being reasonable."[10] The role of French psychiatrists in Réunion has been essentially to authenticate and certify the "illnesses" of the Creole soul and to inculcate a "certain way of being reasonable." Their goal has been to help track down the marginalized, the "abnormal" Creoles. They defined a pathology and designated the culpable: indigence, alcoholism, social and intellectual poverty, and matrifocality. They drew a portrait of the Réunionnais, of the dregs of society, of those who had to be expelled from society, committed to the asylum or put in jail. Tracked since infancy, the "abnormal" Creole became a figure of shame for a people forced to enter modernity on the run.

This reading of psychiatric discourse in Réunion takes as its "patients" the French psychiatrists. It is an observation of those who observe; it is an analysis of those who analyze; it is a reading of the texts of those who "translate" the utterances of the Réunionnais. This reading turns the gaze on those whose gaze has fixed the Creoles into a pathological group. It chooses to correlate facts that psychiatrists have chosen to organize as separate. It looks at the historical conditions of psychiatric discourse's formation that psychiatrists have chosen to ignore. Psychiatry, I contend, is a new form of cultural integration that uses scientific, objective language to construct a normativity. My mode of deconstruction is to trace its lines of filiation and to show how it adopts, in order to adapt to its own goals, theories that were both supporting *and* countering the colonialist's project. The genealogy of my research is by way of the writings of Octave Mannoni, who first directed the gaze on the colonizer's psychology; Frantz Fanon, who studied the psychology of racism in the colonial world; and Albert Memmi, who also insisted on the importance of the colonizer's psychology to explain the colonial relation. Psychiatric discourse has appropriated a one-sided reading of the Mannoni-Fanon-Memmi intervention. My own position turns that intervention on the French male psychiatrists themselves. Psychological discourse is deconstructed by way of psychoanalysis, from which it pretends to borrow concepts and notions.

The assumptions of contemporary psychiatry in the postcolony have their roots in two schools of psychology. One is the "psychology of colonization." In the early twentieth century, colonial administrators and doctors argued that a new field of psychology had to be created and developed to perfect military and administrative colonization. Knowledge of the natives' psyche would explain their resistance to Europeanization in psychological terms. Armed with this knowledge, colonial administrators would know better how to present certain decisions, how to adapt their discourse to the "native soul," and how to integrate native populations into the European project. The theoretical assumption of this psychology was that different peoples have different psyches, more or less sophisticated, more or less capable of abstract thinking and inner reflection. The other school of psychology is the critique of colonial psychology by people such as Mannoni, Fanon, and Memmi, and, related to this critique, the larger critique of psychiatry made by psychoanalysis.

Postcolonial psychiatry in Réunion is thus a mix of the assumptions of colonial psychology and of its critique. Although contemporary psychiatric discourse would like to appear free of any cultural bias, it has revealed itself to be the heir of colonial psychology. It has adopted among its assumptions the hierarchical opposition between prelogical and logical reason, between oral culture (and its alleged incapacity for grasping abstract ideas) and written culture, between scientific medicine and traditional medicine. But it has also integrated the critical vocabulary of anticolonial psychology. It has become fluent in the idioms of Mannonian and Fanonian psychology as well as Lacanian psychoanalysis, and its description of the dominated group has been informed by new approaches in the fields of anthropology and linguistics. The result has been a sophisticated discourse that blends colonial premises with Fanon's denunciation of colonial psychological wounds and Lacan's theory of the three orders. Fanon and Lacan are used and abused to fit the goal of postcolonial psychiatry, which has remained the assimilation of the Creoles into what is conceived to be a higher order of psychological development: a "modern self."

Jean-François Reverzy has argued that the Frenchman's attitude is the result of a *transfert insulaire* (island transference), the site of imaginary projections on human beings and their territory.[11] A successful psychotherapy of the Réunionnais means that the Réunionnais would want to acquire what is presented as a modern psyche: governed by reason, individualistic, turned toward Europe and its values. With this form of psychology, a displacement occurs: instead of looking at socioeconomic and historical reasons to explain the island's situation, authorities concentrate on the "Creole self" and its symptoms. "Creole pathology" has become a familiar referent in Réunion's public discourse. Psychologists and psychiatrists came to Réunion as part of the project of modernization and assimilation announced by the conservative assimilationists in the 1960s. Most of them were young men who had been influenced by the antiauthoritarian and anticolonialist atmosphere of French universities and trained in an era of critical theory. Although some became interested in the history of psychiatry on the island, they never openly contested the purpose of establishing psychological services in which the practitioners were Frenchmen and the patients were poor Réunionnais.

It is not surprising that social workers and psychiatrists now occupy an important place in the elaboration of public policy in Réunion. In the last twenty years, Réunion's society and economy experienced a deep transformation and reorganization. Between 1967 and 1993, the rate of unemployment grew from 13.2 to 37.9 percent.[12] More than one young person out of two was unemployed in 1993.[13] An important part of the population became recipients of welfare. Although Réunion's population represents only 1 percent of France's population, it is the recipient of 10 percent of the total Revenu Minimum d'Insertion (RMI), the financial aid offered to the poorest individuals by the French government after 1988. This population has provided a terrain for a group of experts, people who could describe and analyze its behavior, and, accordingly, prescribe social policies. Its existence has justified the function of the experts, who consequently need to maintain the "needy" population in existence.

The paradigm of progress that dominated the post-1960s era erased the suffering inherent in modernization. Psychiatry played a role in this modernization with a rhetoric that opposed a psyche belonging to a rural, masculine, spirit-filled, backward world in which the other is a potential persecutor, and a psyche belonging to a urban world, in which autonomous individuals have control over their inner life. The narrative of decolonization was no longer the narrative of political autonomy, but a narrative about access to consumption and commodities and about an individual desiring these commodities. Autonomy was no longer a political, social, cultural, and economic question, but a goal for an ahistorical "self." Every Réunionnais could now dream of owning a radio, a VCR, a television, and, most of all, a car. The end of the colonial world was the end of a rural world devoid of comfort and sophistication. Kristin Ross has eloquently shown that the post–World War II modernization of France was to a certain extent the Americaniza-tion of its culture.[14] The modernization of Réunion was its "franci-zation." In France, the figure associated with modernization was the *jeune cadre,* the engineer or executive. In Réunion, the role was performed by the French male civil servant. The site of identifica-tion with modernization was the middle-rank civil servant. In Mo-nique Boyer's autobiographical novel *Métisse,* the black father, whose grandmother was a slave, said to his children: "We are *owners!* I waited for this moment for so long!" His wife is heard to repeat over and over: "I always said that I would marry a civil servant."[15] To this white woman of an extremely poor mountain village, not unlike Yves O.'s village, marrying a postman, even a black one whom she despised, was an escape from poverty, the promise of financial safety, and access to a coveted social status.[16]

The modernization of conservative assimilation turned Ré-union's society upside down. It "depended first on the stabilization of the social order," which in Réunion meant, essentially, contain-ing the Communist Party and the peasants' and workers' unions.[17] But modernization also gave a majority of Réunionnais access to education, household amenities, travel, television. The island and its population became a new object of study and research, and Réunionnais themselves aspired to "understand" their society. They held seminars and workshops, published reviews and journals, in which the history, culture, and politics of the island were examined.[18] Among the discourses of knowledge, psychology seemed to offer a method of investigation that looked promising. Psychological theories could apparently explain the violent and self-destructive acts of the Réunionnais without turning to racist hypotheses. Against a racial and culturalist history, psychology supported the argument that colonized people experienced mental problems because of a past of slavery and colonialism, which wounded their psyche, shattered their world, and subjugated them to physical harm and mental anguish. Yet the way this history was acknowledged, paradoxically, perpetuated its denial.

French psychiatry argued that Réunionnais reveled in dwelling on their past and therefore were unable to turn toward the future and enter modern culture. To say that the Réunionnais' attachment to their past exhibited an inability to enter modernity and culture revealed the desire for forced assimilation behind the psychiatric project. The history adopted by the French psychiatrists has been an "amnesiac history," which has dismissed a popular memory, inhabited by the ghosts of the past—slaves, maroons, social bandits. It has tried to transform a popular memory into a neurotic symptom. At the trials against rioters in 1992, judges and prosecutors spoke of a crowd in which "primary instincts" were unleashed, of youngsters lacking a father figure and therefore seduced by a life of crime. Urban uprisings, which were a response to years of impoverishment and neglect, were denounced as "rioting for fun and profit." Since psychiatrists defined the sources of the Réunionnais' symptoms and delimited their boundaries, the psychiatrists' version of history justified their own intervention. The victims now needed their healers, the psychiatrists. The construction of a postcolonial pathology legitimated the psychiatrists' presence and their expertise. As Foucault has argued, the "power that the asylum gives to the psychiatrist will be justified (as well as being masked as a primordial power) through the production of phenomena which can be integrated into medical science."[19]

Despite a real transformation of social life, modernization left in its wake thousands of people. Education has remained so foreign to the island's language and culture that every year thousands of schoolchildren leave school barely literate. In the last fifty years, in place of economic development, there has been a development of a network of social services, with its array of workers, its hierarchy, its discourse, and its ideal. Among its members, psychiatrists have occupied the top of the hierarchy, and their discourse has become a source of reference for journalists, commentators, judges, psychologists, and social workers. This combination—a poor population and its experts, the psychiatrists—was made possible by the French policy toward the unemployed, the marginalized, and the poor. The metropolitan "dangerous classes" experienced a similar deployment of social services to help, contain, and control them. That the majority of psychiatrists and psychologists are Frenchmen raises the question of neocolonialism. These men occupy, through their functions, social and financial status, and manipulation of scientific concepts, a position not unlike those of colonial administrators: they write about the natives, present themselves as authorities on the natives, and construct metropolitan academic careers on their (post)colonial experience.

Yet, though discipline and assimilation appear to be its main goals, psychiatric discourse contains some observations about the Creoles that cannot be dismissed as mere fantasies. It presents some "truths" about the Creoles: they tend to kill their best friends and fathers, they rape, they seem to express no remorse, they show a tendency to enjoy heavy drinking; women are often single mothers. As Colette Guillaumin has argued: "The activity of categorization is *also* an activity of knowledge. This explains the ambiguity of the struggle against stereotypes and the unexpected discoveries brought by this struggle. The activity of categorization brings knowledge *and* oppression."[20] The reader of Réunion's newspapers would be inclined to agree with the psychiatric diagnosis, for story after story tells of the "frequent criminality, the triviality of the motives, the murderous and always very bloody nature of the brawls" of the Creoles.[21] The critique of French psychiatry in the postcolony requires thus that a distinction be made between the social and political function of psychiatry in the postcolonial territory on the one hand, and the relevance of clinical observations on the other. It is nonetheless impossible to isolate a psychiatric discourse from its historical and cultural formation.

There was a tradition in psychiatry of looking at criminals as biologically and racially deficient from a norm. This tradition traveled to the empire. Colonial doctors were as fascinated by the "psyche" of the natives as their metropolitan colleagues were by the "psyche" of the metropolitan deviants. In the early years of the twentieth century, the interest in the natives' psyche was transformed into a field of scientific studies. The military doctor Antoine Porot, who opened the first psychiatric hospital in Tunisia and went on to create in 1913 the first mental health service of colonial Algeria, became the leader and the theorist of the psychiatrist "School of Algiers," which lasted through the 1950s. He built his reputation on theses about the specificity of "Algerian criminality."[22] His conclusions were that "the Algerian" was more prone to commit blood crimes than other peoples, that "the Algerian" killed savagely and for no reason, that he had no inner life and was naive and susceptible in the extreme, and finally that his verbal expression was reduced to a minimum. The Muslims, Porot wrote, were credulous and degenerate; they showed a weakness of moral and affective life and an innate difficulty with introspection.

Porot's diagnosis, which could be explained by the predominance of neurological psychiatry and the influence of the theory of degeneration, has surprisingly resurfaced in the French neocolonies, despite its obvious obsolescence. This is possible because Réunion is still a dependent territory and French colonial racism has never been fully explored.[23] French psychiatry offers an explanation that seems grounded in the history and culture of the island: magic exists, the family is often female-headed, passivity and fatalism appear to be recurrent behavior among the Creoles, and the language is considered a poor dialect by the legal and medical authorities. A critique of psychiatric discourse requires that we turn to anthropological, linguistic, and historical research to question the assumptions of psychiatry in the postcolony. It demands as well a dialogical position, a readiness to question one's assumptions and projections.

In contrast to political discourses that claim to say what is good for Réunion and to wield the truth about the needs and desires of the community, psychiatry has claimed to present only a scientific truth. When a political discourse presents what it affirms to be good, everyone can give an opinion, contest the grounds on which the claims are made. But a scientific hypothesis claims to be made on neutral scientific grounds, and its conclusions are supposed to be contested by authorities in the scientific domain. It contests the right of the nonscientific to question its assumptions. French psychiatry in Réunion professes to have scientifically observed the

Creoles' behavior and to present an objective truth about their psyche. Psychiatric discourse covertly gives moral references about the way Réunionnais ought to be. The political question in Réunion is "What is good for *us?*" The psychiatric question is "What is good for *them?*" and French psychiatrists contend that they have the answer. To deconstruct the foundations of the psychiatric discourse is to retrieve the genealogy of its diagnosis.

Although I focus on psychiatric discourse, I want to make it clear that there are "in the wings, mute technologies that determine or short-circuit the institutional scene."[24] As Michel de Certeau has argued, "popular (minuscule and daily) procedures play with the mechanisms of discipline," constructing a "counterdiscipline." Réunionnais are not dupes and have often understood the functions of the judge and the psychiatrist. The evasive answers of Réunionnais, said to be the manifestation of their "inability to explore their psychological world," may express their indifference to the psychiatrist's endeavor. What is diagnosed as "sadness and withdrawal may be the result of deciding not to be heard. An agitation may be the expression of fear and anger at not being understood. A tendency to somatize may be the attempt to speak through the body, a language that the psychiatrist should learn."[25] The Réunionnais anthropologist Jacqueline Andoche and the psychologist Yolande Govindama have shown how non-European epistemes about health exist among the population.[26] In the "nocturnal realm," the Creole domain par excellence,[27] a network of practices, removed from the zoreys' gaze, presents a different world from the assimilated, policed diurnal world. These strategies of resistance exist in the margins, in the underground, in the dark of the night. The Réunionnais consults the psychiatrist among other "doctors of the soul," Tamil, Muslim, Yab, Kaf, healers, mixing the diverse diagnostics, taking the diverse medicine. But when confronted with the administration, the Réunionnais is under the gaze of the psychiatrist, whose diagnostic is authoritative.

With its arguments that people have different psyches, different access to language and power to symbolize, to describe inner states, feelings, and sufferings, psychiatry seeks to provide a new vocabulary to designate suffering. The reasons for the specificity of the Creole psyche can be found, many experts have argued, in two interrelated phenomena: the métis origin of the population and the matrifocal family. The former creates confusion about the individual's origins, a confusion leading to a lack of psychological foundations and a weakness of the sense of "self." The latter hinders, psychiatrists contend, individuation, or the possibility for the individual to separate from her or his first object of love, the mother. Together, *métissage* and matrifocality block the access of the individual to language and the law. I want to argue that there is a relation between the notion of blood purity, which informed the idea of community defended by nineteenth-century writers and scientists, and a certain conception of selfhood that stresses wholeness. Racial theories constructed an individual whose purity of blood guarantees a balanced and healthy personality and character; a certain psychological discourse constructs an individual whose mono-ethnic filiation guarantees mental health. The filiation between colonial blood politics and postcolonial psychiatry must be made.

Psychology of Colonization

The Third Republic built its ideology of social regeneration as a response to what it saw as a moral decline in the Second Empire and the military defeat in the 1870 Franco-Prussian War. But it was above all the Commune of Paris that gave the Third Republic the background against which the bourgeoisie built its ideal of the good citizen. In the aftermath of the Paris Commune, "psychological" interpretations of the revolutionaries informed the politics of counterinsurgency.[28] The communards were deviants whose alcoholism had pushed them toward destruction and revolution. The transformation of industry, and therefore of the working class, the project of turning "peasants into Frenchmen,"[29] colonial expansion, the development of social sciences, but also of anti-Semitism, the Dreyfus affair, and the theories about nation and race constituted the stage for the psychological theories of social behavior. Historians have noted the importance of these foundations to understanding the development of the asylum as a place in which individuals dangerous to social order are put out of harm's way. The historian Robert Nye has shown how, toward the beginning of twentieth century, the entire focus was no longer on "seeking to determine simply whether an individual deserved punishment for his crime or cure for his illness," but on determining the degree of danger or threat to society posed by an individual. The "criterion for incarceration or internment ought no longer to be responsibility but 'dangerousness.' "[30] The unification of continental France into a monolingual, monocultural society demanded the repression of regional cultures and beliefs. The school and the army were the institutions in which peasants and workers were made into French citizens. As Daniel Pick has said, "the medico-psychiatric theory of degeneration was a symptom of and a putative solution to a massive uncertainty in the terms of social representation."[31] A new racism was born when the theory about heredity coupled with the psychiatric theory of degeneration.[32]

At the turn of the nineteenth century, the goal of the *psychologie des peuples* was to define a relation between race, culture, and the psyche of the colonized natives. Its approach was influenced by the writings of sociologists and psychologists who had been concerned with finding a link between a social formation and "criminality and revolt, alcoholism and social anarchy."[33] Their subjects of study had been the French working class, the poor peasantry, and the vagrants. These groups were said to be prone to excesses and to display a pathology of degeneration that should be studied in order to deploy preventive strategies. Social psychology was concerned with the consequences of "racial memory," the inherited dissatisfactions said to be "capable of shaking the nation and threatening its healthy body." The study of the symptoms of "racial memory" would expand the understanding of the dynamics of social groups.[34]

Benedict Augustin Morel, in his work *Traité des dégénérescences physiques, intellectuelles et morales de l'espèce humaine* (1857), claimed to describe the "mode of production of degenerated beings, their classification, hygiene and treatment."[35] To men such as the psychologist Hippolyte Taine, the notion of "racial memory" explained that "the normally quiescent subject was overcome by the visual and linguistic experience, thrown back in psychological terms to the evolutionary past."[36] Atavism was the reason for revolution, which bequeathed the process of degeneration. Psychology and psychiatry were developed as sciences to study the "pathology of the dangerous classes."[37] The opposition between the normal and the pathological was tied to the notion that there was a relation among personality, character, anatomy, and racial signs. Race moved from being a "purely biological category to a purely psychological one."[38] French psychology was developed under two approaches, one that owed to Morel the theory about the relation between degeneration, heredity, and madness, and the other that gave psychiatric knowledge a role in the legal system. Article 64 of the *Code Napoléon* situated madness and criminal acts under the control of psychiatry: "There is no crime nor offense when the defendant is in a state of mental disorder during the act, or if he has been under duress." The second legal decision that located madness under the authority of psychiatric knowledge was the 1838 law that allowed the "voluntary or forced institutionalization" of mental patients.

Gustave Le Bon, in *Les Lois psychologiques de l'évolution des peuples* (1894),[39] developed the notion of "psychological race," which was in direct lineage with Gobineau's racist theory and influenced a generation of psychologists. Le Bon made a connection between gender and race, arguing that the "proof of female inferiority, and of similarities between women and Negroes, was provided by craniology."[40] To him, "each people possesses a mental constitution which is as fixed as its anatomical characters," and "each individual is not only the product of his parents, but also, and in fact above all, of his race, or, in other words, of his ancestors."[41] Race was imprinted on memory. Léopold de Saussure pursued Le Bon's approach in his *La Psychologie de la colonisation française dans ses rapports avec les sociétés indigènes* (1899). De Saussure opposed the "moral ideal of assimilation" because it did not "take into account racial heredity":

The acquisition of shared mental characteristics creates veritable "psychological races." The psychological characteristics are as stable as the anatomic characteristics, upon which a classification of the species was made. Psychological characteristics are reproduced, with regularity and constancy, like anatomic ones, through heredity.[42]

The psychiatric theory of degeneration was contested by Freud, who wrote:

Psychiatry, it is true, denies that such things mean the intrusion into the mind of evil spirits from without; beyond this, however, it can only say with a shrug: "Degeneracy, hereditary disposition, constitutional inferiority!" Psychoanalysis sets out to explain these uncanny disorders; it engages in careful and laborious investigations, devises hypotheses and scientific constructions, until at length it can speak thus to the ego: "Nothing has entered into you from without; a part of activity of your own mind has been withdrawn from your knowledge and from the command of your will."[43]

Because they took into account the diversity of cultures, the analyses of the *psychologie des peuples* paradoxically appeared to be more attentive to non-European peoples than the colonial universalist project was. Yet their project was imperial as well, since they insisted on the hierarchy of cultures.[44] Difference was the sign of inequality. The notion developed by Durkheim of "collective representations"—culture, language, institutions—and of their importance in the structuring of individual consciousness was applied by Lucien Lévy-Bruhl to the system of thought of "primitive peoples." In *La Mentalité primitive* (1922),[45] Lévy-Bruhl declared that the "primitive mentality" ought to be studied as a "whole conceptual system, that regulates the ways of thinking, feeling, and acting of primitive peoples, and gives them sense and logic."[46]

The advocates of a psychology of colonization borrowed from Lévy-Bruhl his critique of universalism. They argued that it was necessary to learn about the traditions, language, and culture of native societies and endorsed a psychology that borrowed its facts from ethnological studies. They advocated the education of native mediators and informers for the dissemination of psychological knowledge. In 1912 Dr. Reboul and Dr. Régis spoke in favor of training colonial psychiatrists, elaborating legislation that would take into account local conditions, constructing asylums in the empire, and creating a network of psychiatric assistance adapted to local needs.[47] Although colonial psychologists wanted to base their studies on clinical observations, their biases led them to conclusions that ultimately argued a constitutional inferiority of the colonized.[48] The psychology of colonization competed with the other components of the colonial discourse because it subscribed to a progressive assimilation through seduction rather than through a subjugation by force. The *Revue de Psychologie des Peuples,* founded in 1946, offered a forum to its promoters. Published by the Institute of Sociology on the Economy and Psychology of Peoples, based at Le Havre, an important harbor and place of trade for the French colonial empire, the review, along with texts about psychology, carried advertisements for shipping companies, companies that sold "exotic woods," and other businesses trading with the colonies.[49]

In July 1947, Georges Hardy published in the *Revue de Psychologie des Peuples* a very influential article entitled "La psychologie des populations coloniales." Hardy, who was a colonial administrator, a member of the Académie des Sciences Coloniales, and a prolific writer, pursued throughout his life the goal of defining a coherent and detailed psychology of the races.[50] He criticized the ways in which "primitive populations"—whom he preferred to call *populations attardées* (backward populations)—have been studied: "Everything is judged in the light of one criterion of civilization, which has never been clearly defined, and which expressed only a naive egocentrism."[51] Hardy called for a "new exploration of Africa, Asia, and Oceania" to investigate "the native soul."[52] A "colonization without psychology would only be violence without a future." Hardy criticized the notion of "Negro soul" or "Muslim soul," because, he wrote, the differences between individuals were too great to justify such generalizations.

How is it possible that we stubbornly believed in the virtues of assimilation, when the colonial populations, and even those who are sincerely claiming their close ties with France, are passionately asserting their personalities and refuse any form of fusion? A better study of their psychology would have told us this sooner.[53]

Hardy, who preferred the notion of "ethnic family" to the notion of "race," lobbied for the union of psychology and politics in the colony. Such a union would enhance the understanding and cooperation between peoples:

We saw barbarism in the ideas and practices different from our own, and we were convinced that to throw a European light on these shadowy parts would be sufficient to modify them. We had to renounce this form of colonization, because the souls of the native populations, even when those who appeared to submit, have continued to move in their familiar atmosphere, and, by opposition to us, have adopted a different consciousness.

Colonization has progressively rejected the forms of subjugation which, in its beginnings, transformed its enterprise into a modern form of enslavement. Now, colonization does not rely solely on force. It has transformed domination into tutelage; it has proposed, as its ends, association, reciprocal trust, and now colonization dreams of grafting European buds on these exotic roots. Colonization must know well the human groups on which it is working and psychology has become a preparatory school whose necessity is evident.[54]

Hardy's work exemplified the theoretical approach of the psychology of colonization, its positivism and its assimilative project. It announced ethnopsychiatry and its culturalism, and it constructed a matrix from which colonization was justified. Hardy's claims of scientific objectivity, his apparently sincere respect for other cultures, and the vocabulary of psychology gave to his project a legitimacy that the colonial discourse of conquest had not been able to reach. The conquering soldier ceded his place to the psychologist, militaristic rhetoric to humanist rhetoric. The land had been conquered; the soul of the native was the new territory to map and describe. Colonial psychology produced an idiom whose scientific terminology was easily adopted by the medical profession.[55]

Marius and Ary Leblond, the Réunionnais writers and the creators of the "Creole myth," were extremely influenced by the psychology of colonization. Their writings on Madagascar contained the familiar tropes, the notions of a native "soul" and a language that could not symbolize: "To the intonations of the language corresponds, in the Malagasy spirit, the incapacity to express ideas in a direct way."[56] The Leblonds looked at Réunion's practices of magic, at the *monde de la nuit,* the world of the spirits, but also of slaves' conspiracies, with their characteristic attitude of fascination and repulsion. The Leblonds' goal was to civilize the descendants of the slaves, construct a "serviceable citizen,"[57] and conquer the monde de la nuit. In *Ulysse Cafre, histoire dorée d'un noir* (1924), the world of the spirits was defeated. "The priests teach the children of the Night about the God of Light, and the schoolteacher shows them the Sun of Education, which shines for all. They rush up to mass and to school; they say their prayers and their lessons. To the Whites, the Day . . . But to the Blacks, the Night!"[58] In contrast to Hardy, who supported a form of indirect colonial rule—separation of groups in the name of respect for the differences of psyches—the Leblonds supported assimilation through psychological assimilation. The colonized, whose psyche was the psyche of a child, would acquire through assimilation the psyche of the adult, as well as abstract thinking, emotions, feelings. Hardy, for his part, thought that the colonized were already "adults," with cultural and psychological representations of their own. Studying and understanding these representations while respecting them would facilitate colonization.

The conclusions of the psychology of colonization rested on a series of observations and assumptions. On the one hand, it asked the vexed question about the relationship between culture and the psyche: did culture determine the psyche, or were there universal human psychological mechanisms? On the other hand, it proposed a series of features characterizing the colonized: a poor language, and consequently an inability to conceptualize, a faith in magic, a belief in spirits, fatalism, credulity, and mimicry. Its objects of study were the natives, whose atavistic psychological features made them "natural" criminals and permanent children. Psychological theories developed in the United States opted for similar descriptions to argue the psychological inferiority of blacks. The psychiatrist John E. Lind wrote in 1916 about blacks: "The precocity of children, the early onset of puberty, the *failure to grasp subjective ideas,* the strong sexual and herd instincts with the few inhibitions, the *simple dream life,* . . . the low resistance to such toxins as syphilis and alcohol, the sway of superstitions, all these and many other things betray the savage heart beneath the civilized exterior."[59]

The colonial relation was conceptualized as an unequal relation, in which the colonizer paternally led the colonized to adulthood and psychological maturity. The rhetoric of paternal benevolence masked a policy of death and dispossession. Colonial psychologists claimed to "describe" what they "saw." They were accurately reproducing the utterances and gestures of the colonized. Their scientific gaze was a guarantee of neutrality and objectivity. Their language was "charged with a double function: with its value as precision, it establishe[d] a correlation between each sector of the visible and an expressible element that corresponde[d] to it as accurately as possible; but this expressible element operate[d], within its role as description, a denominative function, which, by its articulation upon a constant, fixed vocabulary, authorize[d] comparison, generalization, and establishment within a totality."[60]

The Decolonization of Colonial Psychology

A definitive departure from the dominant view of the psychology of the colonial relation was proposed after World War II.[61] Starting with Octave Mannoni, the new approach was characterized by the belief that the colonial relation was one that "chained the colonizer *and* the colonized into an implacable dependence."[62] There was a shift in focus, and the colonizer's motives were analyzed. Colonizers had gone to the colonies not with benevolent intent but because they were seeking a facile position of racial, economic, and political privilege. Their psychological complexes made them perfect colonizers; they arrived in a country that had been militarily conquered and found, awaiting them, a social function, cheap labor, and sexual and economic privileges. Being a colonizer brought invaluable narcissistic benefits. Fanon remarked that the "white colonial is motivated only by a desire to put an end to a feeling of unsatisfaction on the level of Adlerian overcompensation."[63] The couple colonizer/colonized was not what the psychology of colonization had construed: an unselfish individual moved by the desire to uplift the backward and lazy native. The colonial relation was now understood dynamically. The portrait of the colonized as lazy, criminal, and dumb was a construction of the colonizer's projections and anxieties. There was no truth to it other than the need to rationalize racial and political subjugation. The colonizer's violence was not a hereditary trait but the result of the psychological violence of the colonial relation.[64] The new theories cast suspicion on the long-held opinion that there was one road to "psychological development" that mirrored the "European psyche," and that there was a psychological solution to the political and economic situation produced by colonialism. Yet these new theories insisted on a psychological analysis of the colonial relation, for this relation had been translated into metaphors, tropes, iconographic material, whose content and consequences exceeded a strictly political analysis of conflictual forces. The colonial relation had been suffused with images of sexuality, bodies, and family relations.[65] As Fanon said, the "problem of colonialism includes not only the interrelation of objective historical conditions but also human attitudes toward these conditions."[66] Psychology, it was said, could be a weapon against colonial psychology.

Mannoni, who served as a colonial administrator in the French colony of Madagascar for twenty years, collaborated in *Revue de Psychologie des Peuples* and *Psyché*, in which he explored the "Madagascan personality" from a psychoanalytical perspective.[67] The object of his research was to show the "existence of a long misunderstanding in inter-racial relations." To Mannoni, a "colonial situation is essentially characterized by the fact that the difference of structure among personality types is greater than in any other situation."[68] Since, according to him, social structures were in agreement with the individual's personality, Mannoni drew conclusions about the Madagascan personality from his observations of their customs, social organizations, and traditions, and their relations with the colonizer. The French psychoanalyst contrasted the prescription for autonomy of the Western individual to the continuous dependence of the Madagascan. If the dictum for the Western individual was "You will leave your father and mother," for the Madagascans it was "You will remain with your father and mother."[69]

In 1948 Mannoni finished a book that expanded on the remarks he had made in his previous articles. The book, published in 1950 in Paris with the title *Psychologie de la colonisation,* generated considerable controversy. Written when France was experiencing the loss of its colonial empire, the book was read by its critics as an apology for colonialism. Mannoni, though he wrote that self-understanding was an "essential preliminary for all research in the sphere of colonial affairs," offered no details about his life in Madagascar and his functions.[70] He was the head of the information services of the colony and was present during the 1947 anti-colonialist Madagascan rebellion, one of the "bloodiest episodes of colonial repression," which resulted in more than 100,000 deaths among the Madagascans. About the rebellion, Mannoni said only that it was as if a "veil was torn aside and for a brief moment a burst of dazzling light enabled one to verify the series of intuitions one had not dared to believe in."[71] Mannoni's thesis was that colonization was the encounter between two neurotic personality types that supported each other. The European going to the colony would become, Mannoni argued, regardless of his former self, a "typical colonial," that is, a racist and mediocre person.[72] "No one becomes a real colonial who is not impelled by infantile complexes which were not properly resolved in adolescence."[73] Colonizers presented a "grave lack of sociability combined with a pathological urge to dominate,"[74] an urge "which is infantile in origin and which social adaptation has failed to discipline."[75] Colonial life was "simply a substitute for those who are still obscurely drawn to a world without men—to those, that is, who have failed to make the effort

necessary to adapt infantile images to adult reality."[76] The colonizer's world lacked "awareness of the world of Others, a world in
which Others have to be respected."[77] The European colonial had
fled a world in which "his misanthropy, melancholy, sense of guilt
towards his father, projection of his faults on to others, [and] repressed affection for a daughter whose sex he preferred to ignore"
could not find a favorable terrain.[78] There was no "inferiority complex of the colored races," but a "dependence complex."[79] The
dependence complex constructed between the colonizer and the
colonized a web of ties in which the colonized felt entitled to the
protection of the colonizer. Withdrawing this protection would
lead to resentment and violence. So long as dependence was maintained, social peace would be preserved in the colony. The anthropologist Maurice Bloch, an expert on Madagascar, challenged
Mannoni's claims about French colonial policies in Madagascar
and Madagascan mores and culture.[80] What was more prejudicial
to Mannoni's argument, Bloch argued, was his lack of "any real
basis for his evaluation of the psyche either of the French colonials
or of the Madagascans."[81] Mannoni, who did not speak Malagasy
properly, further misunderstood many of the cultural and social
features of Madagascan pluri-ethnic society.[82]

Mannoni was also criticized for his reduction of colonial history
to the expression of psyches, making psychology the science of
history. Bouillon argued that Mannoni's theoretical lineage was the
positivism of colonialists such as Emile Caillet, who had, in 1926,
published *Essai de Psychologie du Hova*.[83] Caillet claimed that the
position of subjection, inherent to the Madagascan's psyche, had to
be transferred to the European colonizer so that the colonial conquest would be completed.[84] Mannoni's essay ended up belonging to a discourse in which colonization and its discontents were
analyzed as symptoms of psychological behavior, and in which
psychology was supposed to offer new methods for colonial administration. Mannoni was careful to insist that colonization had
economic and political reasons, but he offered ambiguous conclusions. Once he had presupposed that there was a Madagascan essence to which French colonization had precisely answered, Mannoni's essay could easily be read as an apology for colonization. It
was in his 1966 article "The Decolonization of Myself" that Mannoni finally reflected on his 1950 study.[85] Mannoni wrote that he
would no longer use the term *dependence,* for it put too much

emphasis on the Madagascans, whereas he intended to "describe a situation in which both 'natives' and Europeans were involved." He would also try to understand the strength of the anticolonialist forces, which he had neglected. Yet these were details compared to analyzing why he had sought a "purely psychological explanation to the problems and difficulties born of colonization."

This is where I must pursue the decolonization of myself—in an attempt to discover at what point I had neglected or rejected a crucial element in the situation. The fact is, no doubt, that every attempt to find a solution in the destruction of racism, inevitably leads on to a universalist theory: namely, that all men are essentially alike, just as they are all supposedly endowed with an immortal soul. Here what is in fact only the optimistic denial of the terms of the problem is presented as its solution.[86]

Toward the end of *Prospero and Caliban,* Mannoni warned his readers: "We cannot draw political conclusions or deduce a method of administration from psychological analyses; they simply do not warrant such use."[87] The only "genuine collective psychotherapy," Mannoni added, "is what is known as politics."[88] Mannoni's dilemma, to turn to psychology to understand human relations in a colonial situation yet to affirm that the solution to colonialism was political and not psychological, haunted postwar psychological analyses of colonial relations. It was a dilemma, because though it was clear that psychology shed light on personality structures in a situation of racial inequality, a situation in which mediocre Europeans could acquire wealth and status more easily than in their own country, it could not help resolve the problems and difficulties of the colonial relation.

The most violent attack on Mannoni's thesis came from a young Martinican psychiatrist, Frantz Fanon.[89] In his first book, *Peau noire, Masques blancs,* Fanon rejected Mannoni's conclusions with the argument that "all forms of exploitation resemble one another. . . . All forms of exploitation are identical because all of them are applied against the same 'object': man."[90] Colonial racism was therefore "no different than any other racism," and whites had gone to the colony not because of an "inferiority complex" but because it was "possible for them to grow rich quickly there." Fanon, who was not consistent in his criticism of Mannoni and read him selectively, wanted essentially to challenge an interpretation of colonial violence that tended to transform this violence into expressions of the colonized's fantasies. Fanon had a point, since *Psychology of Colonization* was written after the violent repression of the Madagascan rebellion in 1947. Yet he also subscribed to Mannoni's psychological approach to the colonial relation, and Fanon's goal was similar, to "explain that in the *psychoanalytic* sense the colonial situation generates a unique set of social relationships."[91] Mannoni and Fanon were both convinced that an economic explanation could not fully comprehend the dynamics of the colonial relation and that a partly conscious, partly unconscious set of symbols shaped that relation.[92] Yet Fanon had a greater ambivalence than Mannoni toward psychoanalysis and its ability to explain racism and the colonial relation. Fanon wrote, "Indeed, I believe that only a psychoanalytical interpretation of the black problem can lay bare the anomalies of affect that are responsible for the structure of the complex," but he added that the "black's man alienation is not an individual question. Beside phylogeny and ontogeny stands sociogeny." Fanon often contradicted himself, stressing both the importance of psychoanalysis for understanding colonial relations and its inability to explain colonial and racial relations; he insisted that the neuroses of the Negro were socially determined while giving examples of sources of neurosis that were not social. Fanon wrote: "Psychoanalysis is a pessimistic view of man. The care of the person must be thought of as a deliberately optimistic choice against human reality."[93]

The division of the colonial subject was located, for Fanon, in the split created by racism. The male colonial subject was divided between a white image (the white mask) and a black subjectivity (the black skin). The way to end this division, which Fanon often called "hallucination," was for the black man to understand that he was "his own foundation." The Martinican wanted to build a "new humanism," a world in which differences of color would not have cultural and social consequences. Fanon situated the division of the colonial subject in the social world. What happened in infancy, between the Antillean mother and her child, who seemed to have no sexual identity, produced a sense of fusion and safety. It was the white world that made the "Negro." Fanon fully embraced Jean-Paul Sartre's analysis in *Réflexions sur la question juive*, in which Sartre affirmed that "it is the antisemite that makes the Jew."[94]

To explain why the black adopted a white mask, Fanon borrowed Jacques Lacan's notion of the mirror stage.[95] To Lacan, the mirror stage allows the subject to realize a specular unity of the ego where the other has no place: "In this world, we will see, there is no other."[96] The subject restores the lost unity of the self (a fictional unity), a unity experienced through the symbiotic relation with the mother. This specularity is, Lacan said, the most intuitive form of affective unity, of identity. "What the subject salutes in this representation is the mental unity that is inherent in this very representation."[97] Fanon argued that "only for the white man is the other perceived on the level of the body image, absolutely as the not-self—that is, the unidentifiable, the unassimilable."[98] When the (white) subject experiences anxiety and suspicion, oneness is threatened, the "Other takes a hand," and the fantasy of the Negro as "murderer" intervenes.[99] There is hallucination, and the subject, instead of seeing his own imago in the mirror, sees the imago of the Other, who is black and threatening (because of the "white collective unconscious").[100] In the Fanonian approach, the Other for the white *must* be black, and vice versa, because of the dialectic that Fanon embraces: the Other is the *hallucinated* projection in the mirror of what the subject desires and rejects—the woman for the man; the Jew for the anti-Semite; the black for the white. The self is constituted by the look of the Other: *L'autre me voit donc je suis.*[101] The Other *is* the mirror in which one sees oneself. With this approach, the "consciousness of the other can be satisfied only by Hegelian murder."[102] In Fanonian psychology, difference can only be invidious, and the unconscious is the negative of consciousness; it masks the consciousness. The goal is therefore to destroy the white mask on black consciousness. Behind the mask is the truth.

Fanon disavowed the Creole filiation: the enslaved father and the raped mother could not be his parents.[103] To Fanon, emancipation was the recovery of a wounded masculinity. In Algeria, Fanon found the virile male that would belie the colonial construction of emasculated masculinity. With the Algerian nationalist fighter, Fanon found a man whose masculinity had been wounded but who had, in contrast to the black man of the Antilles, the courage to attack the castrating master, the Frenchman, and to castrate him in return. Albert Memmi has argued that for Fanon, "identification with the Algerian fatherland replaced an impossible identification with the Martinican fatherland."[104] To Fanon, the Antilleans were caught in the realm of the Imaginary. The relation to the Other was skewed because the Other was always the white who occupied the position of the Symbolic, of language, and of the Law. And it was the native mother who had hindered the subject's access to a black authentic Symbolic. Fanon spoke of "lactation," or nursing by the mother, to designate the alienated desire for whiteness. The mother impregnated the child through her milk with the alienated desire for whiteness.[105] Fanon derided the Martinicans' struggle and declared to a friend in 1958: "One of these days, France will force you to take your independence by kicking your ass. You will owe it to Algeria, our Algeria."[106]

To Fanon, the Antillean man was weak; he was dancing, singing, mimicking the white man when he had to seize the gun and fight. Fanon dismissed the resistance of the populations of the French overseas departments because it did not take the form that he expected: heroic armed struggle to create a nation-state. The Fanonian analysis marked the Creoles with the image of unheroic assimilated *évolués* at a moment when, around the world, colonized people, taking arms and freeing themselves, were calling into question the colonialist representation of the undefeated white man and of the cowardly colonized. Fanon invented a romance of men, of brothers in arms. Virile and decolonized fraternity would defeat European fraternity, whose racism and hypocrisy would be exposed.

To Memmi, a Tunisian Jew, the colonizer had constructed a "mythical and degrading portrait" of the colonized that the latter ended up accepting and living to a certain extent.[107] The colonizer had no other choice than to enter into relation with the colonized, whom he despised, because "it is this very alliance which enables him to lead the life which he decided to look for in the colonies; it is this relationship which is lucrative, which creates privilege."[108] Racism was a "consubstantial part of colonialism," the "highest expression of the colonial system and one of the most significant features of colonialism."[109] Memmi, like Fanon, thought that a revolution was needed to accomplish decolonization. "Only the complete liquidation of colonization permits the colonized to be free," but this liquidation was "nothing but a prelude to complete liberation, to self-recovery."[110] Their goal was the creation of a new man on the disappearance of racial differences. Fanon and Memmi rejected the thesis that history could permanently determine identity. "The body of history does not determine a single one of my actions. I am my own foundation," Fanon wrote.[111] To which

Memmi added, "Having recovered all his dimensions, the former colonized will have become *a man like any other.*"[112]

The Fanonian political project and psychology carried a utopian dimension.[113] Fanon's messianic message, his Manichaeanism, and his revolutionary romanticism produced a powerful, yet ultimately flawed, discourse of emancipation. Fanon proposed an autonomous self, uninhibited by the ties of desire and love, except for the abstract love of the undifferentiated oppressed. Memmi argued against this illusion and contended that the question for the colonized was to end a form of dependence that was nefarious and dangerous and to construct new ties with the former metropole and the rest of the world. To him, the refusal to answer the question of interdependency in positive terms led the postcolonial states to embrace a rhetoric of resentment and continuous debt to the metropole. Dependence followed domination, Memmi wrote, though aspects of domination lingered.

With the translation of Georges Devereux's essay "Essais d'ethnopsychiatrie générale" in 1970, anthropologists made their contribution to the debate about psychology and colonialism. They tried to answer the question: does a society favor certain forms of mental illnesses more than others? Although the question was not altogether different from colonial psychology's, ethnopsychiatry purported to adopt a radically different approach. To ethnopsychiatry, "normal or pathological behaviors, far from being the product of a conditioning by society, are *individual* acts, informed by culture yet not reducible to it."[114] It supported an interdisciplinary approach between ethnology and psychiatry.[115] With the arrival of people from former colonies in the metropole and the development of psychiatric services in the postcolony, the school of ethnopsychiatry gained authority, for concrete questions emerged about how to treat people whose cultural references and understanding of illness differed from the metropole's. However, what was often a methodological problem was transformed into a theoretical insight.

Culturalism, or the notion that the psyche is determined by culture, pervaded ethnopsychiatry. The ethnologist François Laplantine spoke of the problems of enthopsychiatry: the sociohistorical and psycho-affective presuppositions of the researchers, which often remain unexplained; the difficulty of adopting a critical stance toward familiar behavior, or of confronting unfamiliar behavior; the fact that ethnographic material is analyzed by psychologists and psychiatrists, who have no idea of what constitutes field research; and finally the lack of an explicit theoretical framework.[116] But ethnopsychiatry gave to postcolonial psychiatrists a legitimacy in the postcolonial world, in which questions of cultural differences have become central. They drew their legitimacy from the suspicion cast over psychoanalysis and its universalism, which was in many cases rejected by the scholars of the decolonized world. Who had said that the Oedipus complex was universal? On what studies did this assumption rest? And why should family relations of love, envy, and jealousy in the non-European world be like those observed in the European family? Manonni, Fanon, and Memmi argued that colonialism caused specific mental disorders and thought that psychology would explain the suffering of colonized people. But their desire to show that politics and psychology were inseparably linked led to a psychologization of the politics of decolonization. Problems related to identification, filiation, and sexual life would not be resolved with political independence. Human alienation (Lacan's *méconnaissance*) and its consequences (depression, frustration, neurosis) perdured. What could be a "decolonized self"?

The Birth of the Clinic in Réunion

The first mention of mental illness in Réunion appeared in a 1760 document that described why a French retired sailor, Philippe Hébert, subject to hallucinations, was committed to the colonial hospital. The island was still the property of the Company of the Indies, and the decision about the mental health of a free individual was made by the Conseil Supérieur de Bourbon. Slaves exhibiting mental imbalance were either sent to Madagascar, whether it was their country of origin or not, or abandoned in the forest. After the purchase of the island in 1764 by the king of France, its judicial organization was thoroughly revised. Prisons, asylums, and hospitals were built. The hospital of Saint-Paul received the incurably ill.[117] In 1803 a specific institution was created, the Assistance de Bienfaisance, to deal with the indigent.

The French psychiatrist Gérard Mouls connected two themes in his study of the birth of the clinic in Réunion. One was the favorite theme of nineteenth-century French psychology, that poverty led to mental illness. The other, inspired by Foucault, saw the asylum as a means to discipline dangerous classes. Mouls saw a connection between the economic transformation experienced on the island in the 1840s and the emergence of madness. The pauperization of an important part of the population generated mental disorders and pushed people to resort to charitable institutions: "Physiologically, this population exhibited malnutrition, the alcoholism specific to the poor, and physical deficiencies; psychologically, pauperization led to the intellectual poverty of poor whites and the loosening of social ties."[118] The asylum did not receive a separate budget until 1848, and it was in 1852 that the first mention of a specific ward for mental patients appeared in administrative documents. The ward took the name of Asile des Aliénés in 1869 and was put under the control of the Assistance Publique. After the abolition of slavery, the distinction between wards for whites and wards for blacks was repeated. The 1838 French law on voluntary internment and *placements d'office* was applied on the island in 1918. The decree of March 19, 1912, published in the *Journal Officiel* of the colony, laid out in detail the regulations of the asylum.[119] Patients could work if the doctor agreed; women could do domestic work for the hospital, and men could make repairs, garden, and clean the wards. Both could use the daily wage they received—men received 0.25Fr, and women 0.20Fr—to "ameliorate their everyday fare."

At a psychiatric congress in 1912, doctors Vincent and Merveilleux, both of the French army medical services, described Réunion's asylum. Situated in a region in which malaria was rampant, the asylum had two sections with a total of forty-five cells for men, and one section of thirty cells for women. Between 1852 and 1911, a majority of asylum patients were men. More than two-thirds of the patients were métis Creoles.[120] Poor whites were the second most numerous group of patients. Only six male patients were Europeans, and there were no European women. Vincent and Merveilleux insisted on the role of alcoholism in the pathology of the Creoles.[121]

Réunion's asylum did not attract a lot of interest from the colonial administration until 1949. Three years earlier, the island had become a French department. Despite appalling conditions, described in a 1949 report, there had been in 1946 an increase of the demands for internment: in 1935 there were twenty entries per year; in 1946, one per week. In 1951 Doctor Calen, a Frenchman whose training in psychiatry had consisted of a year in the psychiatric services of colonial Tunisia, arrived at Saint-Paul. Calen introduced electroshock therapy and chemical drugs such as Largactil and Theralene. The school of nursing trained its first class of psychiatric nurses. In 1953 Dr. Le Mappian was the first doctor with a diploma in psychiatry to be nominated director of Saint-Paul. Under his direction, admissions to the asylum increased rapidly. His first gesture was to change the sign at the entrance from Asile des Aliénés to Hôpital psychiatrique.[122]

In the hospital's annual report, the director of Saint-Paul described the state of the hospital in 1960: "Dilapidated, cluttered, destitute. There are no mattresses for the patients. They sleep on a mat. The cells have no toilets and the patients relieve themselves on the floor on which other patients sleep."[123] That year, windows were pierced in the cells. In 1961 mattresses, sheets, and covers were given to the patients. By 1966 the demand for psychiatric expertise became widespread. Although the 1966 report noted the necessity for a practitioner to learn Creole and to know the socioeconomic conditions of the patient, it added that "Creole was barely adequate on the semantic level for expressing feelings and sentiments." Creoles had adopted psychiatric assistance as another form of welfare, and this adoption was facilitated by the "lack of jobs, the low wages, as well as moral and socio-economic factors."

The terrain for psychiatric order was prepared by the policy of departmentalization, which revolutionized the health services. The institutionalization of free care, Assistance Médicale Gratuite (AMG), brought new patients to the psychiatric hospital by facilitating the detection of mental illness.[124] Social workers and doctors learned to "detect mental illness" and to prescribe the institutionalization of patients.[125] The other factor that explained the increased number of patients was a transformation in the population's attitude toward madness. With urbanization, the tolerance toward people exhibiting mental disorders diminished. To the psychiatrist Jean-François Reverzy, another element explained the rapid development of psychiatric care in the island: the 1975 law on disability and the introduction of neuroleptic drugs.[126] As the 1975 law gave disability benefits to people suffering from "mental disorders," people saw psychiatry as another source of welfare. Madness has never been, among the poor, a shameful state. Therefore going to the asylum and having a clean place to sleep, being guaranteed three free meals, and receiving some drugs that would help one to forget one's misery was acceptable behavior. Psychiatric drugs constituted another form of survival.

Although psychiatry was brought to Réunion by young men who prided themselves on being politically progressive democrats and on the side of anticolonialists, it had a similar concern to psychiatry in the metropole: to discipline and reform the "dangerous classes,"—women, workers, vagrants—and to create a pedagogy of training and correction. Starting in the 1970s, in place of doing their military service, young French men came to do their medical internship on the island.[127] They often pushed for the transformation of rigid institutions. Many had been influenced by the antipsychiatry movement, and by the general atmosphere of challenging authority and questioning colonialism that prevailed in France after May 1968. The consequences of their arrival, whether unexpected or secretly desired, were that the incorporation of the psychiatrist and the psychologist into legal and social procedures, and the definition of the individual therein, changed the structures and the vocabulary of social control and punishment on the island to those then common in France.

The development of psychiatric order was part of the assimilative policy of the 1970s. The men, who constituted the majority of patients of the asylum, were those rejected by the modernization of the economy and agriculture, illiterate men, carriers of an oral culture in a world in which the written word, the word of the law, and of the word of administration were the words of Frenchmen. In thirty years, the rural, feudal world of the plantation was transformed into a world in which the skills of the majority of the island's workforce were no longer needed, and where no programs of reconversion were developed to respond to a growing demand for jobs.

The "extenuating circumstances" evoked by the district attorney at Yves Olivier's trial conjure up the history of men and women whose grandchildren would become the defendants at the criminal court more than a century later. These circumstances were the economic and social conditions created by a capitalist restructuring of the island's economy in the 1850s. After the abolition of slavery in 1848, rich landowners seized the fertile land of the coast and pushed poor whites to the mountains, where they were joined by free slaves who tried to make a living on their own. The "virtuous life" of Yves O.'s father lauded by the president was the life of a man born in poverty, two years into this century. Yves O.'s father had accepted, like his father before him, the rules of colonial society: poverty, exploitation, illiteracy, and a life with no future. In the forty years after 1946, Réunion's peasantry became obsolete.[128] In 1946, 66 percent of jobs were in the agriculture industry; in 1994, between 5 and 6 percent. Peasants and small farmers lost their lands; workers lost their jobs.[129] Economists who expressed doubts about the long-term viability of an agricultural economy inherited from colonialism saw their predictions verified.[130]

Similarities between the policy of disciplining the dangerous classes in France and the island should not hide the differences in both situations. The issue of the Creole language, of psychological treatment connected to welfare and financial survival, and the racist assumptions of psychology in the colony affect the nature of the strategies of discipline and control. Moreover, the psychiatry that arrived in Réunion was a psychiatry that had gone through a crisis of legitimacy. Its legitimacy had been contested by young psychiatrists on the ground that its institution did not serve a humanistic goal but served as social repression, whether in the metropole or the colony.[131] To the critics of psychiatry, "madness was not an illness but a *history,*" the history of a "situation that was the translation of social or family alienation." Fanon's denunciation of the colonial psychiatric diagnosis of the criminality of the North African—"a reaction written into the nature of things, of *the thing* which is biologically organized"[132]—had situated the sources of alienation in the social organization of colonialism. Coming after this critical moment, French psychiatry in Réunion established a "soft psychiatry," with pharmaceutical medicalization on the one hand, and programs of social prevention on the other hand.[133] In a way, it was faithful to the psychiatric tradition of "moral treatment": reconcile the sick with the social world, help them to find in themselves the strength to go back to that world, and use the resources of that world to get free of the disease.[134] But where Pinel, who invented moral treatment, thought that the "mad" was a *sujet* (subject), postcolonial psychiatry proposed a moral treatment in which moralization was the principle and there was no sujet. The goal of the psychiatry in Réunion has been to "avoid hospitalization at any cost."[135] Postcolonial psychiatry wants to be humanist.

Historians of the clinic in France have not investigated the history of colonial psychology. The laws about the asylum that were applied to the postcolony were the laws applied in the metropole. There never existed exceptional laws for the colony. What produced a difference between the metropole and the colony was that these laws were grafted onto a history of social relations determined by slavery, racism, and colonialism, and that they came to the island with welfare and modernization. The birth of the clinic took place much later on the island, around the 1970s, whereas in France, it had taken place a century earlier.[136] In France, psychiatrists were called to testify in court as experts on the mental condition of accused criminals after 1832,[137] whereas in the island of Réunion, they started to fulfill this function in the late 1960s.

Hence, in the postcolony, the reforms of psychiatric institutions in the late 1970s and the 1980s—encouraging short-term stays, group therapy, greater availability of psychotropic drugs, decentralization of the psychiatric hospital—promoted psychiatry as another preventive form of care. Psychiatry arrived "soft," "benevolent," in the colony. Today the overwhelming majority of psychologists and psychiatrists are Frenchmen, and the majority of the psychiatric nurses and the patients are Creole men. Although the psychiatrist claims that he has no colonial goal, that he only wants to explain the patient's psyche, his goal appears as teleological as the colonial policies were. The pathological Creole produces the French male psychiatrist's raison d'être, as the pagan native was the missionary's raison d'être. The goal is to take the colonized through a developmental process whose result should be the creation of a "modern" individual. A "correct" psychological definition of the Creoles will inevitably be reached if sufficiently qualified people have the opportunity to observe the patient in the neutral, rule-oriented scene of the psychological interview.

In their majority, French psychiatrists in Réunion do not question their participation in the economy of discourses that have created the trope of the pathological Creole. The encounter between the Réunionnais and the Frenchmen is an encounter fraught with difficulties, in which the Creole is put in the position of demand and dependence. The difference is not merely cultural, a difference that psychologists are prompt to recognize, but the product of a long history of socioeconomic and political relations of inequality. It is also about two different epistemes, two different approaches to illness. The politics of the psychology of recolonization is about recognizing the *difference* of the Réunionnais so that they would want, themselves, to evolve toward what is presented as desirable: the "modern European self." The psychiatrist participates, certainly with good intent, in a new stage in the long project of assimilation of the Réunionnais to a European model.

It is not that theories about the psyche are in essence about the "European psyche" because they were discovered by Europeans and, therefore, could not be applied to study the symptoms of the Réunionnais. Rather, one must ask if it is possible to open a dialogical interpretive space in Réunion in which the Réunionnais' voices, language, and texts would enter in dialogue with the representatives of a French institution. To raise this question means that one must consider the interaction of a series of phenomena: the rapid modernization of psychiatric services in the island, the increasing intervention of psychologists in different institutions (school, marriage, law), and the high consumption of medical drugs (Réunion has the highest rate of consumption of medical drugs of all the French departments). One would also have to consider the fact that an important group of the population resorts to psychiatric services because a diagnosis of mental illness guarantees a disabled status and, consequently, access to welfare. One would have to question the narcissistic satisfaction of men who, as European experts, can "see" madness and deficiencies in non-European men.

Gilles Deleuze has distinguished between a disciplinary society and a control society.[138] The principal technique of the disciplinary society was *enfermement* (prison, hospital, school, factory, barracks). Now, Deleuze argues, we have entered a society that functions through "continuous control and instantaneous communication." Incarceration might become less necessary because the individual is constantly watched by a complex and multifarous organization of social services. In postcolonial Réunion, these two strategies have concurrently occurred. New types of sanction, education, and care have constructed a web of control around the Creoles, and along with the creation of a vast social network of control, there has been a multiplication of prisons, a criminalization and psychologization of politics.

Yet asking for psychiatric help has become another sign of the Réunionnais' dependence. In 1966 the director of the psychiatric hospital of Saint-Paul wrote in his annual report: "The disability act has become a bonus for sickness. It is often given to crude and uneducated beings, who exhibit a tendency, in front of difficulties, to immediately de-compensate on a hysterical mode. This does not help for a real social reinsertion of mental health patients."[139] In 1988 a psychiatrist analyzed the Creole patient in these terms: "The resistance to a cure, which is a characteristic of madness, has existed ever since madness has existed. In Réunion, this resistance is reinforced by a social mythology which attaches great value to the pension for disability. To receive money from the government is assimilated with being a civil servant. This attitude is often pushed to the extreme. The demand is shocking for persons who come from a Western culture and whose psychical organization is based on a mastered anality and an unbridled search for autonomy."

The scene of psychological interpretation is occupied by two men in Réunion: the poor Creole and the French psychiatrist.[140] The Réunionnais somatizes; the Frenchman interprets. The Réunionnais hallucinates; the Frenchman interprets. Throughout Réunion's history, poor men have been the asylum's patients. Free slaves and poor white farmers were the "indigents" of the hospital. Poor men are still the majority of patients and have been since 1946. In 1965, 63 percent of the patients were men; in 1991, 61 percent. A good third of the men at Saint-Paul were unemployed. They were also very young. Among female patients, the majority were homemakers or women on welfare.[141] Patients came freely.[142]

Why are the majority of patients men? A number of different responses to that question have been given, responses that perhaps need to be considered together, rather than as excluding each other. One of the answers is that the colonial relation has been constructed as a mortal duel between men, in which the dominant would go to any length to degrade and humiliate the dominated. One way to degrade and humiliate a man is to mock, challenge, question, taunt his manhood. The male colonized *body,* his sex, is the target of aggression. The colonizers' gendering of masculinity opposed their own construct, a masculinity constructed around work and morality, to the colonized masculinity—unreliable, violent, immature.

Fanon argued that the relation between colonialism and masculinity (in its psychological sense) entailed a profound destabilization of colonial men. When Fanon arrived at the colonial hospital of Blida, the majority of his patients were poor, rural, Muslim men.

The diagnosis was the same as it was for the poor men of Réunion: they were "hysterical." In 1918 Porot had said that North African men were hysterical. The French psychiatrist Gérard Mouls declared in 1982 that "hysteria reigns in Réunion" and went on to explain its link with the processes of identification in Creole culture: "Identification is skewed in Réunion and this can be explained by the multiplicity of ethnic groups, religions, heterogeneous beliefs, where the son cannot identify with a father who is often absent and when he is present, is negatively judged by the collective Superego (black, slave, alcoholic, unemployed, poor, brutal). The image of the father is far from being satisfying. Every social worker, schoolteacher, knows it and usually describes the mother as someone much more balanced, affective, but often destroyed by the father." Colonized men suffered a disease marked with its relation to femininity in European psychology.[143]

Fanon was right about the ways in which colonialism had configured colonized masculinity as feminized, emasculated, but his solution was misogynist and held out an impossible ideal for colonial men. Rather than understanding the Creole male sphere as a site of resistance to a European conception of masculinity, Fanon gendered decolonized masculinity and saw it emulating virile qualities. Colonialism prevented colonized masculinity from becoming modern by branding it with the mark of the premodern. Decolonized masculinity would be modern and heroic. To Memmi, the colonized man had to flee his native land to free himself from the sterile colonial world.[144] To the Indian Ashis Nandy, the British colonial mirror led the Indian to construct a martial past, a heroic virility to belie the image of the weak, feminized, cowardly Indian.[145] And Aimé Césaire rewrote *The Tempest* to make Caliban a black revolutionary.

Male anticolonialists countered the taxonomic categories of colonialism with new categories. They contested a narrative that mocked their masculinity through dehumanization. They sought to reconstruct their *masculinity* in the name of a shared *humanity*. They said: "We are *men* like you because we are *human* like you." But they also refused to consider that the ways in which colonized men had constructed their masculinity could constitute forms of resistance. The solution, they insisted, was the reconstruction of man. Women could be integrated into the narrative of decolonization, so long as they identified with the figures of heroism. Yet phallic masculinity, as it was deployed through war or moments of intense political mobilization, sustained the construction of a fearless, courageous masculinity but did not offer the foundations for a decolonized masculinity.

Scholars have shown how fragile are the foundations of phallic masculinity.[146] The images and stories linked to heroic masculinity have tended to hide the more complex ways through which colonized men answered to the colonial hegemonic discourse. The heroic soldier, the fearless leader, are tropes that set up their opposite as the unheroic, weak man, who implicitly belongs to the colonial past. Fanon's binarism, hero or passive accomplice, foreclosed masculinity, imprisoned its expressions within virilism. Post-Fanonian psychiatry has appropriated Fanon's insight about the feminization of colonized men, but to its own ends. The collective mirror that the French psychiatrists have presented to the postcolonial male Creoles reflects two images: the Frenchman as modern, educated, capable of inner reflection, and the Creole man as incestuous, inarticulate, drunk, uncouth, childish. Men's masculine identity seemed to suffer more from modernization because French men had a narcissistic stake in demasculinizing black men, rather than in attacking women's femininity. The attack on women would take another form.

French psychiatrists explained that men were the majority of patients because before 1946, the organization of the family was "half-patriarchal, half-matriarchal, with some aspects of clan organization."[147] Then the "site of power was displaced from the father, the master of the plantation, to the mother, the Mère-Patrie who feeds, assists, protects, but also smothers and maintains an infantile status of dependence."[148] The Creoles became the "orphans of a paternalist universe that was dying." Men who headed rural families and lived a hard life rested their authority and masculine legitimacy on their ability to provide for their families. Daniel Waro, a popular Réunion folksinger, remembered his father, a very poor geranium farmer, as someone who "always worked to insure the family's survival. There was no radio at home, no flowers in the garden. The criteria was: is it useful?"[149] To Waro, his father's resilience and his courage as a communist activist in the 1960s were important to inscribe a filiation. Yet to Waro, his father's masculinity lacked an essential component: the ability to show tenderness and affection.

The social and cultural values of conservative assimilation rejected the values of Réunion's masculinity. A majority of Réunion's men, facing the disintegration of their world, turned to
self-destruction. The French National Institute of Statistics spoke
in 1994 of a "masculine handicap that is one of the highest in the
world."[150] Suicide, alcoholism, and mental illness are the main
reasons for masculine mortality.[151] Réunion's men have resisted the
world and the ideal of modernity by killing themselves.

However, even when a Creole man adopts the ideal of modern
masculinity offered by departmentalization, the outcome is not
always a successful assimilation. Monique Boyer's *Métisse* again
offers a reference.[152] Boyer recounts the deep contempt of her
mother for her father, and the consequent promise that her father
made, to leave his wife once the education of their two children
had been secured. Thanks to the father's job in a state institution,
the post office, Boyer's family will own a house, modern appliances,
and a car, the 1960s signs of the Creole's escape from rural poverty.
Her father's mission accomplished, he leaves his wife, who has
always hated him because he is a *Kaf,* a black man. Years later, the
father explains his behavior to his daughter: "I did not want to
shame you! Do not come to see me again, do not even greet me in
the street. Nobody would know that your father is a *Kaf!*"[153] The
mother, mortified by her husband's abandonment, finally expresses
her long-lasting hatred and resentment with the insult: "*Espèce de
cafre!*"[154] To Boyer, "The terrible words uttered by my mother, who
had been humiliated by my father, were not hers: they belonged to
the women and men who had lived on our island. And the courage,
the admirable strength, that she showed when she was twenty
and married my father, when she faced social opinion, saved my
brother and myself from poverty."[155] The social success of the
father could not erase the fact that he was a black man in a society
in which race and masculinity intersected. Modern masculinity
was embodied in the white and European man. The black man
retreated to the dark of his house, withdrawing from a society that
had not accepted him.

The modernity brought by conservative assimilation—an ideal
of communication based on understanding and care, of equality in
the couple, of a certain attention to children—questioned the ideal
of Réunionnais masculinity. The values of masculinity were no
longer found in political courage, hard farmwork, and physical

force but were found in social success, new family organization, and adoption of "metropolitan" attitudes. To postcolonial French psychiatrists, the Creole family was creating Creole pathology. The psychiatrist was the mediator, the observer of the pathological Creole couple. The evolution of the colonial couple according to psychology could be described thus: (1) in the first period, the civilized European and the backward native, the former observing the latter, describing his symptoms (Porot), and leading him to psychological maturity (Porot, Hardy); (2) two individuals, with different psychological motives (Mannoni, Fanon, Memmi); (3) the native couple, producer of pathology, observed by the European psychiatrist.

Psychiatry has served to explain the behavior not only of impoverished individuals but of impoverished groups as well. Its discourse has been adopted by judges, prosecutors, and political commentators to displace the responsibility for impoverishment from economic and political conditions to psychological ones. For instance, the February 1991 urban uprising at Le Chaudron was still the consequence of a "conspiracy" planned by the Communist Party.[156] But when, in December 1992, Le Chaudron was again the site of a violent uprising, the vocabulary of the media and the conservatives changed. Now the riots were the result of moral failure, lack of parental guidance, and a culture of welfare. The journalist Yves Mont-Rouge wrote that "throwing stones, burning, looting stores have nothing to do with legitimate demands. Groups find in rioting the means to gratuitously release their frustrations, to unwind."[157] The prosecutor declared that he regretted that the penal code did not contain a term to designate "primary instincts, violent behavior without reasons."[158] To the conservative Jean-Pierre Bosviel, the uprising was the result of "ten years of state demagogy, when the values of work and effort had been replaced by welfare." Both uprisings were the responses to years of neglect. They were responses to the violence of a consumer culture flaunted before the poor. Le Chaudron contained the greatest number of people collecting welfare in Saint-Denis. Yet it was at the limits of this neighborhood that a "Night of the Porsche" was organized, to celebrate fifty Réunionnais who had bought one of these cars, each of which costs 600,000Fr.

When the poor people of Los Angeles had rebelled in May 1992, U.S. conservatives had used a similar vocabulary: poverty was the result of dependence on the welfare state, moral failure, and lack of responsibility. In both cases, poverty and discrimination, "seen in the past as problems requiring state action, were now seen as the *results* of state activity. What was once the solution (activist social policies) became the problem (dependence)."[159] The widely shared conservative opinion about "fatherless families" in poor communities leading children to a life of crime and laziness was directed against the population of the ghettos of the postcolony of Réunion and the United States. In both cases, state intervention on the behalf of poor groups—an intervention that had not come naturally but had been won by years of activism—was now said to be the cause of poverty.

To Réunion's conservatives, if people revolted, it was because they had become accustomed to welfare and a life of idleness. They also had a penchant for alcohol. Alcoholism was, as early as 1764, blamed for the impoverishment of the islanders' minds, which were "so precocious and premature that one witnessed senility before an individual's old age."[160] In the documents that first reported in detail the reasons for which people were sent to Saint-Paul, alcoholism was listed as the main cause. In the 1960s, there was a greater focus on the causes and effects of alcoholism.[161] The island's administration and the medical and legal professions took a keen interest in prophylaxy.[162] Presentations made at a 1987 colloquium with the emphatic title of *Alcoolisation et Suralcoolisation à La Réunion* testified to the long interest of the medical profession in alcohol-related syndromes.[163] Dr. Amode Ismael-Daoudjee constructed, on Dr. Vincent Bassot's research, a picture of the alcoholic Réunionnais[164] and concluded that one could talk of a "cultural form of alcoholism in Réunion" that explained why "the mode of psychotic de-compensation of an alcoholic individual is a way of realizing the Ego, or, rather it is a mode of survival for an Ego, which is often immature and ambivalent, as well as overwhelmed by the Réunionnais anxiety."[165] Again, it was shown that the poorest men were the main consumers of rum.

The connection between alcoholism and poverty and their link with degeneration and rebellion informed French policies toward the poor and workers in the mid–nineteenth century. Alcoholism in France was not considered a disease until after the Paris Commune, which was attributed to "a monstrous outburst of acute alcoholism."[166] The bourgeois discourse, which had first connected the radical politics of the working class to its penchant for drunk-

enness, came to see drunkenness as a national and medical problem.[167] In Réunion, alcoholism remained attached to poverty and
criminality. On the island, wealth was made from sugarcane, from
which rum is extracted. Slaves were forbidden to drink rum. Rum
was associated with festivities and special occasions, such as bap-
tism, marriage, and funerals. It was said to have curative effects[168]
and was the favorite drink at the end of the day, the drink around
which men gather at the *boutik sinwa.* Rum and Creole masculinity were linked in the Creole popular imagination. To drink rum
and to hold it was a sign of good and strong Réunionnais manhood. With the modernization of the island, new liquors were
imported, such as whiskey, considered less "backward," less associated with the *petit peuple.* The analysis of the discourse about rum
consumption revealed a class bias. Reformist movements have
emerged from the Réunionnais petite bourgeoisie, allied with the
psychiatrists. There is no doubt that there was, among them, a
genuine concern for the health and welfare of the population and
alarm about the increasing danger that alcohol consumption represented. Violence in the family and deadly car accidents increased
because of rum consumption. The relation that was made between
poverty, powerlessness, and alcohol consumption was true. Yet the
discourse about the poor and their penchant for liquors revealed a
shame toward those who "disgrace" the community and a moralis-
tic tone. Creole men drank themselves to death not because of
"their immature and ambivalent Ego" but because they sought
oblivion, self-destruction.

Creole Language and the Symbolic

In 1955 Dr. Le Mappian blamed the pauperism of the island for the
population's health condition, a population burdened with syphilis, malaria, parasitosis, and alcoholism. Creoles adopted a passive
and fatalistic attitude, Le Mappian claimed, to confront the dis-
mal, monotonous character of their harsh life. Yet what appeared
to the French psychiatrist as a considerable handicap, greater than
the symptoms he described, was the Creole language:

The majority of our patients, who are not very sophisticated, speak only
Creole. The question of language is extremely disconcerting. Creole is

practically incomprehensible. To understand it does not resolve the difficulties. To understand the patient does not mean to be understood by
him. The Creole vocabulary is poor. Its imprecise terms cover a wide
range of meanings. When the patient must express inner feelings and
affects, this language is totally defective, because it is aimed only at rudi-
mentary social relations. It was never destined for what the psychiatrist
intended. . . . Our patients ignore introspection and they cannot verbal-
ize what they experience. . . . Mental activity and subjectivity are not
formulated, and barely recognized as such.[169]

Le Mappian insisted, though, that he did not doubt the intellectual capacities of his patients and argued that the conditions of
living were responsible for most of the symptoms exhibited by the
Réunionnais. Yet he followed the dominant colonial paradigm that
denied to the language of the colonized the capacity to conceptualize or express inner feelings. As a reformer, he advocated the training of native assistants to compensate for that difficulty. The assistants would be Creole women versed in the knowledge of Creole
language and mores: "Only a female social worker of Creole origin
would be the perfect auxiliary, so useful to the metropolitan male
psychiatrist."[170] Le Mappian imagined the social and gendered
couple caring for the Creole male patient: the doctor was a man, a
zorey; the assistant, a Creole, a woman. The psychiatric diagnosis
of the Creoles echoes the colonial diagnostic about the "primitive
mind." To J. V. Roumeguere, "The Réunionnais lives totally withdrawn into himself. No maturation, no personal idea. He has no
access to conceptualization and therefore tends to find refuge behind a leader, who is the most astute and intelligent person of the
group. He obeys his directives, blindly following him, and trusts
the leader's critical mind because he is totally deprived of such
ability."[171] To the psychiatrist Jean-Philippe Cravero, there is
an "absence of an existential goal" among the Creoles, who exhibit
a submission to impulses, and a difficult relationship to time and
space.[172] Cravero, with Thierry Dionot, has claimed to have defined the "basic personality" of the population, characterized by
externalization, projection, and self-depreciation. They have observed, they wrote, a "rarity of authentic feeling of guilt," among
the Réunionnais, who tend to live their conflicts essentially as
the result of persecution.[173] The family, as well as social and psychological structures, explains the propensity to depressive moods

among Réunionnais and produces a "basic personality" that is defined through

a relation to time that is marked by the instantaneous (a more immediate structuration of time, inscribed in repetition or sequential succession rather than in continuity; this approach occurs at the expense of apprehending the past as the foundation of the present and as projection of the future); fatalism, passivity, humility, a sense of inferiority, a latent depressive position together with a sense of lack, and an aggressivity that is barely mediated (this aggressivity is not integrated into competitive behavior, but expressed through passivity and freeing itself through behavioral outbursts). One can also observe a certain prevalence of apprehending objects as external, phenomena related to magic thinking, in which insight is not preeminent.[174]

The French psychiatrist Patrick Bensoussan contends that Réunion's society is in infancy and that Creole culture is insular, a culture characterized by "language, cuisine, the power of the Imaginary and of the sorcerer, a poor expression, frequent acting-out, all of this with rum as the background."[175] According to Bensoussan, there is a "Creole way of acting out," which is "impulsive, neither premeditated nor elaborated, and whose causes, as well as its effects, are not up to the gesture, because the conflict remains unresolved."[176] Acting out, according to Freud, is the "action in which the subject, in the grip of his unconscious wishes and fantasies, relives these in the present with a sensation of immediacy which is heightened by his refusal to recognize their source and their repetitive character."[177] It is a neurotic symptom, often related to the "return of the repressed," and can cover a wide range of actions, from violent, criminal acts to more subdued forms of expression. The individual yields to the compulsion to repeat, which replaces the compulsion to remember. Otto Fenichel speaks of an "intolerance of tensions" among neurotics who tend to act out. The patients "cannot perform the step from acting to thinking, that is, from an immediate yielding to all impulses to reasonable judgment."[178] There cannot be a *Creole* form of acting out because acting out *is* impulsive, neither premeditated nor elaborated. Acting out cannot be ethnically defined. Acting out refers to the individual being "acted" on by fantasies. The question in Réunion might be: what is the *repressed* that *returns?* What are the fantasies, the wishes that are acted out? What *is* repeated? But if the

French psychiatrists are convinced that the Creoles cannot express their inner feelings, their internal conflicts, that they are *under* the rule of their impulses, incapable of reasonable judgment, this research cannot be done. The acts of violence perpetuated by Creoles, which French psychiatrists propose as proofs of the "Creole acting out," sometimes pale in comparison to the violence of a text that deprives a people of the ability to symbolize their suffering.

Creoles act out, psychiatrists claim, because they do not accede to symbolized language, to sublimation. They remain in a fusional relation with the mother, in a state of infantile orality. Their impulses are not channeled and transformed into creative acts, because they are like infants who need to have immediate satisfaction. French psychiatrists have applied a strategic adaptation of Lacanian categories to the local ideological struggle. Lacan's three orders, which are profoundly heterogeneous, have been adapted to fit the goals of the psychiatric discourse in the postcolony. In the psychiatric translation of these terms, the *Imaginary,* the world of images, conscious or unconscious, perceived or imagined, is yesterday's "primitivism," or the inability to think in concepts and ideas, and oral culture is intimately associated with this dimension. The Imaginary is opposed, still in the psychiatric translation, to the *Symbolic,* the determining order of the subject, which has become yesterday's rational thinking and writing.[179] Here are some examples of this strategic adaptation of Lacanian vocabulary: the psychologist Jean-Pierre Cambefort contends that Creoles are disinvested from the Lacanian "symbolic function"; that is, they do not understand taboos and laws and are prisoners of the Imaginary.[180] The psychiatrist Gérard Mouls speaks of a "symbolic deficiency" among Réunionnais. They are said to be caught in an intersubjectivity in which mimetic identifications dominate. When these experts contend that there is a supremacy of the Imaginary in Réunion—the register of alienation and méconnaissance in Lacan—they say that the Réunionnais remain prisoners of their identifications, unable to free their *langage premier,* the language of desire. The Réunionnais' Imaginary is understood as the world of the magico-religious, whereas the possibility of reason under the rule of the Symbolic, the order of assumed subjectivity, is associated with the technique of modern psychology. The ideological contest between oral culture and magico-religious belief *and* written culture and reason is rewritten under the sign of the psyche. Psychoanalytical concepts are borrowed to lend to psychology a veneer of respectability and neutral intellectualism. Throughout this process, psychiatry is "psychologized," and Réunionnais are said to be caught in an intersubjectivity in which mimetic identifications dominate.

Cazalis de Fondouce, a child psychiatrist, argues that Creole is a language that uses more the "imagination than the ability to conceptualize." Delassus and Verrière write: "In Creole language, there is no *Je,* (I) but *Moi,* (Me) to designate the subject. . . . The 'I' is a conceptual force. The 'Me' is a simple state. The consequence is that the Creole has no proper culture and that the neurosis inherent to social commitment is very reduced, when it exists at all."[181] The French psychiatrists' remark about Creole language implies that Creoles have no dreams, create no metaphors.[182] In Creole, there are four terms to designate the subject or object of the action: *mwin, mwa, amwim, mi.* Moreover, as the Réunionnais linguist Ginette Ramassamy has shown, the subject in Réunionnais Creole can be assumed through personal pronouns (*mwen la travay pou out gran-per,* I worked for your grandfather), names (*letsi, koméla lé piké,* Litchies are now rotten); nominal syntagmas (*mon granmèr, mon matant té i yaprann a-mwen zistwar,* my grandmother, my aunt told me stories); and propositions (*ti-gason mwen té i yèm la pati madagaskar,* the young man I loved left for Madagascar).[183] Ramassamy has noted that the recurrent omission of the subject in the Creole sentence questions the definition of the subject as "obligatory determinant of the predicate." Creolophones assume that the context, the situation, or a shared understanding compensate for this omission.[184]

The French psychiatrists' conclusion about Creole language reveals a narrow, neocolonial view of language. Mannoni's observation that symbolization is not reduced, as some would like, to the world of concepts opens up the way we look at symbolization. A transitional object, he says, is already part of symbolism. But French psychologists in Réunion deploy a confusion between *language* and *communication.* The difficulties in communication because of language and status are translated into conceptual insufficiencies of the language. The Creole language is faulted for lack of terms and words that would allow the individual to express feelings and emotions. But what do French psychiatrists hear? Certainly more studies remain to be done about the ways Réunionnais symbolize, but what can be said about the motives of experts who seem to revel in being the observers of an exceptional phenomenon: a people whose language prevents them from expressing their internal feelings, dreams, emotions; that exhibits the highest rate of incest, rape, family-related crime, and alcoholism; with families in which the father is absent, the mother too present? It seems that the remark of the Réunionnais cultural critic Carpanin Marimoutou, that the métis has the "false choice between an assimilative mimesis or the derision of the monkey,"[185] is what is proposed by psychiatry. Either you mimic us, or you mock us, but in both cases, you are a monkey.

Returning to Yves Olivier's trial, we find an example of "speaking for the native." The district attorney speaking of Yves O. asks the psychiatric expert: "Yves does not say 'I regret that I killed my father,' but 'I am ashamed.' He shows that he is more sensitive to the opinion of the others, than to the consequences of his act." To which the psychiatrist answers: "He does not exist outside of the others' look." The meaning of the expression "I am ashamed" for the subject, Yves O., is dismissed. In what chain of signifiers does Yves O. inscribe his sentence? Lacan, whom psychiatrists in the postcolony like to quote, said that the "function of language is not to inform but to evoke."[186] What was Yves O. evoking with his expression? Judges and psychiatrists could not listen to what Yves O. was saying about himself and his life when he said: "After throwing the stone, I said to myself: *J'ai tué papa* [I killed Daddy] and I was afraid of being beaten by my sisters and brothers." They could not listen because to listen would mean that they would have to free themselves from the power of the psychiatric discourse, from the ideals they made theirs, a life of dependence on the French state, disguised as freedom. The psychiatrist, who had said of Yves O. that he was a prisoner of magic thinking, was the prisoner of the psychiatric discourse. All his humanistic approach, all his concern for the Creole, would not change the rules imposed by the order he served, which perpetuates the image of the Creoles as monsters.

There has been, among psychiatrists, a fascination with data that enforced the image of a perverted and sick population. An attorney general declared in 1985: "Réunion's population is the most prone to crime of all French regional populations."[187] Experts present the proofs of the population's degeneration: "Its consumption of strong alcohol is among the highest of all French regions."[188] "There is a specific type of Réunionnais suicide";[189] the proportion of parricides is significantly higher than in France;[190] rape and incest occur more frequently than in France. Although they often lack the expertise to do an anthropological study of the society, French psychiatrists fascinated by the degree of the population's métissage have imposed a grid of interpretation on the ethnic composition of the population that, they say, has an impact on the group's psychology. Réunion's population is diverse, and ethnic groups have retained certain specific cultural traditions and religious ceremonies or beliefs. Yet the boundaries among groups are porous, and studies have shown how people circulate among religions and customs.[191] The description of Réunion's society by French psychiatrists echoes colonial stereotypes. Here is how Jean-Michel Porte describes Réunion's society: The zoreys, who are "harbingers of hope and civilization, are both admired and detested. The *malabars,* slender and sophisticated, have European traits.[192] The *Cafres,* tall and big, are like children. Their stereotyped values are physical force and sexual brutality. Their women have the reputation of being easy."[193] The social organization of a pluri-ethnic society is psychologized, and a hierarchy, based on assumptions about what is a desired psychological development, is instituted. At the top of the scale is the Frenchman, the model, the ideal to the Creoles. In the words of the psychologist Cambefort, the Frenchman is the "Other, who, with his radical difference, represents the principle of heterogeneity with whom the island's subject has an ambiguous relation of identification and rivalry."[194] This "Other embodies another psychical instance: the Symbolic, not because he represents objectively this symbolic, but because what he embodies corresponds to this particular psychical register. He represents the Law, the attachment in reality to a tutelary country." To the question of journalist Michèle Autheman about Réunion's psychological problems, the psychiatrist Doctor Chevreau answers: "The Réunionnais presents the following specificity: *métissage* and its related problems. As a consequence, the Réunionnais exhibits a lack of individuality and culture."[195] Processes of identification cannot, it is said, unfold normally because the (racial, ethnic) origin is not clear. These opinions reinforce the French male's narcissism and class and race status.

In 1979 Bernard Biros wrote a psychiatric thesis that claimed to lay down the problematic and characteristics of the "Creole identity,"[196] and his conclusions have been adopted by many psychiatrists.[197] His study is exemplary of postcolonial psychiatry in Réunion because it carefully blends ethnocentric assumptions with Mannoni's and Fanon's insights. The study presents a balance between scientific observations, undeniable facts, and personal interpretation. Réunion's history of slavery and colonialism is acknowledged; the psychiatrist often confesses his incapacity to understand, to intervene; and the tone is constantly one of concern—"Shall we not think that a psychiatric practice issued of the metropole's sociocultural conditions, brought without reflection or an adaptive effort to a new cultural context can only lead to failure?" The result is a work that finds its legitimacy in a self-critical tone and the borrowing of post-Mannonian psychology.

Biros's method was intermediate between classical psychiatry and ethnopsychiatry, because in "Réunion, French and Réunion cultures are inseparable."[198] To Biros, the métissage of the population, which forbade the overlap of the notion of class with race, "literally blurred the image of the relation between ethnic groups and social classes, stabilizing the social structures and hindering the efforts to transform society." Analyzing the case of his patients, the French psychiatrist observed that among all the Creoles whom he had interviewed, it was the *bipolarity of their identity* that was at the center of their discourses. Pursuing his study of what constituted Creoleness, Biros came to the following conclusion: the Creoles are those who have renounced their culture of origin; they have a "dramatic sense of inferiority"; they tend to have a negative opinion about their own community (Creoles, they like to say, are "jealous, proud, lacking good character"); and, in contrast, they value everything zorey.[199] Biros's conclusion, inspired, he said, by Memmi's remarks, seems to draw as well on Fanon's remarks that the white defines the black. But Biros conveniently forgets that Memmi insisted on the portrait of the *colonizer,* even started his essay with this portrait, because to describe the colonized is to describe the colonizer's daily privileges.

The psychiatrist's remarks on Creoles' "self-definition" were based on interviews that he made with "normal [*sic*] Réunionnais,"[200] and on a debate, organized by Daniel Lauret, a Réunionnais linguist, in which a woman, a *Kafrin* working as a maid, a *Kaf* worker, a white Creole man, and a métis man discussed the theme "What is a Réunionnais?" These conversations offered only *indica-*

tions about the ways in which Creoles defined their identity. We know that cultural and social identities are constantly renegotiated, historically formed and transformed. Biros was right when he says that zoreys have been made the desirable figures of identification, but he exaggerated the impact of assimilation and attraction for the zoreys. To be sure, the Réunionnais petite bourgeoisie and bourgeoisie have adopted many of the elements of the French image of themselves. They are often the most virulent critics of their own society, of a Creoleness that they feel is keeping them from acceding to modernity and Europeanness. They gladly offer their support to the project of assimilation led by the French state. At a conference on psychiatry in Réunion, Gisèle Calmy-Guyot decried the fact that "we [the Réunionnais] like to say that we are victims of history. We must sweep away all these repetitive speeches about the past and work so that the future is better."[201] The linguists Ramassamy and Lauret have shown that it is often among Creole schoolteachers that they found the greatest resistance to bilingualism at school. French civil servants can allow themselves to be more open to "regional" cultures, to the specificity of Creoleness, because regionalism does not threaten the unity of the metropole and offers them a field of study to boost their careers.[202]

Biros claims that Creole culture offers only ambiguous images, and therefore the cultural identity of the Creole is governed by ambiguity. Creole culture does not propose a clear set of identifications.[203] Biros constructs an imaginary situation to explain the process of identification. Imagine a play, he says, directed by the Frenchmen who, to obtain the participation of the Creoles in a play whose theme and roles they have not chosen, use the media. The media have made the zorey the most desired object, Biros asserts, and the Creoles play the role that has been chosen for them: to wear the mask of the zorey on their Creole persona.[204] To declare that a society does not propose a clear set of identifications shows a misunderstanding of the processes of identification. Identifications are negotiated, renewed, and proposed to the individual through historical or family figures. Biros's play "Creole self, zorey mask" reveals the author's paradigm: Fanonian theory of alienation and a psychiatric understanding of identification (a given set of figures, rather than a process).

To Biros, passivity has been assigned to the Creoles. The psychiatrist provides as proof of "Creole passivity" the attitude of hospital patients who tend to "expect from the medical doctor help and support that go beyond the medical function." It is not the model of the master-slave that can explain this behavior, he says, but the model of mother-abandonic child.[205] Germaine Guex's notion of the "neurosis of abandonment" defines Creole behavior.[206] To Guex, the "abandonic patient," who has never entered the Oedipal phase, exhibits an unlimited need for love, which is the result of an affective attitude on the mother's part, experienced by the child as a refusal of love. "Threat of separation, rupture, menace of isolation, solitude, lack of love are the terrors of any abandonic."[207] Biros adapts Guex's observations to the Creole patient who "refuses to express his desire, to engage his initiative in the therapeutic project."[208] The zorey occupies the place of the mother, from whom all is expected because "he is the holder of social power, and of material power." Guex clearly situates the source of abandonment neurosis in the family.[209] Biros argues that it is the result of a social and historical formation. He catalogs the different aspects of the abandonic behavior of the Creoles, arguing that they are expressed as a "lack of self-actualization, an over-evaluation of the *zorey,* a tendency of the Creole to judge from appearances, a fear of responsibilities, the absence of a precise and rigid system of taboos, and the fear of being abandoned."[210] Biros then shifts his focus onto the organization of the family, the role of the father and the mother and the consequences for the Creole psyche. The importance of the mother in the Creole's life further frustrates access to the Oedipal stage, or access to the law, that is, submission to a series of taboos that make culture and society possible. Gilbert Duval, in his study of suicide in Réunion, in which métissage and recent social transformations constitute the background of the symptom, claims that the family structure produces anxiety: a "veritable phallic mother" maintains her son in a situation of dependence while an absent father tries to maintain his power through seduction and violence. Lack of communication and impulsiveness push the Creole male individual to suicide.

Creole Women, Creole Mothers, and State Power

Although métissage is the foundation of Creole pathology, what really is its source is the Creole woman. Creoles, psychiatrists argue, remain under the power of their mothers; hence they cannot reach autonomy. A 1993 official document sent to schoolteachers and school psychologists says: "The maternal function has been perverted. The power in the family, which should be patriarchal, is therefore matriarchal. . . . The father expresses himself either through violence or alcoholism. There is a nostalgia about the past and the past (slavery) weighs on society. It is necessary to forget the past. Creole culture is poor."[211] On Mothers' Day in 1993, a newspaper ran an article entitled "Men Expelled from Home," in which a doctor deplored the absence of the father in homes led by a single mother: "We see children who have no sense of what a *real* family is. We have a test in which pigs and chickens are represented. Children are asked to classify them by category but they are incapable of organizing the animals by family because, at home, they cannot distinguish the true family cell among the uncles, stepfathers, cousins, half siblings."[212]

Normative ideas about the family intersect with a narrative about the culture of poverty and the pathology of dependency. The narrative of French psychiatrists echoes the narrative of the Moynihan Report in the United States, which has defined federal and state policy about the African American community. There are similarities and differences between these two discourses, which take a group in a society that has known slavery and, while acknowledging the impact of slavery, affirm that family is the unit that produces deviance. It is an "ideological war by narrative means," as Wahneema Lubiano puts it,[213] which in recent years, in postcolonial Réunion, has established the poor woman, the single mother, as the synecdoche of poor Creole culture.

What became known as the Moynihan Report was a confidential report issued in 1965 and entitled *The Negro Family: The Case for National Action.* Written by Daniel Patrick Moynihan, who was then working at the Office of Policy Planning and Research of the Department of Labor, the report concluded that the "fundamental problem [of the African American community] is that of family structure."[214] The report claimed to use "fundamental insights of psychoanalytic theory" to argue that the Negro child and the Negro man were both victims of a pathological family. The "Negro community has been forced into a matriarchal structure which, because it is so out of line with the rest of the American society, seriously retards the progress of the group as a whole, and imposes a crushing burden on the Negro male, and in consequence, on a great many Negro women as well."[215] At the center of a "tangle of pathology" was a family structure that was *a contrario* with a "society which presumes male leadership in private and public affairs." Moynihan, who decried slavery and racism, claimed that the "pathology" of the African American community was characterized by an increase of illegitimate births, welfare dependency, lack of a strong father figure, and the inevitable consequences: drunkenness, crime, corruption, family disorganization, juvenile delinquency. The state had to step in and offer Negro males an "utterly masculine world," a "world away from women, a world run by strong men of unquestioned authority, where discipline, if harsh, is nonetheless orderly and predictable." The proclaimed goal was to "bring the Negro American to full and equal sharing in the responsibilities and rewards of citizenship." The Moynihan Report influenced the public discourse and policies about African Americans to the extent that we still speak today within the boundaries the report set. As Lubiano has argued, "seeing and hearing the behaviors and economic position of poor African Americans laid at the door of their 'problematic' family structure and/or culture" constructed the "welfare mother [as] the root of greater black pathology."[216] The "welfare queen represents moral aberration and an economic drain," Lubiano has written, "but the figure's problematic status becomes all the more threatening once responsibility for the 'American way of life' is attributed to it."[217]

In Réunion, though the narrative about the welfare single mother appeared later than in the United States, it gained as much authority. It was developed by psychiatrists and repeated by the police, the judges, the social workers, the scholars. It has become a "truth," a text whose assumptions and methodology are not even questioned. It based its conclusions on the theory about matrifocality, or the structure of the family elaborated around a maternal pole. The first writings about matrifocality sought to explain the foundations of "abnormal" behavior among groups with a high rate of concubinage, "illegitimate" births, and a tendency for "sexual promiscuity."[218] Feminists have criticized the assumptions of the scholars using the notion of matrifocality. Arlette Gauthier and Barbara Bush for the Caribbean, and Clélie Gamaleya for Réunion, have shown that women had no real economic or social power, either under slavery or after abolition.[219] Although I think that this debate is very important, my goal is not to add to it but rather to present the social, cultural, and political project carried by the narrative about matrifocality in Réunion.

Like the Moynihan Report, the French psychiatric narrative has blamed slavery for the role and function of the mother. A female superintendent of police affirmed: "Despite the incentives to create a patriarchal family unit, the descendants of slaves became vagabonds. . . . The temptation to have an enslaved workforce, an immoral and dishonest but human reflex, favored debauchery. It is important to grasp this historical element, because it has marked the behavior of the group and the individual as well as the collective unconscious, and has been perpetuated under the name of sexual freedom and loose morals."[220] Through the campaign about the normalization of the family, what emerges is the "imperative of a new relationship between parents and children, a new economy of intra-familial relations: a strengthening and intensification of the relations father-mother-children (at the expense of the multiple relations that characterized the extended family)."[221]

Lubiano has shown that there are two demonized black female figures in the United States: the "welfare queen" and the "black lady" (the successful black woman), and their victim is black manhood. In Réunion, there is the welfare mother, and Creole manhood is her victim, but there is no "black lady." The single mother is a demonized female figure who retards the development of the child because the "Réunionnais mother denies the existence of the child's personality. She ignores the importance of prime infancy and of the role she has to play at that moment."[222] She debases the father and instills in her children an indifference, if not a contempt, for masculine power.[223] The Creole mother is the repository of negativity, along with the "hysterical communist."

The female figure which is celebrated is the *métisse* beauty queen. Métissage has been incorporated in discourse through the aestheticization of young Réunionnais women. They constitute the trope of the tropical beauty. "Their exoticism, their tanned skin, their racial mixing" have made them the "most beautiful women of France," the *Memorial de La Réunion* claims.[224] The métisse beauty queen has joined the gallery of women who throughout history have populated the dreams of European men, exotic but not too foreign, not white but submissive. She is an ahistorical subject, no words being spoken on the conditions that brought her parents to the island. The black father remains locked in his room so that the métisse daughter can find her place in a French-dominated society. The black mother is ignored. To be accepted, métissage must become a trope of a new aesthetic, in which the historical conditions of its formation are ignored. Métissage becomes reconciliation between the former colonial power and its former subjects, a reconciliation of which a female body is the sign. As such, it has become the sign, created and developed by the socialists, of a multiracial France. Their métissage is a trope through which the universalistic discourse of France seeks to cover over a past of slavery and colonialism and a present of racism and imperialism. France remains thus the leader of a new French Union, constituted by its overseas territories and its former colonies.

To the narrative tropes of welfare mother, communist woman, and métisse beauty queen, experts have added the victimized Creole woman. Although women's organizations in Réunion have denounced rape and other forms of violence against women, it has been the words of male French legal and psychiatric experts that have shaped the structures of the discourse about domestic violence. French experts have used rape as a framework to capture both the ways in which Creole women experience sexual harassment and the ways in which the French law protects them. The configuration is different from the U.S. configuration, where, as Kimberlé Crenshaw has argued, white feminists have created a rape trope oblivious to the dimension of race. Yet as Crenshaw has said, "rape and other sexual abuses in the work context, now termed sexual harassment, have been a condition of black women's work life for centuries."[225] Réunion's women, slaves, indentured workers, were sexual objects for the masters. In the postabolition feudal colonial society, women workers, maids, agricultural workers, remained sexual objects. Yet the narrative about rape in Réunion has constructed the rapist as the poor Creole man, whose masculinity is essentially bestial. The rape victim is the Creole woman, her rapist a Creole man, and her protector a Frenchman. Rapes of maids and of saleswomen by their bosses, the sexual harassment of women prevalent in the workplace,[226] do not appear in the studies about violence that focus on poor Creole men, who are easier to catch and accuse. The violent rape in 1986 of a young black woman by four French paratroopers never appeared, even as a footnote, in psychiatric reports.[227]

The politics of race and class inform the psychiatric discourse about rape in Réunion.[228] But behind the rapist, behind Creole male bestiality, French psychiatrists and legal experts contend, is the Creole woman's behavior. According to Nicole Hamann, a police inspector at Saint-Denis, the passivity of the Creole woman, her resentment, and her repressed sexuality lead the Creole man to violence, a violence that can be classified according to ethnic origin. Hamann, citing Mouls, asserts that three kinds of male delinquent behavior may be distinguished: "The African type, where the man has been marked by nostalgia for his primal infancy, and a form of oral mothering; the Asian type, where the family is extremely hierarchical, and in which the man can become susceptible, distrustful, and rigid, even paranoid; the European type, where rural pauperism accentuates severity and inhibition, individualism and depravity."[229] Women are the source of the male pathological violence or mental disorder. The Creole female, herself pathologically passive, produces a pathological, violent son, to whom she does not teach respect for the father, nor for other women. The son, in turn, attacks the Creole woman because his mother has not encouraged in him autonomy and access to symbolization. The psychoanalyst Jacques André, who did a psychoanalytical and ethnological study of blood crimes in the French Antilles, has argued that there is in these Creole societies a "focal incest," that is, a matrifocal structure that fosters a psychotic attachment to the mother.[230] "Nothing prepares the boy to confront the law," André writes; his destiny is to become the "hero of his mother."[231] The Antillean man "will never cease to be a son," and his "encounter with castration will be avoided, deferred—which explains his weak relation to the rule, the law. He will be assured of an infallible, faultless maternal support that will shield him from the 'affronts' which reality will certainly inflict."[232]

The French male psychiatrist who presents the matrifocal structure and its consequences promises his help, but his goodwill and humanistic concern will not succeed alone. He needs the help of the Creole women. To begin with, Creole women must "abandon their fatalistic passivity,"[233] show more respect for the father, and learn about the psychological development of the child. Only under these conditions will the Creole woman become a good auxiliary to the French psychiatrist. The integration of the cultural values of French civil servants will be complete once the Creole family fulfills its role: a mother, fluent in child psychology, a father, stern but loving, both teaching their children the values of an assimilating consumer culture.

The discourse about pathological matrifocality in Creole society is also about displacing the focus from the tutelary mother, La Mère-Patrie, generous but severe, attentive but capricious, to the native mother, who is bad. The colonizing mother has withered away, and the colonized native mother is now at the center of public discourse. To Richard D. E. Burton, who writes about Martinique, there has been not a displacement but rather the fulfillment by the Creole mother of the assimilative role. The "assimilative project is imposed through maternal violence," Burton claims. "Inspired by the White Father, adopted by the colored father, the civilizing mission is realized, in the absence of the father, by the colored mother, who, more than the father, incarnates the French normativity—and the violence thereof—for her children."[234] Burton, who sees the 1946 project as essentially a "passionate desire to assimilate," makes the Antillean mother the accomplice of the French state. Burton does not seek the causes of the failure of political integration in racism and the legacy of colonialism. He blames the failure squarely on the community that has been excluded from the nation.

The discourse about pathological matrifocality has a great seductive power. It posits characters that are easy to identify: the powerful mother, the powerless father, the protected son, and the subjugated daughter. Its stories sound familiar. It has created a rhetorical field and a vocabulary in which anyone can become fluent. Proverbs, tales, and daily events are used to support its hypotheses, for misogyny and celebration of the son are connected phenomena. The mother, who exercises power through the control over her daughters' sexuality and through her son, is a mythological figure whose existence is verified daily.[235] Feminists have questioned the misogynist dimension of this trope, yet there remains something to explore about maternalist ideology. Réunion's society is certainly not different from other societies constructed on the celebration of the reformed mother and at the expense of the woman. Are the crimes committed in Réunion "Creole crimes"? Christian Lesne has asked why out of "complex social phenomena, whose pathological effect should be seen as extremely limited (so much so that single mother–headed families are in a minority), only one model is retained about the Creole family, a family without a father which is said to be the source of psychological abnormalities."[236] To Lesne, the separation of this discourse from anthropological studies is possible only because "evidence that would sustain this particular thesis is selected from a multiplicity of cultural data that are complex, interactive, even contradictory, and often vary from one group to another."[237]

The locus of subjectivity is still a contested territory in Réunion. Yesterday Debré claimed that the Réunionnais was a French person. Today psychiatrists claim to have unveiled the foundations of the Reunionnais' subjectivity, the pathology that stood in the way of Debré's aspiration. Medical, juridical, magical, and empirical knowledges confront and mimic each other in the struggle over the bodies, the souls, and the utterances of the Réunionnais in the power struggle for the self-definition of a people in the postcolonial empire of France.

We can now return to Yves Olivier. This is how I read Yves O.'s case, what I heard that day in the air-conditioned tribunal of Saint-Denis; and what I heard in the story, in the crime of this young man, was different from what the psychiatrist, the judge, and the prosecutor, with all their goodwill, had understood. Yves was from Salazie, the legendary refuge of the maroons, high mountains surrounding a depression dug by rivers and torrents. This geographical depression caused by the caving in of mountains when the island was creating itself through the fire and thunder of volcanoes was a natural refuge. But nights fall earlier than on the coast, and they are much more silent. The ramparts of the mountains seem to close in on the villages. But Yves was not Frême, the young maroon whose story opened this research. Conservative assimilation set up a new imperative, a new economy of social relations between women and men. The psychiatric narrative about Creole men suggested that their resistance to the new paradigm was the consequence of their Creoleness, of their Creole tendency to passivity, laziness, and violence. Yves Olivier, in the words of the district attorney, "made no effort, enjoyed idleness, and played the mad person to escape hard work and be cared for." Yet one could ask what the perspectives of the life of a poor sharecropper could be. Why was a passive rejection of such an ideal of servitude presented as the sign of a proclivity to criminality? The district attorney's judgment rested on the notion that a passive acceptance of poverty was the sign of good behavior. Yves O. resisted the ideal of servitude adopted by his father, who, a gendarme had testified, "never disturbed the peace." But that peace was the peace of a countryside condemned to misery and oblivion. Yves O.'s attitude also disturbed the inhabitants of his village, who petitioned to have him expelled from La Mare à Citrons. The small and poor community, whose life was constructed around harshness and the rules that implicitly followed—one must accept in silence a life of misery because it is too painful to confront its grimness—saw in Yves O. the outcome of resistance: madness and isolation. Between the villagers and Yves, what was played out was the effect of an anxiety, the anxiety of a group whose unity depends on a strict internal control. Yves was a scandal because he did not fit in either of two accepted alternatives: he was neither like his siblings, who had left the village, gone to the coast, and integrated themselves as best as they could into the departmentalized society, nor like his father, who had accepted the village's life and laws. Yves roamed through the mountains, neither man nor woman, but a desexualized boy in a dress, cursing the skies, desperately looking for human contact.

Yves O. was "spoken by" the psychiatric expert, the judge, the gendarme, robbed of his subjectivity and agency. The French civil servants, judges, and psychiatrists could not help showing impatience and irritation with Yves O. Why did he refuse to become a member of their society? Why did he refuse the dream offered by assimilation: dependence and modernity? Why did he not "seize the chance of psychotherapy which had been offered to him," as the district attorney said? In other words, why did Yves refuse the ideal that they offered him? Réunion's criminals, the general district attorney Marcel Rostagno declared in 1985, "are sending us messages. They question us. Their malaise is a form of failure to adapt to the contemporary world." This "contemporary" world was none other than the world of global capitalism, in which, effectively, people like Yves O. and his father had no place, except as a dying breed. As Rostagno said: "The Creole rural society is condemned to disappear." Held under the power of their discourse, a discourse of modernization and Europeanization, judges, gendarmes, and psychiatrists could not imagine an alternative for Creole peasants other than marginalization or else forced assimilation into their world. They were deaf to Yves O.'s world. They could not understand why one would not share their ideal of emancipation—*participate in your own cure, become one of us.*

Yves O. had explained his act by saying: "My father put the devil in me. I had to punish him. He was always singing." The psychiatric expert, the judge, and the district attorney never reflected on the relation between a father and his son, who, wearing a dress, cooked for his father and slept at his feet. The son, who seemed to have been feminized by the father, felt persecuted by him. Although the father had enough money to endow his daughters and live in some comfort, he had Yves sleep on the ground. He used his feebleminded son as a servant. Yves O. had killed a patriarch who had thrown insults at him—"Pimp, bastard!"—and insulted his mother: "F— your mother!" But Yves also killed a man in whom he could recognize his own servitude. How could his father sing when life in Salazie was like life in a prison? Although his intentions remain obscure, by killing his father, Yves O. gave him an identity, an existence. The life of a poor sharecropper, totally ignored by Réunion modern society, was told in a public space, appeared in the newspapers. Yves O.'s crime gave back to the lives of two poor Creole men an identity that society had refused them. His crime made him a subject, the subject of a community that has been marginalized, ignored, and medicalized by the state and yet is alive with its mythology, its memory, its drama and tragedies.

Yves O.'s act evokes Pierre Rivière, the young French peasant who, in 1835, killed his father, mother, sister, and brother.[238] Both Yves and Pierre are victims of a world in which "the abstract violence of money exercises its power. The peasant and the native are now defined as the negative of the ruler. Only the latter is '*notable,*' that is, can be located in a scale of values established by himself, which is said to be the scale of *humanity.*"[239] Outside the scale of this so-called humanity, the poor peasants, the natives, the women, kill "to make themselves heard."[240] They are social bandits, "primitive rebels" committing crimes that, as Fanon has described, are expressions of passive resistance against an order that has crushed them. Their crimes are speech, cries against a world that in its hypocrisy tells them they are humans yet refuses them full humanity. Réunionnais had been told that they were French, but when they wanted fully to enjoy the rights associated with this identity, they were rejected. And when they tried to create an identity as Réunionnais, they were punished. Now they say their difference through their crimes and ask the French psychiatrists and judges: *If we are who you say we are—monsters, beasts, insane—and yet we are your equals, who are you?*

Epilogue:

A Small Island

❦

I started with the fictional story of Frême, the African-born maroon resisting slavery and mobilizing the slaves of Réunion in the struggle for liberty and fraternity. Frême established his headquarters in the mountains of the Salazes, becoming the leader of an army of maroons who threatened the white colonial world of the plantation. I ended with the real story of Yves-Joseph Olivier, a poor Creole man, roaming through the Salazes, condemned to a pathetic life of poverty, who committed parricide and was sent to prison. By ending a narrative about *métissage* and emancipation in Réunion with Yves O., was I implying that the fate of the Creole man was madness, crime, and solitude? It would appear that way. The promise of 1848 seemed to have brought misery, repression, and powerlessness. Yet throughout my research, fiction and facts have woven a more complex story of the men of Réunion. Slavery made women and men the property of men. Becoming a maroon signified rejecting the terms of private property under slavery. Post-emancipation society enforced the respect for private property, work, and bourgeois propriety to maintain and perpetuate racial inequalities and social hierarchy, but now with the pretense of a social contract. Peasants, workers, and vagabonds were not always heroic men, inheritors of Frême. Some were crushed by capital. Others found other ways of resisting the new order. Some killed or were killed; others survived in isolated villages in the mountains. Some challenged the colonial relation; others resigned themselves to survival. Yves O. is a Creole man, like the fictional Frême. Yves's story, told by psychiatrists, lawyers, and judges, is the story of Creole men as much as the story of Raymond Vergès.

Political history, Joan Scott tells us, "has, in a sense, been enacted on the field of gender. It is a field that seems fixed yet whose meaning is contested and in flux."[1] Gender, Scott continues, must be treated as "something contextually defined, repeatedly constructed." Although I have told a story in which men have been the actors, gender has been at the center of my analysis. Visions of masculinities in the colony must be contextually defined. In Creole *métisses* societies, born of colonization and slavery, the question of the place of the "black" father and the "black" mother[2] in the narrative of the society's formation has been a contentious issue. Métissage, as Senghor remarked, was always the product of an encounter between French men and women of color, never the other way around. And more than often, the source of métissage was the rape of the woman of color. The violent circumstances of the *métis* origin have haunted the imagination of Creole societies. It is no surprise then that men have tended to respond to the absence of the black father by celebrating the figure of the *marron,* the slave who escaped and resisted the white master, a father figure, black and heroic.

> Cimendef: "I say zanguebar."
> Mussard: "I say navarre."
> Cimendef: "I say makondé."
> Mussard: "I say vendée."
> Cimendef: "I say sofola, mikidani, bagamoyo."
> Mussard: "I say angoumois, quercy, saint-malo."[3]

This verbal match, imagined by the Réunionnais poet Boris Gamaleya in his poem *Vali pour une Reine Morte,* set up Cimendef, a legendary leader of the maroons in Réunion, against Mussard, his legendary poor white hunter. It illustrates the historical contest between two men who aspire to mark the space of the island.

Paternity is a contested site, and women and men have responded to the absence of the native father in different ways. Fanon blamed the black woman who "desires" the white man. His resentful and bitter reproach found an echo among postcolonial critics, who when they celebrated a woman chose a strong, motherly figure, especially a grandmother, a woman who has "lost" her sexuality. The masculinity of the black Creole man has to be reaffirmed and his place in the family romance solidified. Writing the story of the heroic maroon, they take revenge on history. The black son avenges his father, who was not one of those slaves who died on the plantations and accepted the whip of the master. He went to the mountains, took his wife and children with him, built another world, and threatened the class of white landowners.[4]

The narratives of the heroic maroon and of the spirited and resilient mother are creative efforts to reimagine a world whose archives are human memory or the masters' documents. The colonial primal scene has held under its power the imaginary of writers and poets. Through its constant retelling, this congenitally conflictual scene is symbolized, but no *single* narrative could exhaust its potency. I have offered one. The oral tradition on the island offers others. African slaves believed that Europeans were taking them away to eat them. Whites were cannibals, they thought.[5] Their narrative was a reversal of the European myth. Slaves invented a destiny for their masters, and their stories belied the dominant official narrative. For instance, official history has transformed Madame Desbassyns, an infamous slave owner known for her cruelty, into a shrewd businesswoman, a "feminist" before her time who was "paternal" with her slaves. Oral tradition, by contrast, has reimagined her, condemned to dance naked in the burning inferno of the volcano, forever dancing for the men she sent to the hell of slavery. She is also said to haunt the countryside at night, clanking the chains that she used on her slaves. Ghosts and figures of abjection populate the Réunionnais discourse. Poets write their stories working through the conflictual relation between the language of Réunion's ghosts, Creole, and French.[6] Writing "Réunion" is taking the island as the *source,* the *matrix* of Réunion's people. The mother is not France but the island, its mountains and its coast. The Réunionnais are the island's children, and understanding the conditions of their formation is to take the island as a starting point and from this point to look at the diversity of the elements that contributed to make them.

The history of Réunion's women remains to be told, and this study has not given them their due. I also think of the Creole language and its ways of symbolizing, of oral poetry and songs, this vast reservoir of imagination and conceptualization. There are the religious beliefs and their multifarious practices. There are the testimonies of those who, because they were not part of the educated elite, remain to be written. And, of course, the island and the ocean, the cyclones and the volcano, whose roles in the population's dreams, songs, and imagination reveal that they are more than just a background to the métis-Creole narrative, the *Île-écriture,* as the poet Carpanin Marimoutou calls it. A small island.

Notes

❧

Preface: Bitter Sugar's Island

Arundhati Roy, *The God of Small Things* (London: Flamingo, 1997), p. 53. In 1963 a documentary film was shot in Réunion. It was called *Sucre Amer* ("Bitter Sugar"; the title was inspired by *Bitter Rice*) and received an award at the Berlin Film Festival. The French government forbade the film's distribution in French territory (metropolitan and postcolonial).

1 Jamaica Kincaid, *A Small Place* (New York: Plume Book, 1988), pp. 79–80.

2 This is how the Haitian thinker Patrick Bellegarde-Smith put it at the Conference on Pan-Africanism Revisited, Pomona College, 9 April 1988. Cited in Françoise Lionnet, *Autobiographical Voices: Race, Gender, Self-Portraiture* (Ithaca, N.Y.: Cornell University Press, 1989), p. 6.

3 Ibid.

4 See, for instance, the issue of *Dedale* 5–6 (spring 1997), "Postcolonialisme: Décentrement, Déplacement, Dissémination."

5 Homi Bhabha, "Minority Maneuvers and Unsettled Negotiations," *Critical Inquiry* 23 (spring 1997): p. 434.

6 With its 600,000 inhabitants, Réunion is the most populated of the French overseas departments. The total population of the French overseas departments is 1,459,000.

7 The first colonial empire was constituted *before* the French Revolution.

What is generally known as the French colonial empire—Indochina, Algeria, countries of sub-Saharan Africa, Madagascar—began to be constituted in the mid–nineteenth century. The conquest of Algeria began in 1830.

8 Today, besides the overseas departments, France controls the overseas territories of New Caledonia, Polynesia, Wallis, and Futuna, as well as the island of Mayotte (Comoros Islands) and the islands of Saint-Pierre and Miquelon. On the history of Réunion, see Marcel Leguen, *Histoire de l'Île de La Réunion* (Paris: L'Harmattan, 1979); André Scherer, *Histoire de La Réunion* (Paris: PUF, Que Sais-Je?, 1966); Auguste Toussaint, *Histoire des Îles Mascareignes* (Paris: Berger-Levrault, 1972). For the revolutionary period, see Claude Wanquet, "Révolution Française et Identité Réunionnaise," *Revue française d'histoire d'outre-mer* 282–83 (1989): pp. 35–74; "Les débuts de la Franc-Maçonnerie à La Réunion," in *Problèmes religieux et minorités en Océan Indien* (Aix-en-Provence: IHPOM, 1981), pp. 30–44; *Histoire d'une révolution: La Réunion, 1789–1803*, 4 vols. (Marseille: Jeanne Laffitte, 1984); Claude Wanquet and François Julien, eds., *Révolution française et Océan Indien: Prémices, paroxysmes, héritages et déviances* (Paris: Université de La Réunion/L'Harmattan, 1994). Throughout this book, the translation of French texts and documents is mine unless otherwise indicated.

9 On the French monarchy's policy of colonization, see Jean Meyer et al., *Histoire de la France Coloniale: Des Origines à 1914* (Paris: Armand Colin, 1991).

10 The island was described as an "Eden" by Arab, Portuguese, and British navigators. See the descriptions of the island left by Da Cunha, 1528; Davis, 1599; Van Neck, 1599; Bontekoë, 1619. See also François Leguat, *Aventures aux Mascareignes: Voyage et aventures de François Leguat et de ses compagnons en deux îles désertes des Indes Orientales, 1707, suivi du Recueil de quelques mémoires servant d'instruction pour l'établissement de l'île d'Eden par Henri Duquesne, 1689* (Paris: Éditions de La Découverte, 1984); Alfred North-Coombes, *La Découverte des Mascareignes par les Arabes et les Portuguais* (Port-Louis, Mauritius: Service Bureau, 1979); Paul Kaeppelin, *Les Escales françaises sur la Route de l'Inde, 1638–1731* (Paris: A. Challamel, 1908). About the Indian Ocean before its "discovery" by Europeans, see *Historical Relations across the Indian Ocean* (UNESCO, 1980); *Voyages de Vasco de Gama: Relations des expéditions de 1497–1499 et 1502–1503* (Paris: Editions Chandeigne, (1995). About the act of ownership of Réunion, see my "Merveilles de la prise de possession," in *L'Insularité: Thématiques et Représentations,* ed. Jean-Claude Marimoutou and Jean-Michel Racault (Paris: Université de La Réunion/L'Harmattan, 1995), pp. 213–22.

11 White men were forbidden to marry black women because, the ordinance said, it would encourage blacks to "despise domesticity and black men to marry white women." According to a 1686 census, the majority of families were mixed: ten families in which both husband and wife were French, or a total of fifty-three persons; twelve families in which the husband was French and the wife was Indio-Portuguese, or sixty-six persons; fourteen families in which the husband was French and the wife was Malagasy, or seventy-eight persons; eight families in which both husband and wife were from Madagascar. Cited in Rose-May Nicole, *Noirs, Cafres, et Créoles: Étude de la représentation du Non-Blanc Réunionnais. Documents et Littératures Réunionnaises, 1710–1980* (Paris: L'Harmattan, 1996), p. 110. The first Indians arrived on the island in 1674. They came as sailors, carpenters, and agricultural workers. See Jean Defos Du Rau, *L'Île de La Réunion: Étude de Géographie Humaine* (Bordeaux: Institut de Géographie, 1960), p. 136.

12 Although the king of France had forbidden the Company of the Indies to partake in the slave trade, "slavery is as old as the island's colonization," as Jean Defos du Rau has written. According to Rose-May Nicole, the first document that mentions the sale of a slave is dated May 1687: François, a young Indian, age twelve, was sold. Cited in Nicole. See also J. V. Payet, *Histoire de l'esclavage à l'île Bourbon* (Paris: L'Harmattan, 1990), p. 21. Payet gives the following numbers: in 1735, among the slaves, there were 3,855 Madagascans, 725 Africans, 487 Indians, and 1,503 Creoles (slaves born on the island). On December 1, 1674, the governor Jacob de la Haye issued the first ordinance forbidding marriages between persons of different races.

13 See Louis Sala-Molins, *Le Code Noir ou le calvaire de Canaan* (Paris: PUF, 1987).

14 In 1704, according to Antoine Boucher, African and Madagascan men were 13 percent of the slave population; Indians, 24 percent. In 1708, 36 percent of male slaves and 20 percent of female slaves were from India. The Indians constituted the nucleus of the group named Libres (free slaves). In 1779 there were 465 Libres, 6,464 whites, and 22,611 slaves. Among the female bonded population, 63 percent were from Madagascar in 1709. By 1808 African slaves were more numerous than Malagasy slaves: 41.5 percent of the slaves were from Africa, 26.4 percent from Madagascar. "Creole slaves" (slaves born on the island) constituted an important minority, around 30 percent of the slaves. They were responsible for the "creolization" of new slaves. Among the Creole slaves, women were proportionally more numerous than men. In 1765, of the Creole slave group, 43 percent were female slaves, 31 percent male.

15 I use the term *race* even though I am very well aware that there is no such thing as a "race" scientifically and biologically speaking. I make no claims about racial biology, yet given the political reality of the French

colonial and postcolonial world, I refer to the idea of "race" as a social, political, economic, and cultural fact.

16 Because there are fewer Hindus (called "coolies") in the Antilles than in Réunion, their effect on West Indian culture and religious beliefs has been minor, compared to the influence of the Hindu and Tamil communities on Réunion. The proximity of Mauritius Island and India has also helped these communities to maintain cultural and religious ties to their native countries that are closer than those of Antillean Hindus.

17 See the testimony of the descendant of an *engagé* (the name given to the indentured worker) in Jean Benoist, *Paysans de La Réunion* (Aix-Marseille: Presses Universitaires, Fondation pour la Recherche et le Développement dans l'Océan Indien, 1984). Benoist cites, among others, Gabriel Francinet, eighty-two years old: "My father came from India, when he was a child. He told me one day how it happened. He was in the fields with members of his family, not his parents. Men came and took them away, and they said that they could not leave this child alone in the fields. So they took him too. He never saw his parents again, no other member of his family either. When he arrived in Réunion, they gave him to Monsieur de Villèle. . . . My father later met a Creole woman and lived with her. But they did not marry and this is why I have the name of my mother. . . . My mother had seventeen children, but only four survived. . . . It was misery, it was slavery."

18 On the policies about indentured workers, their living and working conditions, and their culture, see Christian Barat, *Nargoulan: Culture et rites malbars à La Réunion* (Saint-Denis, Réunion: Editions du Tramail, 1989); Firmin Lacpatia, *Boadour* (Saint-Denis, Réunion: AGM, 1978) (this novel is the account of the life of Lacpatia's Indian grandmother), and *Les Indiens de la Réunion,* 2 vols., (Saint-Denis, Réunion: ND, 1982); Raoul Lucas, *L'Engagisme indien à La Réunion* (Sainte-Clotilde, Réunion: Les Cahiers du CRI, 1986); Michèle Marimoutou, *Les engagés du sucre* (Saint-Denis, Réunion: Éditions du Tramail, 1989); Jacques Weber, "L'Émigration indienne des comptoirs, 1828–1861," in *Migrations, minorités et échanges en Océan Indien, XIXe–XXe siècles* (Aix en Provence: IHPOM, 1979). On Chinese workers, see Huguette Ly-Tio-Fane Pineo, *La Diaspora chinoise dans l'Océan Indien occidental* (Aix en Provence IHPOM, 1981); Edith Wong-Hee-Kam, *La diaspora chinoise aux Mascareignes: Le cas de La Réunion* (Paris: Université de La Réunion, L'Harmattan, 1996). On the Muslim immigration, see Jacques Nemo, *Musulmans de La Réunion* (Saint-Denis, Réunion: ILA, 1983).

19 Sixty-six percent of the arable lands are occupied by sugarcane. The mechanization of the harvest has pushed thousands of agricultural workers out of work, and tenant farmers have been unable to compete with large companies that control the land and factories and set prices.

20 Réunion is the French department with the greatest disparity in incomes. See *Tableau Économique de La Réunion: Édition 93/94* (Saint-Denis, Réunion: INSEE, Région Réunion, 1994).

21 The stories of people from North Africa and Africa about the French immigration services are an example of the widespread practice of humiliating immigrants.

1. The Family Romance of French Colonialism and *Métissage*

1 The notion is taken from Antoine de Baecque, "La Révolution française: Régénérer la culture?" in *Pour une histoire culturelle*, ed. Jean-Pierre Rioux and Jean-François Sirinelli (Paris: Seuil, 1997).

2 I do not imply that feminist and anticolonialist movements remove individuals from serious intellectual enterprise, but that was the case for the groups in which I was an activist.

3 The demand for recognition and the aspiration for dignity are connected. The aspiration for dignity is a demand of recognition as a "human being," the demand to be treated like one as opposed to being treated "like a dog." *Dignity* is a term often used by oppressed people around the world to express a demand for "respect." In Salvador, during the war, I met a women's group whose name was Mujeres por la Dignidad y la Vida (Women for Dignity and Life).

4 *Métissage* is the French word for the Spanish *mestizaje* and the English *miscegenation*.

5 Lynn Hunt, *The Family Romance of the French Revolution* (Berkeley: University of California Press, 1992), p. xiii. See also the discussion with Hunt in John Renwick, ed., *Language and Rhetoric of the Revolution* (Edinburgh: Edinburgh University Press, 1990), pp. 42–49.

6 Hunt, *Family Romance*, p. 199.

7 Sigmund Freud, "Family Romances (1909) [1908]," in *The Standard Edition of the Complete Works of Sigmund Freud*, vol. 9 (1906–1908) (London: Hogarth Press, 1959), pp. 235–44, 238. The notion of "family romance" first appeared in the 1909 edition of Otto Rank's *Der Mythus von der Geburt des Helden* (*Myth of the Birth of the Hero*, 1913), which argued that there is a relation between the child's ego and the hero of the legends. In 1899 Freud mentioned this fantasy in a letter to Wilhelm Fliess. Freud first thought that it was a pathological symptom related to paranoia; he gave this symptom the name *Entfremdungsroman* to express the idea of a psychotic denial of reality. Later, he affirmed that this was a normal and universal phenomenon of infantile life. Family romance, he said, is pathological only when an adult still believes in it. As Freud explained, "the liberation of an individual, as he grows up, from the authority of his parents is one of the most necessary though one of the most painful results brought about by the course of his development."

8 Marthe Robert, *Roman des origines et origine du roman* (Paris: Gallimard, 1972), p. 45.

9 Ibid., p. 46.

10 Antoine de Baecque, "The Allegorical Image of France, 1750–1800: A Political Crisis of Representation," trans. Marc Roudebush, *Representations* 47 (summer 1994): p. 137.

11 About the prerevolutionary empire, see Marc Ferro, *Histoire des colonisations: Des conquêtes aux indépendances, XIIIe–XXe siècle* (Paris: Seuil, 1994); Philippe Haudrère, *L'empire des rois, 1500–1789* (Paris: Denoël, 1997).

12 See Édouard Glissant, *Introduction à une poétique du divers* (Paris: Gallimard, 1996); *Poétique de la relation* (Paris: Gallimard, 1990); "Beyond Babel," *World Literature Today* 63, no. 4 (autumn 1989): pp. 561–63.

13 Paolo Viola, "Introduction à la commission 'Les républiques soeurs' du colloque Révolution et République, l'exception française," cited in Sophie Wahnich, *L'impossible citoyen: L'étranger dans le discours de la Révolution française* (Paris: Albin Michel, 1997), p. 356.

14 My reading of the colonial family romance diverges from Richard Burton's in his book *La Famille coloniale: La Martinique et la Mère-Patrie, 1789–1992* (Paris: L'Harmattan, 1994). Burton, who applies to the Antilles a literal reading of the romance, suggests that the lasting "success" of the colonial familialist rhetoric can be explained by the matrifocal organization of the family in Martinique. The black Martinican single mother has integrated the values of the "French or European superego" and teaches these values to her children. Her behavior supports the project of colonial familialism. Burton's shift from La Mère-Patrie to the native mother as the force that hinders autonomy reduces the dynamics of the colonial relation to the power of the native mother over the powerless son. My goal is different: I study the vicissitudes of the colonial family romance. See also Burton's article "Maman-France doudou': Family Images in French West Indian Colonial Discourse," *Diacritics* 23, no. 3 (1993): pp. 69–90.

15 On the notion of *patrie,* see Colette Beaune, *Naissance de la nation France* (Paris: Gallimard, 1985); Marie-Madeleine Martin, *Histoire de l'unité française: L'idée de Patrie en France des origines à nos jours* (Paris: PUF, 1982). On France as a female and maternal figure, see Maurice Agulhon, *Marianne au combat: L'Imagerie et la symbolique républicaine de 1789 à 1880* (Paris: Flammarion, 1979); *Marianne au Pouvoir: L'Imagerie et la symbolique républicaine de 1880 à 1914* (Paris: Flammarion, 1989); Antoine de Baecque, "The Allegorical Image of France, 1750–1800: A Political Crisis of Representation"; Lynn Hunt, *Politics, Culture, and Class in the French Revolution* (Berkeley: University of California Press, 1984); Michel

Vovelle, ed., *Les Images de la Révolution française* (Paris: Publications de la Sorbonne, 1988).

16 The French word *don* is translated as "gift" in English, which does not carry the dimension of *don* as devotion, sacrifice, favor, or grace.

17 The expressions are Toni Morrison's, in "Friday on the Potomac," in *Race-ing, Justice, En-gendering Power: Essays on Anita Hill, Clarence Thomas, and the Construction of Social Reality,* ed. Toni Morrison (New York: Pantheon Books, 1992), pp. vii–xxx, xxvi.

18 Etienne Balibar, "Ambiguous Universality," *Differences* 7 (spring 1995). See also Etienne Balibar, "Algérie, France: Une ou deux nations?" *Lignes* 30 (February 1997): pp. 7–22.

19 Françoise Bloch and Monique Buisson, "La circulation du don entre générations, ou comment reçoit-on?" *Communications* 59 (1994): pp. 55–72, 56. "Ainsi, lorsque le donataire glisse de cette position à celle de donateur, l'acte de donner s'initie dans le sentiment d'avoir reçu, allié ou non à celui d'avoir manqué: mais le *don ne sera reconnu comme tel par le destinataire que s'il s'inscrit dans une relation intersubjective où les partenaires se reconnaissent mutuellement comme sujets, c'est-à-dire comme semblables et autre,* répondant ainsi à une condition essentielle de l'existence humaine, qui est de se constituer en identité par rapport à autrui et d'engager à cette fin un rapport social." See also Françoise Bloch and Monique Buisson, "Du don à la dette: la construction du lien social familial," *MAUSS* 11 (1991): pp. 54–71; Marcel Gauchet, "La dette du sens et les racines de l'État," *Libre* 2 (1977): pp. 5–43; Jacques Godbout and Alain Caillé, *L'Esprit du don* (Paris: La Découverte, 1992); Aldo Haesler, "La preuve par le don," *MAUSS* (1993): pp. 174–93; Pierre Legendre, *L'Inestimable Objet de la transmission: Études sur le principe généalogique en Occident, Leçons IV* (Paris: Fayard, 1985).

20 This secular model is the heir of Christianity, which imagined human beings to be the children of *one* parent, God.

21 Monique Boyer, *Métisse* (Paris: L'Harmattan, 1992). Boyer has declared: "I was born *métisse*. . . . In me, I had China, I had Africa, France, and who knows, India, Portugal. In me, I had the *whole world.*" Cited in Halimi. Emphasis mine. In Edith Halimi, "Renaître métisse et exorciser ses malaises," *JIR,* 12 December 1992, p. 15.

22 Boyer's purpose in writing her book was, she said, to celebrate her black *métis* father, a man whose "moral strength and dignity" she admired, but who had to endure the racism of her white mother and of a society defined by slavery and colonialism. Boyer, *Métisse,* p. 139. See the interviews with Monique Boyer: Edith Halimi, "Renaître métisse et exorciser ses malaises"; Fabrice Boulard, "Le métissage, richesse et souffrance mêlées," *Quotidien,* 11 November 1992, p. 12.

23 The writer Yachar Kemal advocates the notion of grafting, arguing

that *métissage* is a term that cannot be translated in many languages: "It is interesting to note that the term *métissage* does not exist in all languages. I would prefer the metaphor of graft: what is important for us is to notice the ways in which cultures have impregnated each other." *Le Monde,* 13 July 1993, p. 2.

24 The notion of *Peuple banyan* has been used in Réunion: the banyan is a tree whose branches become roots, creating a very large tree with multiple trunks. Hindu temples used to be built under banyan trees. See Paul Vergès, *D'une Île au monde: Entretiens avec Brigitte Croisier* (Paris: L'Harmattan, 1993), pp. 105–6.

About métissage, see Jean-Loup Amselle, *Logiques métisses: Anthropologie de l'identité en Afrique et ailleurs* (Paris: Payot, 1990); Jean-Luc Bonniol, *La Couleur comme maléfice: Une illustration créole de la généalogie des Blancs et des Noirs* (Paris: Albin Michel, 1992); Françoise Lionnet, *Autobiographical Voices: Race, Gender, Self-Portraiture* (Ithaca: Cornell University Press, 1989), and *Postcolonial Representations: Women, Literature, Identity* (Ithaca: Cornell University Press, 1995).

About postcoloniality, a comprehensive bibliography would require more than a footnote. Among the essays, see "Identities in Search of a Strategy," *Socialist Review* 21, nos. 3–4 (1991); Kwame Anthony Appiah and Henry Louis Gates Jr., eds., "Identities," *Critical Inquiry* 18, no. 4 (1992); "Gayatry Spivak on the Politics of the Postcolonial Subject, Interview by Howard Winant," *Socialist Review* 3 (1990); Françoise Lionnet and Ronnie Scharfman, eds., "Post-Colonial Conditions: Exiles, Migrations, and Nomadisms," *Yale French Studies* 82–83 (1993); Padmini Mongia, introduction to *Contemporary Postcolonial Theory* (London: Arnold, 1996), pp. 1–19; Anne McClintock, "The Angels of Progress: Pitfalls of the Term 'Post-Colonialism,'" *Social Text* 10, nos. 2–3 (1992): pp. 84–98.

25 Glissant, *Poétique de la relation,* pp. 26–27.

26 See Glissant's presentation at the conference "36 heures pour la Caraïbe," 20 and 21 June 1997, at Lamentin (Martinique) in *Justice* and *Témoignages.* Glissant argues that if one can foresee the result of métissage, the result of creolization remains unforeseeable.

27 Glissant, *Le Discours antillais,* p. 422. This is where Jean Bernabé, Patrick Chamoiseau, and Raphaël Confiant have entered the debate with the notion of *Créolité,* "Creoleness," which they argue "expresses not a synthesis, not a *métissage,* or any other kind of unity," but a "kaleidoscopic reality." Jean Bernabé, Patrick Chamoiseau, and Raphaël Confiant, *Éloge de la Créolité* (Paris: Gallimard, 1989), p. 28. Trans. Mohamed B. Taleb Khyar as "In Praise of Creoleness," *Callaloo* 13 (1990): pp. 886–909. See also Laure Colmant, "Patrick Chamoiseau: Le système scolaire doit exalter la diversité," *Le Monde de l'Éducation,* September 1994, pp. 47–48; René de Cecatti, "La Bicyclette créole ou la voiture française: Entretien

avec Raphaël Confiant," *Le Monde: Carrefour des littératures européennes,* November 1992, p. 3. Confiant says: "For us [the Antilleans] what is normal is difference, diversity."

28 Antonio Benítez-Rojo, *The Repeating Island: The Caribbean and the Postmodern Perspective,* trans. James E. Maraniss (Durham: Duke University Press, 1992), p. 126. In the Spanish-speaking postcolonial world, the debate around métissage has known a similar development. See Nancy Morejón, *Nacion y mestizaje en Nicolás Guillen* (Havana: Union, 1982); Roberto Fernández Retamar, *Caliban and Other Essays,* trans. Edward Baker (Minneapolis: University of Minnesota Press, 1989). For a critical and feminist reading, see Vera M. Kutzinski, *Sugar's Secrets: Race and the Erotics of Cuban Nationalism* (Charlottesville: University Press of Virginia, 1993).

29 See, for instance, Stefan Zweig's opinion of métissage. In 1939 Zweig had escaped Nazism and gone to Brazil, where in 1940 he wrote *Brasilien, ein Land der Zukunft* (Brazil, Land of the Future). The discovery of a métisse society represented to Zweig, horrified by the Nazi ideology, the hope of humanity. Zweig killed himself the same year.

30 Ranajit Guha has asked, "Can we afford to leave anxiety out of the story of empire?" in "Not at Home in Empire," *Critical Inquiry* 23 (spring 1997): pp. 482–94.

31 The fear of miscegenation was often an obsession among colonial whites throughout the world. See J. M. Coetzee, "Blood, Taint, Flaw, Degeneration: The Novels of Gertrude Millin," in *White Writing: On the Culture of Letters in South Africa* (New Haven: Yale University Press, 1988), pp. 136–62.

32 The Bible contains numerous commandments forbidding métissage between tribes. Pierre Brocheux and Daniel Hémery claim that the prejudices against métis were stronger among Vietnamese than among Laos and Khmers. In *Indochine, la colonisation ambiguë: 1858–1954* (Paris: Éditions La Découverte, 1995), p. 184.

33 James Baldwin, "East River, Downtown: Postscript to a Letter from Harlem," in *Nobody Knows My Name: More Notes of a Native Son* (New York: Penguin Books, 1964), pp. 68–76, 70.

34 See Pierre Clastres, "On Ethnocide," trans. Julian Pefanis and Bernadette Maher, *Art and Text* 28 (1980): pp. 51–58. In his analysis of ethnocidal violence as the essence of the State, Pierre Clastres proposes to understand what makes Western civilization more ethnocidal than other societies by looking at its *system of economic production.* Clastres wrote: "Races, societies, individuals; space, nature, seas, forests, subsoil: everything is useful, everything must be utilized, everything must be productive, have a productivity driven to its maximum rate of intensity."

35 See Jean Borreil's critique of "nostalgic politics" in *La Raison nomade* (Paris: Payot, 1993), pp. 142–65.

36 Ibid., p. 165.

37 Laplanche and Pontalis, p. 349.

38 Octave Mannoni, *Le racisme revisité: Madagascar 1947* (Paris: Denoël, 1997), p. 171. I discuss in chapter 4 the criticisms against Mannoni's thesis. Mannoni thought that the métis' lives were more difficult than others' because they were rejected by both communities.

39 Frantz Fanon, *Black Skin, White Masks,* trans. Charles Lam Markmann (New York: Grove Press, 1967), pp. 9–10.

40 Albert Memmi, *The Colonizer and the Colonized* (New York: Orion Press, 1965), p. ix.

41 Frantz Fanon, *Black Skin, White Masks,* p. 84.

42 Ibid., p. 3.

43 The most recent group has come from the Comoros Islands, and their arrival has revived an Islam originally brought to the island by their ancestors and by Muslims from India in the 1870s.

44 Joan W. Scott, "Experience," *Feminists Theorize the Political,* ed. Judith Butler and Joan W. Scott (New York: Routledge, 1992), pp. 22–40, 34. Emphasis mine.

45 Teresa de Lauretis, *Technologies of Gender: Essays on Theory, Film, and Fiction* (Bloomington: Indiana University Press, 1987), p. 26.

46 Michel Foucault, *Il faut défendre la société* (Paris: Gallimand/Seuil, 1997), p. 146.

47 De Baecque, "The Allegorical Image of France," p. 114. Emphasis in text.

48 Ibid., p. 7. Emphasis in text. Foucault, *The Archaeology of Knowledge and the Discourse on Language* (New York: Harper, 1972).

49 Frantz Fanon, "On National Culture," in *The Wretched of the Earth,* trans. Constance Farrington (New York: Grove Press, 1968), p. 36.

50 Fanon, *The Wretched of the Earth.* Colonialism was murderous, and there was the necessity to put an end to it. I am discussing here the ways in which political struggle (which may be violent, decisive) is narrated in terms of psychological and symbolic transformations. To be sure, there is a psychological and symbolic transformation with the end of the colonial status, but the idealization of this transformation denies the interdependency of cultures and societies. See the discussion of this argument by Benita Parry, "Problems in Current Theories of Colonial Discourse," in *The Post-Colonial Studies Reader,* ed. Bill Ashcroft, Gareth Griffiths, and Helen Tiffin (London: Routledge, 1995), pp. 36–44, 43.

51 Psychoanalysts and psychiatrists have studied the impact of traumatic events such as death, torture, and imprisonment. They have tried to bring out the reasons why some people seem more able than others to integrate and interpret these traumatic moments, whereas others cannot escape the hold of the memories on their psyche. For a theoretical approach, see

Nicholas Abraham and Maria Torok, *L'Écorce et le noyau* (Paris: Flammarion, 1987), particularly pp. 229–75; Sigmund Freud, "Mourning and Melancholia," and "Thoughts for the Times on War and Death," in *Collected Papers,* vol. 4, ed. Joan Riviere (London: Hogarth Press, 1948), pp. 152–70, 288–317; Jacques Hassoun, *La Cruauté mélancolique* (Paris: Aubier, 1995).

52 Karl Marx, "The Eighteenth Brumaire of Louis Bonaparte," in *Surveys from Exile* (New York: Vintage Books, 1974), pp. 143–249, 146.

53 Gail Caldwell, "Author Toni Morrison Discusses Her Latest Novel *Beloved*" [1987], in *Conversations with Toni Morrison,* ed. Danille Taylor-Guthrie (Jackson: University Press of Mississippi, 1994), pp. 239–45, 241. On "writing slavery" see also Toni Morrison, *Playing in the Dark: Whiteness and the Literary Imagination* (Cambridge: Harvard University Press, 1992); and, of course, her novel *Beloved* (New York: Plume, 1988).

54 Fanon is here the true heir of Césaire. He sees the colonial experience as producing an essentially alienated subject. For a different view of the wounds of slavery, racism, and colonial experience, see the texts of James Baldwin and Ralph Ellison. In his sharp critique of Aimé Césaire's speech at the 1956 Conference of Negro-African Writers and Artists, James Baldwin wrote: "He [Césaire] had certainly played very skillfully on their emotions and their hopes, but he had not raised the central, tremendous question, which was, simply: What had this colonial experience made of them and what were they now to do with it? For they were all, now, whether they liked it or not, related to Europe, stained by European visions and standards, and their relation to themselves, and to each other, and to their past had changed." To Baldwin, this experience could not simply be reduced to negativity.

55 Nicolas Abraham and Maria Torok have proposed a distinction between *conservative repression* and *constitutive repression* that offers a way out of the dilemma between melancholic memory and repression. Constitutive repression is dynamic repression, in which there exists a "desire that seeks its way through detours and finds it in symbolic realizations." In conservative repression, the past is buried but is neither transformed into ashes nor capable of being retrieved. See Abraham and Torok, *L'Écorce et le noyau,* p. 255.

56 Elsie B. Washington, "Talk with Toni Morrison," in *Conversations with Toni Morrison,* p. 235.

57 Historians have shown how in the nineteenth century, white Creoles made themselves innocent of the crime of slavery and insisted that they had been forced into the slave trade and the use of a workforce in chains by the state. See Hubert Gerbeau, "Fabulée, Fabuleuse, la traite des Noirs à Bourbon au XIXe siècle."

58 De Certeau, "L'opération historique," p. 34, in *Faire de l'histoire: Nou-*

veaux problèmes, ed. Jacques Le Goff and Pierre Nora (Paris: Gallimard, 1974), pp. 3, 41.

59 Ibid.

60 Ernesto Laclau, "Universalism, Particularism, and the Question of Identity," *October* 61 (summer 1992): pp. 83–90, 89.

61 Xiaomei Chen, *Occidentalism: A Theory of Counter-Discourse in Post-Mao China* (New York: Oxford University Press, 1995), p. 17.

62 Jacques Derrida, "The Laws of Reflection: Nelson Mandela, in Admiration," in *For Nelson Mandela,* by Jacques Derrida and Mustapha Tlili (New York: 1987), p. 17.

63 Michel de Certeau, *L'écriture de l'histoire* (Paris: Gallimard), p. 325.

64 Octave Mannoni, "Administration de la folie, folie de l'administration," in *Un commencement qui n'en finit pas: Transfert, interprétation, théorie* (Paris: Éditions du Seuil, Champ Freudien, 1980), p. 137.

65 Ibid.

66 The comparison with the discourse on African Americans (illustrated by the Moynihan Report) is examined in chapter 5 of this book, "Single Mothers, Missing Fathers, and French Psychiatrists."

67 I have published elsewhere articles about the struggle of Réunion women. See *Combat Réunionnais, Témoignages.*

68 In the colonial Spanish world, the figure of the *mulata* has been investigated as a trope of betrayal, mediator, colonial sexuality, harbinger of the future. See Antonio Benítez-Rojo, *The Repeating Island: The Caribbean and the Postmodern Perspective,* trans. James E. Maraniss (Durham: Duke University Press, 1992); Vera M. Kutzinski, *Sugar's Secrets: Race and the Erotics of Cuban Nationalism* (Charlottesville: University Press of Virginia, 1993).

69 See *des femmes en mouvements hebdo* (1979–1982) and *Femmes et Russie 1980* (Paris: des femmes, 1980); *Des femmes russes* (Paris: des femmes, 1980); *Des chiliennes* (Paris: des femmes, 1981).

70 When I worked at the monthly and weekly review *des femmes en mouvements,* we published numerous articles about women's struggles *in the world* (Egypt, Salvador, Eritrea, Soviet Union, Guatemala, Chile, United States) but very few about immigrant women in France or about the remnants of the French colonial empire. It must be said that feminists of the Trotskyist groups were more mobilized than our group around these issues.

71 Chandra Talpade Mohanty, "Under Western Eyes: Feminist Scholarship and Colonial Discourses," in *Third World Women and the Politics of Feminism,* ed. Chandra Talpade Mohanty, Ann Russo, and Lourdes Torres (Bloomington: Indiana University Press, 1991), pp. 51–80.

72 See Graziella Leveneur's speech at the Congress of Réunion Women, 1997.

73 Jacques Rancière, "Politics, Identification, and Subjectivization," *October* 61 (summer 1992): pp. 58–64.

74 Jean-François Bayard, *The State in Africa: The Politics of the Belly,* trans. Mary Harper, Christopher Harnson, and Elizabeth Harnson (London: Longman, 1993). Originally *L'Etat en Afrique: La politique du ventre.*

75 Jacques Rancière, *Les mots de l'histoire: Essai de poétique du savoir* (Paris: Seuil, 1992), p. 193.

2. Contested Family Romances: Slaves, Workers, Children

1 *Oeuvres d'Évariste Parny,* tome I, 5th song (Paris: Debray, 1838).

2 Proclamation of Sarda Garriga, "To the Workers," 20 December 1848. Archives Départementales de La Réunion (ADR), 11M.

3 Proclamation of Sarda, 20 December 1848, ADR. Emphasis mine.

4 *Macadam* means tar. This term was used to designate forced work because most of the people condemned to disciplinary work were sent to construct roads, railways, harbors, and bridges on the island. For a comparison with the postabolitionist period in the United States, see the recent and remarkable study, *Scenes of Subjection: Terror, Slavery, and Self-Making in Nineteenth-Century America,* by Saidiya V. Hartman (New York: Oxford University Press, 1997).

In 1998, the one-hundred-fifty-year anniversary of the abolition of slavery in the French colonies offered an occasion to revise the history of slavery and abolitionism in France. However, the commemoration has not really triggered the interest of French historians and intellectuals. Slavery remains a blind spot in French thought; the figure of the black slave as a foundation of (white) citizenship is still ignored; the complicity of French republicanism with colonialism and racism continues to be disavowed.

The Socialist government chose to celebrate the republican principles that led to the end of slavery, to honor a leading nineteenth-century French abolitionist, and to praise the French model of integration. Few official discourses addressed the slave trade as a source of economic wealth, colonial racism as a source of French nationalism, and slaves' resistance as a source of the abolition of slavery.

Postcolonial critics in the overseas departments and in France have criticized how the commemoration has been organized. They have pointedly remarked that the history of slavery and of Creole societies is still not included in school readers. They have denounced a discourse of reconciliation and social harmony that disregards a history of violence and denial and refuses to confront the intimate relation between abolitionism and the imperial project.

On May 23, 1998, more than 20,000 Martinicans, Guadeloupeans, Guyanese, and Réunionnais marched silently through the streets of Paris to honor their enslaved ancestors. It was an unprecedented event organized by the Comité pour une commémoration unitaire de l'abolition de l'esclavage des Nègres dans les colonies françaises. Édouard Glissant has launched an international campaign to have slavery recognized as a "crime against humanity."

On the commemoration, see Louis Sala-Molins, "Le Cent Cinquantenaire de quoi?" *Le Monde,* April 16, 1998, p. 13; Françoise Vergès, "I Am Not the Slave of Slavery: The Politics of Reparation in (French) Postcolonies," in *Frantz Fanon: Critical Perspectives,* ed. Anthony Alessandrini (New York: Routledge, 1999), and "Une citoyenneté paradoxale: Affranchis, Colonisés et Citoyens des Vieilles Colonies," in *Anthologie de textes abolitionnistes* (Brussels: Éditions Complexe, 1998).

5 For other pre-emancipation utopias and projects, see the articles of Tristan Picrate in *Témoignages,* 1995–1997.

6 Louis-Timagène Houat, *Les Marrons* (Saint-Denis, Réunion: CRI, 1989), p. 135.

7 See the most recent essays by Jean-François Sam-Long, *Le défi d'un volcan: Faut-il abandonner la France?* (Paris: Stock, 1993), and by Paul Vergès, *D'une île au monde: Entretiens avec Brigitte Croizier* (Paris: L'Harmattan, 1993).

8 See Lynn Hunt, *The Family Romance of the French Revolution* (Berkeley: University of California Press, 1992), p. 99.

9 In 1804 Napoleon invalidated the decree of emancipation and re-established slavery in the French colonies. Slave trade lasted up to the late years of the nineteenth century. On the first abolition, see Claude Wanquet, *La France et la première abolition de l'esclavage, 1794–1802* (Paris: Karthala, 1998).

10 The notion of republican fraternity contains a notion of equality: brothers are now equal, no longer subjected to the power of the patriarch or of the firstborn. This notion of equality must be distinguished from the notion of social equality.

11 The "colonial pact" referred to an ensemble of rules that regulated commerce between the metropole and its colonies. The pact gave the metropole the entire power to determine import and export taxes and to control the amount and sources of import and export goods in the colony.

12 Carole Pateman, *The Sexual Contract* (Stanford, Calif.: Stanford University Press, 1988), p. 36.

13 Ibid., p. 221.

14 Juliet Flower MacCannell, *The Regime of the Brother after the Patriarchy* (London: Routledge, 1991).

15 Ibid., p. 12.

16 Ibid., p. 176.

17 This argument rests on Freud's remark that "Children . . . (or at any rate, boys) attribute the same male genital to both sexes. If, afterwards, a boy makes the discovery of the vagina from seeing his little sister or a girl playmate, he tries, to begin with, to disavow the evidence of his senses." Sigmund Freud, "Infantile Organization of the Libido," in *The Standard Edition of the Complete Works of Sigmund Freud,* vol. 19, trans. James Strachey et al. (London: Hogarth Press, 1953), p. 312.

18 MacCannell, p. 18.

19 See also the discussion by Luce Irigaray, *Speculum of the Other Woman,* trans. Gillian C. Gill (Ithaca: Cornell University Press, 1985). See Hunt's critique of Pateman's analysis of the masculinism of liberal revolution in *The Family Romance of French Revolution,* pp. 99–100, 201–3.

20 There are in Freud, Jacques André writes, two geneses of the social bond: one is the struggle between the father and the oldest son, the other between the mother and the younger son. Jacques André, *La révolution fratricide: Essai de psychanalyse du lien social* (Paris: PUF, 1993), pp. 13–38.

21 Hunt, p. 203.

22 This may explain why in Réunion women sided with men in the anticolonial struggle rather than seeking to obtain specific rights. It was in the seventies that more specifically feminist issues such as rape, domestic violence, and sexism were taken up by women's groups. See Clélie Gamaleya, *Filles d'Heva,* which presents women's struggle in Réunion from the beginnings of colonization to the present.

23 See the critique of Pateman's theory by Chantal Mouffe, "Feminism, Citizenship, and Radical Democratic Politics," in *Feminists Theorize the Political,* ed. Judith Butler and Joan W. Scott (New York: Routledge, 1992), pp. 369–84.

24 Mouffe, p. 382.

25 Conference given by Lynn Hunt at the École des Hautes Études en Sciences Sociales, Paris, 15 June 1994. Hunt does not take into account the Christian origins of the order of fraternity.

26 Jacques Derrida, *Politiques de l'amitié* (Paris: Galilée, 1994).

27 *Métis* derives etymologically from the Latin *mixtus,* "mixed," and its primary meaning refers to cloth made of different fibers, with no animal or sexual implication. Cited in Françoise Lionnet, *Autobiographical Voices: Race, Gender, Self-Portraiture* (Ithaca: Cornell University Press, 1989).

28 I use indiscriminately *mulatto* and *métis* to designate persons born in the colonies of parents of different ethnic groups. *Mulatto* was more in usage than *métis* in the second part of the nineteenth century, but the two term were interchangeable. The term *Creole,* which came to designate the people of Réunion, appeared much later, in the early twentieth century. Race would be a reductive term insofar as it would collapse together peo-

ples that were taken from the coasts of Madagascar (an island where there were already different ethnic groups), people taken from different parts of Africa, and people taken from India and China. The Treaty of Paris in 1814 had forbidden the slave trade, and if this ban was not always respected, it had made the work of slave traders more difficult. England abolished slavery in 1833. In the first years of the July Monarchy, timid measures were taken toward emancipation. For instance, the Royal Ordinances of March 1, 1831, and July 12, 1832, facilitated the process of manumission. Until 1848, emancipation could be reached through the following processes: children born of free parents were born free, and emancipation could be bought by slaves. Emancipations were also given by the masters. More women than men were emancipated, particularly those who were domestic servants. In Réunion, between 1832 and 1845, 1,703 women and 873 men were emancipated. Sudel Fuma, *L'esclavagisme à La Réunion, 1794–1848* (Paris: L'Harmattan–Université de La Réunion, 1992), p. 148.

29 The Greeks had already conceptualized the métis. See Françoise Letoublon, "Un cercle d'ébène sur son bras d'ivoire: L'antiquité grecque face au métissage," pp. 83–98, and Jean Peyras, "Identités culturelles et métissages ethniques dans l'antiquité," in *Métissages: Littérature-Histoire*, vol. 1 (Paris: L'Harmattan–Université de La Réunion, 1992), pp. 183–98.

30 Frédéric de Godefroy, *Dictionnaire de l'ancienne langue française du XIe. au XVe. siècle* (Geneva: Slatkine, 1982).

31 Montaigne, *Essais* (1595): II.1.3.

32 Honoré de Balzac, *La Peau de chagrin* (1831; Paris: Union Générale d'Éditions, 1962).

33 The French adopted the term in 1598 to refer to the offspring of Portuguese colonists and Indian women in the Portuguese ports of India or to the offspring of Europeans and natives of the Americas. They used *mûlatres*, "mulattoes," for the offspring of Africans and Europeans, although as the linguist Robert Chaudenson has noted, *mûlatres* and *métis* were often interchangeable terms. See Robert Chaudenson, "Mûlatres, Métis, Créoles," in *Métissages: Littérature-Histoire*, vol. 1, pp. 23–37. Chaudenson refers to a 1598 text: "There are in the island of Danabon some mulattoes or *métis*, persons born of unions between white men and black women."

34 See Michèle Duchet, *Anthropologie et histoire au siècle des Lumières* (Paris: Maspéro, 1971).

35 Diderot, "Le rêve d'Alembert," in *Oeuvres Complètes*, vol. 8, pp. 97–98. "Tous les êtres circulent les uns dans les autres. Tout est un flux perpétuel et il n'y a qu'un seul grand individu: c'est le tout."

36 Kant wrote in 1790: "The bastard products have debased the good race without elevating in proportion the bad race." This unpublished excerpt was in "Worin besteht der Forstchritt zum Besseren im Menschgeslechte?" (1914). Cited in Giuliano Gliozzi, "Le métissage et l'histoire de l'espèce humaine: De Maupertuis à Gobineau," In *Métissages,* vol. 1, pp. 51–58. See also Alexis Philonenko, *La théorie kantienne de l'histoire* (Paris: Vrin, 1986), pp. 177–78.

37 The doctrine was supported by monotheist religions, which declared that the human species had descended from *one* created pair.

38 Jean-Marie Desports, *De la servitude à la liberté: Bourbon des origines à 1848* (Saint-Denis, Réunion: Océan Éditions, 1989), p. 50.

39 Louis Sala-Molins, *Le Code Noir, ou le calvaire de Canaan* (Paris: PUF, 1987), p. 109. Spanish colonies had a similar code. See Manuel Lucena Salmoral, *Los Códigos Negros de la América Espanola* (Paris: Universidad de Alcalá/Ediciones UNESCO, 1996).

40 See Christian Barat, Robert Gauvin, and Jacques Nemo, "Société et culture réunionnaises," *Les Dossiers de l'Outre-Mer: Réunion, Guyane. Sociétés pluriculturelles* 85 (1986): pp. 50–79, 54; Robert Chaudenson et al., *Encyclopédie de l'Île de La Réunion* (Saint-Denis, Réunion: Livres Réunion, 1980); André Scherer, *Histoire de La Réunion* (Paris: PUF, Que Sais-Je?, 1966). In 1671 there were seventy-six adults on the island, of whom thirty-seven were Malagasy, and three métis children.

41 I have decided not to capitalize the terms *black* and *white,* which designate in the racial rhetoric people of different skin color.

42 See Yves Benot, *La Révolution française et la fin des colonies* (Paris: Éditions La Découverte, 1988). State discrimination against blacks and métis persisted after the French Revolution. A ministerial instruction taken on August 5, 1818, informed whites that they were forbidden to bring black or métis servants to France. Cited in Sala-Molins, *Le Code Noir ou le Calvaire de Canaan,* p. 276.

43 We find the same anxiety and concern in the colonial Americas. See Magnus Mörner, *Le métissage dans l'histoire de l'Amérique Latine* (Paris: Fayard, 1971); Russell Thornton, *American Indian Holocaust and Survival: A Population History since 1492* (Norman: University of Oklahoma Press, 1987). "Meanwhile, mixed offspring presented an important definitional problem for Europeans, particularly the Spanish," Thornton says. Mexican and Brazilian scholars have also studied the questions raised by *mestizaje* (métissage). Contemporary Chicana feminists have reappropriated the term and expanded it. In the United States, laws against miscegenation were maintained long after the abolition of slavery. See John David Smith, ed., *Anti-Black Thought, 1863–1925: Racial Determinism and the Fear of Miscegenation* (New York: Garland Publishing, 1993).

44 Cited in Hans-Jürgen Lüsebrink, "Métissage: Contours et enjeux d'un concept carrefour dans l'aire francophone," *Études Littéraires* 25, no. 3 (winter 1992–1993): pp. 93–106, 94.

45 "Free coloreds" refer to emancipated blacks or métis. The island was

renamed Bourbon in 1810 under the British occupation and kept that name until 1848, when the republican name of Réunion was reestablished by the Second Republic.

46 Quoted in Claude Prudhomme, *Histoire religieuse de La Réunion* (Paris: Éditions Karthala, 1984), p. 66.

47 Subtitle of the *Revue des Colonies.*

48 The revolution of July 1830 overthrew the Bourbon monarchy, which had been restored in 1815, and replaced it with the constitutional, or July, Monarchy, with Louis-Philippe as its king (1830–1848). Louis-Philippe swore fidelity to the Charte, a document that guaranteed freedom of the press. The conservative party, *le parti des notables,* imposed its antirepublican program of bourgeois social order. The petite bourgeoisie, the industrial bourgeoisie, the peasant class, and the workers were excluded from political power. The opposition, united by a common refusal of the July Monarchy, organized societies to propagate republican principles, as the September 1835 laws had forbidden republican propaganda.

49 See Mercer Cook, "The Life and Writings of Louis T. Houat," *Journal of Negro History* 30 (1945): pp. 185–98; Eric Mesnard, "Les mouvements de résistance dans les colonies françaises: L'affaire Bissette (1823–1827)," in *Les abolitions de l'esclavage de L. F. Sonthonax à V. Schoelcher, 1793, 1794, 1848* (Paris: Presses Universitaires de Vincennes/Editions UNESCO, 1995), pp. 293–97; Nelly Schmidt, "Aspects des répercussions de la Révolution aux Caraïbes au XIXe siècle: Histoire et mythes en situation coloniale," in *Le XIXe siècle et la Révolution Française* (Paris: Éditions Créaphis, 1992), pp. 281–95, 288–89.

50 *Revue des Colonies,* no. 2 (1834): p. 5.

51 Schmidt, p. 289.

52 The complaint is addressed to white men, yet the black man looks at the sky, taking God as his witness. The representation used both Christian and secular references. It is a reproduction of the famous pitcher designed by Josiah Wedgwood, c. 1790.

53 "Diviser pour régner," *Revue des Colonies,* March 1836, p. 397.

54 Ibid.

55 The editors argued that the "landlords or aristocrats, were aware that the political doctrines defended by the *petits blancs* [poor whites] or *marrans,* as they call them, would necessarily have resulted in their alliance with mulattos. Therefore, the aristocrats have sought to cut short this progress and this common aspiration for equality." *Revue des Colonies,* March 1836, p. 400.

56 Text of the accusation in "Un procès politique à l'île Bourbon," *Revue des Colonies,* March 1837, pp. 359–60.

57 Slaves who heard of a conspiracy were required to report it to authorities, according to a law of September 1825.

58 The *Revue des Colonies*, in December 1835, reported that the Colonial Council of Bourbon had confiscated issues of the review because it was "dangerous and a threat to public order. It could give to slaves ideas about freedom that the slaves do not have" (p. 363).

59 *Revue des Colonies*, March 1837, p. 355.

60 Ibid.

61 *Revue des Colonies*, April 1837, p. 397.

62 *Revue des Colonies*, September 1836, pp. 118–19.

63 *Revue des Colonies*, September 1836, p. 122.

64 Barbaroux was a liberal. A partisan of the 1830 revolution, he signed the petition of July 26, 1830, that demanded the respect of the Charter by the new king, Louis-Philippe.

65 Ogé was in Paris during the French Revolution advocating the rights of mulattoes. At the end of 1789, he went back to Saint Domingue and demanded equal rights for the mulattoes. When the colonial administration rejected his demands, he organized in October 1790 a revolt that failed. He took refuge in the Spanish part of the island but was handed by Spanish authorities over to the French colonists in January 1791. He was publicly executed by the white colonists in February. See Benot, pp. 75–78, 223. On Ogé, see also J. Saintoyant, *La colonisation française pendant la Révolution, 1789–1799* (Paris: 1930).

66 Memoirs of Barbaroux père, quoted in *Revue des Colonies*, April 1837, p. 395.

67 The ordinance of August 21, 1825, that had reorganized the colonial administration gave three men the role of assisting the governor, who himself had large powers: the director of the interior, in charge of the police and taxes; the commissar in charge of war administration, marine, and treasury; and the state prosecutor. In André Scherer, *Histoire de la Réunion* (Paris: PUF, 1966), p. 54. Barbaroux issued the order banning the *Revue des Colonies*. In 1832 he was the prosecutor at the trial of the "conspirators of Saint-Benoît," a slaves' conspiracy. Of the four revolt leaders condemned to death, two were pardoned and two were executed in front of more than a thousand slaves. See P. L. Roques, "1815–1848: La vie politique à Bourbon. Les institutions et les hommes" (M.A. thesis, University of Provence, 1972), p. 100.

68 All quotes are from the "Acte d'Accusation dans l'affaire des hommes de couleur de Bourbon," *Revue des Colonies*, March 1837, pp. 359–72.

69 *Revue des Colonies*, April 1837, p. 361.

70 Ibid., p. 409. "Nous le verrons dire quand on lui rappelle les événements de Saint-Leu, que si, jusqu'ici, aucune révolte d'esclaves n'a réussi, c'est que les mulâtres n'en étaient pas" [We will see that Houat declared: if no slaves' revolt has succeeded until now, it was because mulattoes were not participating].

71 Ibid., p. 398.

72 Ibid., p. 399.

73 "Within the low ranks of this class, where feelings of inequality have been compounded with the grief of being nothing, where wounds of pride, always made more bitter by impotency gave more attraction to the desire of raising socially." Ibid., p. 400.

74 Ibid., p. 402.

75 Ibid.

76 Ibid., p. 403.

77 Prudhomme.

78 A letter of February 16, 1820, sent by the governor Milius to Paris explained that it was necessary to organize contract work "to give the Colony the arms whose lack is felt because of the strict application of the laws that prohibit slave trade." Quoted in Hubert Gerbeau, "Le cyclone et la liberté," in *Fragments pour une histoire des économies et sociétés de planta-tion à La Réunion,* ed. Claude Wanquet (Saint-Denis, Réunion: Publica-tions de l'Université de La Réunion, 1989), pp. 159–224, 171.

79 See Sudel Fuma, *L'esclavagisme à La Réunion, 1794–1848,* and *Esclaves et citoyens, Le destin de 62,000 Réunionnais* (Saint-Denis, Réunion: Fon-dation pour la recherche et le développement dans l'Océan Indien, 1982); Michèle Marimoutou, *Les engagés du sucre* (Saint-Denis, Réunion: Édi-tions du Tramail, 1989); Jacques Nemo, *Musulmans de La Réunion* (Saint-Denis, Réunion: ILA, 1983).

80 *Revue des Colonies,* November 1836, p. 204.

81 The governor had the power to ignore the amnesty and banish mulat-toes from the island.

82 *Un proscrit de l'Île de Bourbon à Paris* (Paris: Imp. Félix Malteste, 1838).

83 During his imprisonment, Houat had started to write poetry, and his poems were published in the *Revue des Colonies.* One of his poems was addressed to "L," who according to the Réunionnais critic Rose-May Nicole was certainly the poet Auguste Lacaussade, with whom Houat identified because Lacaussade too had been denied justice because he was a métis. See Rose-May Nicole, "1838: Louis Timagène Houat: Un proscrit de l'île Bourbon à Paris," *Expressions* 3 (August 1989): n.p.

84 *Mémoire* of Houat, p. 68.

85 "A la France," in *Un proscrit,* p. 20.

86 Ibid.

87 Ibid., p. 21.

88 See Houat's poem "Un éxilé sur mer," in *Un proscrit,* p. 17. He wrote: "Weeping on our miseries / I soothed the pains / And culpable brothers / Have dug my grave!"

89 "A la France," p. 19.

90 Ibid., p. 21.

91 Ibid. The colonial sister was not a rival. She did not threaten the brother, who expressed his sadness about leaving her among hateful men.

92 Houat's poems were written when the feminine representation of republican France reemerged to mark the opposition of the Left to the July Monarchy. The July Monarchy, even though it claimed to be the heir of the Revolution, feared the power of revolutionary symbols, and the regime chose to build monuments and statues that were not female allegorical figures, for they would evoke 1789. Jean Garrigues, "Les images de la Révolution de 1830 à 1848: enjeux politiques d'une mémoire," in *Le XIXe siècle et la Révolution Française* (Paris: Éditions Créaphis, 1992), pp. 91–103. Garrigues writes that for this reason, Louis-Philippe chose a male, rather than a female, figure for the statue on the top of the Column of July on the Place de la Bastille built to commemorate the July 1830 revolution. See also Maurice Agulhon, *Marianne au combat.* In the chapter "La déesse et le Roi-Citoyen, 1830–1848," Agulhon makes a similar argument (pp. 55–83).

93 "Memoir for Louis Timagène Houat and his companions, all men of color, illegally deported from Bourbon despite the royal amnesty of 1837." *Mémoire pour Louis Timagène Houat et pour ses compagnons d'infortune, tous hommes de couleur illégalement déportés de l'île Bourbon au mépris de l'amnistie royale de 1837.* Paris, 1837. Centre des Archives d'Outre-Mer (CAOM) Aix-en-Provence. Service Geog. C. 102. d. 726.

94 *Mémoire pour Louis-Timagène Houat,* p. 22.

95 The date on the memoir is 10 May 1838 (p. 49).

96 Ibid., p. 48. Ogé Barbaroux answered Houat's memoir with *De l'application de l'amnistie du 8 Mai 1837 aux condamnés de l'île Bourbon et du mémoire de M. Houat, l'un des amnistiés* [About the application of amnesty of May 8, 1837, to the condemned of Bourbon and about the memoir of Mr. Houat] (Paris: Imp. Gratiot and Gros, 1837).

97 Houat, *Les Marrons.* The novel was not successful. Some contemporary critics have argued that compared to two novels that addressed métissage—Victor Hugo's *Bug Jargal* (1832) and Alexandre Dumas père's *Georges* (1843)—Houat's novel was stylistically weak. But Houat's novel was different from Hugo's and Dumas's. *Bug Jurgal,* situated in Saint Domingue, tells the story of a black leader, Bug Jurgal, who is in love with a white woman and dies to save her and her white lover. *Georges* is the story of a métis of Mauritius. He is in love with Sara, a white woman, but her father is against their marriage. Georges leads a slave revolt. Arrested, he is condemned to death. On the morning of his execution, Sara agrees to marry him, and Georges leaves the island with her. Dumas's *Georges* responded to the archetype of the métis: his white side was rational, moral, and had given him beauty, whereas his black side pushed him toward uncontrolled desire and anger. See the critique of *Georges* by Pat-

rick Girard, "Le mûlatre littéraire ou le passage au blanc," in *Le couple interdit,* ed. Léon Poliakov (Paris: Mouton, 1980), pp. 191–214. See also Gérard Gengembre, "De Bug-Jargal à Toussaint Louverture: Le Romantisme et l'esclave révolté," in *Les abolitions de l'esclavage,* pp. 309–16. The novel *Les Marrons* was rediscovered and published in 1989 by a Réunionnais scholar, Raoul Lucas.

98 One can compare Houat's project to the project of Cuban poet Nicolás Guillén, who wrote about métissage a century later. Antonio Benítez-Rojo argues about Guillén's project: "Guillén desired a Cuba that was *mulata;* that is, a form of nationality that would resolve the deep racial and cultural conflicts by means of a reduction or synthesis that flowed from the proposal of a creole myth; that is, the *mestizo* reality understood as 'unity,' not as a sheaf of different and coexistent dynamics" (Antonio Benítez-Rojo, *The Repeating Island: The Caribbean and the Postmodern Perspective,* trans. James E. Maraniss [Durham: Duke University Press, 1992], p. 126).

99 Frantz Fanon, *Peaux noires et masques blancs* (Paris: Seuil, 1975). The Symbolic in Fanon is not Lacan's. Lacan's Symbolic is the "determining order of the subject, and its effects are radical: the subject, in Lacan's sense, is himself an effect of the symbolic. In the symbolic, there is a relation between the subject and the signifiers, speech, language." In Fanon, the Symbolic is a determining order of the subject, but the subject still has agency, freedom to determine his or her existence. See Jacques Lacan, *Écrits: A Selection,* trans. Alan Sheridan (New York: W. W. Norton, 1977).

100 See Lynn Hunt's chapter, "The Rise and Fall of the Good Father," in *The Family Romance of the French Revolution* (Berkeley: University of California Press, 1992), pp. 17–52. Hunt shows that already in the novels of the prerevolutionary years, a shift had occurred that introduced heroes without fathers.

101 Priests held registers on which they noted the birth of "so-and-so, born of so-and-so, Slave." There were no patronymic names. This is not to say that a memory about genealogy and filiation was not kept by the slaves. Nor do I want to claim that slaves could not assume a paternal function. I am addressing the fact that slavery barred access to the paternal function in the social-legal order.

102 Pierre Legendre, *L'inestimable objet de la transmission: Étude sur le principe généalogique en Occident* (Paris: Fayard, 1985), pp. 74–316.

103 Françoise Hurstel, "La fonction paternelle, questions de théorie ou: des lois à la Loi," in *Le Père. Métaphore paternelle et fonctions du père: L'Interdit, la Filiation, la Transmission* (Paris: Denoël, 1993), pp. 235–62.

104 Ibid., p. 249.

105 Freud writes in *Civilization and Its Discontents* that "Women soon come into opposition to civilization and display their retarding and restraining influence—those very women who in the beginning, laid the foundations of civilization by the claims of their love. Women represent the interests of the family and sexual life" (p. 103).

106 Article 13 of the *Code Noir:* "If the male slave has married a free woman, their children, male or female, will follow their mother's condition and will be free like her regardless of their father's servitude; if the father is free and the mother a slave, the children will be slaves." Cited in Sala-Molins, p. 116.

107 Hortense J. Spillers, "Mama's Baby, Papa's Maybe: An American Grammar Book," *Diacritics* (summer 1987): pp. 65–81, 76.

108 Ibid., p. 80.

109 Ibid.

110 The opening of the novel repeats Barbaroux's description of the alleged conspiracy at Houat's trial: it is night, and the conspirators are seated in a circle. The meeting is a transgressive act because article 16 of the *Code Noir* forbade any gathering of slaves "day or night," and "especially in roads or places that are away from plantations." When caught, disobedient slaves were subjected to corporal punishment and, in case of frequent recidivism, put to death. Sala-Molins, p. 122.

111 *Les Marrons,* p. 3. The term *Creole* refers here to slave *born* on the island.

112 Ibid., p. 23.

113 Ibid., p. 24.

114 The Salazes are a range of high mountains in Réunion.

115 *Les Marrons,* p. 55.

116 Houat follows the cultural and social conventions that connected black male leadership to a noble origin. Frême fits the parameters set by the Romantic aesthetics for the black male. If Frême is "black," he still has a "noble and beautiful figure" (pp. 84–85). Frême is a prince, albeit a black prince.

117 The Treaty of Paris in 1814 had forbidden slave trade, and by 1832, the ban was sometimes enforced. See Serge Daget, *La Répression de la traite des Noirs au XIXe siècle* (Paris: Karthala, 1997).

118 *Les Marrons,* p. 68.

119 Jean-François Sam-Long has noted that the anagram of Frême is *Ferme* (Firm or determined). Jean-François Sam-Long, *Le roman du marronage* (Saint-Denis, Réunion: Éditions UDIR, 1990), p. 35. If naming performs a cultural reterritorialization, and the young African is made French by virtue of a name, Houat gives his hero a name that grounds him in the conflictual history of colonialism. He is standing "firm" against the masters. Sam-Long investigates the textual strategies of the novel about marronage through Houat's novel, *Les Marrons,* and *Bourbon pittoresque* by Eugène Dayot, which was published in 1848 and was, Sam-Long writes, *the* Réunion novel of the nineteenth century.

120 Slaves were forbidden to learn to read and write. Frême transgresses the prohibition.

121 *Les Marrons,* p. 72.

122 Ibid., pp. 132–34. I read this dream as expressing Houat's central fantasy. The centrality of Câpre's dream is noted as well by Martine Mathieu in "Créolisation et Histoire de Famille: Remarques sur les conceptions littéraires réunionnaises," *Études Créoles* 10, no. 1 (1987): pp. 62–71, and by Jean-François Sam-Long, *Le roman du marronnage.*

123 Research has shown that the first women on the island were Madagascans or Indo-Portuguese.

124 See Sigmund Freud, "Some Psychical Consequences of the Anatomical Distinction between the Sexes," in *The Standard Edition of the Complete Psychological Works of Sigmund Freud,* vol. 19, and "The Loss of Reality in Neurosis and Psychosis," *Collected Papers,* vol. 2, p. 277.

125 "Foreclosure" in Laplanche and Pontalis, pp. 166–69.

126 The novel implies that Jean was the grandfather that Câpre was looking for.

127 *Les Marrons,* p. 100.

128 Ibid., p. 103.

129 Ibid., p. 105.

130 Ibid., p. 160.

131 Ibid., p. 62.

132 Ibid.

133 Otto Rank, *Le mythe de la naissance du héro* (Paris: Payot, 1983), p. 89.

134 Ibid., p. 147.

135 Jean Laplanche and J. B. Pontalis, *Fantasme originaire. Fantasmes des origines. Origines du fantasme* (Paris: Hachette, 1985), p. 52.

136 Ibid., p. 159.

137 Ibid., p. 160.

138 Sam-Long, p. 36.

139 There was a tradition of a Creole pastoral. Bernardin de Saint-Pierre's description of Bourbon contained the tropes of the pastoral (in contrast to Antoine Boucher's memoir written in 1710, which described the Creoles as degenerate). See Jean-Michel Racault, "Pastorale ou 'Dégénération': L'image des populations Créoles des Mascareignes à travers les récits de voyages dans la seconde moitié du XVIIIe siècle," in Wanquet and Julien, pp. 71–81.

140 Houat's pastoral contrasted with the European pastoral, in which the wild garden was the site of vices and disorder, and the tame garden was the site of virtue and order.

141 In the novel, except for Marie, all the whites are males.

142 The poem was written to celebrate the arrival of the ship *Aimable*

Victoire, which brought the news of the 1837 amnesty ordering the liberation of all political prisoners ("Une action de grâce," in *Un proscrit,* pp. 11–13).

143 Ibid., p. 12.

144 See Clélie Gamaleya, *Filles d'Héva.* Heva was one of the first women to be a maroon. She lived for fourteen years with Anchaing, a maroon, with whom she had eight daughters. Two of them are remembered: the firstborn, Simangavole, wife of Matouté, who sat at the council of maroon leaders, and Marianne, wife of Cimendef.

145 The Bible. At the end of the Flood, "God gave Noah the rainbow sign, No more water, the fire next time!"

146 Agulhon says that Marianne is the conflation of Marie, the Virgin Mother, and Anne, Marie's mother.

147 See Sarah Kofman, *The Enigma of Woman: Woman in Freud's Writings,* trans. Catherine Porter (Ithaca: Cornell University Press, 1985), p. 74.

148 Fanon, *Black Skin.*

149 See Mary Douglas, *Purity and Danger* (London: Routledge and Kegan, 1966).

150 Pierre Grimal, *Dictionnaire de la mythologie grecque et romaine* (Paris: PUF, 1958), p. 168. Cited in André (1992), p. 129.

151 We could also interpret Frême's blood as the blood of Christ, which lactates and gives birth. Medieval writers spoke of "Jesus as a mother who lactates and gives birth. They called the wound in Christ's side a breast." See Caroline Walker Bynum, " 'The Body of Christ in the Later Middle Ages': A Reply to Leo Steinberg," *Renaissance Quarterly* 39 (1986): pp. 399–439, 424.

152 *Les Marrons,* p. 132.

153 Lacan, "The Mirror Stage as Formative of the Function of the I as Revealed in Psychoanalytical Experience," in *Ecrits: A Selection,* p. 2.

154 *Les Marrons,* p. 134.

155 Rose-May Nicole, "La partenaire blanche des couples mixtes dans *Les Marrons* (1844) et dans *Eudora* (1955)," in *Métissages: Littérature, Histoire,* vol. 1 (Paris: L'Harmattan, 1992), pp. 161–68.

156 Rose-May Nicole, "Quelques facettes de la représentation du Noir (1822–1840)," in *Îles et fables: Psychanalyse, Langues et Littérature,* ed. Jean-François Reverzy and Jean-Claude Carpanin Marimoutou (Paris: L'Harmattan, 1990), pp. 147–54, 147.

157 Mary Louise Pratt, *Imperial Eyes: Travel Writing and Transculturation* (New York: Routledge, 1992), pp. 86–107, 97.

158 Ibid., p. 101.

159 Vera M. Kutzinski, *Sugar's Secrets: Race and the Erotics of Cuban Nationalism* (Charlottesville: University Press of Virginia, 1993), p. 168.

160 Sam-Long notes that the term *brother* is used frequently: he counts forty-three occurrences of the term in the single dialogue between Câpre and the Madagascans that opens the novel. Sam-Long, p. 34.

161 See Paul Bénichou, *Le Temps des prophètes: Doctrines de l'âge romantique* (Paris: Gallimard, 1977).

162 Monique Schneider, "Freud entre le mythe et le roman," in Groupe de recherches sur la critique littéraire et les Sciences Humaines, "Le roman familial," *Cahiers de l'Université* 5 (1985): p. 151.

163 For a study of the maroon character in Réunion literature, see Jean-François Sam-Long, *Le roman du marronage;* Michel Beniamino, *L'imaginaire Réunionnais* (Saint-Denis, Réunion: Éditions du Tramail, 1992).

164 Edgar Burrows and Michael Wallace, "The American Revolution: The Ideology and Psychology of National Liberation," *Perspectives in American History* 6 (1972): pp. 167–306, 200.

165 See Wanquet 1984.

166 See Zita Nunes, "Anthropology and Race in Brazilian Modernism," in *Colonial Discourse/Postcolonial Theory,* ed. Francis Barker, Peter Hulme, and Margaret Iversen (Manchester: Manchester University Press, 1994), pp. 115–25.

167 Scheider, pp. 146–55, 150. In one of the few critical discussions of *Les Marrons,* Martine Mathieu read Houat's novel as the mythological tale of the birth of a native race on an island that had no natives before colonization. This race can only be métisse, and for Mathieu, this reveals a fantasy of autogenesis: "This new generation could only be daughter of itself." Mathieu, "Créolisation et histoire de familles: Remarques sur les conceptions littéraires réunionnaises," *Études Créoles* 20, no. 1 (1987): pp. 62–71, 66. It is clear that my analysis differs from Mathieu's.

168 "L'abolition de l'esclavage à La Réunion," in *L'Épopée coloniale de la France racontée par les contemporains,* ed. Georges Guenin (Paris: Larose, 1932), p. 254.

169 In January 1848, the breakdown of the population was 62,151 slaves; 40,433 free coloreds and whites. Free coloreds were estimated to be around 12,211. The sex ratio in the enslaved population was three men for two women. See Sudel Fuma 1982, p. 14; *Le Memorial de la Réunion,* vol. 3, p. 53. About the abolitionist movement in France, see Robin Blackburn, *The Overthrow of Colonial Slavery, 1776–1848* (London: Verso, 1988); Michel L. Martin and Alain Yacou, eds., *Mourir pour les Antilles: Indépendance Nègre ou esclavage, 1802–1804* (Paris: Éditions Caribbéennes, 1991); Nelly Schmidt, *Victor Schoelcher et l'abolition de l'esclavage* (Paris: Fayard, 1994), and *L'engrenage de la Liberté: Caraïbes—XIXe siècle* (Aix en Provence: Publications de l'Université de Provence, 1995); Philippe Vigier, "La recomposition du mouvement abolitionniste français sous la monarchie de Juillet," in *Les abolitions de l'esclavage,* pp. 285–91. Vigier shows the role of the Protestants in the French abolitionist movement and the influence of the British abolitionist movement.

170 Karl Marx, "On the Jewish Question," in *Early Writings* (New York: Vintage Books, 1975), pp. 212–42, 212.

171 In Réunion, the communities of maroons were exterminated by the colonialists around 1775. Marronnage started with the first arrival of slaves on the island in 1663 and soon became a serious threat to the colonial order. Maroons raided the plantations, but more importantly, they offered the slaves an alternative to their condition. Punishment for marronnage was severe. It was carried out publicly: Jean was whipped by all the slaves of Saint-Paul; Henri was condemned to carry a weight of twenty-five pounds for five years. Yet slaves continued to maroon. They fled to the mountains with their female companions. They set up camps and lived off of the forests or raids. In 1725 the *Conseil supérieur* of Bourbon ordered slave hunters to kill maroons who refused to surrender. The following year, it offered money for their capture. Finally, in 1729, the council organized armed groups to go "into the forests looking for maroons," and in 1742 nineteen armed detachments were formed. For each maroon captured, the captor received a slave as a reward. The war against the camps of maroons was relentless. The maroons had leaders—Cimendef, Anchaing—and they formed a council to plan and organize counterattacks. But the maroons were outnumbered, and above all, they lacked arms. They suffered large losses. According to the historian Jean-Marie Desport, the last organized attack against a camp of maroons took place in 1765.

172 Sudel Fuma gives the following numbers about the repartition of slaves for cultures for the area of Sainte-Marie: slaves working in sugarcane industry, 3,000; in coffee, 1,000; in other jobs, 1,079. Adult men were twice as numerous as women. Fuma and Prosper Eve have pointed to the ethnic divisions among slaves. Slave owners were always careful to mix groups that had different languages, traditions, and religions, and they encouraged divisions among them. Fuma, who has studied the ethnic distribution of slaves on fourteen plantations between 1829 and 1830, wrote that 57 percent were of African origin, 23 percent were Creoles, 17 percent Madagascans, and 3 percent Malays. The imbalance of the sex ratio was greater among Africans and Madagascans than among Creole slaves. The sex ratio among slaves was Creoles: 64 percent men, 36 percent women; Malagasy: 78 percent men, 22 percent women; Africans: 84 percent men, 16 percent women. Creole slaves were often domestics, craftsmen, or carpenters, whereas Africans and Madagascans were *Noirs de pioche* (working in the fields). In *L'esclavagisme à La Réunion, 1794–1848* (Paris: L'Harmattan, 1992), pp. 35–38.

173 Ibid., p. 56.

174 Gerbeau, "Le cyclone et la liberté," pp. 159–224. About plans for indentured work, see also "Memoir of the Governor Cuvillier," ADR, IJ 141; "Étude de Patu de Rosemont sur le travail libre," *L'Indicateur colonial,* 17 May 1845, 26 April 1845. On the political institutions of pre-emancipation years, see the dissertation of Pierre-Louis Roques.

175 *Feuille Hebdomadaire de Bourbon,* 1 February 1843, no. 1257, ADR, I PER 5/19.

176 Patu de Rosemont, 26 April 1845.

177 Ibid.

178 *La gazette de l'île Bourbon* of 2 January 1830 signaled that the company Gamin *fils* offered three hundred Indians to the planters, and the company Fabre et Weiss, fifty. Cited in Fuma 1992, p. 106. Sudel Fuma points out, however, that the slave trade did not end in 1848. He writes: "Until the end of the nineteenth century, the islands of the Indian Ocean, and particularly the island of Réunion, continued to receive by the thousands African slaves who were bought on the eastern coast of Africa, with or without the complicity of the colonial authorities" (*Expressions,* January 1989).

179 A decree in July 1829 defined the status of the indentured workers. There were regulations about their housing, food, and salaries. At the end of 1830, there were 3,102 indentured workers from India in the colony. A commission was created to enforce these regulations (Fuma 1992, p. 108).

180 Cited in Fuma 1992, p. 115.

181 *L'indicateur colonial,* 20 September 1845, and *Feuille Hebdomadaire de Bourbon,* 24 September 1845, reported that on the plantation Piteveau at Bras-Panon, an Indian had physically attacked the owner, and following this, a dozen contract workers had found refuge in a building. Fuma reports other instances of resistance by Indians. Cited in Fuma 1992, pp. 119–21.

182 Letter of the governor to the minister of navy and colonies, 1842, ADR 57 M1.

183 Jacques Denizet, *Sarda Garriga: L'homme qui avait foi en l'homme* (Saint-Denis, Réunion: Éditions CNH, 1990), p. 57.

184 *Feuille Hebdomadaire de Bourbon,* 4 July 1843.

185 *Feuille Hebdomadaire de Bourbon,* 31 July 1844.

186 *Feuille Hebdomadaire de Bourbon,* 26 February 1845. Also, *L'indicateur colonial,* 20 September 1845. "Experience has shown that Blacks from eastern Africa are the best [slaves]."

187 *Feuille Hebdomadaire de Bourbon,* 16 October 1844. "We have been surprised that there were no women among the Chinese imported in the colony. This mode of immigration is immoral and contrary to the principles of civilization. These women would have found work right away as domestics. . . . Why deprive the Chinese of his woman who would attach him to this land?"

188 *Feuille Hebdomadaire de Bourbon,* 6 August 1845. "Whites who live in poverty could find in Madagascar new opportunities."

189 To justify the attack on Madagascar's sovereignty, newspapers insisted on the "historical rights" of France to the island. They presented Madagascan society as cruel and allowing slavery. Queen Ranavalona I, who became queen in 1828, was demonized. At the beginning of her reign, Ranavalona I had good relations with France and Great Britain, the two colonial powers interested in her island. She was supported by the class of merchants, which lobbied for good relations with the two powers. The French government wanted commerce privileges; it was not interested in colonization. However, during the Restoration, a wealthy landowner of Bourbon, the Count de Villèle, who was a minister of Charles X, pushed for the occupation of Madagascar and for the recognition of the "historical rights of France upon the west coast of Madagascar." The July Monarchy pursued a policy of accommodation, trying to find alliances with the merchant Madagascan class. Again, the landowners of Bourbon pushed for colonization and obtained satisfaction. See Pierre Boiteau, *Contribution à l'histoire de la nation malgache* (Paris: Éditions Sociales, 1958).

190 On February 22, 1848, the people of Paris took to the streets. The National Guard fraternized with the revolutionaries, King Louis-Philippe dismissed the Guizot cabinet. On February 24, Louis-Philippe abdicated. The same day, a provisory government was constituted. Arago, Louis Blanc, and Lamartine were among its members. See Maurice Agulhon, *Les Quarante-huitards* (Paris: Julliard Archives, 1975).

191 Marcel David, *Le printemps de la Fraternité: Genèse et vicissitudes, 1830–1851* (Paris: Aubier, 1992), p. 172.

192 There was more than one understanding of fraternity; see Agulhon, *Les Quarante-huitards;* David; Mona Ozouf, "Liberté, Égalité, Fraternité," in *Les Lieux de mémoire. III: Les France. 3: De l'archive à l'emblème,* ed. Pierre Nora (Paris: Gallimard, 1992), pp. 583–629.

193 The decision to inscribe the republican triad on public buildings was only made in 1880. Ozouf, "Liberté, Égalité, Fraternité."

194 Ozouf remarks that the iconography of fraternity accentuated its specificity. "Children, flowers, kisses, doves accompany the third goddess, always more soothing and radiant than the two others" (p. 595).

195 Discourse of Barère, 28 messidor, An II. Quoted in Ozouf, p. 598.

196 Ozouf, p. 608. The motto would know another setback under the Second Empire. The Third Republic definitely formulated it as we know it. See also David on the history of fraternity.

197 Speech of A. Crémieux. Festival of 27 February 1848. Quoted in David, p. 175.

198 Circular of Lamartine to the agents of the French Foreign Service, 4 March 1848. Quoted in David, p. 181.

199 David, p. 319.

200 After the dissolution of the National Workshops on June 21, 1848, the workers took to the streets. The proletarian insurrection was crushed. It is not possible here to give a full bibliography of the 1848 revolution. For the memoirs of contemporaries, see J. Benoit, *Confessions d'un prolétaire* (Paris: Éditions Sociales, 1968); Louis Blanc, *Histoire de la Révolution de 1848* (Bruxelles, 1870); Lamartine, *Histoire de la Révolution de 1848* (1850; Paris: Vent du Large, 1948); Alexis de Tocqueville, *Souvenirs,* vol. 12 (Paris: Gallimard, 1964).

201 Karl Marx, *The Class Struggles in France: 1848 to 1850,* p. 47. Italics in the text.

202 Cited in Aimé Césaire, "Victor Schoelcher et l'abolition de l'esclavage," in *Esclavage et colonisation* (Paris: PUF, 1948), pp. 1–28, 11.

203 "Rapport fait au Ministre de la Marine et des Colonies par la Commission Instituée pour Préparer L'Acte d'Abolition Immédiate de l'Esclavage" (Paris: Imp. Nationale, 1848). Quoted in *Esclavage et colonisation,* p. 152.

204 Schoelcher, p. 144. His report contained recommendations to enforce work in the colonies. Schoelcher proposed that a decree, not a popular consultation, put an end to slavery. A group of young Creoles from Réunion immediately signed a petition to support his proposition. See "Le 20 décembre 1848 . . . de Paris, l'action de Leconte de Lisle, Auguste Lacaussade, Lépervanche, Amelin . . . ," *Les Cahiers de La Réunion et de l'Océan Indien* (1 November 1972): pp. 77–80.

205 *Aux Peuples.* Bibliothèque Nationale, Paris. Cabinet des Estampes. Although there is no date, it seems that the engraving was done after June 1848. Reproduced in David. Agulhon, David, and Ozouf have commented on the 1848 shift toward a more Christian iconography than that used during the French Revolution.

206 Sketch attributed by Michel Vovelle to Monsiau and by Jean-Marie Desport to Charles Thévenin. The sketch is at the Musée Carnavalet, Paris. Vovelle remarks that it was one of the better-known representations of this event. Desport, p. 97; Michel Vovelle, *La Révolution française: Images et récits,* vol. 2, *Octobre 1789–September 1791* (Paris: Messidor, 1986), p. 242.

207 Musée de Versailles.

208 *Adresse et protestation à l'Assemblée Nationale de France par l'Assemblée des délégués des Communes, March 1848.* Cited in Volsy Focard, *Dix-huit mois de République à l'île Bourbon, 1848–1849* (Saint-Denis, Réunion, 1863), p. 118.

209 Denizet, pp. 24–25. Sarda Garriga was born December 13, 1808, the son of Gauderic Sarda, a shepherd, and of Marie Garriga. Adopted at birth by a wealthy landowner, the child escaped a world of poverty and received a bourgeois education. Denizet suggests that there was some doubt about the child's paternity, which would explain his adoption by Jean Arnaud, the wealthy landowner. When Sarda married in 1838, he added to his father's name, Sarda, the name of his mother, Garriga.

210 In 1821, the Société de la Morale chrétienne, advocating emancipation of the slaves, was founded by members of the Protestant elite in France. Constant was a member of this Société. About Constant's ideas, see Benjamin Constant, *Écrits politiques* (Paris: Gallimard, 1997), and *Principes de politique* (Paris: Hachette/Pluriel, 1997); Tzvetan Todorov, *Benjamin Constant, la passion démocratique* (Paris: Hachette, 1997).

211 The charge was "conspiracy against the State" because the society had celebrated the anniversary of the Trois Glorieuses, the three days of July 1830 when the people of Paris revolted and brought down the Restoration.

212 Denizet, p. 43.

213 Discourse of Sarda Garriga cited in Benjamin Laroche, *Histoire de l'abolition de l'esclavage dans les colonies,* vol. 1, *La Réunion* (Paris: Firmin Didot, 1851), p. 24.

214 Ibid.

215 Édouard Glissant, *Le discours antillais* (Paris: Seuil, 1981), pp. 45–47. See also Aimé Césaire for a critical analysis of the discourse on emancipation in the French Caribbean.

216 Sarda concluded his first declaration with: "The support that all social classes have spontaneously offered to my presence is the evidence that the alliance of order and liberty in connection with work is finally established in your beautiful colony." Laroche, p. 26.

217 Declaration of Sarda, 17 October 1848. Cited in Laroche, p. 25. Emphasis mine.

218 See Jacques Derrida's analysis of the production of the legitimated and authorized signature in the Declaration of Independence of the United States, in *Otobiographies: L'enseignement de Nietzsche et la politique du nom propre* (Paris: Galilée, 1984).

219 Declaration of Sarda, 17 October 1848, cited in Laroche, p. 24.

220 Ibid., p. 25.

221 Cited in Prudhomme, p. 110. It must be said, however, that some priests took a radical position against the landed aristocracy and were expelled because of their "communist" views.

222 Auguste Cochin, *L'abolition de l'esclavage,* vol. 1 (Paris: Lecoffre, 1861), p. 311.

223 Ibid., p. 346.

224 Mondon, p. 33.

225 Prudhomme, p. 115.

226 Laroche, p. 27. The idea of the institution of forced work was an old one. In 1839 Alexis de Tocqueville had proposed that forced work be

organized between the moment of emancipation and the moment when emancipated slaves would enjoy civil rights. Blacks had to learn to "withstand liberty," Tocqueville wrote. He said that the emancipated slaves should be denied access to private property so that they would have to sell their labor. Cited in Césaire, p. 9.

227 Decree of 27 April 1848. Those condemned to the disciplining workplaces had every moment of their lives regulated. Workdays were nine hours and thirty minutes long in winter, ten hours and thirty minutes in summer; work had to be done in silence; food was rationed (80 g. of rice per day; 15 g. of salt); women and men were housed in different quarters; the condemned received a religious instruction; there were rewards for good behavior: (1) honorable mention, (2) permission to talk and smoke, (3) 62 g. of codfish or salt beef, or tobacco, (4) less painful jobs. CAOM. C379. d.3200.

228 *Le Mémorial de la Réunion,* vol. 3, p. 54.

229 Declaration of Sarda Garriga, cited in Laroche, pp. 53–54.

230 *Le Moniteur de l'Île de La Réunion,* 4 November 1848.

231 Prosper Eve, personal communication, December 1992.

232 Civil authorities in Saint-Paul, an important urban center, forbade the sale of alcoholic beverages from December 18 to December 19, 1848. Similar measures were taken in Saint-Joseph, Sainte-Marie, and other cities. Cited in Fuma 1982, p. 17.

233 Laroche, p. 47.

234 Speech of Lamartine at the Constitutive Assembly, 4 September–4 November 1848. Cited in David, p. 318.

235 Ibid., p. 320.

236 Yves Perotin, "Comment on s'habillait au temps de Sarda-Garriga," in *Chroniques de Bourbon* (Nerac: Couderc, 1957), pp. 197–203.

237 I. Chauvac et al., *Étude sur les registres d'affranchissement des esclaves à Saint-Denis* (Saint-Denis, Réunion: École Normale, 1973).

238 Recent works by French psychologists studying Réunion or the Antilles echo this view. Creole societies are said to be pathological because of the lack of the Name of the Father. Their views are discussed in chapter 5.

239 Spillers, "Mama's Baby," p. 80. Emphasis in the text.

240 Ibid.

241 See, for instance, James Baldwin, *Notes of a Native Son;* Thelma Golden, ed., *Black Male: Representations of Masculinity in Contemporary American Art* (New York: Whitney Museum of American Art, 1994); Robert Gooding-Williams, ed., *Reading Rodney King, Reading Urban Uprising* (New York: Routledge, 1993); Hortense Spillers, ed., *Comparative American Identities: Race, Sex, and Nationality in the Modern Text* (New York: Routledge, 1991).

242 Michel Foucault, *Discipline and Punish* (New York: Vintage Books,

1979); *L'impossible prison: Recherches sur le système pénitentiaire au XIXe siècle réunies par Michelle Perrot* (Paris: Seuil, 1980). On discipline, see also Michel de Certeau, *The Practice of Everyday Life* (Berkeley: University of California Press, 1988); Gilles Deleuze, *Pourparlers* (Paris: Éditions de Minuit, 1990), particularly pp. 229–47; Patrick Brantlinger and Donald Ulin, "Policing Nomads: Discourse and Social Control in Early Victorian England," *Cultural Critique* 25 (fall 1993): pp. 33–64.

243 The back of the knee of maroons was cut to hinder new attempts to escape.

244 The point made by Brantlinger and Ulin on vagrants in early Victorian England could be made about vagrants in late-nineteenth-century Réunion. I applied to the postslavery maroons their use of the concept of "nomadology." The concept of nomadology was developed by Gilles Deleuze and Félix Guattari in *A Thousand Plateaux*. Deleuze and Guattari wrote: "History is always written from the sedentary point of view and in the name of a unitary state apparatus . . . even when the topic is nomads. What is lacking is a Nomadology, the opposite of a history." Cited in Brantliger and Ulin, p. 35. On the repression of vagrancy in France in another postrevolutionary moment, see Kristin Ross, *The Emergence of Social Space: Rimbaud and the Paris Commune* (Minneapolis: University of Minnesota Press, 1988), particularly pp. 56–59. Ross notes that later on, the French government would apply a more effective treatment to vagrancy: sending the vagabonds as colonists to its overseas colonies.

245 For instance, in the county of Sainte-Suzanne, the population of emancipated was 3,445 in 1849 but only 1,382 in 1860. They migrated to Salazie and La Plaine des Palmistes, both mountainous places. Cited in Fuma 1992, p. 164.

246 *Le colon,* 11 November 1852.

247 See *Le colon,* 11 November 1852; *Le Moniteur de l'Île de La Réunion,* 15 December 1845 and 29 January 1853.

248 *Feuille Hebdomadaire de Bourbon,* 14 February 1852.

249 *Bulletin Officiel de l'Île de La Réunion,* decree of 24 October 1848.

250 Declaration of Sarda Garriga, 17 February 1849, cited in Laroche, p. 59.

251 Ibid., p. 60.

252 Ibid.

253 See Jacques Berchtold and Michel Porret, eds., *La peur au XVIIIe siècle, discours, représentations, pratiques* (Genève: Droz, Faculté de Genève, 1994); Prosper Eve, *Île à peur: La peur redoutée ou récupérée à La Réunion des origines à nos jours* (Saint-Denis, Réunion: Océan Éditions, 1992).

254 *Le Moniteur de l'Île de La Réunion,* 17 November 1849.

255 *Le Moniteur de l'Île de La Réunion,* 6 January 1849.

256 *Le Moniteur de l'Île de la Réunion,* 17 November 1849.

257 Michel Foucault, *Histoire de la sexualité: La volonté de savoir* (Paris: Gallimard, 1976).

258 See Jacques Rancière, *La nuit des prolétaires* (Paris: Fayard, 1981).

259 A report of the general prosecutor to the commissioner of the republic of December 3, 1849, insisted on the need to educate the emancipated so that they understood punishments (CAOM, Série Géog. C.18, d.114).

260 See the catalog of these pictures, Fuma, *Chambre noire, Chants obscurs,* with texts by Sudel Fuma and Jean-Claude Carpanin Maritmoutou (Saint-Denis, Réunion: Conseil Général, 1994). See also Pascal Blanchard et al., *L'autre et nous: "scènes et types"* (Paris: Syros/ACHAC, 1995).

261 *Chambre noire,* pp. 39–41. Between 1848 and 1865, of the indentured workers arriving in Réunion, 37,777 were from India, 26,748 were from Mozambique, and 423 were from China.

262 Edward W. Said, *Orientalism* (New York: Vintage Books, 1979), p. 55.

263 André Scherer, *Histoire de La Réunion,* p. 73.

264 See the excellent study of Jean-Claude Laval, *La justice répressive à La Réunion de 1848 à 1870* (Saint-Benoît, Réunion: Université Populaire, 1986). Laval says that the port of Saint-Pierre was practically entirely constructed by macadam convicts. In 1865, 5,421 days of 5,959 days of work by the convicts were for the construction of the port. The same year, the convicts worked for a total of 274,000 days free of charge for the colony (pp. 41–42).

265 Declaration of Sarda Garriga on the incoming elections, September 1849, cited in Laroche, p. 66. During his tour, Sarda rewarded a "good" emancipated slave who had continued to work for his master after emancipation and, after his master's death, had stayed to work for his master's widow and her five children. Official historiography seems to have favored this story, which constructs the image of a "good" and faithful servant who is naive and awed by power. He is said to have chosen as his last name Lacollé (Be Embraced) to celebrate Sarda's embrace. It is a pun on Creole stupidity. Sarda had said, "Let me shake your hand. . . . No, it is not enough, let me embrace you fraternally" [laisse-moi te donner *l'accolade* fraternelle]. See Auguste Brunet, *Trois cent ans de colonisation: La Réunion* (Paris: Éditions de l'Empire Français, 1948), p. 145; Laroche, p. 71; *Le Mémorial de La Réunion,* vol. 3, p. 62.

266 Laroche, p. 68.

267 Cited in Fuma 1982, p. 45.

268 Ibid., pp. 46–50.

269 On these elections, see Jean-Claude Balducchi, "Le personnel politique à l'Île de La Réunion, 1848–1860" (M.A. thesis, University of Aix en Provence, 1973). The results of these elections show that Houat received

69.2 percent in the eastern part of the island, whereas Barbaroux and Greslan, both candidates of the Colonial party, received only 44.3 percent in this region. It was the vote of the western part of the island that gave the Colonial party its final victory (p. 71).

270 The colony learned in February 1852 that there had been a coup d'état in Paris on December 2, 1851. The coup put an end to the Second Republic and brought Louis Bonaparte to power. The notables swore fidelity to the empire. Newspapers greeted with joy the repressive measures about suffrage. Balducchi cites an article of May 22, 1852, of the *Moniteur de l'Île de La Réunion:* "The France of the colonies now depends on the Senate; in this assembly, only distinguished men sit. There, at least, the disastrous and stupid theories of democratic *negrophilism* will not penetrate as they did until recently in the national assembly" (cited in Balducchi, p. 94).

271 Scherer, p. 74.

272 W. E. B. DuBois, *The Souls of Black Folk* (New York: Fawcett Publications, 1903), pp. 23–41. Excerpts cited in Joanne Grant, ed., *Black Protest: 350 Years of History, Documents, and Analyses* (New York: Fawcett Columbine, 1968).

273 Letter of Judge Coulon, 12 November 1852, Archives du parquet du Procureur Général, ADR 21 11 631 N775.

274 Ibid. "Free" work was waged work. Emphasis in the text.

275 Fuma 1992, pp. 177–78.

276 Decree of 22 November 1865. An agent of this brigade was paid 480F per year, four times more than any other worker in the colonies. Cited in Laval, p. 37.

277 "Circulaire du Directeur de l'Intérieur sur la recherche et la répression du vagabondage aux Maires de l'île," 29 November 1865, ADR. *Bulletion Officiel de l'île de La Réunion,* 1865, pp. 345–51.

278 Cited in Laval, p. 124. See similar testimonies, pp. 125–27.

279 File Santé Publique et Hygiène, "Luttes contre les maladies vénériennes: Circulaires, réglementations de la prostitution, 1852–1942," ADR 5 M48.

280 Ibid.

281 File Santé Publique et Hygiène, "Lutte contre les maladies vénériennes: Contrôle sanitaire des prostituées, 1853–1854," ADR 5M49.

282 Denizet, p. 119.

283 In January 1850, an order from the French government put an end to Sarda's mission. He left the island in May and received the mission of organizing a penal colony in Guiana. Sarda's new motto was "Repentance Is Salvation." His goal was to "humanize" the penal colony. He worked at his project until March 1853, when he returned to France. In 1858 the General Council of Réunion allocated a life pension to Sarda Garriga. He died on September 8, 1877. See Denizet.

Louis-Timagène Houat turned to medicine after the publication of *Les Marrons* and his failed attempts at a political career. In 1863 he published *Études et Sciences Spirites*. Houat lived for a while with his wife and daughters in Saint Petersburg, then studied the writings of the founder of homeopathy, Samuel Hahneman. Back in Paris, Houat published works on homeopathy in 1866, 1868, and 1883. He spent his last years in Pau (southern France) and died in the late 1880s. See Woodson.

284 See Sophie Wahnich, *L'impossible citoyen: L'étranger dans le discours de la Révolution française* (Paris: Albin Michel, 1997). Although Wahnich looks at the French Revolution, her analysis of republican fraternity enlightens the analysis of republican (imperial) fraternity in the 1840s.

285 Ibid., p. 356.

3. Blood Politics and Political Assimilation

1 I will use this name throughout this chapter to distinguish these territories from the other colonized territories of Africa, Asia, and the Pacific.

2 Archives de l'Assemblée Nationale, *Annales de l'Assemblée Nationale Constituante, 1945.*

3 The Charter of the United Nations was signed on June 26, 1949, by fifty founding countries, with France among them. The charter expressed the countries' commitment to help the populations under colonial control to "develop their capacities to govern themselves."

4 See Yves Benot, *Massacres coloniaux* (Paris: Éditions La Découverte, 1994); Boucif Mekhaled, *Chroniques d'un massacre: 8 mai 1945. Sétif, Guelma, Kherrata* (Paris: Syros, 1995); Philippe Devillers, ed., *Paris, Saigon, Hanoi: Les archives de la guerre, 1944–1947* (Paris: Archives Gallimard, Julliard, 1988). Devillers presents in these archives—some of them were opened in recent years—documents that show the responsibility of the French army and of the colonial administration in the Indochinese war. Devillers publishes notes of the Vietnamese nationalists that prove their will to find a political solution with the French state and avoid the war.

5 Women as well as men can occupy this position of the masculine hero in arms. The image of armed women is attractive. It disrupts the traditional image of the woman as nurturing, partisan of peace, guardian of the house, and responds to the desire and the will of women to join the liberation struggle. I am not defending a "nurturing female position" in anticolonialist and anti-imperialist struggles, but rather I want to point to the gendered rhetoric that accompanies the heroic position. Again, I want to insist on the fact that the French state refused more than once to consider a political solution with the anticolonialist forces and that armed struggle was the only way out of an unbearable situation. But to conceive the history of emancipation solely as a story of virile heroes is to repress important events.

6 See Frantz Fanon, *Black Skin, White Masks,* trans. Constance Farrington (New York: Grove Press), and *The Wretched of the Earth,* trans. Constance Farrington (New York: Grove Press, 1963); and my "To Cure and to Free: The Fanonian Project of Decolonized Psychiatry," in *Fanon: A Critical Reader,* ed. Louis R. Gordon et al. (Oxford, U.K.: Blackwell, 1996), pp. 85–99, and "Chains of Madness, Chains of Colonialism: Fanon and Freedom," in *The Fact of Blackness: Frantz Fanon and Visual Representation,* ed. Alan Read (London: ICA, 1996), pp. 46–75.

7 Benot, p. 56.

8 A comparison could be made with the Declaration of Independence in the United States and its exclusion of slaves from the community of equals. A further comparison could be made between the movement for integration in the Old Colonies and the movement for integration in the United States. Yet integration was not always the response to exclusion in slave societies. (The British Caribbean islands asked for independence.) Could we then say that the demand for political integration was partly the consequence of the revolutionary discourse in France and the United States? The weight of names—liberty, equality, independence—and the revolutionary promise led excluded groups to desire integration into the republican community.

9 Sophie Wahnich, *L'impossible citoyen: L'étranger dans le discours de la Révolution française* (Paris: Albin Michel, 1997).

10 See Pascal Blanchard, "Nationalisme et Colonialisme: Idéologie Coloniale, Discours sur l'Afrique et les Africains de la Droite Nationaliste française des années 30 à la Révolution nationale" (Ph.D. diss., University of Paris I, 1994).

11 Édouard Glissant, *Le Discours antillais* (Paris: Seuil, 1981), p. 58.

12 Raphäel Confiant, *Aimé Césaire: Une traversée paradoxale du siècle* (Paris: Stock, 1994), p. 32.

13 Ibid., p. 37. Emphasis mine.

14 Sigmund Freud, *Moses and Monotheism* (London: Hogarth Press, 1939), p. 109.

15 Sigmund Freud, *The Interpretation of Dreams,* vol. 6 of *The Standard Edition of the Complete Works of Sigmund Freud,* trans. James Strachey (London: Hogarth Press), p. 197.

16 Sigmund Freud, "Letter to Romain Rolland, A Disturbance of Memory on the Acropolis," *Standard Edition,* vol. 22, p. 247.

17 Cited in Marianne Krüll, *Freud and His Father,* trans. Arnold J. Pomerans (New York: W. W. Norton, 1986), p. 155. Emphasis mine.

18 Hannah Arendt, "Truth and Politics," in *Between Past and Future* (New York: Penguin Books, 1977), pp. 227–64, 241.

19 Ibid., p. 241.

20 Michel de Certeau, *L'écriture de l'histoire* (Paris: Gallimard, 1975), p. 22.

21 Confiant's choice of Delgrès as a "true" ancestor rather than (or with) Césaire, or some Réunion activists' choice of the maroon Cimendef as ancestor rather than (or with) Raymond Vergès, show how this temptation remains powerful. About the need for heroes in the national narrative, see Anna Makolkin, *Name, Hero, Icon: Semiotics of Nationalism through Heroic Biography* (New York: Mouton de Gruyter, 1992).

22 Jacques Hassoun, *Les contrebandiers de la mémoire* (Paris: Syros, 1994).

23 Aimé Césaire, Archives de l'Assemblée Nationale, *Annales de l'Assemblée Nationale Constituante,* March 1946. Discussion on the classification of Guadeloupe, Martinique, Réunion, and French Guiana as French departments.

24 Ibid.

25 Raymond Vergès, Archives de l'Assemblée Nationale, *Annales de l'Assemblée Nationale Constituante,* March 1945. As Caroline Oudin-Bastide and Prosper Eve have shown, the doctrine of assimilation was associated, in France and in the colonies, with the republicans, whereas autonomy was traditionally the demand of the landed aristocracy. Prosper Eve, *Le jeu politique à La Réunion de 1900 à 1939* (Paris: L'Harmattan–Université de La Réunion, 1994); Caroline Oudin-Bastide, "L'assimilation, La stratégie du pouvoir: la lutte des colonies," *CARÉ* 7 (February 1981): pp. 89–119. Full incorporation in the French state challenged the arbitrary administration that had been instituted by the 1852 constitution. The Constitution of 1852 put the administration of the Old Colonies and Algeria under the control of the French Senate, which ruled by decrees. There was not, therefore, a general comprehensive policy for the colonies, but rather decisions taken when the situation demanded it.

26 Jacques Rancière, "The Image of Brotherhood," trans. Kari Hanet, *Edinburgh Magazine* 2 (1977).

27 In the 1946 constitution's preamble, the proposal of the French Union was: "France shall form with the peoples of her Overseas Territories a Union based upon equality of rights and privileges, without distinction of race or religion." Yet among these equal units, one was designated as more than equal: France, which, "faithful to her traditional mission, shall guide the peoples for whom she has assumed responsibility, toward freedom to govern themselves and toward the democratic administration of their own affairs." See Hubert Deschamps, *The French Union: History, Institutions, Economy, Countries, and Peoples—Social and Political Changes* (Paris: Éditions Berger-Levrault, 1956). Deschamps writes: "The 1946 Constitution includes a Preamble and twelve titles. The longest of the latter, Title VIII (articles 60 to 82 inclusive), is devoted to the French Union" (p. 91). The excerpt that I reproduce is from the last three paragraphs of the preamble.

28 Jean-François Lyotard, "Notes on Legitimation," *Oxford Literary Review* 9, nos. 1–2 (1987): pp. 106–18, 113.

29 The Third Republic ended in 1940 when Marshal Pétain took the French collaborationist government to Vichy after surrendering to the Nazis.

30 The struggle to end colonial status had started in 1936, when for the first time workers demonstrated with banners asking for "Reunion, French Department!" At the end of the nineteenth century, the elected representatives of the Old Colonies had demanded assimilation, but large social and popular movements did not mobilize around this demand. On March 17, 1883, Dislère, a representative of the colonies at the French National Assembly, introduced a project to the Commission of the Colonies: "The colonies of Guadeloupe and Martinique will be assimilated with the metropole." The proposition was rejected.

31 See Gaston Monnerville's speech, 14 March 1946, *Annales de l'Assemblée Nationale*.

32 Jacques Rancière, "Politics, Identification, and Subjectivization," *October* 61 (summer 1992): pp. 58–64, 58.

33 René Gallissot, "Les thèses du 'Socialisme colonial' en Tunisie: Colonisation socialiste et formation d'une nouvelle patrie par le mélange des races. Le discours de J. Durel au Conseil National du Parti Socialiste S.F.I.O. de Juillet 1928," *Pluriel* 12 (1977): pp. 53–59, 54.

34 Ibid., p. 58.

35 Ibid.

36 Ibid., p. 56.

37 "Appel de l'Union Intercoloniale aux populations des colonies," *Le Paria* 5 (August 1922): p. 1. For the history of movements of colonized peoples in France during the 1930s, see Philippe Dewitte, *Les Mouvements nègres en France, 1919–1939* (Paris: L'Harmattan, 1985); Roger Toumson and Simonne Henry-Valmore, *Aimé Césaire, le nègre inconsolé* (Paris: Syros, 1994).

38 "Des droits politiques pour les indigènes," *Le Paria* 2 (May 1922): p. 1. See also *L'Action Coloniale* (1918–1928), which published numerous articles defending a fraternal and just colonization against colonialism. The civil servants in the colonies were accused of being "monsters lost in vice, soaked in alcohol, degenerated with syphilis." Assimilation was defended in the name of justice against the arbitrary rule of the colonial governor.

39 "Une visite à René Maran," *Le Paria* 20 (November 1923): p. 2.

40 *Les problèmes des Antilles et de La Réunion*, 22 July 1948. Personal archives of Paul Vergès.

41 In 1945 the Gaullist representative at the San Francisco meeting that inaugurated the United Nations strongly opposed the American proposition of an international trusteeship of the colonies to ensure their transition to independence. De Gaulle's government distrusted the U.S. government and feared that the United States would take advantage of the trusteeship to advance its interests in the French empire. See Benot. The anticolonialists of the French Antilles used the United States' interest in their argument for assimilation: Was it better to be under the control of U.S. imperialism or within the French republic?

42 *Les problèmes des Antilles et de La Réunion,* pp. 7–8. Emphasis mine.

43 *Annales de l'Assemblée Nationale Constituante,* no. 210 (March 1946).

44 See the analysis of republican fraternity by Lynn Hunt, *The Family Romance of the French Revolution* (Berkeley: University of California Press, 1992): Jacques André, *La révolution fratricide: Essai psychanalytique sur le lien social* (Paris: PUF, 1993).

45 Robert Delavignette, a French colonial writer, administrator, and ethnologist, regarded the representations of African theater at the 1937 Colonial Exhibition at Paris as "one of the first convincing demonstrations of the emergence of Eurafrican *métisse* culture overcoming previous antagonisms." Delavignette wrote: "The theater they will do at Gorée will not be cut off from the agrarian experience to which they have been connected; the theater is permeated by this experience; it is rooted in their soil and will give them the sense of an Africa that evolves but remains essential. . . . They return to their mother tongue that gives them the theme they will create and they express in French what the theme that inhabits them suggests. It is more than a double translation." Robert Delavignette, "Le Théatre de Gorée et la culture franco-africaine," *Afrique française* 10 (October 1937): pp. 471–72.

46 On racialized medical ideology, see Sander Gilman, *Difference and Pathology: Stereotypes of Sexuality, Race, and Madness* (Ithaca: Cornell University Press, 1985); *Freud, Race, and Gender* (Princeton, N.J.: Princeton University Press, 1993).

47 Details of Raymond Vergès's life come from personal interviews with Laurence, Paul, and Jacques Vergès. I also consulted Chantal Lauvernier's M.A. thesis, "Ban-Baï, Raymond Vergès, 1882–1957" (University of Réunion, 1992).

48 *Vergès* means "small orchard" in Catalan.

49 Vergès opened a night school to train Chinese technicians and skilled workers. He tutored sixty students, and their degrees in engineering were approved by the Chinese Ministry of Transportation. Six of these students followed him to France in 1912 and returned to China with French degrees in engineering. Three thousand workers took his classes in drawing, geometry, and algebra.

50 Raymond Vergès, "Les Grands Jours de la Révolution Chinoise," *La Vie* 1 (February 1912): p. 24.

51 Ibid. Emphasis in the text.

52 Raymond Vergès, "Le choc des races de Charles Géniaux," *La Vie* 4 (March 1912): pp. 120–21.

53 Raymond Vergès, "Le caoutchouc en Cochinchine," *La Vie* 3 (March 1912): p. 87.

54 The distinction between the project and the individuals that carry it out is not particular to republican colonialism. Servants of an institution want to believe that what they serve is right, the problem being the quality of the servants. We find this distinction among Christians who do not blame the church but blame its servants for abuse or misuse of its teachings, or among members of a political party. The fallibility of human beings often offers a satisfying explanation for the failings of a project. By adopting such a position, the individual does not question the structure itself. Does the structure encourage a certain behavior? Is it mainly attracting a certain type of individual whose behavior reflects in fact the qualities demanded by the structure? Hence, was it possible to have good individuals in the colonies?

55 Vergès was asked to teach hygiene, geology, and geometry for fourteen hours per week and to offer nine hours of doctor's consultations.

56 Raymond Vergès, "L'action médicale de la France aux Colonies," in *La Réunion vous parle: Semaine de la France d'Outre-Mer à l'Île de la Réunion, 15–21 Juillet 1941* (Saint-Denis, Réunion: 1941), pp. 136–51, 142.

57 Ibid., p. 149.

58 Charles Renouvier, *Manuel républicain de l'homme et du citoyen* (Paris: Éditions Garnier Frères, 1981), p. 113. This manual, even though it was written in 1848, presented the republican vision of the citizen's role and duties, and its lessons were reappropriated by the Third Republic. Among these lessons, augmented by the experience of the Second Empire, were the ideas that "the political lack of education of the rural population, the pressure by the wealthy, the priests, and the prefects" harmed the republic. The goal was to educate and enlighten the rural population so that a popular majority would elect a republican Chamber. See Maurice Agulhon, introduction to Renouvier, pp. 9–31.

59 See Michel Foucault, *Discipline and Punish: The Birth of the Prison* (New York: Vintage Books, 1979); *L'impossible prison: Recherches sur le système pénitentiaire au XIXe siècle réunies par Michelle Perrot* (Paris: Seuil, 1980).

60 Femininity was reconstructed as well by feminists who made their ideology a "problematic of the Third Republic," as Laurence Klejman and Florence Rochefort remark in *L'égalité en marche: Le féminisme sous la Troisième République* (Paris: des femmes, 1989), p. 22. Like many French scholars, Klejman and Rochefort do not seem interested by colonialism and its impact on the redefinition of masculinity and femininity in the metropole. On feminism in the Third Republic, see also Geneviève

Fraisse and Michelle Perrot, eds., *Histoire des femmes: Le XIXe. siècle* (Paris: Plon, 1991); Claire Moses, *French Feminism in the Nineteenth Century* (Albany: New York State University Press, 1984); Marilyn Boxer and Jean H. Quataert, eds., *Socialist Women: European Socialist Women in the Nineteenth and Early Twentieth Centuries* (New York: Elsevier-Holland, 1978).

61 A. Clayton, *Contes Franco-Annamites: Livre de lecture pour les écoles du Tonkin* (Hanoi: Imprimerie F. H. Schneider, 1887). Preface by Georges Dumoutier, inspector for the Écoles Franco-Annamites, in charge of the organization of education in the Tonkin. Cited in *Pluriel* 12 (1977): pp. 60–62.

62 Arthur Girault, *Principes de Colonisation et de Législation Coloniale* (Paris). Girault's book went through five editions between 1894 and 1927. Cited in Martin Deming Lewis, "One Hundred Million Frenchmen: The Assimilation Theory in French Colonial Policy," *Comparative Studies in Society and History* 4, no. 2 (January 1962): pp. 129–53, 132.

63 Cited in Lewis, p. 134.

64 Cited in Jean Fremigacci, "L'État colonial français, du discours mythique aux réalités, 1880–1940," *Matériaux pour l'histoire de notre temps* 32–33 (July–December 1993): pp. 27–35, 28.

65 The French governor general of Indochina Albert Sarraut rejected colonization for conquest alone in his book *Mise en valeur des colonies françaises* with these words: "For a long time now, France has repudiated the brutal conception of the old colonial pact that rested upon the eternal inequality of races and the right of might, an operation of colonization conceived uniquely for the interest of the conqueror." In *La Mise en valeur des colonies françaises* (Paris: Payot, 1923), p. 19.

66 Cited in Fremigacci, p. 29.

67 Paul-Leroy Beaulieu, *De la Colonisation chez les peuples modernes,* 3d ed. (Paris: Librairie Guillaumin, 1886), p. xvi.

68 Fremigacci has noted the continuity of the French policy toward its former empire. The concepts of "development" and "cooperation" that have defined post-decolonization policies are the heir of Sarraut's notions.

69 Sarraut, p. 89.

70 Speech of Paul Bert, published in *Le Saïgonnais,* 1 April 1886. Reproduced in M. P. De La Brosse, *Une des grandes énergies françaises: Paul Bert* (Hanoi: 1925), pp. 121–27. On the conquest of Indochina, see Georges Taboulet, *La Geste française en Indochine: Histoire par les textes de la France en Indochine des origines à 1914,* vol. 1 (Paris: Adrien Maisonneuve, 1955), p. 876. For the ideas that governed the colonization of South Asia, see Jules Harman, *Domination et colonisation* (Paris: Ernest Flammarion, 1910). Harman was, with Leroy-Beaulieu, a tireless lobbyist for French colonial expansion. Colonial expansion was justified by the "superiority"

of the European race even though a "controlled" participation of the natives in local colonial administration was advocated. Colonization, these men wrote, which had always been a "natural human activity," had now to be scientifically organized. See also Georges Hardy, *Histoire de la colonisation française* (Paris: Librairie Larose, 1928); G. Guenin, *L'Épopée coloniale de la France racontée par les contemporains* (Paris: Librairie Larose, 1932); Henri Russier and Henri Brenier, *L'Indochine française* (Paris: Armand Colin, 1911). On the history of Vietnam, see Pierre Brocheux and Daniel Hémery, *Indochine, La colonisation ambiguë: 1858–1954* (Paris: Éditions La Découverte, 1995); Jean Chesneaux, *Contribution à l'histoire de la nation vietnamienne* (Paris: Éditions sociales, 1955); Lê Thanh Khôi, *Le Vietnam* (Paris: Éditions de Minuit, 1955). On colonial society and its "mediocrity," see Jean Tardieu, *Lettre de Hanoï* (Paris: Gallimard, 1997); Léon Werth, *Cochinchine: Voyage* (Paris: Viviane Hamy, 1997). Werth's text is a violent attack on colonial society, its narrowness, lack of intellectual life, and racism. On the construction of Indochina in the French imaginary, see Denys Lombard, Catherine Champion, and Henri Chambert-Loir, *Rêver l'Asie: Exotisme et littérature coloniale aux Indes, en Indochine et en Insulinde* (Paris: Editions de l'École des Hautes Études en Sciences Sociales, 1993); Panivong Norindr, *Phantasmatic Indochina: French Colonial Ideology in Architecture, Film, and Literature* (Durham, N.C.: Duke University Press, 1997).

71 Fremigacci, "L'État colonial français," p. 27.

72 Ibid., p. 27.

73 In the empire, groups of natives demanded either their assimilation and the status of the Old Colonies or full access to French citizenship. But the colonial authorities responded with decrees of 1909 in Madagascar and of 1912 in West Africa. They retained the right to grant the status of citizen and granted it individually and exceptionally. The majority of the populations in the French colonies had the status of *indigène*, which kept them in an inferior position vis-à-vis the French (Fremigacci, p. 29).

74 Benjamin Stora, "Passé colonial et représentations françaises de la guerre d'Algérie: le masque de l'universalisme républicain," Communication at the 16th Congress of IPSA, Berlin, August 1994.

75 Raphaël Barquissau, *Les Conquérants d'âme*, p. 6.

76 On the development of French colonial policy, see Winfried Baumgart, *Imperialism: The Idea and Reality of British and French Colonial Expansion, 1880–1914* (Oxford: Oxford University Press, 1982); Hubert Deschamps, *The French Union: History, Institutions, Economy, Countries, and Peoples—Social and Political Changes* (Paris: Éditions Berger-Levrault, 1956); René Girardet, *L'Idée Coloniale de la France* (Paris: La Table Ronde, 1972); Jean-Louis Miège, *Expansion européenne et décolonisation de 1870 à nos jours* (Paris: PUF–Nouvelle Clio, 1973); Mort Rosenblum, *Mission to*

Civilize: The French Way (San Diego: Harcourt Brace Jovanovich, 1986). The French republican government founded the École Coloniale in 1889 to develop the "technologies and science" of colonization. The Colonial Army was created in 1893, and the Ministry of the Colonies in 1894. Colonial propaganda often showed medical progress in the empire to justify its project in the name of humanism. The Vichy regime also promoted medicine as a justification of empire. See, for instance, *L'Empire français,* January–April 1942, whose cover represents a white nurse weighing a black baby.

77 *Le Progrès,* 28 August 1928.

78 Conference of Raymond Vergès, "La matinée des Sciences et des Arts," *Le Peuple,* 1 October 1928, p. 1.

79 Raymond Vergès, "L'action médicale de la France aux Colonies," p. 138.

80 Leconte de Lisle, *Catéchisme Populaire Républicain* (Paris: Alphonse Lemerre, 1870).

81 Serge Halimi, "Sisyphus Is Tired: The French Left and the Exercise of Power (1924–1986)" (Ph.D. diss., University of California at Berkeley, 1990). Published under the title *Sysyphe est fatigué: Les Échecs de la Gauche au pouvoir* (Paris: Robert Laffont, 1993).

82 Albert de Pourvouville, *Histoire populaire des colonies françaises: L'Indochine,* p. 216.

83 Dr. Gaide, *L'Assistance Médicale et le Protection de la Santé Publique.* Exposition Coloniale Internationale. Indochine Française. Inspection des Services Sanitaires et Médicaux de l'Indochine (Hanoi: Imprimerie d'Extrême-Orient, 1931), p. 417.

84 Conference of Raymond Vergès, "La matinée des Sciences et des Arts," *Le Peuple,* 1 October 1928, p. 1.

85 Ibid.

86 Ibid.

87 Raymond Vergès, "L'action médicale de la France aux Colonies," p. 138.

88 Ibid., p. 139.

89 Raymond Vergès cited in the bibliography used for his presentation works that celebrated the action of the colonial health service. Dr. Paul Erau, *Trois siècles de Médecine Coloniale Française* (1931 [year of the Colonial Exhibition in Paris]); Commissariat de l'Exposition Coloniale de Paris, *Le Service de la Santé aux Colonies* (1931); Ministère de la Guerre, *L'Oeuvre du Service de Santé Militaire en Algérie* (1931); Exposition Coloniale de Paris, *L'Assistance Médicale et la Protection de la Santé Publique en Indochine* (1931). The colonial health service gave birth to an important literature. See Dr. Charles Grail, *Hygiène coloniale appliquée: Hygiène de l'Indochine* (Paris: Librairie J. B. Baillière et Fils, 1908), in which Grail, in

great detail, laid out the multiple activities of colonial doctors and of their native help.

90 CAOM, series A GGF, Raymond Vergès.

91 In 1907 the colonial medical assistance opened a program to train native doctors and nurses. Since European doctors did not speak the native languages and did not know the customs and the traditions, they would not be able to convince the native patients of the virtues of medical principles about hygiene and prophylaxy. Therefore, it was the role of the native doctor to "interpret" to the natives these principles. The European doctor's role was "to guide and to control" the native doctor. See Dr. Gaide, p. 29.

92 In 1924 Vergès launched a campaign of vaccination against pox and taught the nurses and the population the use of quinine against malaria. Vergès wanted to build wards to receive lepers, but the colonial administration rejected his proposal. One of his goals was to reduce infant mortality, but pregnant women refused to see him individually. He proposed then to hold consultations in groups, and women agreed to be examined.

93 See Lion Murard and Patrick Zylberman, *L'hygiène dans la République: La santé publique en France ou l'utopie contrariée, 1870–1918* (Paris: Fayard, 1996).

94 Yvonne Knibiehler and Régine Goutalier, *Femmes et colonisation: rapport terminal au Ministère des relations extérieures et de la coopération* (Aix-en-Provence: Université de Provence, Institut d'Histoire des Pays d'Outre Mer, 1986), p. 6.

95 Ibid., pp. 26–27. Health was a mobilizing domain for men and women alike in the colonies. Native women became the favorite group targeted by the colonial health service.

96 Archives Diplomatiques du Ministère des Affaires Étrangères, Nantes, carton 174, Dossier général, 1924; CAOM, cartons 39757 and 32919.

97 Devillers.

98 Devillers writes that "the regime installed by the French was for the sixty years that it lasted a bureaucratic dictatorship. A very powerful French administration helped by local auxiliaries, who often were mediocre, and by Europeans colonists pursued an economic policy that benefited first the French interests. It created a remarkable infrastructure (harbors, cities, roads, hospitals) with fiscal resources that weighed heavily upon the Indochinese. . . . Poverty, however, remained the lot of the majority of the population." Any form of opposition was severely repressed (pp. 27–29).

99 CAOM, Gouvernement Général de l'Indochine, Siam, Direction des Affaires Politiques, no. 42424: 37.

100 Charles Meyer, *Des Français en Indochine, 1860–1900* (Paris: Hachette, 1985), p. 263.

101 Nguyên Xuân Tué has remarked that Vietnamese never used this term with the meaning given it by the French. They called women living with French *me tây*, a "flattering word" meaning "European or French mothers." The congaï was represented as one of the rewards of colonization. Colonial literature constructed the congaï as a devious woman, attracted by money. Nguyên Xuân Tué, "*Congaï*, une race de femmes annamites, produit de la colonisation," *Reflets Littéraires: Indochine*, 1992, pp. 69–77, 69.

102 The following excerpts encapsulate the trope of the congaïe in colonial culture: "The charm of absolute possession is enhanced by an aesthetic appeal. The congaies' miniature bodies, their exquisite modeled hands and feet, have an elegance and grace that is part of the heritage of their civilization. . . . A Western man may win a congaie without effort, beauty, or intelligence. . . . He is forever charmed by the obedience, discretion and detailed attention with which he is surrounded, by the delightful creature whom he owns. . . . Soon the supple slave becomes the task mistress. Sulking proves a successful weapon and is effectively repeated." The congaïe held the Western man in ways that he did not even suspect: "Her family eventually comes to live in the house: confusion, dirt, and noise then reign supreme. The arrival of progeny supplies the finishing touch and the European's servitude is now complete." Virginia Thompson, *French Indo-China* (New York: Macmillan, 1942), pp. 443–45.

103 In colonial literature, "Eurasian" children were, like other métis, described in negative terms. Thompson writes: "Writers are unanimous in attributing to the Eurasian certain moral defects, notably a pride that degenerates into touchiness or arrogance, a disdain of manual labor that might betray his native origin, and a retention of injuries and humiliations that leads to ultimate revenge" (p. 447).

104 CAOM, File Rougni, 42425.

105 Declaration of Doctor Trancière, 4 August 1929, to the colonial authorities at Saigon, CAOM, File Rougni, 42425.

106 On the reconfiguration of Otherness with the Orient as Other, see Lisa Lowe, *Critical Terrains: French and British Orientalisms* (Ithaca: Cornell University Press, 1991); Edward Said, *Orientalism* (New York: Vintage Books, 1979), and *Culture and Imperialism* (New York: Alfred A. Knopf, 1993). About race and empire, see Ann Laura Stoler, *Race and the Education of Desire: Foucault's History of Sexuality and the Colonial Order of Things* (Durham, N.C.: Duke University Press, 1995).

107 Bumgart, p. 57.

108 On Morel's ideas, see Sander L. Gilman, *Difference and Pathology: Stereotypes of Sexuality, Race, and Madness,* pp. 60, 192–93, 225; Richard D. Walter, "What Became of the Degenerate? A Brief History of A Concept,"

Journal of the History of Medicine and the Allied Sciences 2 (1956): pp. 422–29; Daniel Pick, *Faces of Degeneration: A European Disorder, c.1848–c.1918* (Cambridge: Cambridge University Press, 1989), pp. 37–59.

109 Benedict Augustin Morel, *Traité des Dégénérescences Physiques, Intellectuelles et Morales de l'Espèce Humaine et des Causes qui produisent ces variétés maladives* (Paris: J. B. Baillère, 1857).

110 Ibid., pp. 424–26.

111 Ibid., p. 425.

112 Pick, p. 59.

113 Léon Poliakov, *Le Mythe aryen* (Paris: Éditions Complexes, 1987), p. 255.

114 Arthur de Gobineau, *Essai sur l'inégalité des races humaines* (Paris: 1853). English translation: *The Moral and Intellectual Diversity of Races, with Particular Reference to Their Respective Influence in the Civil and Political History of Mankind* (Philadelphia: Lippincott, 1856). Michael Rogin has pointed out the switch in the translation of the title: "inequality" in the French title becomes "diversity" in the English title.

115 Gobineau was influenced by the views of the scientist Bichat, who contended that all nations were condemned to disappear because of métissage. See Poliakov, pp. 23–24.

116 We saw in chapter 2 that the scientists of the Enlightenment defended the notion of the hybrid as sterile.

117 Gobineau, p. 29.

118 Gobineau's views were largely endorsed by scientists, politicians, and even feminists such as Clémence Royer whose writings "constructed a hierarchy of peoples where the connection between science and racial theories was evident." Clémence Royer, *Du groupement des peuples et de l'hégémonie universelle* (Paris: 1877). Cited in Knibiehler and Goutalier 1986, p. 38.

119 Pierre-André Taguieff, "Doctrines de la race et hantise du métissage," *Nouvelle Revue d'Ethnopsychiatrie* 17 (1991): pp. 53–100, 58. The works devoted to race doctrines and fear of métissage emerged with the eugenics movement. French books were translated into English and vice versa. A writer who greatly influenced French racial theorists, such as René Martial, was Lothrop Stoddard, a Harvard professor who wrote *The Rising Tide of Color against White World-Supremacy* (New York: Charles Scribner's Sons, 1920). Stoddard contended that mixed-bloods were inferior to whites and that they were potential revolutionaries because of their inherent bitterness. See also Jean Finot, *Préjudice de la race,* trans. by Florence Wade-Evans as *Race Prejudice* (London: Archibald Constable, 1906). Finot advocated the assimilation of people of color into the white world so that "when exposed to the action of the factors which have fashioned the soul of the Whites, the same stupid Negro, careless and often cannibal,

will assimilate the mentality and the intellectual conceptions of the latter." It was assimilation without métissage.

120 Similar concerns agitated the scientific and political world in the United States. See Thomas F. Gossett, *Race: The History of an Idea in America* (Dallas, Tex.: Southern University Press, 1963); John S. Haller Jr., *Outcasts from Evolution: Scientific Attitudes of Racial Inferiority, 1859–1900* (Chicago: University of Illinois Press, 1971); Sandra Harding, ed., *The "Racial" Economy of Science: Toward a Democratic Future* (Bloomington: Indiana University Press, 1993).

121 Dr. Bérillon, "Le métissage: son rôle dans la production des enfants anormaux," *Revue de Psychologie appliquée* 1 (January 1927): pp. 3–5. See also "Le problème psycho-biologique du métissage dans les races humaines," *Revue de Psychologie appliquée* 6 (June 1926): pp. 81–83; 7 (July 1926); 8 (August–September 1926): pp. 114–15; 11 (November 1926): pp. 138–45; 12 (December 1926): pp. 156–157; 1 (January 1927): pp. 3–5; 4 (April 1927): pp. 52–54. In these articles, Bérillon argued that métis were biologically inferior to the respective races (June 1926, p. 83). Even the métissage between white races would give birth to defective individuals, devoid of moral sense and with a tendency to become revolutionaries (August 1926, p. 115). Two kinds of policies had to be enforced: (1) The organization of strategies of control that would be accomplished by the police, the judges, and the physicians; their goal would be to eliminate "undesirable" individuals; (2) A policy of adaptation and progressive naturalization of the métis. The aim would be the final exclusion of bad, hostile, and dubious individuals (December 1926, p. 156). In the same vein, Charles Richet, a Nobel Prize winner in biology, demanded, in the name of progress and civilization, the rigorous interdiction of sexual intercourse between blacks and whites.

122 Martial defined the object of anthropo-biology as the study of human races, using the insights of history, biology, and psychology. René Martial was a prolific advocate of racial control, and many of his books went through many editions. Martial admired Georges Vacher de Lapouge (1854–1936), the founder of "anthroposociology," a theory that claimed to demonstrate a relation between the size and form of the skull and social status. To Vacher de Lapouge, class struggle was "more than a struggle between groups, [it was] a race struggle." One could prove that "morphological differences existed between classes which reveal greater 'ethnic' differences than between ethnic groups." See Georges Vacher de Lapouge, *Race et milieu social* (Paris: Marcel Rivière, 1909), p. xxix. About Vacher de Lapouge's ideology, see André Béjin, "Le sang, le sens et le travail: Georges Vacher de Lapouge darwiniste social, fondateur de l'anthroposociologie," *Cahiers Internationaux de Sociologie* 53 (1982): pp. 323–43.

Among René Martial's writings, see *Race, Hérédité, Folie,* 4th ed. (Paris:

Mercure de France, 1943); "L'immigration et les fous," in *Bulletin de l'Académie des Sciences Morales et Politiques* (Paris: Alcan, 1932); "Étude de l'aliénation mentale dans ses rapports avec l'immigration," *Hygiène Mentale,* nos. 2–3 (1933); *La race française* (Paris: Mercure de France, 1935); "Race, groupements sanguins et hygiène mentale," *Hygiène Mentale,* no. 8 (1935); "Race et Immigration," *Bulletin de l'Académie des Sciences Morales et Politiques,* 1936; "Métissage et Immigration," at the Première réunion des Eugénistes de l'Amérique Latine, 1937. Martial greatly admired the United States immigration policy and lobbied for similar measures in France. To him, the Immigration Restriction Act of 1924 was a model of immigration control. During the debate in the House and the Senate, eugenics arguments framed the question of immigration as a biological, not economical, issue. Among the arguments for a strict control of immigration, the mixing and interbreeding of races was presented as a degenerate process, a threat to national strength and security. See Kenneth Ludmerer, *Genetics and American Society: A Historical Approach* (Baltimore: Johns Hopkins University Press, 1972); Mark Haller, *Eugenics: Hereditarian Attitudes in American Thought* (New Brunswick: Rutgers University Press, 1963).

123 René Martial, *Race, Hérédité, Folie: Étude d'anthroposociologie appliquée à l'immigration* (Race, Heredity, Madness: Anthroposociological Study Applied to Immigration) (Paris: Mercure de France, 1938), p. 101. Similar projects about "good" métissage appeared in the United States. Haller presents the views of Frederick L. Hoffman, who "believed that intermarriage among races of similar cultures resulted in physical and psychical advantages for both stocks but that mixture of Germans and Italians, English and Spaniards, Swedes and Turks, let alone Caucasians and Negroes, was altogether another matter" (p. 64).

124 René Martial, *Les Métis* (Paris: Flammarion, 1942), p. 26.

125 Ibid., pp. 104–5. Martial supported this singular argument by drawing a parallel between bad métissage and breast feeding: "To feed an infant with the milk of a mother whose blood type is different from his can produce allergy in the infant." One could infer that similar consequences could arise with métissage.

126 Ibid., p. 44.

127 Ibid., p. 45.

128 The Nazi racial laws of 1935 included an article about the *Mischlinge,* the métis. The Nazi regime ordered the forced sterilization and then the extermination of all métis born of the soldiers of the French colonial army—soldiers from Senegal, Antilles, Madagascar—and German women. See Poliakov, pp. 4–5.

129 As Sander Gilman has shown, male Jews were uncanny to medical science because they "superficially appear to be males but are not because of the altered form of the genitalia." Male and female métis were uncanny because while superficially appearing normal, they were not normal because of the duality of bloods. Gilman, *Difference and Pathology,* p. 51.

130 French travelers had been first repulsed by the "nondifferentiation" between women and men. "Asexual race; androgynous race," they wrote. See Paul Bonnetain, *Les Petites épouses* (Paris: Calmann Lévy, n.d.). In his study of Indochinese exoticism in French literature, Malleret gives many examples of descriptions that demonstrate the fear of sexual nondifferentiation (see pp. 70–76); Thoung Vuong-Riddick, "La Découverte de l'Indochine et des Indochinois," *Reflets Littéraires,* pp. 27–33.

131 Hans-Jürgen Lüsebrink, "Métissage culturel et société coloniale: Émergence et enjeux d'un débat, de la presse coloniale aux premiers écrivains africains (1935–1947)," in *Métissages,* vol. 1, pp. 109–18.

132 Denise Bouche, "Autrefois, notre pays s'appelait la Gaule: Remarques sur l'adaptation de l'enseignement au Sénégal de 1817 à 1960," *Cahiers d'Études Africaines* 8, no. 2 (1968): pp. 110–12.

133 Gunther Hecht, *Die Bedeutung des Rassengedankens in der Kolonialpolitik,* 1937. On the Nazi colonial project, see Charles-Robert Ageron, "L'idée d'Eurafrique et le débat colonial franco-allemand de l'entre-deux guerres," *Revue d'Histoire Moderne et Contemporaine* 22 (1975); Alexandre Kum'a N'Dumbe III, *Hitler voulait l'Afrique: Le projet du 3e Reich sur le continent africain* (Paris: L'Harmattan, 1980), and *Négritude et Germanité: L'Afrique Noire dans la littérature d'expression allemande* (Dakar: Nouvelles Éditions Africaines, 1983); Julius Rohrbach, *Das neue Deutsche Kolonialreich: Umfang, Aufgaben und Leistungmöglichkeiten* (Berlin: 1940).

134 Ousmane Socé, *Mirages de Paris* (1937; Paris: Nouvelles Latines, 1964), p. 147.

135 Léopold Sedar Senghor, "Le problème culturel en A.O.F.," *Le Périscope Africain* 382 (September 1937): pp. 1–3, and 383 (October 1937): p. 3.

136 Fily Dabo Sissoko, "Les noirs et la culture," *Congrès International de l'Évolution culturelle des peuples coloniaux: Rapport et compte-rendus,* Exposition Internationale de Paris, 1937 (Paris, 1938), pp. 108–22; and, "À propos du Congrès de l'Évolution culturelle des peuples coloniaux: Réponse à Ousmane Socé," *Paris-Dakar,* 27 January 1939, pp. 1, 5.

137 See Martine Astier-Loufti, *Littérature et colonialisme* (Paris: Mouton, 1971); Léon Farroudh-Siefer, *Le mythe du nègre et de l'Afrique Noire dans la littérature française de 1800 à la Deuxième Guerre Mondiale* (Dakar: Nouvelles Éditions Africaines, 1980); Pierre Jourda, *L'Exotisme dans la littérature française depuis Chateaubriand* (Paris: Boivin-Université de Montpellier, 1956); Ada Martinkus-Zemp, *Le Blanc et Le Noir: Essai d'une description de la vision du Noir par le Blanc dans la littérature française de l'entre-deux guerres* (Paris: A. G. Nizet, 1975).

138 Robert Randau, *Le chef des porte-plumes: Roman de la vie coloniale* (Paris: Éditions du monde nouveau, 1922).

139 Sander L. Gilman, "Sexology, Psychoanalysis, and Degeneration," in *Difference and Pathology*, pp. 191–216. Gilman has examined the relation in Europe between theories about crime, mixed marriages, degeneration, and incest at the time of Freud. To the medical European world, the figure of the degenerate was the Jew. See *The Case of Sigmund Freud: Medicine and Identity at the Fin de Siècle* (Baltimore: Johns Hopkins University Press, 1993), pp. 169–215.

140 De Pourvouville, *Histoire populaire des colonies françaises. L'Indochine,* p. 380.

141 Vu Trong Phung, *Ky nghê lây Tây* (Job: Marrying a European) (Hanoi: Édition Phuong Dông, 1936; reedited, Hanoi: Nhà xuât ban, 1989). Cited in Nguyên Xuân Tué. Asian women went from being horrible and abject to being the "desirable Oriental." At first, Vietnamese women were particularly abject to the Europeans. They provoked horror and fascination. One writer described them as like Medusae with their "black mouths, which look when open like the mouth of a snake: it is like the grave of love" (Bonnetain, p. 136). "Women are particularly horrible. . . . They are shameless and licentious. . . . As if nature has not made them ugly enough, they add to the feeling of disgust that they inspire to any European by chewing something that dyes their teeth, lips, and mouth in red," traveler Philippe Aude wrote (Letters of Philippe Aude, "À la suite de l'Amiral Charner: Campagne de Chine et de Cochinchine [1860–1864]," published by Louis Cadière in *Bulletin des Amis du Vieux Hué,* 1932, pp. 72–75; cited in Pierre-Jean Simon, "Portraits coloniaux des Vietnamiens [1858–1914]," *Pluriel,* 1 [1977]: pp. 29–54, 36). Simon presents an interesting typology of the colonial descriptions of the Indochinese. On the trope of the "Eurasian métis," see also Ida Simon-Barouh, "Identités eurasiennes," *Pluriel* 21 (1980): pp. 69–80.

142 See Henri Sambuc, "Enquête sur la question des métis," *La Revue du Pacifique.* Sambuc writes: "White races have produced a burden we must suffer and confront: the burden of the fusion of races. The facts have demonstrated that it is vain to try to fight it. What is possible though is to limit it" (p. 95).

143 Ernest Babut, "Le Métis franco-annamite," *Revue Indochinoise,* July 1907, pp. 897–908.

144 Dochet, *Métis et congayes d'Indochine* (Hanoi: 1928), cited in Le Huu Khoa, *L'Interculturel et l'Eurasien* (Paris: L'Harmattan, 1993), p. 84.

145 Henri Sambuc, "Les Métis franco-annamites en Indochine," *La Revue du Pacifique,* April 1931, pp. 194–209. Sambuc cites the "Première Enquête sur les caractères intellectuels et moraux des métis," published in *Bulletins et Mémoires de la Société d'Anthropologie de Paris,* December 1910, and the "Enquête sur les métis," done by the Société d'Anthropologie de Paris at the demand of Governor-General A. W. Ponty of

French West Africa. Published in *Revue d'Anthropologie* 9–10 (September–October 1912).

146 As early as 1895, a Société de Protection de l'Enfance de la Cochinchine was founded in Saigon. In 1931, the society had 167 children under its control. It opened two orphanages: one in Cholon for boys, one in Saigon for girls. In 1898 an Association de Protection des enfants métis du Tonkin was founded in Hanoi. Boys were sent to professional schools; girls were taught domestic skills.

147 Knibiehler and Goutalier, p. iii.

148 Ibid., p. 34.

149 Ibid., p. 37. See also Ann Laura Stoler, "Carnal Knowledge and Imperial Power: Gender, Race, and Morality in Colonial Asia," in *Gender at the Crossroads of Knowledge: Feminist Anthropology in the Postmodern Era,* ed. M. di Leonardo (Berkeley: University of California Press, 1991).

150 Knibiehler and Goutalier, p. 36.

151 See Bonifacy; Babut "Le Métis"; Mazet *Lacondition juridique*; Sambuc "Enquête sur la question des métis."

152 Bonifacy.

153 Mazet *La condition juridique.*

154 Babut, "Le Métis," p. 899.

155 Cited in Pierre-Jean Simon, "Un village franco-indochinois en Bourbonnais: Aspects de la colonization et de la décolonisation de l'Indochine orientale" (Ph.D. diss., University of Lille, France, 1974), pp. 114–15.

156 Albert de Pourvouville, *Le mal d'argent* (Paris, 1926). Among novels where métis figure prominently as tragic, devious, and threatening, see Henry Casseville, *Thi-Nhi, autre fille d'Annam* (Paris: Figuière, 1922); Jehan Cendrieus, *François Phuoc, Métis* (Paris: Bibliothèque Charpentier, 1929); Clotilde Chivas Baron, *Trois femmes annamites* (Paris: 1922); *Confidences de métisse* (Paris: 1927); Olivier Dirayson-Seylor, *Amours d'Extrême-Orient* (Paris: Carrington, 1905); *Demi-Blanc* (Paris: 1912); Claude Farrère, *Les civilisés* (Paris: Librairie Paul Ollendorf, 1908); Christiane Fournier, *Homme jaune et femme blanche* (Paris: Flammarion, 1933); Jeanne Marquet, *Le jaune et le blanc* (Paris: 1927); Herbert Wild, *L'autre race* (Paris: Albin Michel, 1930). These novels were popular. Many of them went through numerous editions. Some were published in newspapers.

157 The French state enacted a series of laws to define the legal status of the métis. The laws of 1897 stated that any individual born of a French is a French. The law of November 4, 1928, said: "Any *métis* born in Indochina of a father who has not recognized the child but is French has the right to judicial recognition as a French." December 4, 1930: "Any individual born of a French woman, even in the colonies, is French." To Jacques Mazet, thanks to these laws, "From now on, French blood will prevail over foreign or indigenous blood." Mazet, *La condition juridique des Métis*

(Paris: Domat-Montchrestien, 1932), p. 54. See also A. Girault, *Rapport sur un projet de décret concernant les métis* (Paris: 1928); "La condition juridique des métis dans les colonies françaises," *Revue politique et parlementaire,* 10 April 1929, pp. 124–31. Comparisons were made with the Dutch colonies, where métissage was encouraged by the colonial administration and the métis group had proved to be no trouble. Sociologists were also interested in the social and psychological condition of métis. See René Maunier, *Sociologie Coloniale: Introduction à l'étude du contact des races* (Paris: Éditions Domat-Montchrestien, 1932), English translation by E. O. Lorimer, *The Sociology of Colonies: An Introduction to the Study of Race Contact* (London: Routledge and Kegan Paul, 1949); *Sociologie Coloniale: Psychologie des expansions* (Paris: Éditions Domat-Montchrestien, 1936). Maunier distinguished three steps through which different peoples brought into contact were going. Opposition preceded imitation, which in turn preceded "aggregation." The last step would take humanity toward "universal civilization," and the "City of God" founded on the unity of humankind (1932, p. 194). Progress was "exchange and mixing" (1936, p. 420). Maunier also insisted on the necessity of inscribing the métis in the paternal lineage. Maunier's bibliographies are full of references to the literature about colonization, métissage, and the "psychology of natives."

158 Métis boys and girls were destined to different tasks. Boys could become "low-ranking civil servants or employees, which is the ideal of the respectful Annamite" (Pourvouville, p. 380). Girls could learn to become good wives or enter religious orders. The colonial school had therefore a specific task, and the state had an essential role in their education. Pourvouville thought that it was fundamental to "save the franco-annamite child from the bad influences of an unworthy native mother."

159 Jehan Cendrieus, *François Phuoc, Métis,* p. 171.

160 Maria Torok and Nicholas Rand, "Reading *The Sandman,*" in *Speculations after Freud: Psychoanalysis, Philosophy, and Culture,* ed. Sony Shamdasani and Michael Münchow (London: Routledge, 1994).

161 Frantz Fanon remarked: "In a general sense the white man behaves toward the Negro as an elder brother reacts to the birth of a younger." See Fanon, *Black Skin, White Masks,* trans. Charles Lam Markmann (New York: Grove Press, 1967), p. 157. Fanon drew from Jacques Lacan's theory of the fraternal complex his remark on colonial jealousy. Jealousy, Lacan said, emerges as the "archetype of social feelings." To the older brother, the younger brother is an intruder. "The narcissistic structure of the fraternal complex is revealed through the more paranoid themes of intrusion, influence, splitting, and all the wild transmutations of the body." See Jacques Lacan, "La famille," in *Encyclopédie Française,* vol. 8, (Paris: Librairie Larousse, 1938). Lacan's contribution to the eighth volume of the encyclopedia, entitled "La Vie Mentale," was edited under the direction of Lucien Febvre as *Les complexes familiaux dans la formation de l'individu* (Paris: Navarin, 1984).

162 See "Secrets de famille et pensée perverse," *Gruppo: Revue de psychanalyse familiale et groupale* 8 (1992); Paul-Claude Racamier, *Le génie des origines: Psychanalyse et psychoses* (Paris: Bibliothèque Scientifique Payot, 1992); François Vigouroux, *Le secret de famille* (Paris: PUF, 1993).

163 Regarding the social laws acquired by women between 1874 and 1968, see Maïté Albistur and Daniel Armogathe, *Histoire du féminisme français,* vol. 2 (Paris: des femmes, 1978), pp. 576–85.

164 Michael Paul Rogin, *Subversive Genealogy: The Politics and Art of Herman Melville* (New York: Alfred A. Knopf, 1983). Rogin shows how similar anxieties agitated Jacksonian America.

165 Khoa, p. 87.

166 CAOM, Gouvernement Général de l'Indochine, Siam, Direction des Affaires Politiques, File 42424. See also Document 26 of 30 June 1929. Doctor Fancière, sent to check on the accusations against Vergès, reported new accusations. His report detailed a story that the declaration of birth of Jacques and Paul was falsified. A rumor said that Jacques had been born at Savannakhet and Paul at Oubone. The report did not explain why Vergès would have wanted to falsify the dates of his sons' births. See also a report of 21 December 1929 concluding that doubts remain that Vergès has played his role to "develop French influence."

167 Letter of Raymond Vergès to the governor of Indochina, Ventiane, 24 June 1929. In this letter, Vergès reports that his wife was very sick in Réunion and that the rumors about their future have "aggravated her illness and she has died the day before our departure for Indochina."

168 Jean-Paul Sker, *Boscot, sous-off. et . . . assassin?* (Saigon: Imprimerie C. Ardin, 1930; reprint, with a preface by Françoise Vergès and a postface by Jean-Claude Carpanin Marimoutou, 1996). Sker announced the publication of other novels: *Jaune: Roman vécu, documentaire et actuel d'un mariage annamite* (Yellow: Documented and Actual Testimony of a Franco-Annamite Marriage); *Mes connaissances de l'Est* (My knowledge of the East); *Métis* (Indochinese Studies); and *Dans la boue du Delta* (In the Mud of the Delta).

169 Vergès, *Boscot,* pp. 24–27.

170 Ibid., p. 27.

171 Ibid., p. 37.

172 Ibid., p. 31.

173 Eugène Pujarniscle, *Philoxène ou de la littérature coloniale* (Paris: Firmin Didot, 1931).

174 Ibid., p. 15.

175 Cited in "Itinéraires et Contacts de Cultures," in *Le Roman Colonial* (Paris: L'Harmattan, 1987), p. 217.

176 Malleret, p. 245. Louis Malleret, in his study of Indochinese exoticism in French literature since 1860, claimed that the first novel to investigate "native psychology" appeared in 1910. It was Emile Nolly's *La barque annamite* (1910). Nolly was the pseudonym of Captain Détanger.

177 Edward Said, *Orientalism* (London: Routledge and Kegan Paul, 1978), p. 78.

178 Lowe.

179 Marius Leblond, *Après l'exotisme de Loti, le Roman Colonial* (Paris: Buissière, 1926), p. 46.

180 Jean-Claude Carpanin Marimoutou, "Le triste fardeau de l'homme blanc, les colonies désenchantées: Raymond Vergès et le roman colonial," postface to Jean-Paul Skler, *Boscot, sous-off. et . . . assassin?* (Saint-Denis, Réunion: Grand Océan, 1996), pp. 189–211.

181 Ibid., p. 209.

182 Ibid., p. 211.

183 The newspaper *La Bataille Sociale* described, in a January 1915 article, the popular neighborhoods of the capital in these terms: "Our city exhibits a spectacle of poverty that makes one cry. . . . Walk through the streets of Petite Ile, the Camp Ozoux, La Source, the Camp Giron. . . . You will see appalling slums where entire families live. . . . This urban proletariat is totally ignorant. It lives in awful promiscuity with the animals it raises." Cited in Prosper Eve, *La Première Guerre Mondiale vue par les poilus réunionnais* (Saint-Denis, Réunion: Éditions CNH, 1992), p. 26. The rate of infant mortality was 268 per thousand in 1901; 145 per thousand in 1946. In France, it was 37 percent. Among adults, 22 to 39 percent of deaths were caused by malaria. Raymond Vergès, alarmed by the endemic character of malaria, decided to produce pills from the bark of the quinquina trees. The rate of malaria among schoolchildren went from 21 percent in 1934 to 11.5 percent in 1938. See Prosper Eve, *Tableau du Syndicalisme à la Réunion* (Saint-Denis, Réunion: Éditions CNH, 1991), pp. 42–44. Jean-Claude Balducchi gives similar numbers. In 1931, in a population of 197,933 inhabitants, the mortality rate was 32.87 percent. The infant mortality rate was 37.4 percent for children between zero to two years and 78.53 percent for children between two and five years old. Balducchi writes that the "population was undernourished, alcoholic, subjected to fevers, tuberculosis, and, generally in a deplorable physiological state." See Jean-Claude Balducchi, "La vie politique et sociale à La Réunion, 1932–1939," 2 vols. (Ph.D. diss., University of Aix en Provence, 1984).

184 Ligue des Droits de l'Homme et du Citoyen, "Causerie faite par le Citoyen Dr. Raymond Vergès, le 16 Octobre 1932 à la Section de Saint-Denis" (Saint-Denis, Réunion: Imprimerie Industrielle, H. Vavasseur, 1932).

185 Ibid., p. 6.

186 Raymond Vergès was a friend of the Leblonds, the leading figures of the Creole myth; he collaborated in their review *La Vie* in the 1910s.

187 Marius and Ary Leblond were not related. Marius was born Georges Athénas on February 26, 1877, at Saint-Denis in a family of Greek origin. Ary was born Aimé Merlo on July 30, 1880, at Saint-Pierre in a family that had come from Provence. The name that they chose, Leblond (the blond, the white), could be read as a political gesture. It expressed the wish to associate Réunion with whiteness. It also marked their aspiration to a form of fraternity that was not based on blood ties. They reinvented themselves as *white brothers.* Their texts were signed either Marius-Ary Leblond, realizing a complete fusion of both persons, or Marius Leblond and Ary Leblond.

188 Another myth that emerged about Réunion during the same period was that of "Lémuria." Réunion was said to be a remnant of the continent of Lémurie. See Jean-Louis Joubert, "Pour une exploration de la Lémurie: Une mythologie littéraire de l'Océan Indien," *Annuaire des Pays de l'Océan Indien* 3 (1976): pp. 51–63.

189 Marius-Ary Leblond, "L'île de La Réunion," in *L'île de la Réunion,* ed. Raphaël Barquissau, Hippolyte Foucque, Hubert Jacob de Cordemoy (Paris: Émile Larose, 1925), p. 43.

190 Ibid., p. 53.

191 Ibid.

192 Ibid., p. 119.

193 Ibid., p. 120.

194 Jules Herman cited in Robert Chaudenson et al., *Encyclopédie de l'Île de La Réunion,* vol. 7 (Saint-Denis, Réunion: Livres Réunion, 1980), p. 79.

195 Leblond 1926, p. 7.

196 Raphaël Barquissau, *Les îles* (Paris: Grasset, 1942), p. 17.

197 Auguste Brunet, "Trois cent ans de colonization française," in *Encyclopédie de l'Empire Français* (Paris: 1947), pp. 282–92, 292.

198 Fanon, *The Wretched of the Earth,* p. 211.

199 Eve, *Tableau du Syndicalisme,* p. 54; Balducchi, pp. 76–77. Railroad workers formed a union in April 1936. In August, schoolteachers opened a branch of the Syndicat National des Instituteurs (SNI, National Union of Schoolteachers). On November 11, 1936, six thousand workers and peasants demonstrated in the streets of Saint-Denis.

200 Eve 1994, pp. 145–70.

201 Eve, *Tableau du Syndicalisme,* p. 47.

202 CAOM, Fonds FOM, C.310 and C.311. In July 1941, the governor Aubert (who was pro-Vichy) visited the island. At Salazie, Raymond Vergès organized demonstrations of the youth. The Leblonds also appeared in the demonstrations organized during the war.

203 Michael Lambert has noted, "Far from having overriding concerns with social ostracism or the political and economic injustices of French imperialism, the *négritude* authors focused on culture and French representations of blacks." Michael C. Lambert, "From Citizenship to Négritude: 'Making a Difference' in Elite Ideologies of Colonized Francophone West Africa," *Society for Comparative Study of Society and History* 35, no. 2 (April 1993): pp. 239–62, 243.

204 Ibid., p. 256.

205 *Annales de l'Assemblée Nationale Constituante,* Archives de l'Assemblée Nationale, 1945.

206 Ibid., March 1946.

207 Vergès ignores the presence of Madagascans in the first days of colonization.

208 In this speech, Vergès celebrated the memory of Sarda Garriga. When Vergès was the mayor of Saint-Denis, he proposed that what had been the "Esplanade Pétain" be renamed "Place Sarda Garriga." This was the place where slaves had danced on December 20, 1848, to celebrate their liberty. The vote of the city council was unanimous (Decree taken 19 March 1946, *Journal Officiel,* 21 March 1946).

209 Ibid.

210 Raymond Vergès, Session of 10 July 1947, *Annales de l'Assemblée Nationale, Quatrième République, no. 222,* Archives de l'Assemblée Nationale.

211 Aimé Césaire, *Annales de l'Assemblée Constituante, no. 210,* Archives de l'Assemblée Nationale, March 1945.

212 Raymond Vergès, *Annales de l'Assemblée Constituante, no. 210,* Archives de l'Assemblée Nationale, March 1945.

213 Jean-François Lyotard, *The Differend: Phrases in Dispute,* trans. Georges Van Den Abbeele, Theory and History of Literature, vol. 46 (Minneapolis: University of Minnesota Press, 1988).

214 Ibid., p. 27.

215 The histories of colonialism and the abolitionist movements in France and Great Britain were different. See Robin Blackburn, *The Making of New World Slavery from the Baroque to the Modern, 1492–1800* (London: Verso, 1997), and *The Overthrow of Colonial Slavery, 1776–1848* (London: Verso, 1997). Blackburn insists on the origins of abolitionism and its sources in the Scottish Enlightenment. He also shows the role of the Baptist, Methodist, and Morovian churches in the British colonies, which welcomed blacks and allowed them to fulfill the functions of pastors. In the French colonies, the Catholic Church supported slavery.

216 See Prosper Eve, *De La Réunion coloniale au département: La concrétisation d'un désir* (Saint-Denis, Réunion: Association "Notre Département a 50 ans," 1996).

217 Karl Marx, *Critique of Hegel's Doctrine of the State: Early Writings,*

trans. Rodney Livingstone and Gregor Benton (New York: Vintage Books, 1975), p. 129.

218 Oudin-Bastide, p. 107.

219 *Le Progrès,* 26 June 1951.

220 Cited in Michel Robert, *La Réunion: Combats pour l'Autonomie* (Paris: L'Harmattan, 1976), p. 36.

221 Raymond Vergès, *Annales de l'Assemblée Nationale,* Archives de l'Assemblée Nationale, no. 234, session of 9 July 1948.

222 See Raymond Vergès's speeches, July–August 1948, 12–21 July 1949, in the *Annales de l'Assemblée Nationale.*

223 Raymond Vergès, *Annales de l'Assemblée Nationale,* Archives de l'Assemblée Nationale, no. 243, Fourth Republic, session of 30 June 1949.

224 Lewis, p. 149.

225 Fanon, p. 60.

226 *Témoignages,* 21 March 1949.

227 The expression is of course Benedict Anderson's in *Imagined Communities: Reflections on the Origin and Spread of Nationalism,* rev. ed. (London: Verso, 1991). The Creoles described by Anderson are not the Creoles of Réunion. As I have said in the text, the fact that there was no native population in Réunion before colonization by French and Madagascans has always affected the mythology constructed in Réunion. Furthermore, Anderson's central question, "Why was it precisely *creole* communities that developed so early conception of their nation-ness—*well before most of Europe?*" (p. 50), cannot be applied to Réunion, where Creoleness did not bring nation-ness. Anderson also points to the importance of printing in the emergence of nationalism. Raymond Vergès bought, with his first salaries as representative, a printing press. He sent it to Réunion and hired a German technician who had been a political refugee of Nazism in France. Vergès founded a newspaper whose goal was to defend *workers'* rights. Printing in Réunion was associated with class, rather than with nation.

228 Vera M. Kutzinski, *Sugar's Secrets: Race and the Erotics of Cuban Nationalism* (Charlottesville: University Press of Virginia, 1993), p. 194. Although Kutzinski is speaking of the creation of Cuban *nationalism* on the figure of the mulatta, her analysis echoes some of my concerns.

229 Kwame Anthony Appiah, *In My Father's House: Africa in the Philosophy of Culture* (New York: Oxford University Press, 1992), p. 180.

230 In Réunion, Paul Caubet, a professor of history and geography at the Lycée Leconte de Lisle, publicized the 1917 revolution. See Eve, *Tableau du Syndicalisme,* pp. 51–52.

231 Poster for the elections of October 1951 for the candidates of the Communist Federation of Réunion that Vergès helped to create in 1947. The Communist Federation of Réunion was affiliated with the French Communist Party. The poster claimed: "The communists have fought

against the preparation for war and against the pursuit of the dirty war in Vietnam. Réunionnais, Réunionnaises: You want to put an end to this politics of oppression, war, poverty, and fascism. . . . Vote against colonialism, for the equality of rights, Vote for the modernization of the island, Vote for a politics of economic and social progress, Vote to block the road to fascism and racism; Vote to put an end to the policy of arms-building and preparation to war. For the end of the war in Vietnam and Korea. Vote for peace. . . . All of us, workers, agricultural workers, small farmers, peasants, artisans, traders, civil servants, intellectuals, young and old, democrats, unite!"

232 Jean-Christophe Bailly, "L'isthme," in *La comparution (politique à venir)*, by Jean-Luc Nancy and Jean-Christophe Bailly (Paris: Christian Bourgeois Éditeur, 1991), p. 41.

233 Albert Memmi, *The Colonizer and the Colonized* (New York: Onion Press, 1965), p. 127.

234 Michael Rogin makes a similar argument about civil rights tactics in the United States. See Michael Rogin, *Blackface, White Noise: Jewish Immigrants in the Hollywood Melting Pot* (Berkeley: University of California Press, 1996). For a comparison of the movements of integration in the United States and the Old Colonies, see my essay "Egalite républicaine et réalité (post)coloniale."

4. "Oté Debré, rouver la port lenfer, Diab kominis i sa rentre": Cold War Demonology in the Postcolony

The quote in the chapter title is the first sentence of a communist political song in Creole of the sixties that meant: "Oh Debré! Open the door of Hell, Communist devils are coming!"

1 Eugène Rousse, *Combat des Réunionnais pour la liberté*, vol. 3 (Saint-Denis, Réunion: Éditions CNH, 1994), p. 114.

2 In April 1955, leaders of twenty-four governments convened at the Afro-Asian Conference, held at Bandung, Indonesia. They issued a declaration that stressed the necessity of economic cooperation between Asia and Africa, condemned racism and colonialism, and encouraged cultural exchanges. The Bandung Conference was followed by the Cairo Conference in December 1957. The Cairo Conference reaffirmed the participants' condemnation of colonialism and imperialism and their support for the struggles of national self-determination.

3 December 20, the date of the emancipation of the slaves in the French colonies, was not officially celebrated, and *maloya*, the music of the slaves, was banned on the radio and ignored by historians. Religious traditions that were not Catholic were not acknowledged and, in many instances, were repressed by the Roman Catholic Church. At the founding congress of the Réunionnais Communist Party, the band of Firmin Viry, a descendant of slaves, performed a maloya for the first time in public.

4 Rousse, pp. 115–16.

5 On December 2, 1868, there was a demonstration at Saint-Denis for universal suffrage.

6 According to the colonial pact: (1) the colony must serve the metropole's needs, (2) the colony is a reserved market for the metropole's manufactured goods, (3) the transportation of the goods to and from the metropole is monopolized by French companies.

7 *Annales de l'Assemblée Nationale*, no. 277, 7 October–13 November 1952.

8 *Annales de l'Assemblée Nationale*, no. 283, 12 May–2 July 1953.

9 In 1945, Communists had joined the government, whose head was de Gaulle. De Gaulle resigned in January 1946, and a new government was formed, controlled by the center Left. In May 1947, the communist ministers left the government. Their party was now in the opposition.

10 "Le XXème anniversaire du Parti Communiste Réunionnais," *Les Cahiers de L'Île de La Réunion,* September–October 1979, pp. 31–37.

11 Rousse, *Combat des Réunionnais pour la liberté,* vol. 3, p. 118.

12 Vergès, *Cahiers,* p. 32.

13 See the role of communism in South Africa and Vietnam.

14 Hereafter, PCR. In the French Antilles as well, communist parties were founded in 1959. Aimé Césaire, who had been a member of the French Communist Party since 1946, resigned in October 1956 and founded the Parti Progressiste Martiniquais. In a public letter to Maurice Thorez, the French Communist Party's secretary, Césaire denounced the chauvinism of the French communists and their conviction that their struggle for progress and emancipation was the only one valid and their belief in European superiority. See Rousse, pp. 134–39; Roger Toumson and Simonne Henry-Valmore, *Aimé Césaire, Le Nègre inconsolé* (Paris: Syros, 1994), pp. 131–53.

15 Debré's remarks are cited by Frantz Fanon in "Mr. Debré's Desperate Endeavors," in *Toward the African Revolution: Political Essays,* trans. Haakon Chevalier (New York: Grove Press, 1967), pp. 158–62, 158.

16 Debré was of course not the first French leader to oppose the Algerian nationalists. The socialist governments of the Fourth Republic had clearly expressed their opposition to reform. François Mitterand, minister of the interior in 1954, had declared that "Algeria is France," and Pierre Mendès France had added that the "Department of Algeria belong to the Republic, they are French. . . . Never France, never any government would renounce this principle."

17 Fanon, p. 162.

18 Michel Debré, *Gouverner Autrement: Mémoires,* vol. 4 (Paris: Albin Michel, 1993), p. 21.

19 Ibid., p. 197.

20 When elections became democratic in the late 1970s—that is, when elections were not marred by fraud—the Communist Party's support could be more justly assessed. It commanded between 30 percent and 40 percent of the vote.

21 The expression is Jean Benoist's in *Un développement ambigu: Structure et changement de la société réunionnaise,* Documents et Recherches 10 (Saint-Denis, Réunion: Fondation pour la recherche et le développement dans l'Océan Indien, 1983).

22 *La Nation: Édition spéciale de La Réunion,* no. 3 (1 May 1963): p. 1.

23 Ibid., p. 23.

24 Hanna Fenichel Pitkin, *Fortune Is a Woman: Gender and Politics in the Thoughts of Niccolò Machiavelli* (Berkeley: University of California Press, 1984), p. 7.

25 Ibid.

26 Martin Oswald, *Autonomia: Its Genesis and Early History* (American Philological Association: Scholars Press, 1982), p. 1. The early history of the Greek term from which "autonomy" derived suggests that it signified an attempt to curtail the power of an imperial state and to guarantee to states moving in its orbit the right to define their own laws.

27 Interview of Paul Vergès, general secretary of the CPR, in *La Gauche au pouvoir dans 9 mois? Ce que proposent les organisations démocratiques pour la Réunion: Supplément au Journal* Témoignages *du 4 Juin 1977* (Saint-Denis, Réunion: Juillet, 1977), p. 36.

28 Ibid.

29 Jean-Claude Leloutre, *La Réunion, département français,* Cahiers Libres 134 (Paris: François Maspéro, 1968), p. 50.

30 Exports were sugar, rum, geranium, and vetyver.

31 "Au milieu d'une crise qui s'aggrave, Le Parti Communiste propose: Un plan immédiat de survivre," Conférence Extraordinaire du Parti Communiste Réunionnais, April 1975, p. 6.

32 Ibid., p. 4.

33 Ibid., p. 141.

34 Ibid., pp. 112–26.

35 In 1959 the state funds amounted to more than 2 billion CFA. In 1966 23 billion 690 million FF. In 1971: 42 billion 650 million FF. 1973: 54 billion 300 million FF. The majority of these transfers were used to pay the salaries in the public function. In 1975 state credits to Réunion amounted to a total of 18 billion 325 million CFA; 67.6 percent went to pay the salaries in the tertiary sector. In 1974, 57.5 percent of the active population worked in the third sector; in 1982, 68.4, percent, which represented a 2.8 percent increase per year. In 1984, 70 percent of jobs were in the third sector. The majority of the workers in the tertiary sector

are employees of the state. They are a powerful lobby whose interests have been supported by trade lobbies, for whom state employees constitute reliable customers. They earn more than their counterparts in the metropole (between 53 and 70 percent), pay less in taxes (30 percent less), and receive other bonuses (free trips for the entire family to the metropole, free moves, bonus for the first months, etc.). A 1990 governmental report that proposed to reduce the state employees' subsidies was met with considerable resistance. The Ripert Commission proposed to reduce the bonuses by creating a development fund in which state employees could invest these bonuses. The fund would act as a savings bank, and state employees would earn interest on their savings. State employees' unions strongly opposed these propositions, and the recommendations of the Ripert Commission were ignored. In March 1997, civil servants went on strike, paralyzing the island, to protest against a project of reform of their status.

36 "La Réunion aux Réunionnais. L'Autonomie: Comment y parvenir? Son contenu. Le Programme du Parti Communiste Réunionnais," 21 March 1981, p. 1. See also the most recent communist document on the island's situation, *La Réunion, Égalité et Développement* (October 1990).

37 In 1968, for instance, France was paying only 3.2 percent more than the world price for a kilo of geraniums. See "À propos du commerce extérieur de La Réunion. Comment l'impérialisme français pille notre pays. Réponse à quelques objections," in *Arguments* (Saint-Denis, Réunion: REI, 1970), p. 4.

38 Cercle Éliard Laude, *Réunion 1969: Une Colonie française* (Paris: François Maspéro, 1969).

39 In 1946, one ton of locally produced goods bought 841 kg of imported goods. In 1968, one ton paid for only 534 kg of imported goods.

40 John M. Ostheimer, *The Politics of Western Indian Ocean Islands* (New York: Praeger, 1975), p. 118.

41 Marc Oraison, *Le Parti Communiste Réunionnais et l'Autonomie Démocratique et Populaire* (Saint-Denis, Réunion: Université de La Réunion, 1978), p. 8.

42 Philippe de Baleine, *Les danseuses de la France* (Paris: Plon, 1979), pp. 100–101.

43 See also Josyane Potíer and René Potier, *Étude anthropologique d'une zone sucrière à La Réunion* (Université de La Réunion, 1973).

44 Benoist, p. 82.

45 See "Statistiques et indicateurs économiques," Région Réunion, 1974: "Faits et Chiffres 1988," Région Réunion, 1988; "L'Économie de La Réunion, Panorama 1988," INSEE; "Tableau Économique de La Réunion," INSEE–Région Réunion, 1989, 1991, 1993; Paul Vergès, *Les départements d'Outre-Mer face au choc de 1992: Débat au Parlement Européen et annexes* (Brussels/Parlement Européen, 1992).

46 Recent statistics have shown that there has been no transformation of this pattern: in 1991, 76 percent of the exported goods (sugar) went to France, and 64 percent of the imported goods came from France. Manufactured goods and goods for consumption coming from France were more than one-third of the imports. The island's production is steadily decreasing, and today the island imports items it once produced, such as vegetables and poultry. The percentage of the active population working in industry has decreased by 1.3 percent per year, and the hypertrophy of the tertiary sector has become an impediment to economic transformation.

47 This is still the case, so that during the austral summer, one can learn about snow in the Alps.

48 Between 1946 and 1971, the population of Réunion increased from 225,000 to 454,300. Unemployment increased by 115 percent between 1967 and 1972. Debré declared in 1972: "The direct consequence of ending the policy of emigration will be revolution." To the state, there were three solutions: birth control, emigration to the metropole, and creation of jobs in Réunion. The first solution was opposed by Debré and the Catholic Church. The last solution was put aside because "it is the most difficult task to accomplish," a parliamentary commission wrote. In 1963 the government opened the Bureau for the Development of Migrations in the Overseas Department (in French, it was known by its acronym, the BUMIDOM). In the 1960s, four thousand to five thousand Réunionnais were sent every year to France, where they usually ended up in underqualified and underpaid jobs. However, the balance between the arrivals and the departures in Réunion did not indicate a pattern of relieving the island of a so-called overwhelming population. On the policy of emigration, see Isabelle Tal, *Les Réunionnais en France* (Paris: Éditions Entente, 1975); Parole and Société, *Les oubliés de la décolonisation française,* no. 2 (1973): pp. 204–8; Collectif des Chrétiens pour l'autodetermination des DOM-TOM, *Encore la France Coloniale* (Paris: L'Harmattan, Parole et Société, 1976), pp. 43–54; Alain Lorraine, Wilfrid Bertile, and le Collectif Dourdan, *Une communauté invisible: 175,000 Réunionnais en France métropolitaine* (Paris: l'Harmattan, 1996); Albert Weber, *L'Émigration réunionnaise en France* (Paris: L'Harmattan, 1994).

49 In 1982, 26.15 percent of families, or 125,000 people, were living with an income of less than 1,000 FF, or $200; 58.14 percent had a monthly income between $200 and $600; 1.3 percent were living with more than $2,000 per month. Réunion is the French department with the highest rate of unemployment: 37 percent (higher than the Antilles). The monthly income of the Réunionnais is high compared to the income of surrounding countries (Madagascar, Mauritius). Réunionnais are much better off than their neighbors, but their standard of living rests on very fragile foundations.

50 In 1946, the island had two high schools; it had eighty in 1986.

51 In 1988, 54 percent of Réunion's population benefited from medical aid. Sonia Chane-Kune, *Aux origines de l'identité réunionnaise* (Paris: L'Harmattan, 1994), and *La Réunion n'est plus une île* (Paris: L'Harmattan, 1996). See also Jean Benoist, *Anthropologie médicale en société créole* (Paris: PUF, 1993). In 1989, 60 percent of the budget of the department went to health services; Thierry Simon, "La santé à La Réunion de 1900 à nos jours: D'une colonie cachectique à un département presque comblé" (thesis in medicine, University of Tours, 1990).

52 Wilfrid Bertile, *Le logement dans les départements d'Outre-Mer: Rapport au Premier Ministre* (Paris: La Documentation Française, 1984), p. 13.

53 Sonia Chane-Kune, p. 292. In 1989, 75 percent of the population was suffering from parasitosis.

54 Ibid., p. 291.

55 In 1991, 11 percent of Réunion students obtained the baccalaureat, a percentage that was half that of the metropole.

56 The sociolinguist Pierre Cellier argues that none of the arguments advanced against teaching in Creole has a pedagogical foundation. The arguments are ideological and ethnocentric. Pierre Cellier, "École et société: L'enseignement du français," *Cahiers de La Réunion et de l'Océan Indien* 4 (1974): pp. 21–25. On the repression of Creole language, see Robert Chaudenson, *Lexique du parler créole de la Réunion* (Paris: Champion, 1974); Axel Gauvin, *Du créole opprimé au créole libéré* (Paris: L'Harmattan, 1977); Daniel Lauret, *Le créole de la réussite* (Saint-Denis, Réunion: Éditions du Tramail, 1991); Ginette Ramassamy, "Syntaxe du Créole Réunionnais: Analyse de corpus d'unilingues créolophones" (Ph.D. diss., University of Sorbonne, Paris, 1985). Despite numerous studies by scholars, educators, and child psychologists who have shown that the dropout rate and failure among schoolchildren is the direct result of the policy of forbidding Creole in schools, authorities stubbornly maintain that using Creole in the classroom would impede Réunion children's access to knowledge. Creole parents themselves have often been persuaded that using Creole is bad, and they support the policy. It must be said that the texts defining what must be taught in the French classroom no longer forbid the use of "regional" languages and the teaching of regional culture. The *rectorat,* the administrative authority on education in the department, teachers, and parents are thus responsible for refusing to use Creole in the classroom.

57 Chane-Kune, p. 343.

58 Daniel Sibony, *Écrits sur le racisme* (Paris: Christian Bourgeois Éditeur, 1987), p. 118.

59 Ibid., p. 123. Aimé Césaire has called it "cultural genocide."

60 Michel Debré, *Une politique pour La Réunion* (Paris: Plon, 1974), p. 215.

61 Prosper Eve has shown that after World War I, the church and the republican school, both powerful institutions on the island, spread the message that France was central to the existence and survival of the island. Eve contends that after 1917, schoolteachers were advised to make the idea of *patrie* and love for the fatherland central to their teaching. In Prosper Eve, *La Première Guerre Mondiale vue par les poilus réunionnais* (Saint-Denis, Réunion: Éditions CNH, 1992), p. 77.

62 At the 1942 exhibition on France d'Outre Mer, seven women were chosen to represent the French colonial empire. At the center of the row of women was a young woman with the French flag on her breast and the words "La Réunion, fidèle à La Mère-Patrie" (Réunion Island, faithful to the fatherland). Réunion was the "colony that colonizes." It deserved the recognition of France for its role in the colonial expansion and the spread of colonialism. In *Le Quotidien de l'Île de La Réunion,* 19 March 1986, p. 9. Hereafter cited as *Quotidien.*

63 Frantz Fanon participated in one of these demonstrations in Lyon. He later wrote: "As for Jacques Vergès, a native of Réunion, the French colony, we need only remember how several of us were trampled underfoot in Lyon ten years ago to feel on an equal footing with him. Ten years ago hundreds of Algerian workers and students manifesting their solidarity with a relative of Maître Vergès, who was the victim of a plot in Réunion, were clubbed by the French police and gendarmerie." See "Concerning a Plea," in *Toward the African Revolution: Political Essays,* pp. 73–75, 75.

64 "Comment l'aristocratie du sucre fit assassiner De Villeneuve: Interview du Docteur Raymond Vergès, Député de La Réunion," *La Défense,* 10 January 1947, p. 1.

65 Colonizers were radicalized by their experience in the struggle against Nazism. They saw that white peoples could do to other white peoples what had been done to them: displacements of populations, massacres, internment in camps. To fight against Nazism was also to fight against racism. Colonized soldiers felt entitled to rewards for having participated in the defeat of Nazism and for having joined the Allied armies, even though France did not recognize them as equal citizens. Many went back to their country with a sense of not having been rightly rewarded. On December 1 and 2, 1944, hundreds of Senegalese soldiers who had fought in Europe with the French forces were massacred by the French army at the camp of Thiaroye in Senegal. They had asked for their pay and for the recognition of their status as French veterans.

66 *Étudiants Anticolonialistes,* no. 1 (1949). *Étudiants Anticolonialistes* put out seven issues—the last in August 1950.

67 Max Rivière, "L'île de la Réunion contre le colonialisme," *Étudiants Anticolonialistes,* no. 6 (June 1950).

68 Jacques Vergès, "La lutte des étudiants créoles," *Étudiants Anticolonialistes,* no. 6 (June 1950).

69 The Section Coloniale was criticized for its patronizing methods vis-à-vis the colonized.

70 In France, there were demonstrations against the war, and an appeal was addressed to the draftees to refuse to go to Algeria. The French communists, who had denied the right of the Algerian people to self-determination and had voted the special powers of the government in 1954 (the right of the government to do as it pleased in Algeria without parliamentary control), now supported the antiwar demonstrations. The Communist Party never led the antiwar movement. It was the role of intellectuals—Jean-Paul Sartre, Simone de Beauvoir, Dyonis Mascolo, and François Maspéro, among others—and of thousands of activists.

71 On the history of fraud, violence, and repression during the elections, see Jocelyne Lauret, "Un siècle de fraudes électorales à La Réunion" (M.A. thesis, University of Réunion, 1990); Eugène Rousse; *Le Monde,* 4 May 1963, 7 May 1963; *France-Observateur,* 18 April 1963.

72 The constitution of the Fifth Republic was adopted by referendum in September 1958. De Gaulle was elected president of the republic on December 21, 1958.

73 Speech of de Gaulle, *Mémorial de La Réunion,* vol. 6, pp. 426–27.

74 Interview of Michel Debré on the TV station RFO, Réunion Island, 25 September 1989.

75 Ibid.

76 The decree was originally a clause of a February 4, 1960, law enacted by Debré's government to deal with the opposition to the Algerian War. The decree authorized the French government to take "all necessary measures to maintain order, safeguard the State and the Constitution, and pursue the pacification and administration of Algeria." It was a decree enacted against French civil servants living in Algeria who supported the Algerian nationalist struggle.

77 The decree remained operative until 1972. On the Debré ordinance, see Michel Robert, *La Réunion: Combats pour l'autonomie* (Paris: L'Harmattan, 1976), pp. 119–22; Eugène Rousse, "Le bilan de 25 années de Michel Debré à La Réunion dans le domaine des libertés," *Témoignages,* 1989.

78 Of the thirteen who were the victims of the Debré ordinance in Réunion, seven worked in education.

79 Jacques Vergès, *De la stratégie judiciaire,* 3d ed. (Paris: Éditions de Minuit, 1981).

80 After the war, Jacques Vergès married a young Algerian woman, Djamila Bouhired. Bouhired had participated in the Battle of Algiers (1954–1956), in which she was arrested and tortured by French paratroopers. Condemned to death by a French tribunal, she was defended by

Jacques Vergès. Djamila Bouhired, with other Algerian women condemned to death, was pardoned by President Auriol in 1958. About Algerian women and the war, see Danièle Djamila Amrane-Minne, *Des
femmes dans la guerre d'Algérie* (Paris: Karthala, 1994); Georges Arnaud
and Jacques Vergès, *Pour Djamila Bouhired* (Paris: Éditions de Minuit,
1957); Gisèle Halimi with Simone de Beauvoir, *Pour Djamila Boupacha*
(Paris: Gallimard, 1962).

81 *Le Progrès,* 21 January 1963.

82 The minister, following the recommendation of Réunion's prefect, set
against Vergès the law of state emergency. *Le Monde,* 31 January 1963.

83 "Interview de Michel Debré par Claude Estier," *France-Observateur,*
April 1963.

84 Michel Debré, *Trois républiques pour une France: Mémoires,* vol. 1
(Paris: Albin Michel, 1984), pp. 32, 35.

85 Ibid., p. 37.

86 In his memoirs, Debré devotes a chapter, entitled "Mater, Uxor, So-
ror," to the women who were important in his life. He says: "I owe to my
mother, my wife, my sister, the political will to facilitate the access of
women to high functions and careers." Yet he also insists that "the denial
of women's vocation to motherhood and family life is a sin against the
individual and the human species" (p. 68).

87 Ibid., p. 42.

88 Ibid.

89 Ibid.

90 Ibid., p. 59.

91 Ibid., p. 19.

92 Ibid., vol. 4, p. 195. To Debré, migrant workers, arriving with their
families from the former colonial empire, were not a solution to the de-
crease in the French birthrate because they "came from faraway countries
and brought the *germs* of a different civilization" (p. 199, emphasis mine).

93 Ibid., p. 73. Emphasis in the text.

94 Ibid., p. 27.

95 Michel Debré, *Une politique pour La Réunion* (Paris: Plon, 1974), p. 1.

96 Ibid., p. 17.

97 Until then, young men had joined the army on a voluntary basis.

98 Ibid., p. 19.

99 Ibid., p. 21.

100 Ibid., p. 22.

101 Michael Paul Rogin, *"Ronald Reagan," the Movie: and Other Episodes
in Political Demonology* (Berkeley: University of California Press, 1987),
p. xiii.

102 Ibid., p. 237.

103 In 1963, twenty-four organizations from Guadeloupe, Martinique, and Réunion signed in Paris a manifesto that demanded the status of autonomy for the overseas departments. The gesture was repeated in 1968 with the "Manifesto for Self-Determination." The 1971 Convention at Morne Rouge, Martinique, reaffirmed their will for the creation of a "united anti-colonialist front." For the first time, at this convention, Catholic movements joined the anticolonialists. In Réunion, where the Catholic Church has always exercised its influence in politics, the participation of Catholics in such a conference had considerable impact.

104 In order to examine political demonology in Réunion, I have looked at brochures, leaflets, newspapers, and posters from 1963 to 1993. I have organized vocabulary lists and analyzed the gendered grammar and vocabulary of the texts provided by this corpus. The newspapers, leaflets, posters, and brochures were found at the Archives Départementales de La Réunion. I read the following newspapers published between 1963 and 1993: *Journal de l'Île de La Réunion, Le Progrès, Hebdo-Bourbon, Croix Sud, La Voix des Mascareignes, La Nation, Combat National, Liberté, Quotidien de l'Île de La Réunion, Le Réunionnais.*

105 *Journal de l'Île de La Réunion,* 5, 9, 10, 14 January 1963, 2 March 1963, 19, 20 April 1963, 2, 3 May 1963, 21 November 1963. Hereafter cited as *JIR.*

106 In these beauty pageants, whiteness was rewarded. Beauty was embodied by a young, blond, white woman.

107 See Jean-Claude Balducchi, "La vie politique et sociale à La Réunion, 1932–1939" (Ph.D. diss., University of Aix-en-Provence, July 1984); Prosper Eve, *Le jeu politique à La Réunion de 1900 à 1939,* for examples of the paranoid style in Réunion's politics during the pre–World War II era. Examples of religious political demonology after World War II can be found in Réunion's newspapers, such as *Le Progrès, La Démocratie,* and *Dieu et Patrie.*

108 In 1914, twelve people were killed, and one hundred and fifty people were wounded, during the electoral campaign. In André Scherer, *Histoire de La Réunion* (Paris: PUF, Que Sais-Je?, 1966), p. 92.

109 Prosper Eve, *Île à peur: La peur redoutée ou récupérée à La Réunion des origines à nos jours* (Saint-Denis, Réunion: Océan Éditions, 1992).

110 Ibid., pp. 400–402.

111 *JIR,* 9 March 1963.

112 In 1950 there were 1,900 radios in the island and thirty hours a week of programs. Thirteen years later, there were 25,400 radios and seventy hours a week of programs. See Karine Técher and Mario Serviable, *Histoire de la presse à La Réunion* (Saint-Denis, Réunion: ARS Terres Créoles/URAD, 1991); Brigitte Fontaine, "Historique et point de vue sociologique de la presse écrite et audiovisuelle à l'île de La Réunion des origines à nos jours," (M.A. thesis, University of Réunion, 1982); Bernard Idelson, "De la RTF á RFO" (M.A. thesis, University of Réunion, 1995).

113 It was illegal, according to the French law, to create a private radio or television. In 1982 the French government finally authorized the creation of private radios and televisions.

114 *JIR*, 11 April 1963. In 1967 the prefect attacked the communists and urged the population to make the "right choice" by electing Debré.

115 The mayors of Réunion signed an appeal supporting Debré and offering free public transportation to the first demonstration of the 1960s' countersubversive campaign, on May 1, 1963.

116 *JIR*, 20 April 1963.

117 In Réunion, the Catholic Church launched the anticommunist campaign after World War II. The church was following the Vatican's instructions. In 1949 Catholics were warned that "a catholic cannot be a communist without violating the law of the Church." *Le Progrès*, 12 September 1949. On 16 May 1949: "The Communists have the habit of attacking the Christians, hiding cowardly behind the parliamentary immunity of Papa Vergès [name given to R. Vergès]." On 7 June 1949: "If a Catholic is communist, he goes against the law of the Church." In 1953, the bishop issued a declaration to the believers: "1-There is an obligation to vote; 2-It is forbidden to vote for communism. It is an anti-religious doctrine, condemned by the Church; 3-One must stop communism and vote for the anti-communists. 4-To abstain is to play into the hands of the communists. These directives must be read at all the masses of Sunday 13, 20, and 27, September, without any comment and will remain posted on the doors of the churches and chapels of the district during the entire electoral campaign" (*Le Progrès*, 14 September 1953). The bishop reissued a warning on 26 September 1953. In 1967 the bishop called for a mobilization against communism and to vote for Debré (*Croix Sud*, 26 February 1967).

118 Banner at the May 1, 1963, conservative demonstration. Emphasis in the text. In the movie, *Sucre Amer*, we see women and men, passive and mute, carrying banners.

119 *Hebdo-Bourbon*, 2 March 1967, p. 1.

120 Rogin, p. 284.

121 Donald W. Winnicott, "Discussions of War Aims," in *Home Is Where We Start From: Essays by a Psychoanalyst*, ed. Clare Winnicott, Ray Sheperd, and Madelaine Davies (New York: W. W. Norton, 1986), pp. 210–20, 215.

122 Ibid.

123 Donald Winnicott, "The Capacity to Be Alone," in *Collected Papers: Through Pediatrics to Psycho-Analysis* (London: Tavistock, 1971), p. 205.

124 Winnicott, "Psychoanalysis and Science: Friends or Relations?" in *Home Is Where We Start From*, pp. 13–18, 16.

125 Octave Mannoni, *Prospéro et Caliban: Psychologie de la Colonization* (1949; Paris: Éditions Universitaires, 1984). Trans. Pamela Powesland as

Prospero and Caliban: The Psychology of Colonization (Ann Arbor: University of Michigan Press, 1990), p. 174. Quotes are from the English translation.

126 Ibid., p. 174.

127 Ibid., p. 175.

128 Personal communication, January 1995.

129 Edgar Burrows and Michael Wallace, "The American Revolution: The Ideology and Psychology of National Liberation," *Perspectives in American History* 6 (1972): pp. 167–306, 189.

130 Ibid., p. 275.

131 Pitkin, p. 324.

132 Sigmund Freud, *Inhibitions, Symptoms, and Anxiety,* trans. Alix Strachey (New York: W. W. Norton, 1959), p. 54.

133 Melanie Klein, "A Contribution to the Psychogenesis of Manic-Depressive States," *International Journal of Psycho-Analysis* 16 (1935): pp. 145–74.

134 Jean Laplanche and Jean-Baptiste Pontalis, *The Language of Psychoanalysis,* trans. Donald Nicholson-Smith (New York: W. W. Norton, 1973), p. 107.

135 Sigmund Freud, "Psychotherapy of Hysteria," in Josef Breuer and Sigmund Freud, *Studies on Hysteria 1893–1895,* trans. James Strachey (New York: Basic Books, 1957), pp. 253–306, 269.

136 *JIR,* 3 May 1963.

137 On the phallic mother, see Françoise Couchard, *Emprise et violence maternelles* (Paris: Dunod, 1991).

138 In psychoanalytical parlance, the perfect object of love is an object that persecutes. To Melanie Klein, the introjection of bad and good objects in the child's ego signifies that the infant has successfully overcome the split between good and bad objects. In some instances, though, the ego defends itself against "internalized persecutors by the process of expulsion and projection." It is not only the bad object that persecutes. The good object itself can become persecuting. Its demands are perceived by the ego as "extremely cruel." "The result," Klein writes, "is a conception of extremely bad and extremely perfect objects, that is to say, its loved objects are in many ways intensely moral and exacting." The superego of the individual exercises a "relentless severity." One cannot ever fulfill the strict demands of the perfect love object. There is even a constant uncertainty about the goodness of the love object, but it is an uncertainty that the individual cannot accept because she or he cannot accept the complex nature of love. The ambivalence that one feels toward the imaginary perfecting object is repressed and projected onto others. The beautiful image that one has of the object is separated from the real object. If the idea of perfection is so constraining, Klein argues, it is because it refutes the idea of disintegration. See Melanie Klein, "A Contribution to the Psychogenesis of Manic-Depressive States," p. 151. Klein is writing about the melancholic individual, but I think that her observations can be applied to the kind of love France exacted from the colonized.

139 Since 1946 French people have come to Réunion to occupy high decision-making functions and the majority of posts in education, health service, and the administration. The percentage of zoreys living in Réunion has steadily increased. In 1967 they were 1.4 percent of the population. In 1982 they were 4.1 percent. In 1990 the zoreys were 6.3 percent of the total population. All observers agree that the group of zoreys has profoundly affected Réunion's society. Zoreys hold 69 percent of the posts in education. Today, seven out of ten jobs created in Réunion go to metropolitan French.

140 Benoist, p. 149. See also Chane-Kune, pp. 423–34; Leloutre, pp. 35–38; Jacques Pelletier, "La Chaloupe, Ile de La Réunion, une société créole: Stratégies individuelles et hiérarchies des réseaux" (Ph.D. diss., École des Hautes Études en Sciences Sociales, Paris, 1983).

141 See *Hebdo-Bourbon,* 31 March 1966, 9 June 1966: "Is there really a question about why the *metro* [the French] comes to Réunion? He just wants to get richer."

142 Marcelo N. Vignar, "Violence sociale et réalité dans l'analyse," in *Violence d'État et Psychanalyse,* by Janine Puget et al. (Paris: Dunod, 1989), pp. 41–66, 63. See also, in the same book, Lia Ricón, "L'autoritarisme dans la société argentine et son rôle dans l'apparition de pathologies graves," pp. 67–85.

143 Puget, "État de menace et psychanalyse: De l'étrange structurant à l'étrange aliénant," in *Violence d'État et Psychanalyse,* pp. 1–40.

144 Ibid., p. 13. For the concept of "alienation" adopted here, see Piera Aulagnier, *Les destins du plaisir: Aliénation, amour, passion* (Paris: PUF, 1979).

145 *La Voix des Mascareignes,* 5 September 1963.

146 See *La Voix des Mascareignes,* 5 September 1963, 10 October 1963; *JIR,* 23 February 1967.

147 *JIR,* 23 February 1967. Emphasis in text.

148 *La Nation,* 23 February 1967.

149 *Hebdo-Bourbon,* 18 May 1967, p. 2.

150 *Hebdo-Bourbon,* 2 February 1967, p. 2.

151 *JIR,* 2 March 1963. Communiqué of the association Réunion French Department, p. 1.

152 Ibid.

153 *JIR,* 19 April 1963, p. 1.

154 Allusion to the 1947 trial of Paul Vergès. Vergès had been charged with murder, but the trial ended with a rejection of the indictment.

However, conservatives in Réunion have continued to allude to that indictment to portray the communist leader as a murderer.

155 This is a reference to Jacques Vergès, who defended the Algerian nationalists during the war and adopted Islam after the Algerian independence to marry Djamila Bouhired. Jacques Vergès published a review, *Révolution*, which supported Beijing in its opposition to Moscow and "Soviet imperialism."

156 The term "The Parisian" evokes the image of a man lavishly spending his life in the cafés and bars of Paris while the poor, credulous Réunionnais thought that Vergès was lobbying for them in the French capital.

157 *Popaul* is a pejorative diminutive of Paul.

158 Compilation of names that appeared between 1963 and 1973 in Réunion's newspapers about Debré and Vergès.

159 Spelling the word *comrade* with a *k* and giving communist names a Russian flavor—such as Vergeskoff, Mondonovitch—were recurrent devices of the conservative press to conjure up the alien nature of communism. "Mondonovitch" was Raymond Mondon, a communist who had been elected with Paul Vergès at the 1956 elections to the French National Assembly. Mondon was also a leader of the union of schoolteachers.

160 This was an allusion to the 1947 trial of Paul Vergès.

161 *Hebdo-Bourbon,* 1 December 1966, p. 6.

162 *La Voix des Mascareignes,* 9 March 1967, p. 1.

163 *JIR,* 18 March 1964. The story about the missing *s* does not really make sense. To the conservatives, the mistake in the title signified a rupture with Raymond Vergès, who was the creator of the newspaper and had chosen for its title *Témoignages.* As Debré restated some twenty years later: "At that time [1946] the communists were nationalists. They changed." Interview at RFO, 25 September 1989.

164 "Madame Raymond Vergès qui soutient la candidature de M. Debré expose à *La Nation* les raisons de son attachement à la France," *La Nation,* 29 April 1963, pp. 1–2; emphasis in the text. *La Voix des Mascareignes,* in an article "Cocos la Fraude," reproduced excerpts of speeches in which Joséphine Vergès declared: "Workers, my friends, you know me. I fought alongside Raymond Vergès to better your social conditions. . . . The Communist candidates want autonomy, the independence of Réunion, that will bring you misery. I can ensure you that Raymond Vergès would not have wanted this" (2 May 1963). Joséphine Vergès, though, was not an activist in the 1940s and 1950s.

165 Ibid.

166 *JIR,* 17 February 1967.

167 Michel Pastoureau, "Le coq gaulois," in *Les lieux de mémoire: Les France, De l'archive à l'emblème,* ed. Pierre Nora (Paris: Gallimard, 1992), pp. 507–39.

168 The cock also belonged to the Christian symbolic order. Pastoureau writes: "Numerous texts [at the end of the Middle Ages] talked of the cock in positive terms. Singing at dawn, the cock chases the demons of the night and wakes up the faithful who are sleeping in sinful darkness. It invites to conversion and announces the future resurrection. The biblical episode of the repudiation of Saint Peter (the cock sang three times) serves as the foundation of this valorizing symbolic of the cock" ("Le coq gaulois," p. 516). Besides being the emblem of the nation, the cock was an evangelizing emblem. And as Pastoureau remarks, the cock appears on churches as well as on republican public buildings and monuments to the dead.

169 See the Réunion proverb: "Hide your hens, my cock is on the run."

170 Paul Vergès has said that his father did not like this appellation. "It was said with a lot of affection but he was very uncomfortable with it." In *D'une île au monde: Entretiens avec Brigitte Croisier* (Paris: L'Harmattan, 1993), p. 160.

171 No political leader is today called "Papa." Only among old people who have known Raymond Vergès can one still hear "Papa Vergès. He was our papa."

172 It would be interesting to research the linguistic traditions of the ethnic groups that constituted the Réunion population. What did they call their leaders?

173 "Du lait grâce à Papa Debré," *La Nation,* 26 April 1963, p. 2.

174 *Annales de l'Assemblée Nationale,* no. 244, 12–21 July 1949.

175 See Leloutre, Cercle Éliard Laude, and Robert. Also the introduction of Jean Benoist, *Anthropologie médicale en société créole.*

176 Cited in Cercle Éliard e Laude, p. 79.

177 *JIR,* 2 February 1967.

178 Poster for the 1963 electoral campaign. Archives Départementales de La Réunion.

179 *La Nation,* 26 April 1963.

180 Leaflet distributed to call for a May 1 demonstration at Saint-Denis.

181 Workers, students, housewives were mobilized. Debré wanted an affirmation of the "pro-national" sentiment.

182 Leaflet.

183 *JIR,* 27 April 1963, p. 1.

184 Testimonies of workers in *Sucre Amer.*

185 Speech of Paul Vergès in *Sucre Amer.*

186 *Le Progrès,* 6 March 1963.

187 *Le Monde,* 20 April 1963.

188 *Le Monde,* 4 May 1963, 7 May 1963.

189 It seems that sometimes conservative candidates were not satisfied even with their victory. Robert cites the case of Debré in the elections of

July 23, 1968. On the evening of the election day, the prefect declared that officially 25,000 votes had been cast for Debré. The following day, the number was raised to 33,000 votes, without any explanation (Robert, p. 122).

190 Debré, *Une politique pour La Réunion,* pp. 214–15.

191 According to Chane-Kune, after 1973, the distribution of the votes changed in meaningful ways. Conservatives had claimed between 75 percent and 95 percent of the vote. After 1973, their tally decreased to 45 percent, and the communists, who had received between 1 and 3 percent of the vote, now won around 35 percent of the vote (Chane-Kune, p. 482). Chane-Kune argues that fraudulent practices have persisted. They are more subtle and less violent, but she contends that truly free elections in Réunion still do not exist. Poverty and welfare make an important part of the population sensitive to blackmail. For instance, in the two weeks preceding elections, unemployed people are given, by conservative city councils, temporary jobs in exchange for a "good" vote.

192 *Mémorial de La Réunion,* vol. 6, p. 490.

193 *JIR,* 24 January 1964, p. 1; 8 February 1964, p. 1.

194 Hundreds of Algerians were killed in Paris and drowned in the Seine. The articles reproduced reports that had appeared in two French newspapers, *Le Monde* and *L'Humanité,* whose editors were not indicted by the French authorities.

195 About the state's involvement in the repression in Réunion, see Jacques Foccart, *Tous les soirs avec De Gaulle: Journal de l'Elysée—I, 1965–1967* (Paris: Fayard, Jeune Afrique, 1997), pp. 100, 131, 499, 530.

196 The conservatives' anxiety dictated measures that went beyond a rational concern for public order. In 1969 the prefect severely restricted the screening of the movie *Z* by Costa-Gravas, which depicted the life of an antifascist leader during the military dictatorship in Greece. The movie was shown only in two theaters and was forbidden to individuals under age eighteen, even if they were accompanied by their parents. The movie had not been subjected to similar measures in France. In the overseas departments, a special commission decides movie programming. In 1976 the conservatives protested the scheduling of the movie *Main Basse sur la Ville,* which denounced the scandals of graft and corruption among Italian conservatives. The movie, whose release had been planned a week before district elections, was rescheduled after the elections.

197 More than 20 million francs CFA were spent on the festivities, quite an enormous sum for 1965. (The Franc CFA was the money of the French Union).

198 "Les fêtes du Tricentenaire," in *Le Mémorial de La Réunion: La Réunion d'aujourd'hui, 1964–1979,* ed. Henri Maurin and Jacques Lentge, vol. 7 (Saint-Denis, Réunion: Éditions Australe, 1989).

199 *JIR,* 4 October 1965.

200 "Program of the tricentennial: "1665: Le Tricentennaire—1965.""

201 "La veuve Aimée Gossard declare au Premier Ministre," *La Nation,* 3 May 1963, p. 3.

202 *JIR,* 16 March 1964, p. 1.

203 *Hebdo-Bourbon,* 1 December 1966, p. 6.

204 *Quotidien,* 25 November 1992, p. 2. See also *Quotidien,* 5 August 1991. Testimony of a woman: "Before I was a communist. But they said I was a bad communist because I did not want to hit gendarmes and priests."

205 Paul Vergès, *D'une île au monde,* p. 147.

206 Albert Ramassamy, "Une décision politique, sage et juste," *JIR,* 22 December 1992, p. 2.

207 François Gillet, "Le cercle des électeurs disparus," *Quotidien,* 23 March 1993, p. 9.

208 Jacky Ferrere, "Paul Vergès: L'adversaire politique numéro un," *JIR,* 16 March 1993, p. 6.

209 Jean-Paul Virapoullé, "Le PCR a manipulé les jeunes!" *Quotidien,* 1 March 1993, p. 7.

210 Jean-Jacques Marchat, "Le PCR incontournable aux sénatoriales," *L'Écho,* 24 September 1992, p. 9.

211 "Thill, Vergès et Sudre ne sont pas Zorro," *JIR,* 18 March 1993, p. 9.

212 Jacky Ferrere, "Union sacrée autour de J. F. Bosviel," *JIR,* 23 March 1993.

213 Jean-Louis Rabou, "Question de sincérité," *Quotidien,* 3 March 1993, p. 1.

214 Ferrere, "Au nom du père," *JIR,* 1 March 1993, p. 13.

215 "L'opposition accuse Vergès," *Quotidien,* 11 December 1992, p. 6.

216 "Paulo, dis-moi que ce n'est pas vrai!" *Quotidien,* 25 November 1992, p. 2. Also, on Vergès as a person protecting his "dynasty," see "Adieu Pota, merci Cassam," *JIR,* 23 November 1992. All the letters are anonymous.

217 *JIR,* 1 March 1993, p. 13.

218 Pierre is one of Paul Vergès's two sons. Laurent, his first son, was killed in October 1988.

219 See "Sur la piste de Pierre Vergès: Rapport de gendarmerie sur cinq mois de recherches," *Quotidien,* 28 February 1994, pp. 4–5.

220 *Petit Pierre,* or *Ti Pierre,* was the nickname of Pierre Vergès among his friends and family. It was used in the media as a pejorative appellation.

221 Jean-Louis Rabou, "Des méthodes de voyou," *Quotidien,* 5 April 1993, p. 3.

222 "Du PCR à dynastie: Le nom des Vergès," *Quotidien,* 18 May 1989.

223 Rogin; Cynthia Enloe, *The Morning After: Sexual Politics at the End of the Cold War* (Berkeley: University of California Press, 1993).

224 Enloe, p. 3.

225 Ibid., p. 240.

226 Monique Payet, "La femme mise en chansons: L'image des femmes à travers quelques ségas réunionnais," in *Figures et Paroles de Femmes, Recueil d'articles parus dans* Témoignages, n.d., pp. 15–17.

227 The Law Neuwirth (1967) and the Law Veil (1975) gave women the right to contraception and abortion. The 1975 law on divorce facilitated the divorce procedure for women.

228 Jean-Paul Virapoullé, a leader of the conservatives, liked to challenge male opponents on a terrain charged with masculinist affect: "Camille Sudre [the leader of a populist movement, Freedom, who had won the majority in recent regional elections] should have the courage to accept a man-to-man debate" ("Jean-Paul Virapoullé: Expliquez-vous, Monsieur Sudre!" *Le Réunionnais,* 15 March 1993, p. 3). Women who dare to enter politics encounter extreme misogyny.

229 Marie Gamel, for instance, was deputy major to Raymond Vergès, in the city council of Saint-André. Other women, such as Alice Peverelly, Augusta LeToullec, and Isnelle Amelin, joined the Communist Party's leadership.

230 "Trois femmes devant leur peuple," *Témoignages Chrétien Réunionnais,* no. 163 (10–16 October 1977): p. 9, and personal interview, December 1992.

231 Ibid.

232 "Il faut toujours se rendre utile, est sa devise: Isnelle Amelin, Rebelle de tous les combats à 86 ans," *Quotidien,* 16 September 1993, pp. 16–17.

233 "La situation de la femme à La Réunion: Mémoire présenté par l'Union des Femmes de La Réunion à l'occasion de la visite du Président de la République Française à La Réunion," 17 October 1976, personal archives.

234 *JIR,* 15 February 1967, p. 1.

235 *Hebdo-Bourbon,* 24 March 1966, p. 2.

236 In 1982, 95 percent of Réunion's working women were in the tertiary sector (Catherine Pasquet and René Squarzoni, "Les femmes à La Réunion: Une évolution impressionnante, une situation ambigüe," *Études et synthèses,* no. 1, Observatoire Départemental de La Réunion, p. 35).

237 Feminist scholars have reported similar perceptions in the French Antilles. See France Alibar et Pierrette Lembeye-Boy, *Le couteau seul: Sé Kouto sèl . . . La condition féminine aux Antilles* (Paris: Éditions Caribéennes, 1983); Huguette Dagenais and Jean Poirier, "L'envers du mythe: la situation des femmes en Guadeloupe"; and Catherine Charbit, Yves Charbit, and Catherine Bertrand, "La pluripaternité en Guadeloupe et en Martinique," *Nouvelles Questions Féministes,* 9–10 (spring 1985): pp. 53–84.

238 *Femmes en Chiffre, Réunion* (Saint-Denis, Réunion: Service Régional de l'INSEE, 1988).

239 In 1982, 2.9 percent of women and 4.1 percent of men went to college (Pasquet and Squarzoni, p. 43).

240 Ibid., pp. 41–44.

241 See Gisela Bock and Pat Thane, eds., *Maternity and Gender Policies: Women and the Rise of the European Welfare States, 1880s–1950s* (New York: Routledge, 1994); Claire Duchen, *Women's Rights and Women's Lives in France, 1944–1968* (New York: Routledge, 1994); Seth Koven and Sonya Michel, *Mothers of a New World: Maternalist Politics and the Origins of Welfare States* (New York: Routledge, 1992); CERM, eds., *La Condition féminine* (Paris: Éditions Sociales, 1978).

242 On the history of welfare programs in the United States, see Linda Gordon, *Pitied but Not Entitled: Single Mothers and the History of Welfare, 1890–1935* (New York: Free Press, 1994); Gwendolyn Mink, *The Wages of Motherhood: Inequality in the Welfare State, 1917–1942* (Ithaca: Cornell University Press, 1995).

243 Cited in Frank F. Furstenberg Jr., "Women and Children Last," *New York Review of Books,* 16 October 1994, p. 46.

244 See Eliane Wolf, *Quartiers de Vie: Approche ethnologique des populations défavorisées de l'île de La Réunion* (Saint-Denis, Réunion: CIIRF, ARCA, 1989). Wolf shows that access to publicly funded low-income housing is preferably given to women because women can guarantee a regular income (p. 35).

245 See the report of the Congress of the Union of Women of Réunion, 8–9 October 1983. Personal Archives.

246 Debré's opposition to contraception was attacked in France by French Planned Parenthood and by feminist groups. Debré was often a target of the demonstrations of the French women's movement after 1968 because of his stubborn resistance to the legalization of abortion and contraception.

247 Debré, *Une politique pour La Réunion,* p. 34.

248 Ibid., p. 38.

249 Ibid., p. 39.

250 *La Nation,* 19 April 1963, p. 1.

251 The order in which these three names appear is in itself interesting. Are we going from a minus to a plus? From France to Debré? Or vice versa?

252 Laws about divorce are presented in an official document as an "extension of women's recourse against violent, alcoholic, irresponsible, and inconstant husbands" (Pasquet and Squarzoni, p. 7).

253 Pasquet and Squarzoni write: "We must note that the conquest of rights by women in the metropole has led to the extension of these rights in the overseas departments but also that they were not the consequence of local struggle or local demands" (p. 6). The struggle of the Union des Femmes Réunionnaises was not acknowledged.

254 In the early 1970s, Mauritius, which became independent in 1968, became the favorite destination for cheap vacations, where Réunionnais could act out their fantasies of being rich and "whiter" because they were French. Madagascar knew another fate. In 1974 a nationalist military government came to power, promising its population the end of neo-colonialism and the advent of socialism. Corruption, mismanagement of the economy, and irrational policies brought famine and epidemics to the island's population. Political changes in Madagascar brought an end to the failed experiment. The country has become in recent years both the "Somalia" and the "Thailand" of Réunion. Their Somalia, because Réunionnais can be charitable and feed the poor of Madagascar. Their Thailand, because Madagascans, desperate for money, are selling themselves, sometimes for next to nothing.

5. Single Mothers, Missing Fathers, and French Psychiatrists

1 The trial's quotes are from personal notes taken during the trial, and from Alain Dupuis, "Huit ans pour avoir tué son père," *Le Journal de l'Île de La Réunion,* 26 November 1992, p. 6; Pascal Neau, "D'une prison à l'autre," *Quotidien du Jeudi,* 26 November 1992, p. 5; Florence Vendome, "Huit ans pour un parricide," *Le Réunionnais,* 26 November 1992, p. 4. Notes taken during the 1992–1993 session at the criminal court at Saint-Denis and interviews with psychiatrists and psychiatric nurses and with lawyers and with cultural and social workers provided the material for this chapter. I read the psychiatric theses on Réunion written before 1993 and the articles and comments about the February 1991 and the December 1992 urban uprisings at Saint-Denis.

2 The criminal court, where murders are tried, has three judges: the president and two assessors.

3 Chinese migrants opened small groceries throughout the island, in which they sold food and other goods, often opening monthly credit to their poor customers. Children used to go to *boutik sinwa* (the Chinese store). Men sat by the store in the evening, playing cards or dominoes and gossiping while sipping rum.

4 Article 64 said that if the criminal is declared "mad" when the crime was committed, there is no "crime."

5 Dupuis.

6 Michel Foucault, *Discipline and Punish: The Birth of the Prison,* trans. Alan Sheridan (New York: Vintage Books, 1979), p. 19. Using Foucault requires some explanation. As Ann Laura Stoler has shown, "In short-circuiting empire," Foucault missed "key sites in the production of the discourse" about European sexuality and discounted "the practices that

racialized bodies." I used Foucault for his insights about the psychiatric order to study *colonial and postcolonial* psychiatry, aware of his dismissal of empire. See Stoler, *Race and the Education of Desire: Foucault's History of Sexuality and the Colonial Order of Things* (Durham, N.C.: Duke University Press, 1995).

7 See, for instance, the articles in *JIR* and *Quotidien de La Réunion* after the December 1992 riots at Saint-Denis. "Nuit de pillage," *JIR,* 3 December 1992; "Premières condamnations," *JIR,* 4 December 1992; "Chaudron Bis," *Quotidien,* 3 December 1992; "Le gachis," *Quotidien,* 4 December 1992.

8 Arlette Farge, "Michel Foucault et les archives de l'exclusion," in *Penser la folie: Essais sur Michel Foucault* (Paris: Galilée, 1992), pp. 63–78, 78.

9 Octave Mannoni, "Administration de la folie, folie de l'administration," in *Un commencement qui n'en finit pas: Transfert, interprétation, théorie* (Paris: Éditions du Seuil, Champ Freudien, 1980), pp. 137–57, 137.

10 Ibid., p. 137.

11 Jean-François Reverzy, "Chronique des transferts insulaires: Esquisse des figures du double dans le monde indoocéanique," *Nouvelle Revue d'Ethnopsychiatrie* II (1988): pp. 107–16.

12 "L'emploi et l'activité radicalement transformés en 50 ans," in "L'emploi depuis la départementalisation," *Économie de La Réunion* 71 (1994): pp. 3–5, 3. Between 1982 and 1990, every year 7,500 persons arrived on the job market but only 3,500 jobs were created.

13 This rate was twice the metropole's rate. "L'emploi et l'activité radicalement transformés en 50 ans," p. 4.

14 Kristin Ross, *Fast Cars, Clean Bodies: Decolonization and the Reordering of French Culture* (Cambridge: MIT Press, 1995).

15 Monique Boyer, *Métisse* (Paris: L'Harmattan, 1992).

16 About the transformation of rural and social life in Réunion, see, for instance, Jean Benoist, *Structure et changement de la société réunionnaise* (Saint-Denis, Réunion: Centre universtitaire de La Réunion, 1974), *Un développement ambigu: Structure et changement de la société réunionnaise* (Saint-Denis, Réunion: Fondation pour la Recherche dans l'Océan In dien, 1983), *Paysans de La Réunion* (Aix en Provence: Fondation pour la Recherche dans l'Océan Indien, 1984); Bernard Cherubini, ed., *Le Monde rural à La Réunion: Mutations foncières, mutations paysagères* (Paris: Université de La Réunion/L'Harmattan, 1996); E. Faugère, "Une plantation de canne à sucre à La Réunion: Logiques familiales et logiques en conflit" (M.A. thesis, Marseille, 1993).

17 Luc Boltanski, cited by Ross, makes a similar point about France: "Modernizing the economic apparatus was not a purely technical exercise. It depended first on the stabilization of the greater social order (essentially, containing the rise of the French Communist Party, especially after the

wave of strikes in 1947–48), on the creation of a corporate 'climate' similar to that of American companies, and thus on a transformation in the *mentalité* of the individual engineer/executive" (p. 170). See Luc Boltanski, "America, America . . . le plan Marshall et l'importation du 'management,'" *Actes de la recherche en sciences sociales* 38 (1981): pp. 19–41.

18 See *Les Cahiers de l'île de La Réunion et de l'Océan Indien*, 1972–1976, 1979. This review, launched by the communists and directed by Réunionnais intellectuals, had a great impact on the island's cultural and political debates in the 1970s.

19 Michel Foucault, *Résumé des cours, 1970–1982* (Paris: Julliard, 1989), p. 59.

20 Colette Guillaumin, *L'Idéologie raciste, Genèse et language actuel* (Paris: Mouton, 1972), p. 183.

21 Frantz Fanon, "De l'impulsivité criminelle du Nord-Africain à la guerre de libération nationale," in *Les damnés de la terre* (Paris: François Maspéro, 1981), pp. 215–28. Trans. Constance Farrington as "Colonial War and Mental Disorders," in *The Wretched of the Earth* (New York: Grove Press, 1963). Fanon wondered why the majority of Algerians' victims of crime were Algerians. Rejecting the diagnosis of French psychiatrists, who had detected a "typical Algerian impulsivity," Fanon blamed colonialism.

22 Adolphe Porot published in 1918 his first essay, "Notes de psychiatrie musulmane." His thesis was that the North African, who was "a liar, a thief, and lazy," could be defined as a "hysterical moron, subject to unexpected criminal impulses." According to Berthelier, the influence of the School of Algiers lasted until the 1950s. See Robert Berthelier, "Tentative d'approche socio-culturelle de la psycho-pathologie nord-africaine," *Psychopathologie Africaine* 5, no. 2 (1969): pp. 171–222; "Psychiatres et psychiatrie devant le musulman algérien," *Psychopathologie Africaine* 16, no. 3 (1980): pp. 343–69; Adolphe Porot, "Notes de psychiatrie musulmane," *Annales Médico-Psychologiques* 1 (1918).

23 The editors of the special issue of *Hommes et Migrations*, "Imaginaire Colonial, Figures de l'immigré," have shown the filiation between the colonial racist representations of the "indigènes" and the actual racist representations of the migrant workers in France (May–June 1997).

24 Michel de Certeau, *L'invention du quotidien, Arts de faire* (Paris: Folio, 1990), p. xxxix.

25 Christian Lesne, *Cinq essais d'ethnopsychiatrie antillaise* (Paris: L'Harmattan, 1990), p. 149.

26 Jacqueline Andoche, "Le double récit sorcier: Mythe et réalité dans l'approche de la maladie mentale à La Réunion," in *L'éternel jamais: Entre le monde et l'exil: Anthropologie*, ed. Jean-François Reverzy and Christian Barrat (Paris: INSERM, L'Harmattan, 1990), pp. 181–84; "À partir d'une ethnographie des troubles mentaux: les représentations de la personne et du corps à l'île de La Réunion," *Nouvelle Revue d'Ethnopsychiatrie* 14 (1989): pp. 111–21; "L'interprétation populaire de la maladie et de la guérison à l'île de La Réunion," *Sciences Sociales et Santé* 6, nos. 3–4 (1988): pp. 145–65; Yolande Govindama, "La fonction symbolique de la déesse Pétiaye dans la mentalité des femmes hindoues de La Réunion," in *Cultures: Exils et Folies dans l'Océan Indien,* ed. Jean-François Reverzy (Paris: INSERM, l'Harmattan, 1990), pp. 157–62; and *Psychopathologie Africaine: Sciences Sociales et Psychiatrie en Afrique* 25, no. 2 (1993).

27 The night was the moment during which slaves could gather and talk, perform their rituals, and play their music away from the gaze and ears of the masters. (We might remember that the novel *Les Marrons* opens with a meeting at night between three slaves.) The night has remained an important element in Creole culture: it is usually at night that the Creole storyteller speaks; the wake lasts a night; the annual ceremony for the dead performed by *Kafs* starts at nightfall; maloya belongs to the night.

28 On the ways in which the bourgeois construction of gender and politics was disturbed by the Commune of Paris, see Kathleen Jones and Françoise Vergès, "Aux Citoyennes!: Women, Politics, and the Paris Commune of 1871," *History of European Ideas* 13, no. 6 (1991): pp. 711–32, and "Women of the Paris Commune," *Women's Studies International Forum* 14, no. 5 (1991): pp. 491–503; Gay L. Gullickson, *Unruly Women of Paris: Images of the Commune* (Ithaca: Cornell University Press, 1997).

29 The expression is Eugen Weber's in *Peasants into Frenchmen: The Modernization of Rural France, 1870–1914* (Stanford, Calif.: Stanford University Press, 1976).

30 Nye, *Crime, Madness, and Politics,* p. 257.

31 Ibid., p. 73.

32 Michel Foucault, *Il faut défendre la société* (Paris: Gallimard/Seuil, 1997).

33 Daniel Pick, *Faces of Degeneration: A European Disorder, c. 1848–c. 1918* (Cambridge: Cambridge University Press, 1989), p. 70.

34 About the notion of "race" in the discourse of discipline, see Michel Foucault, *Il faut défendre la société* (Paris: Gallimard/Seuil, 1997). Foucault argues that "race struggle and class struggles became, at the end of the nineteenth century, the two great schemes upon which war and power in society were articulated." The social body was articulated upon the notion of two "races." To Foucault, since the seventeenth century, the idea existed that there was a "race struggle" (a war between two groups), and this idea informed the study of social war. In this discourse, race did not come from somewhere else but was there, infiltrated in the national body. One race was said to be the true one, instituting a norm and fighting the other "race." Foucault analyzed European society and did not include the empire. See Ann Laura Stoler for a critique of Foucault's indifference to the empire.

35 Bernardin Augustin Morel, *Traité des dégénérescences physiques, intellectuelles et morales de l'espèce humaine* (Paris: J. B. Baillière, 1857), p. 7. His conclusions, which were made from his observations of the poor proletariat and of poor agricultural workers around the city of Rouen, drew him to advocate moral education and reform to slow down the process of degeneration.

36 Pick, p. 71.

37 See Michelle Perrot, ed., *L'Impossible prison: Recherches sur le système pénitentiaire au XIXe. siècle* (Paris: Éditions du Seuil, 1980); Pick, *Faces of Degeneration.*

38 Sander L. Gilman, *Freud, Race, and Gender* (Princeton, N.J.: Princeton University Press, 1993), p. 23.

39 Gustave Le Bon, *Les lois psychologiques de l'évolution des peuples* (Paris: Félix Alcan, 1894). Le Bon's works, written around the time of the Dreyfus affair, were translated into ten languages and sold hundreds of thousand of copies.

40 Tzvetan Todorov, *On Human Diversity, Nationalism, Racism, and Exoticism in French Thought,* trans. Catherine Porter (Cambridge: Harvard University Press, 1993), p. 114.

41 Le Bon, *Les lois psychologiques de l'évolution des peuples,* pp. 6, 13.

42 Léopold de Saussure, *La psychologie de la colonisation française dans ses rapports avec les sociétés indigènes* (Paris: F. Alcan, 1899), pp. 14, 38. De Saussure gave as an example of the negative consequences of assimilation what had happened in the "Creole colonies." The abolition of slavery, he wrote, had discouraged the white colonists and encouraged the insolence of the mulattoes. The notion of equality that they learned at school had led blacks and mulattoes to demand the transformation of their islands into French departments (p. 199).

43 Cited in Gilman, *The Case of Sigmund Freud,* p. 162. Freud wrote these remarks in 1917. See Gilman's examination of Freud's reaction to the theses of degeneration, which dominated science in his time (pp. 157–68).

44 See Antoine Bouillon, *Madagascar, Le colonisé et son âme: Essai sur le discours psychologique colonial* (Paris: Éditions l'Harmattan, 1981), p. 111. Bouillon's study is extremely valuable, and his bibliography on French "colonial psychology" is one of the most complete one can find.

45 Lucien Lévy-Bruhl, *La mentalité primitive* (Paris: PUF, 1960). See Paul Bercherie, *Les fondements de la clinique* (Paris: La Bibliothèque d'Ornicar, 1980), pp. 242–43.

46 Lévy-Bruhl. Although his writing often exhibited an imperial approach to the "primitive," Lévy-Bruhl later rejected the hierarchy made between logical and prelogical thought (a hierarchy based on its writings) and emphasized the importance and complexity of "prelogical" thought.

47 Mamadou M'Bodj, "Aspects de la psychiatrie dans le monde," *Psychopathologie Africaine* 14 (1978). See Emmanuel Régis and Henri Reboul, "L'assistance aux alienes aux colonies," in *Rapport au XXII Congrès des Médecins aliénistes et neurologistes de langue française Tunis 1–7 avril 1912* (Paris: Masson, 1912). Reboul and Régis's propositions were adopted in the French colonies. The colonial government of the *Afrique Occidentale Française* issued a decree in June 1938 that established the first *service d'assistance psychiatrique en AOF.*

48 See Henri Aubin, "Introduction à l'étude de la psychiatrie chez les Noirs," *Annales médico-psychologiques* 1 (1939); L. Lauriol, "Quelques remarques sur les maladies mentales aux colonies" (thesis in medicine, Paris, 1938).

49 Among the review's editors was the sociologist Roger Bastide, as well as the general administrator of the Inscription Maritime, a shipping company. Essays in the review foreshadowed the work that would be done by the proponents of "ethno-psychology" (the review was renamed *Ethno-Psychologie* in 1970). About a similar development in the British empire, see Jock McCullogh, *Colonial Psychiatry and the "African Mind"* (Cambridge: Cambridge University Press, 1995).

50 See, for instance, his *Histoire coloniale et psychologie ethnique* (Paris: Revue de l'Histoire des Colonies Françaises, 1925); *La pénétration saharienne et la psychologie du nomade saharien* (Paris: Revue de l'Histoire des Colonies Françaises, 1929); *Psychologie et Colonization* (Paris: Le Monde Nouveau, 1929); *Sur la psychologie de quelques métiers marocains* (Paris: Outre-Mer, 1929); *De la gaieté chez les Noirs d'Afrique* (Paris: Outre-Mer, 1930); *Psychologie avant-tout* (Paris: Outre-Mer, 1934); *Pour une étude de la mimique* (Alger: Revue Africaine, 1936). In a 1948 article "Psychologie et tutelle," Hardy argued that a reason for colonial discontent was that "civil servants who are far from having the same conquering faith, the same fecund illusions as the colonial conquerors," were now making the decisions in the colonies. There was a solution, though: a training in psychology. The article was published in a special issue of the review *Chemins du Monde*, "Fin de L'Ère Coloniale? Peuples et Évolution," in which Aimé Césaire wrote an essay entitled "L'impossible contact."

51 Georges Hardy, *La géographie psychologique* (Paris: Gallimard, 1939), p. 26.

52 Georges Hardy, "La psychologie des populations coloniales," *Revue de Psychologie des Peuples* 3 (1947): pp. 233–61.

53 Ibid., p. 260.

54 Ibid., pp. 233–34.

55 Adolphe Porot, "Notes de psychiatrie musulmane," *Annales Médico-Psychologiques* 1 (1918): pp. 377–84; "Quelques aspects de l'âme indigène," *Conférence à la Ligue de l'enseignement à Oran*, March 1922.

56 Marius-Ary Leblond, *La Grande Île de Madagascar* (Paris: Ch. Delagrave, 1907), p. 411.

57 The expression is Francis Galton's in *Hereditary Genius: An Inquiry into Its Laws and Consequences,* 2d ed. (1892; Gloucester: Peter Smith, 1972), p. 36.

58 Cited in Jean-Claude Carpanin Marimoutou, "Les âmes errantes dans le texte: Ulysse Cafre," *Grand Océan* 4 (1992): pp. 87–106.

59 See Thomas S. Szasz, "The Negro in Psychiatry: An Historical Note on Psychiatric Rhetoric," and "The Sane Slave: An Historical Note on the Use of Medical Diagnosis as Justificatory Rhetoric," *American Journal of Psychotherapy* 25, no. 2 (1971): pp. 469–71; emphasis mine. See also Alexander Thomas and Samuel Sillen, *Racism and Psychiatry* (New York: Brunner/Mazel, 1972). See McCullogh 1995 for similar observations about Africans.

60 Michel Foucault, *The Birth of the Clinic: An Archaeology of Medical Perception,* trans. A. M. Sheridan Smith (New York: Vintage Books, 1973), pp. 113, 114.

61 These writings were discussed in Octave Mannoni, *Prospero and Caliban: Psychology of Colonization,* trans. Pamela Powesland (Ann Arbor: University of Michigan Press, 1990), p. 34. The book was first published in 1950 by the Éditions du Seuil, Paris, under the title *Psychologie de la colonisation.* The first English translation was published in 1956 in London, then in 1964 in New York. It was in the first English edition that the book acquired the title under which it became known, *Prospero and Caliban.* Mannoni's notion of a "complex of dependency" among the colonized was violently attacked by Aimé Césaire in *Discourse on Colonialism,* Frantz Fanon in *Black Skin, White Masks,* and Albert Memmi in *The Colonizer and the Colonized.* Mannoni answered his critics in "The Decolonization of Myself," *Race,* April 1966. In this essay, Mannoni wondered what it meant to look for a psychological explanation to problems inherited from colonization. For an anthropological critique of Mannoni's work, see Maurice Bloch, new foreword to *Prospero and Caliban.* For a critical analysis of Fanon's critique of Mannoni, see Jock McCullogh, "Fanon and Mannoni," in *Black Soul, White Artifact: Fanon's Clinical Psychology and Social Theory* (Cambridge: Cambridge University Press, 1983), pp. 213–21.

Frantz Fanon, *Peau Noire, Masques Blancs* (Paris: Points Seuil, 1975). The first edition of *Peau Noire* appeared in the collection *Esprit,* published by the Éditions du Seuil in 1952. The English translation was by Charles Lam Markmann, with the title: *Black Skin, White Masks* (New York: Grove Press, 1967). Whenever possible I have used this translation. Markmann's translation stresses aspects that in the French version are less marked. For instance, Markmann translates "ce travail voudrait être un miroir à infra-structure progressive, où pourrait se retrouver le nègre en voie de désaliénation" (p. 148) as "This book, it is hoped, will be a mirror with a progressive infrastructure, in which it will be possible to discern the Negro on the road to disalienation" (p. 184). In Markmann, the *reader* discerns the Negro in the mirror that is the book, whereas in Fanon's text, the book is a mirror *to the Negro.*

Albert Memmi, *The Colonizer and the Colonized* (New York: Orion Press, 1965). Originally *Portrait du colonisé précédé du Portrait du Colonisateur* (Paris: Éditions Buchet-Chastel, 1957).

On postcolonial psychiatry, see also Chabani Manganyi, *Being-Black-in-World* (Johannesburg: Spro-Cas/Ravan, 1973); *Treachery and Innocence: Psychology and Racial Differences* (Johannesburg: Ravan, 1991); Ashis Nandy, *The Intimate Enemy: Loss and Recovery of Self under Colonialism* (Delhi: Oxford University Press, 1983), and *The Savage Freud and Other Essays on Possible and Retrievable Selves* (Princeton: Princeton University Press, 1995); Lionel J. Nicholas and Saths Cooper, eds., *Psychology and Apartheid: Essays on the Struggle for Psychology and the Mind in South Africa* (Johannesburg: Vision/Madiba Publication, 1990); Sudhir Kakar, *The Colors of Violence: Cultural Identities, Religion, and Conflict* (Chicago: University of Chicago Press, 1996); *D'un inconscient post-colonial, s'il existe* (Paris: Association Freudienne Internationale, 1995).

62 Memmi, *The Colonizer and the Colonized,* p. ix; emphasis mine.

63 Fanon, *Black Skin,* p. 84.

64 In France, psychology had constructed workers' violent rebellions as the result of atavistic traits, inborn criminality, and alcoholism.

65 Similar work has been done in the United States. On the whites' projections on Indians, see Michael Rogin, *Fathers and Children: Andrew Jackson and the Subjugation of the American Indian* (New York: Vintage Books, 1975); Richard Slotkin, *Regeneration through Violence: The Mythology of the American Frontier, 1600–1860* (Middletown, Conn.: Wesleyan University Press, 1973); *The Fatal Environment: The Myth of the Frontier in the Age of Industrialization, 1800–1890* (Middletown, Conn.: Wesleyan University Press, 1985). Slotkin is inspired by the writings of E. P. Thompson and Raymond Williams. On the psychological relation between English colonizers and American colonists, see Edgar Burrows and Michael Wallace, "The American Revolution: The Ideology and Psychology of National Liberation," *Perspectives in American History* 6 (1972): pp. 167–306.

66 Fanon, *Black Skin,* p. 84.

67 Octave Mannoni, "Ébauche d'une psychologie coloniale: Le complexe de dépendance et la structure de la personnalité," *Psyché* (12 October 1947): pp. 1229–42, and 13–14 (November–December 1947): pp. 1453–79; "La personnalité malgache, Ébauche d'une analyse des structures," *Revue de Psychologie des Peuples* 3 (July 1948): pp. 263–81.

68 Mannoni, "Ébauche d'une psychologie coloniale," pp. 1235, 1238–39.

69 Octave Mannoni, "Colonisation et Psychanalyse," *Chemins du Monde*, October 1948, pp. 89–96.

70 The study of social relationships coincided with research into his own personal problems, Mannoni wrote. Madagascar had profoundly transformed him, he said in 1954. The "psychological analysis had a quite different point for me at the time I was writing this book. I was more interested in my own psychological make-up than in the psychology of the subjects under observation, who presented a less complex problem." In *Prospero and Caliban*, p. 34.

71 Ibid., p. 6. Parts of Mannoni's study were drawn from his observations of the 1947 uprising in Madagascar, which had been violently repressed by the French army. There were 100,000 dead among the Madagascans. Mannoni, who looked at the uprising with sympathy and consequently lost his job in the colonial administration, nonetheless analyzed the 1947 rebellion as an answer to a fear of abandonment among the Madagascans because the French were offering more autonomy. Here Mannoni showed his total ignorance of the political situation in Madagascar and denied the nationalist aspirations of the Madagascans.

72 Mannoni, p. 97. English edition.

73 Ibid., p. 104.

74 Ibid., p. 102. To Mannoni, the "case" of Defoe is "one of misanthropy, melancholy, a pathological need for solitude, the projection of his faults onto others, a sense of guilt towards his father, repressed affection for a daughter whose sex he preferred to ignore" (p. 103).

75 Ibid., p. 108.

76 Ibid., p. 105.

77 Ibid., p. 108.

78 Ibid., p. 103.

79 Mannoni illustrated this complex with his interpretation of an incident with his tennis coach, a young Merina. The author, who had ordered a small supply of quinine to be sent to the young Madagascan, who had gone down with a fever, observed a radical change in his behavior. Mannoni's action was intended to be purely a "helpful gesture," and yet his tennis coach, failing to "appreciate its objective and impersonal nature," saw it "strictly subjectively," setting up a relationship of dependence. Now the two individuals were engaged, not in a relation between a tennis player and his coach, but in a relation between two "selves." Mannoni claimed that if he had broken off this relation, he would have provoked feelings of abandonment, enmity, and even hatred.

80 Maurice Bloch, new foreword to *Prospero and Caliban*, pp. v–xx.

81 Ibid., p. xiii.

82 According to Bloch, the analysis of the episode with the tennis coach, the basis for Mannoni's complex of dependency, was based on a radical misunderstanding of the significance of gifts and demands in the context of Merina culture. Rather than being the signs of dependence, the demands of the tennis coach were expressions of the "typical way in which Merina friends and relatives, standing in an egalitarian relationship, behave toward each other." Demands, in this context, "defined a close relationship of equality." Bloch argued that Mannoni's conclusions were based on his observations of the Merina, one among the Madagascan ethnic groups, and yet, "Mannoni's 'ancestor worship' was totally un-Merina." See pp. xvii–xx. To reassess Mannoni's work fifty years after the Madagascan rebellion, psychoanalysts and postcolonial critics of the southwest region of the Indian Ocean met in November 1997 at the University of Antananarivo and in February 1998 at the UNESCO (Paris). Madagascan psychologists and critics assailed again Mannoni's notion of dependency and confirmed that he had not understood the cult of the ancestors. However, they also recognized many of Mannoni's insights about the colonized's complexes. See particularly Christiane Rakotolahy's contribution.

83 The Hovas are one of Madagascar's ethnic groups.

84 Emile Caillet, *Essai sur la psychologie du Hova* (Paris: PUF, 1926). "To begin with," Caillet wrote, "the ancestor reigns with absolute power. The primitive's life is ruled by customs. Then suddenly, he is confronted with the foreigner who is all powerful. The primitive rushes toward the world of the foreigner which attracts him" (pp. 180–81). Cited in Antoine Bouillon, p. 196.

85 Octave Mannoni, "The Decolonization of Myself," *Race* 4 (April 1966): pp. 327–35. The essay was simultaneously published with the same title in French and English. The French version also appeared in Mannoni, *Clefs pour l'imaginaire* (Paris: Le Seuil, 1969), and *Psychologie de la colonisation*, pp. 207–215.

86 Ibid., p. 331.

87 Mannoni, *Prospero and Caliban*, p. 165.

88 Ibid., p. 171.

89 On Fanon's life, see Pierre Bouvier, *Fanon* (Paris: Éditions Universitaires, 1971); David Caute, *Frantz Fanon* (Paris: Seghers, 1970); Peter Geismar, *Fanon: The Revolutionary as Prophet* (New York: Grove Press, 1971); Irene Gendzier, *Frantz Fanon: A Critical Study* (London: Pantheon Books, 1973); Albert Memmi, "La vie impossible de Frantz Fanon," *Esprit*, September 1971, pp. 248–73, 250, translated as "The Impossible Life of Frantz Fanon," *Massachusetts Review* 14, no. 1 (winter 1973): pp. 9–39; B. Marie Perinbam, *Holy Violence: The Revolutionary Thought of Frantz Fanon* (Washington, D.C.: Three Continent Press, 1982); and of course Isaac Julien's beautiful movie *Frantz Fanon: Black Skin, White Mask* (1997; Mark Nash producer).

For a feminist critique of Fanon, see Gwen Bergner, "Who Is That Marked Woman? Or, The Role of Gender in Fanon's *Black Skin, White Masks,*" *PMLA* 110, no. 1 (January 1995): pp. 75–88; Diana Fuss, "Interior Colonies: Frantz Fanon and the Politics of Identification," *Diacritics* 24, nos. 2–3 (summer–fall 1994): pp. 20–42; bell hooks, "Feminism as a Persistent Critique of History: What's Love Got to Do with It?" in *The Fact of Blackness: Frantz Fanon and Representation,* ed. Alan Read (London: ICA, 1996), pp. 76–85; B. Marie Perinbam, "Parrot or Phoenix? Frantz Fanon's View of the West Indian and Algerian Woman," *Journal of Ethnic Studies* 1, no. 2 (summer 1973): pp. 45–55; Winifred Woodhull, *Transfigurations of the Maghred: Feminism, Decolonization, and Literatures* (Minneapolis: University of Minnesota Press, 1993); Clarisse Zimra, "A Woman's Place: Cross-Sexual Perceptions in Race Relations: The Case of Mayotte Capecia and Abdoulaye Sadji," *Folio,* August 1978, pp. 174–92; Lola Young, "Missing Persons: Fantasizing Black Women in *Black Skin, White Masks,*" in *The Fact of Blackness,* pp. 102–13. See also Lewis R. Gordon, *Fanon and the Crisis of European Man: An Essay on Philosophy and the Human Sciences* (New York: Routledge, 1995); Kobena Mercer, "Decolonisation and Disappointment: Reading Fanon's Sexual Politics," in *The Fact of Blackness,* pp. 114–65; the essays in *Fanon: A Critical Reader* (London: Blackwell, 1996), and the special issue of *History of Psychiatry* 7 (1996), notably Claude Razanajao, Jacques Postel, and D. F. Allen, "The Life and Psychiatric Work of Frantz Fanon," pp. 499–524. Fanon studied psychiatry at the University of Lyon. In 1953 he was offered, a year before the Algerian war of liberation started, the post of director at the hospital of Blida-Joinville, in Algeria. He was diagnosed as having leukemia in 1960 and died in Washington, D.C., in December 1961. Fanon's formal psychiatric articles were written between 1953 and 1959.

90 Fanon, "The So-Called Dependency Complex of Colonized Peoples," in *Black Skin,* pp. 83–108.

91 Jock McCullogh, *Black Soul, White Artifact,* p. 215; emphasis in the text.

92 On the economic conditions in the colony, Mannoni wrote: "Economic questions are certainly important; they may not absolutely determine the future of the colonial peoples, but that future will undoubtedly depend on them to a very great extent. I ought therefore to explain why they are given so little place in this book. It is because economic explanations are too general in their application to account very accurately for the facts of colonization: economic exploitation occurs wherever political and social conditions favor it, in the colonies as elsewhere. In the colonies, however, its character changes and it becomes colonial exploitation." In *Prospero and Caliban,* p. 202. And later: "There is, moreover, considerable danger in adhering too closely to the economic explanation, for it implies that colonization would have been a good thing if it had been economically honest, if lust for gains had not falsified the accounts, if the colonizers had been economically disinterested" (p. 204). Fanon would have agreed.

93 *L'information psychiatrique* 51, no. 10 (December 1975).

94 Jean-Paul Sartre, *Réflexions sur la question juive* (Paris: Folio, 1954), p. 84. Tori Moi argues in her biography of Beauvoir that the influence of *The Second Sex* on *Black Skin* must be acknowledged. "The parallels between the two texts are striking," Moi writes. She remarks that Fanon must have been aware of de Beauvoir's analysis of women's construction by men. Fanon was a faithful reader of *Les Temps Modernes,* and between 1948 and 1949 the journal published excerpts of de Beauvoir's text. As woman is the Other for man, so the black is the Other for the white. Moi, *Simone de Beauvoir: The Making of an Intellectual Woman* (Cambridge, Mass.: Blackwell, 1994), pp. 204–7. For references to Sartre in *Black Skin,* see pp. 27–29, 41, 87, 93, 115, 118–19, 133, 139.

95 Fanon refers here to the notion of the mirror stage that Lacan developed in the chapter on family written for the eighth volume of the *Encyclopédie Française* (1938). Lacan's contribution was reedited in 1984 under the title *Les Complexes familiaux dans la formation de l'individu* (Paris). For more information on Lacan's contributions to the encyclopedia, see Elisabeth Roudinesco, *Jacques Lacan: Esquisse d'une vie, histoire d'un système de pensée* (Paris: 1993), pp. 193–204, and *Histoire de la psychanalyse française, 2, 1925–1985* (Paris: 1986), pp. 156–58.

96 Lacan writes: "Nous voulons pénétrer sa structure mentale avec le plein sens du mythe de Narcisse; que ce sens indique la mort: l'insuffisance vitale dont ce monde est issu; ou la réflexion spéculaire: l'imago du double qui lui est centrale; ou l'illusion de l'image: ce monde, nous l'allons voir, ne contient pas d'autrui." Vol. 8, sec. 40, p. 10. In this paragraph, Lacan explains why there is not other in the mirror stage: Its narcissistic structure, its specularity in which the central figure is the subject's double, produces a world in which there is no alterity.

97 Ibid.

98 Fanon, *Black Skin,* p. 161.

99 Ibid., pp. 161–62.

100 Ibid., p. 162.

101 François Georges, *Deux études sur Sartre* (Paris: Christian Bourgeois Éditeur, 1976). Cited in Martin Jay, "Sartre, Merleau-Ponty, and the Search for a New Ontology of Sight," in *Modernity and the Hegemony of Vision,* ed. David Michael Levin (Berkeley: University of California Press, 1993), pp. 143–85, 156.

102 Jacques Lacan, "The Mirror Stage as Formative of the Function of the I as Revealed in Psychoanalytic Experience," in *Écrits: A Selection,* trans. Alan Sheridan (New York: W. W. Norton, 1977), pp. 1–7, 6.

103 See my "Creole Skin, White Mask: Fanon and Disavowal," *Critical Inquiry* 23, no. 3 (spring 1997): pp. 578–95.

104 Memmi, "La vie impossible de Frantz Fanon," p. 254.

105 Richard Burton's analysis of the "colonial family" is thus very Fanonian.

106 Testimony of Bertène Juminer in "Hommages à Frantz Fanon," *Présence Africaine* 40 (1962): p. 126.

107 Memmi, *The Colonized*, p. 87.

108 Ibid., p. 8.

109 Ibid., p. 74.

110 Ibid., p. 151.

111 Fanon, *Black Skin*, p. 231.

112 Memmi, *The Colonized*, p. 153; emphasis mine.

113 Memmi, Personal communication, 13 and 17 January 1995.

114 François Laplantine, *L'Ethnopsychiatrie* (Paris: PUF, Que Sais-Je?, 1988), p. 27; "Ethnopsychiatrie et ethnoscience: Les problèmes posés par l'étude des savoirs étiologiques et des savoir-faire thérapeutiques concernant les maladies mentales," *Confrontations psychiatriques* 21 (1982): pp. 11–27.

115 The scholar associated with the growth and development of ethnopsychiatry remains Geza Róheim. See *Psychanalyse et Anthropology* (Paris: Gallimard, 1967); *Origine et fonction de la culture* (Paris: Gallimard, 1972); *Les portes du rêve* (Paris: Payot, 1973); *La panique des dieux* (Paris: Payot, 1974). For contemporary ethnopsychiatry in France, see the works of Tobie Nathan.

116 Laplantine, p. 25. About the difference between Devereux's ethnopsychiatry and Tobie Nathan's, see the introduction by Elizabeth Roudinesco in Georges Devereux, *Psychothérapie d'un Indien des plaines* (Paris: Fayard, 1998).

117 See Henri Azéma, *L'assistance publique à l'île de La Réunion;* Georges Boisvert, "Histoire de l'implantation de l'Assistance Psychiatrique dans l'île de La Réunion" (M.A. thesis in psychiatry, University of Caen, 1985); Dr. Maurice Jay, personal communication, 18 November 1992; *L'assistance psychiatrique à La Réunion: Histoire,* n.d.; "L'état actuel et les besoins futurs de l'assistance psychiatrique dans le département de la Réunion," *L'Information psychiatrique* 6 (June 1963): pp. 335–62; Gérard Mouls, "Histoire de l'asile des aliénés de Saint-Paul" (Ph.D. diss., University of Medicine, Cochin-Port-Royal, 1974); Gabrielle Thetiot, " 'Dangereux pour l'ordre public': Les malades mentaux à La Réunion, 1849–1912" (M.A. thesis, University of Réunion, 1987).

118 Mouls, p. 32.

119 *Journal et Bulletin Officiel de l'Île de La Réunion,* 22 March 1912, no. 24, pp. 114–24.

120 Among the 3,285 patients received at Saint-Paul, 2,500 were métis: 1,500 men and 1,000 women.

121 An 1889 study showed that the consumption of alcohol amounted to 10 liters per year and per inhabitant, or 4.5 liters of nondistilled alcohol. Cited in Jay, *L'assistance psychiatrique,* p. 11.

122 Dr. Le Mappian, "La psychiatrie à l'Île de La Réunion," *L'Information psychiatrique,* January 1955, pp. 38–49.

123 Département de La Réunion, Centre Hospitalier Spécialisé. *Rapport annuel de gestion, bilan social.* I thank Doctor Maurice Jay, who generously gave me access to these documents.

124 Maurice Jay, "L'état actuel et les besoins futur," p. 345.

125 In 1989, 60 percent of the budget of the department went to health services. Thierry Simom, "La santé à La Réunion de 1900 à nos jours: D'une colonie cachectique à un département presque comblé" (M.A. thesis in Medicine, University of Tours, 1990).

126 In 1976 the law about the Allocation Adultes Handicappés (Disabled Adults Allowance), which guarantees financial aid to mental patients whose illness is considered a disability, was applied to Réunion. In 1989, 30,000 people benefited from this aid (not all of them were suffering from mental disorders). The number of patients received at the Saint-Paul hospital has steadily increased: 5,149 in 1989; 6,139 in 1990, and 6,539 in 1991.

127 The French government instituted in the late 1960s a Service Militaire Adapté, in which male students could voluntarily do their year of military service in the technical, medical, or teaching cooperation. The overseas departments were a coveted destination.

128 In 1973 there were 29,000 small farms, with sugarcane as the main product; in 1981, 10,600. In eight years, 18,400 farms had disappeared.

129 Products cultivated by small farmers—geraniums, vetiver, vanilla, sugarcane—lost their value, and farmers went bankrupt.

130 The French government did not propose a plan of agricultural reconversion and diversification, arguing that diversification was impossible. Yet Mauritius Island, which shared numerous similarities with her "sister island," Réunion—a small island far away from large markets, whose economy was dominated by the monoculture of sugarcane, and with a rural and métisse population—successfully reconverted and diversified its agriculture during the same period. On Mauritius's economic recovery and its limits, see Catherine Hein, "Jobs for the Girls: Export Manufacturing in Mauritius," *International Labour Review* 123, no. 2 (1984): pp. 251–65, and *Multinational Enterprises and Employment in the Mauritian Export Processing Zone* (Geneva: International Labour Office, 1988); "L'île Maurice: Le tournant des années 90, Comment maîtriser un miracle économique," *Marchés Économiques et Tropicaux,* December 1989, pp. 3702–27.

131 The critique of the notion of "mental illness" and of a psychiatry that was judged pathogenic started in 1959, in England, California, and Italy. As Roudinesco has remarked, the majority of the critics had been involved in radical political movements. David Cooper had fought apartheid in South Africa; Franco Basaglia was a member of the Italian Communist Party; Ronald D. Laing had practiced in India. Élizabeth Roudinesco, "Lectures de *l'Histoire de la folie* (1961–1986)," in *Penser la folie*, pp. 11–35. For the history of psychiatry in France, see Klaus Doerner, *Madmen and the Bourgeoisie: A Social History of Insanity and Psychiatry* (Oxford: Blackwell, 1981); Jacques Postel, *Genèse de la psychiatrie* (Paris: Le Sycomore, 1981); Gladys Swain, *Le sujet de la folie: Naissance de la psychiatrie* (Toulouse: Privat, 1977). For the antipsychiatry movement, see the writings of Franco Basaglia, David Cooper, and R. D. Laing.

132 Fanon, *The Wretched of the Earth*, p. 303; emphasis in the text.

133 Personal interview with Dr. Jean-François Reverzy, 21 April 1993. The island is now divided into five sectors, each controlled by a psychiatric team. In 1993 a new plan was presented in which the expansion of psychiatric services was announced. The goal was to "entirely cover" the island, so that no villages remain untouched by psychiatric services. "Le CHU s'humanise," *Le Réunionnais*, 25 January 1993, p. 12.

134 Gladys Swain, against Foucault, has shown the importance of the reformist thought in the history of psychiatry. See *Le Sujet de la folie* and *Dialogue avec l'insensé* (Paris: Gallimard, 1994).

135 Declaration of Michel Brun, director of Saint-Paul, in "Le CHS s'humanise," *Le Réunionnais*, 25 January 1993, p. 12.

136 See Michel Foucault, *Histoire de la folie à l'âge classique* (Paris: Gallimard, 1991); Swain, *Le sujet de la folie*.

137 See Foucault, *Discipline and Punish: The Birth of the Prison;* Robert A. Nye, *Crime, Madness, and Politics in Modern France: The Medical Concept of National Decline* (Princeton, N.J.: Princeton University Press, 1984).

138 Gilles Deleuze, *Pourparlers* (Paris: Éditions de Minuit, 1990), pp. 236–37.

139 Département de La Réunion, Centre Hospitalier Spécialisé, *Rapport annuel de gestion, bilan social,* 1966.

140 For a comparison with the situation of migrant workers meeting with French doctors, see Frantz Fanon, "The North African Syndrome," in *Toward the African Revolution* (New York: Grove Press, 1967), pp. 3–16. First published in *Esprit,* February 1952, under the title "Le syndrome nord-africain." In this essay, Fanon questioned the preexisting framework of the French medical personnel vis-à-vis the North African workers.

141 See "Quelle psychiatrie à La Réunion?" 1981.

142 In France, there are three types of hospitalization: *libre,* through the demand of another party, and *placement d'office.* The mayor and the

prefect must give their authorization in the two last cases. In 1991, at Saint-Paul, 94 percent of the patients were *libres*.

143 In Gérard Mouls, *Études sur la sorcellerie à La Réunion* (Saint-Denis, Réunion: Éditions UDIR, 1982). In the metropole, according to the historian Susanna Barrows, the majority of patients were usually women. See Susanna Barrows, *Distorting Mirrors: Visions of the Crowd in Late Nineteenth-Century France* (New Haven: Yale University Press, 1988).

144 See Albert Memmi, *La statue de sel* (1972; Paris: Folio, 1993).

145 Ashis Nandy, *The Intimate Enemy: Loss and Recovery of Self under Colonialism* (New Delhi: Oxford University Press, 1983).

146 On masculinity and war, see Sandra Gilbert, "Soldier's Heart: Literary Men, Literary Women, and the Great War," in *Behind the Lines: Gender and the Two World Wars;* Susan Jeffords, *The Remasculinization of America: Gender and the Vietnam War* (Bloomington: Indiana University Press, 1989); Michael Rogin, "Kiss Me Deadly: Communism, Motherhood, and Cold War Movies," in *"Ronald Reagan," the Movie: and Other Episodes in Political Demonology* (Berkeley: University of California Press, 1987), pp. 236–71; Klaus Theweleit, *Male Fantasies: Women, Floods, Bodies, History,* trans. Stephen Conway (Minneapolis: University of Minnesota Press, 1987).

147 Bernard Biros, "Essai sur l'identité créole" (Ph.D. diss., Paris, Faculté de Médecine, Necker, 1979).

148 Ibid., p. 97.

149 Personal interview, 14 December 1992.

150 INSEE, *Tableau Économique de La Réunion, 1993–1994,* p. 66. In France, the difference in death rate between women and men is eight years; in Mauritius, six years.

151 For men age thirty-five and older, mental illnesses and alcoholism kill ten times more in Réunion than in France. INSEE, p. 66.

152 Monique Boyer, *Métisse* (Paris: L'Harmattan, 1992). See also Rose-May Nicole, *Laetitia* (Peuples Noirs, peuples africains, n.d.) In both novels, racism destroys the father.

153 Boyer, *Métisse,* p. 133.

154 Ibid., p. 128. The insult could be translated as "Nigger!" The term *Cafre*—in Creole *Kaf,* and for the feminine, *Kafrine*—comes from the Arab word *Kafir* (nonbeliever). It was applied to the blacks of sub-Saharan Africa, transformed into "Cafres" by the French, and adopted in the Creole language of Réunion to designate people of dark skin, usually the descendants of Madagascan or African slaves. The term can be derogatory and an insult. Yet it is also a term to express affection and love, as in *Mon Kaf, Mon Kafrine.* In recent years, it has also been reclaimed as a term of political resistance and cultural identity.

155 Ibid., p. 130.

156 The prefect, Daniel Constantin, asserted that the demonstrations and following violence that had caused twelve deaths and billions in property damages were "perfectly orchestrated" by a political organization that wanted to destabilize the island. Ibrahim Issa, "Un mouvement parfaitement orchestré," *Quotidien de La Réunion,* 25 February 1991; Y. M., "Ce sont des casses organisés," *JIR,* 2 February 1991.

157 Yves Mont-Rouge, "Galets gratuits pour vignette trop chère," *JIR,* 3 December 1992, p. 7.

158 "Premières condemnations, *JIR,* 4 December 1992.

159 Michael Omi and Howard Winant, "The Los Angeles 'Race Riot' and Contemporary U.S. Politics," in *Reading Rodney King, Reading Urban Uprising,* ed. Robert Gooding-Williams (New York: Routledge, 1993), pp. 97–114.

160 R. P. Caulier, *Fragments sur l'île Bourbon.* Cited in Mouls, p. 7.

161 See Dr. Maurice Jay, "L'alcoolisme à La Réunion," *Annales médico-psychologiques* 2, no. 1 (1965): pp. 29–52.

162 Dr. Maurice Jay was particularly interested in the causes and effects of alcoholism in Réunion; ibid. In 1960 men institutionalized for alcoholism were 36 percent of the total of entries; women, 7 percent. A year later, men entering for alcohol-related symptoms were 42 percent of the total of patients admitted.

163 One of the first theses of psychiatry that took Réunion's population as its subject of research devoted an entire chapter to alcoholism. See Paulette Collin, "La psychiatrie à l'île de La Réunion en 1960" (M.A. thesis, University of Lille, 1963). Jay said that for a long time, researchers did not know if the specific alcohol-related symptoms were caused by culture, ethnicity, diet, or rum. Research conducted in the French Antilles and Réunion concluded that rum led to specific kinds of auditory and visual hallucinations.

164 Vincent Bassot, "Aspects particuliers de l'alcoolisme à La Réunion," 1977. Cited in Dr. Amode Ismael-Daoudjee, "Quelques aspects du vécu culturel et sociologique de l'alcoolisme à La Réunion," *Alcoolisation et Suralcoolisation à La Réunion* (Région Réunion: Comité de la Culture, de l'Éducation, et de l'Environnement, 10–11 July 1987).

165 Ismael-Daoudjee, p. 147.

166 Jules Bergeron, "Rapport sur la répression de l'alcoolisme," *Annales d'hygiène publique et de médecine légale* 38 (1872): p. 6. Cited in Nye, *Crime, Madness, and Politics in Modern France,* p. 155.

167 Ibid., pp. 154–58. The medicalization of alcoholism, Nye has shown, developed gradually, and doctors "appeared on the rolls of anti-alcoholic organizations in disproportionately large numbers from the very start of the movement."

168 See Jean Benoist, *Les carnets d'un guérisseur réunionnais,* Documents et Recherches 7 (Saint-Denis, Réunion: Fondation pour la Recherche et le Développement dans l'Océan Indien, 1980); Jean-François Sam-Long, *Sorcellerie à La Réunion* (Saint-Denis, Réunion: Anchaing, 1979).

169 Le Mappian, pp. 42–43.

170 Ibid., p. 40.

171 J. Y. Roumeguere, *La migration des ressortissants des départements d'outre-mer: Aspect médicaux et psycho-sociologiques* (Nice: IDERIC, 1972).

172 Jean-Philippe Cravero, "Contribution à l'étude de la sorcellerie réunionnaise" (CES de Psychiatrie, Faculté Kremlin Bicêtre, 1979).

173 Similar remarks were made about Africans. Henri Collomb and his students at the Centre Hospitallier de Fann at Dakar, Senegal, studied the absence of self-accusation and neurotic guilt, as well as the rarity of depressive states among Senegalese, and concluded that they were the consequences of efficient mechanisms of projection and the protective role of the family. The point, therefore, was not to see this absence as a lack but to see it as another way of dealing with mental illness. See Danielle Storper-Perez for an assessment of the work at the Fann Hospital in *La folie colonisée* (Paris: François Maspéro, 1974); Marie-Cécile and Edmond Ortigues, *Oedipe Africain* (Paris: L'Harmattan, 1984).

174 J. P. Cravero and Th. Dionot, "Modalités expressives des dépressions à l'Île de La Réunion," *Psychopathologie Africaine* 17, nos. 1–3 (1981): pp. 64–72, 66.

175 Patrick Bensoussan, "Le mouvoir des mots: Essai d'approche transculturelle du passage à l'acte en pays créole," *Psychopathologie Africaine* 11, no. 1 (1986–1987): pp. 5–18, 7.

176 Ibid., p. 9.

177 Jean Laplanche and Jean-Baptiste Pontalis, *The Language of Psychoanalysis,* trans. Donald Nicholson-Smith (New York: W. W. Norton, 1973), pp. 4–6.

178 Otto Fenichel, *The Psychoanalytical Theory of Neurosis* (New York: W. W. Norton, 1972), p. 507.

179 The symbols referred to are signifiers, elements that acquire meaning only in their mutual relations. The *Real* is what is refractory, resistant to the other orders.

180 "Dialectique de l'intersubjectivité dans le cas de l'insularité réunionnaise," paper presented at the International Colloquium "Insularités: Thèmes et Représentations," at the University of Réunion, April 1991.

181 J. M. Delassus and E. Verrière, "La santé mentale à La Réunion," *Bulletin d'information Cenaddom,* no. 69 (1983): pp. 20–30.

182 Denizot said at Yves Olivier's trial that the defendant spoke in metaphors but had no vocabulary to speak of his feelings. This quite surprising comment (do we not talk in metaphors?) is largely shared in Réunion. Fanon shared this view about Creole and thought that the poetic merit of

Creole and its ability to express complex ideas was dubious. See "The Negro and Language," in *Black Skin,* pp. 17–40. To Fanon, the problem of the Antillean Negro was his desire to adopt French as a superior language. Fanon's attitude toward Creole was ambivalent. On the one hand, Fanon questioned the attitude of Antilleans who "cling together in their dialect [*patois*]," and on the other hand, he thought that "to speak a language is to take on a word, a culture."

183 Ginette Ramassamy, "Syntaxe du Créole Réunionnais: Analyse de corpus d'unilingues créolophones" (Ph.D. diss., University of Paris-Sorbonne, 1985), pp. 251–54.

184 See also Roger Annibal, Jean-Paul Bomel, and Marysette Virassamy, "Reflexions sur les repérages d'isolement en pedo-psychiatrie," Intervention 7 July 1984, at the Conference on Psychiatry in Réunion.

185 Jean-Claude Carpanin Marimoutou, "Écrire Métis," in Cahiers CRLH-CIRAOI, *Métissages,* vol. 1 (Paris: L'Harmattan, 1991), pp. 247–60, 252.

186 Lacan, p. 86.

187 Declaration of attorney general Marcel Rostagno in *Les affaires de la Cour d'Assises à La Réunion en 1984. Audience solennelle de rentrée,* 8 March 1985.

188 Colloque International: Alcoolisation et Suralcoolisation à La Réunion, 10–11 Juillet 1987 (Région Réunion: Comité de la Culture, de l'Éducation, et de l'Environnement). Réunion's consumption is 19.9 liters of alcohol per adult per year. The consumption of alcohol has increased since the 1960s, thanks to more regular income.

189 In Réunion, suicide touches young men in greater numbers than in France. The median age of the suicide is thirty-nine in Réunion, fifty-three in France. See Gilbert Duval, "Suicides, tentatives de suicide, violences à la Réunion: Abord clinique, épidémiologique, sociologique, culturel," *L'Espoir Transculturel: Des communautés d'origine aux nouvelles solidarités,* 1988; Jean-François Reverzy, "L'Envers du volcan: Études d'anthropologie psychanalytique des positions et des registres du symptome-suicide à l'île de La Réunion," *L'Espoir Transculturel: Des communautés d'origine aux nouvelles solidarités,* 1988; Jean-François Reverzy et al., "Suicide et insularité: la réalité réunionnaise," *Psychologie médicale* 19, no. 5 (1987): pp. 623–28, and *Suicide et tentatives de suicide à La Réunion* (Saint-Denis, Réunion: CORI, INSERM, 1989).

190 Bernard Tabone, "Violence sociale, violence dans la clinique," n.d., p. 4.

191 See Jacqueline Andoche; Christian Barrat, *Nargoulan: Culture et rites malbars à la Réunion* (Saint-Denis, Réunion: Éditions du Tramail, 1989); Prosper Eve, *La religion populaire à La Réunion* (Université de La Réunion: Institut de Linguistique et d'Anthropologie, 1985); Jean-François

Reverzy, ed., *Cultures, Exils et Folies dans l'Océan Indien* (Paris: INSERM, L'Harmattan, 1990).

192 *Malabars* is the name given to the descendants of Hindu indentured workers. See also the description in Jean-Philippe Cravero, "Contribution à l'étude de la sorcellerie réunionnaise" (CES of psychiatry, University Kremlin-Bîcetre, 1979). Cravero, though he warns that (1) his data are simply the average of those proposed by the works cited in his bibliography, (2) that there is no precise census of ethnic groups, (3) that métissage is important, and (4) that ideology often dictates the interpretation of data, nonetheless proposes his own tableau of Réunion's population with the usual stereotypes: Chinese are hardworking, Kaf are poor, and so forth.

193 *Cafres* is the name given to the descendants of African or Malagasy slaves.

194 J. P. Cambefort, "Dialectique de l'intersubjectivité dans le cas de l'insularité réunionnaise," in *L'Insularité: Thématique et Représentations,* ed. Jean-Claude Marimoutou and Jean-Michel Racault (Saint-Denis: Université de La Réunion, 1995), pp. 345–52.

195 In "La Nef des Fous," *Télé 7 Jours,* 30 September–6 October 1989, pp. 15–20.

196 Biros, "Essai sur l'identité creole."

197 See Evelyne Thiebaut and Frank Waserhole, "La Violence à l'île de La Réunion: Criminalité et interculture créole" (CES of psychiatry, University of Grenoble, 1982).

198 Biros, p. 7.

199 Ibid., pp. 65–70.

200 Ibid., p. 47.

201 Cited in Annibal, Bomel, and Virassamy, "Reflexion sur les repérages d'isolement en pédo-psychiatrie."

202 See Jean Borreil, "Des politiques nostalgiques," in *La Raison nomade* (Paris: Payot, 1993), pp. 142–65.

203 Biros, pp. 76–77.

204 Ibid., p. 80.

205 "Abandonic" is the term used in Laplanche and Pontalis, *Vocabulary of Psychoanalysis,* to translate *abandonnique*. Abandonic is chosen to make a distinction with "abandoned" because the "abandonic" subject "may not necessarily have been the victim of abandonment during his childhood" (p. 270).

206 Germaine Guex, *Le syndrome d'abandon* (Paris: PUF, 1973).

207 Ibid., p. 51; translation mine.

208 Biros, p. 92.

209 Guex writes: "The symptoms of abandonment anxiety are essentially linked to a familial cause: errors, incomprehension and lack of love from the parents" (p. 111).

210 Biros, pp. 99–100. Biros harks back to Mannoni's infamous remarks on the "fear of abandonment" among the colonized.

211 In "Comité Académique des programmes, Commission Transversale Conditions Psycho-Sociales et Contenus d'Enseignement," 1993.

212 There is something surprising when experts use pigs and chickens to represent families! See Sylvie Andreau, "Les hommes rejetés du foyer," *Quotidien,* 4 June 1993, p. 12; emphasis mine. The total number of families in 1990 was 141,173. The total number of households was 157,853, and women were the head of 34,946 households. Among the households headed by a single woman, 16,165 were working women, and 12,347 were women without a job (Data INSEE, 93/94, p. 81).

213 Wahneema Lubiano, "Black Ladies, Welfare Queens, and State Minstrels: Ideological War by Narrative Means," in *Race-ing, Justice, Engendering Power: Essays on Anita Hill, Clarence Thomas, and the Construction of Social Reality,* ed. Toni Morrison (New York: Pantheon Books, 1992), pp. 323–64.

214 See Lee Rainwater and William L. Yancey, eds., *The Moynihan Report and the Politics of Controversy* (Cambridge, Mass.: MIT Press, 1967).

215 Ibid., p. 29.

216 Lubiano, p. 335.

217 Ibid., p. 338.

218 See J. Blake, *Family Structure in Jamaica: The Social Context of Reproduction* (Glencoe: Free Press, 1961); Richard D. E. Burton, *La famille coloniale: La Martinique et la Mère-Patrie, 1789–1992* (Paris: L'Harmattan, 1994); E. Clarke, *My Mother Who Fathered Me* (London: G. Allen and Unwin, 1966); Fritz Gracchus, *Les lieux de la mère dans les sociétés afro-américaines* (Paris: Éditions Caribéennes, 1987); Livia Lesel, *Le Père oblitéré: Chronique antillaise d'une illusion* (Paris: L'Harmattan, 1995); R. R. Randolph, "The 'Matrifocal Family' as a Comparative Category," *American Anthropologist* 66, no. 3 (1964): pp. 628–31; N. L. Solien Gonzalez, "Toward a Definition of Matrifocality," in *Afro-American Anthropology: Contemporary Perspectives* (New York: Free Press, 1970); Elaine Wolf, *Quartiers de vie: Approche ethnologique des populations défavorisées de l'île de La Réunion* (Saint-Denis, Réunion: CIIRF, ARCA, 1989). About matrifocality in Creole societies, see Francis Affergan, *La Pluralité des mondes: Vers une autre anthropologie* (Paris: Albin Michel, 1997); Jacques André, *L'Inceste focal dans la famille noire antillaise* (Paris: PUF, 1987). For a feminist critique of the narrative of matrifocality in the French Antilles, see Arlette Gauthier, ed., "Antillaises," *Nouvelles Questions Féministes,* 1985.

219 Barbara Bush, *Slave Women in Caribbean Society, 1650–1838* (Bloomington: Indiana University Press, 1990); Arlette Gauthier, *Les soeurs de Solitude: La condition féminine dans l'esclavage aux Antilles du XVII au XIX* *siècle* (Paris: Éditions Caribéennes, 1985); Clélie Gamaleya, *Filles d'Héva* (Saint-Denis, Réunion: UFR, 1984); Marietta Morrissey, *Slave Women in the New World: Gender Stratification in the Caribbean* (Lawrence: University Press of Kansas, 1989).

220 Nicole Hamann, inspector of police, "Commission traitant des violences intra-familiales," c. 1990.

221 Foucault, *Résumé des cours,* p. 78.

222 Georges Xiberras, "La mère et l'enfant," in *L'enfant réunionnais et son milieu* (Saint-Denis, Réunion: CDDP-CREAI, 1979).

223 More studies must be done to define the paternal function in Réunion in its complexity and historicity. Réunionnais children have an image of the "father." According to the child psychologist Olivier Douville, who designed a series of questions for children between ages six and twelve, the representation of the father is not as censored as psychiatric reports claim.

224 "Les plus belles filles de France," *Memorial de La Réunion* 7 (1964–1979): pp. 250–54.

225 Crenshaw, p. 411. About violence against African American women, see also Angela Davis, *Women, Race, and Class* (New York: Random House, 1982).

226 See the study by the Union des Femmes de La Réunion.

227 On September 13, 1986, a young woman (she was eighteen) was kidnapped by four paratroopers as she was leaving a dancing hall near Saint-Pierre. They took her to a sugarcane field, raped her, tortured her, and, after tying her to their car, dragged her on the road. She survived and was accused of being a "loose woman." The Union of Réunion Women defended her. See "Un crime raciste," *Témoignages,* 27 September 1986, pp. 2–3; "A propos du viol," *Témoignages,* 24 October 1986, p. 6; Stéphane Barbier, "Le calvaire de Marie-Claire Angama," *Libération,* 27–28 September 1986.

228 On the construction of the black man as rapist in the United States, see Angela Davis, "Rape, Racism, and the Myth of the Black Rapist," in *Women, Race, and Class.*

229 Hamann, p. 5.

230 André.

231 Ibid., p. 69.

232 Ibid., p. 70.

233 Hamann, p. 28. Mouls draws this connection between ethnicity and crime in *Études sur la sorcellerie à La Réunion.*

234 Burton, p. 234.

235 See Françoise Couchard, *Emprise et violence maternelle* (Paris: Dunod, 1991), and "On bat une fille," *Revue Française de Psychanalyse* 3 (1993): pp. 773–50; Béatrice Marbeau-Cleirens, *Les mères imaginées: Hor-*

reur et vénération (Paris: Les Belles Lettres, 1988); Gabrielle Rubin, *Les sources inconscientes de la misogynie* (Paris: Robert Laffont, 1977).

236 Lesne, p. 143.

237 Ibid., p. 144. Similar criticisms have been made about the Moynihan Report.

238 See Michel Foucault, ed., *Moi, Pierre Rivière, ayant égorgé ma mère, ma soeur, et mon frère . . . Un cas de parricide au XIXe. siècle* (Paris: Julliard, Collection Archives, 1984).

239 Jeanne Favret and Jean-Pierre Peter, "L'animal, le fou, la mort," in Foucault, *Moi, Pierre Rivière,* pp. 243–64, 254.

240 Ibid., p. 254. See also Frantz Fanon, "Colonial War and Mental Disorders"; Jacques Lacan, "Motifs du crime paranoïaque: Le crime des soeurs Papin," *Le Minotaure* 3–4 (1933): pp. 25–28. In this essay, Lacan analyzes the crime of two sisters who in 1933 savagely killed the woman they worked for and her daughter. The sisters had killed, according to Lacan, to destroy the ideal of the master, which they had internalized. They were model servants who had internalized the ideal of servitude.

Epilogue: A Small Island

1 Joan W. Scott, "Gender: A Useful Category of Historical Analysis," in *Coming to Terms,* pp. 81–100, 100.

2 Black is here understood according to the Réunionnais critic Rose-May Nicole's understanding of Réunionnais identity, that is, "nonwhite."

3 Boris Gamaleya, *Vali pour une Reine Morte* (Saint-Denis, Réunion: REI, 1973), pp. 26–27. Cimendef is crying African and Madagascan names, and Mussard, French ones.

4 To the critic James Arnold, the paradigm of the maroon constructed a supermale, an idealized figure, a redemptive figure against the emasculated, feminized male figure constructed by the colonial romance. James Arnold, "The Gendering of Créolité," paper presented at the Francophone Caribbean Colloquium: Expanding the Definition of Créolité, University of Maryland, 22–23 October 1993, in *Repenser La Créolité,* ed. Madeleine Cottenet-Hage and Maryse Condé (Paris: Éditions Karthala 1995), pp. 21–40.

5 Gerbeau, "Fabulée, Fabuleuse, la traite des Noirs à Bourbon au XIXe siècle," p. 479. Gerbeau writes: " 'To eat me, Sir' [*Para comer, Senor*] was the answer in 1856 of a Black from Mozambique to the question of a European about the goal of his trip." This opinion, which survived, Gerbeau says, the emancipation of the slaves, was widespread among the slaves of the Indian Ocean's islands. In Madagascar, in the Comoros Islands, people believed that whites were anthropophagous.

6 See Michel Beniamino, *L'Imaginaire Réunionnais* (Saint-Denis, Réunion: Éditions du Tramail, 1992); Jean-Claude Carpanin Marimoutou, "Créolisation, Créolité, Littérature," in *Cuisines, Identités,* ed. Daniel Baggioni and Jean-Claude Carpanin Marimoutou (Saint-Denis, Réunion: Publications de l'Université de La Réunion, 1988), pp. 99–101; "Quartier 3 Lettres/Kartyé Trwa Let: La réécriture du sujet," in *Culture(s) Empirique(s) et Identité(s) Culturelle(s) à La Réunion,* by Daniel Baggioni and Martine Mathieu (Saint-Denis, Réunion: Publications de l'Université de La Réunion, 1985), pp. 101–5; Jean-Claude Carpanin Marimoutou, "L'île-Écriture: Écriture du désir, écriture de l'île, mauvaise conscience et quête de l'identité dans la poésie réunionnaise de langue française" (Ph.D. diss., University of Montpellier, 1980); Martine Mathieu, "Le Discours créole dans le roman réunionnais d'expression française" (Ph.D. diss., University of Provence, 1984). Literary criticism in Réunion often presents symptoms similar to that of the psychiatric discourse: a profound conviction that people of the island are not "open" to the world, are "too attached" to their island, and that therefore their literature lacks the "quality" shown by other literatures born in similar conditions, such as that of the French West Indies.

Bibliography

❧

Archives and Documents

Annales de l'Assemblée Nationale Constituante. 1945
Annales de l'Assemblée Nationale Constituante. Archives de l'Assemblée Nationale. 1945
Annales de l'Assemblée Nationale Constituante. No. 210. March 1946
Annales de l'Assemblée Nationale. No. 277. 7 October–13 November 1952
Annales de l'Assemblée Nationale. No. 283. 12 May–2 July 1953
Archives Départementales de La Réunion (ADR)
Archives de l'Hôpital Psychiatrique de La Réunion
Archives du Parti Communiste Réunionnais (PCR)
Centre des Archives d'Outre-Mer (CAOM)
Jacques Vergès Personal Archives
Paul and Laurence Vergès Personal Archives

Réunion Newspapers and Journals (1963–1994)

Les Cahiers de l'île de La Réunion
Le Combat National
Croix-Sud

La Démocratie
Économie de la Réunion
Femmes en Chiffre, Réunion
La Feuille Hebdomadaire de l'Île Bourbon (Hebdo-Bourbon)
Le Journal de l'Île de La Réunion (JIR)
Liberté
La Nation
Le Progrès
Le Quotidien de l'Île de La Réunion (Quotidien)
Le Réunionnais
Témoignages
Témoignages Chrétien de La Réunion
La Voix des Mascareignes
"Statistiques et indicateurs économiques," *Région Réunion*, 1974.
Tableau Économique de La Réunion. Éditions 1989, 1991, 1992, 1993–1994.
 Saint-Denis, Réunion: INSEE.

Books and Articles

Abraham, Nicolas, and Maria Torok. *L'Écorce et le noyau*. Paris: Flammarion, 1987.

Affergan, Francis. *La Pluralité des mondes. Vers une autre anthropologie*. Paris: Albin Michel, 1997.

Ageron, Charles-Robert. "L'idée d'Eurafrique et le débat colonial franco-allemand de l'entre-deux guerres." *Revue d'Histoire Moderne et Contemporaine* (1975): 22.

Agulhon, Maurice. *Les quarante-huitards*. Paris: Julliard Archives, 1975.

——. *Marianne au combat: L'Imagerie et la symbolique républicaine de 1789 à 1880*. Paris: Flammarion, 1979.

——. *Marianne au Pouvoir: L'Imagerie et la symbolique républicaine de 1880 à 1914*. Paris: Flammarion, 1989.

Albistur, Maïté, and Daniel Armogathe. *Histoire du féminisme français*. Vol. 2. Paris: des femmes, 1978.

Alibar, France, and Pierrette Lembeye-Boy. *Le couteau seul: Sé Kouto sèl . . . La condition féminine aux Antilles*. Paris: Éditions Caribéennes, 1983.

Amrane-Minne, Danièle Djamila. *Des femmes dans la guerre d'Algérie*. Paris: Karthala, 1994.

Amselle, Jean-Loup. *Logiques métisses: Anthropologie de l'identité en Afrique et ailleurs*. Paris: Payot, 1990.

Anderson, Benedict. *Imagined Communities: Reflections on the Origin and Spread of Nationalism*. London: Verso, 1991.

Andoche, Jacqueline. "L'interprétation populaire de la maladie et de la guérison à l'île de La Réunion." *Sciences Sociales et Santé* 6, nos. 3–4 (1988): pp. 145–65.

——. "À partir d'une ethnographie des troubles mentaux: les représentations de la personne et du corps à l'île de La Réunion." *Nouvelle Revue d'Ethnopsychiatrie* 14 (1989): pp. 111–21.

——. "Le double récit sorcier: Mythe et réalité dans l'approche de la maladie mentale à La Réunion." In *L'éternel jamais: Entre le monde et l'exil: Anthropologie,* ed. Jean-François Reverzy and Christian Barrat, pp. 181–84. Paris: INSERM, L'Harmattan, 1990.

André, Jacques. *L'Inceste focal dans la famille noire antillaise.* Paris: PUF, 1987.

——. *La révolution fratricide: Essai de psychanalyse du lien social.* Paris: PUF, 1993.

Andreau, Sylvie. "Les hommes rejetés du foyer." *Quotidien de La Réunion,* 4 June 1993, p. 12.

Annibal, Roger, Jean-Paul Bomel, and Marysette Virassamy. "Reflexions sur les repérages d'isolement en pédo-psychiatrie." Intervention, 7 July 1984, at the Conference on Psychiatry in Réunion.

"Appel de l'Union Intercoloniale aux populations des colonies." *Le Paria* 5 (August 1922): p. 1.

Appiah, Kwame Anthony. *In My Father's House: Africa in the Philosophy of Culture.* New York: Oxford University Press, 1992.

Appiah, Kwame Anthony, and Henry Louis Gates Jr., eds. "Identities." *Critical Inquiry* 18 (1992): pp. 625–29.

"À propos du commerce extérieur de La Réunion. Comment l'impérialisme français pille notre pays. Réponse à quelques objections." In *Arguments.* Saint-Denis, Réunion: REI, 1970.

"A propos du viol." *Témoignages.* 24 October 1986, p. 6.

Arendt, Hannah. "Truth and Politics." In *Between Past and Future,* pp. 227–64. New York: Penguin Books, 1977.

Arnaud, Georges, and Jacques Vergès. *Pour Djamila Bouhired.* Paris: Éditions de Minuit, 1957.

Astier-Loufti, Martine. *Littérature et colonialisme.* Paris: Mouton, 1971.

Attorney General Marcel Rostagno in *Les affaires de la Cour d'Assises à La Réunion en 1984. Audience solennelle de rentrée.* 8 March 1985.

Aubin, Henri. "Introduction à l'étude de la psychiatrie chez les Noirs." *Annales médico-psychologiques* 1, no. 1 (1939): pp. 1, 213.

Aulagnier, Piera. *Les destins du plaisir: Aliénation, amour, passion.* Paris: PUF, 1979.

Azéma, Henri. *L'assistance publique à l'île de La Réunion. Bulletin de l'Académie de l'Ile de La Réunion,* 5 (1923): pp. 3, 22.

Babut, Ernest. "Le Métis franco-annamite." *Revue Indochinoise,* July 1907, pp. 897–908.

Bailly, Jean-Christophe. "L'isthme." In Jean-Luc Nancy and Jean-Christophe Bailly, *La comparution (politique à venir).* Paris: Christian Bourgeois Éditeur, 1991.

Balducchi, Jean-Claude. "Le personnel politique à l'Ile de La Réunion: 1848–1860." M.A. thesis, University of Aix en Provence, 1973.

——. "La vie politique et sociale à La Réunion, 1932–1939." 2 vols. Ph.D. diss., University of Aix en Provence, July 1984.

Baldwin, James. *Notes of a Native Son.* Boston: Beacon Press, 1957.

Balibar, Etienne. "Ambiguous Universality." *Differences* 7 (spring 1995).

——. "Algérie, France: Une ou deux nations?" *Lignes* 30 (February 1997): pp. 7–22.

Balzac, Honoré de. *La Peau de chagrin.* 1831. Reprint, Paris: Union Générale d'Éditions, 1962.

Barat, Christian. *Nargoulan, Culture et rites malbars à La Réunion.* Saint-Denis, Réunion: Editions du Tramail, 1989.

Barat, Christian, Robert Gauvin, and Jacques Nemo. "Société et culture réunionnaises." *Les Dossiers de l'Outre-Mer: Réunion, Guyane. Sociétés pluriculturelles* 85 (1986): pp. 50–79.

Barbaroux, Ogé. *De l'application de l'amnistie du 8 Mai 1837 aux condamnés de l'île Bourbon et du mémoire de M. Houat, l'un des amnistiés* [About the Application of Amnesty of May 8, 1837, to the Condemned of Bourbon and about the Memoir of Mr. Houat]. Paris: Imp. Gratiot and Gros, 1837.

Barbier, Stéphane. "Le calvaire de Marie-Claire Angama." *Libération,* 27–28 September 1986.

Barquissau, Raphaël. *Les îles.* Paris: Grasset, 1942.

Barrows, Susanna. *Distorting Mirrors: Visions of the Crowd in Late Nineteenth-Century France.* New Haven: Yale University Press, 1988.

Bassot, Vincent. "Aspects particuliers de l'alcoolisme à La Réunion." Medicine thesis, Paris, 1978.

Baumgart, Winfried. *Imperialism: The Idea and Reality of British and French Colonial Expansion, 1880–1914.* Oxford: Oxford University Press, 1982.

Bayard, Jean-François. *The State in Africa: The Politics of the Belly.* Trans. Mary Harper, Christopher Harnson, and Elizabeth Harnson. London: Longman, 1993. Originally, *L'État en Afrique: La politique du ventre.*

Beaulieu, Paul-Leroy. *De la Colonisation chez les peuples modernes.* 3d ed. Paris: Librairie Guillaumin et Cie, 1886.

Beaune, Colette. *Naissance de la nation France.* Paris: Gallimard, 1985.

Béjin, André. "Le sang, le sens et le travail: Georges Vacher de Lapouge:

Darwiniste social, fondateur de l'anthroposociologie." *Cahiers Internationaux de Sociologie* 73 (1982): pp. 323–43.

Beniamino, Michel. *L'imaginaire Réunionnais.* Saint-Denis, Réunion: Éditions du Tramail, 1992.

Bénichou, Paul. *Le Temps des prophètes: Doctrines de l'âge romantique.* Paris: Gallimard, 1977.

Benítez-Rojo, Antonio. *The Repeating Island: The Caribbean and the Postmodern Perspective.* Trans. James E. Maraniss. Durham: Duke University Press, 1992.

Benoist, Jean. *Les carnets d'un guérisseur réunionnais.* Documents et Recherches 7. Saint-Denis, Réunion: Fondation pour la Recherche et le Développement dans l'Océan Indien, 1980.

——. *Un développement ambigu: Structure et changement de la société réunionnaise.* Documents et Recherches, 10. Saint-Denis, Réunion: Fondation pour la Recherche et le Développement dans l'Océan Indien, 1983.

——. *Paysans de La Réunion.* Aix-Marseille: Presses Universitaires, Fondation pour la Recherche et le Développement dans l'Océan Indien, 1984.

——. *Anthropologie médicale en société créole.* Paris: PUF, 1993.

Benoit, J. *Confessions d'un prolétaire.* Paris: Éditions Sociales, 1968.

Benot, Yves. *La révolution française et la fin des colonies.* Paris: Éditions La Découverte, 1988.

——. *Massacres coloniaux.* Paris: Éditions La Découverte, 1994.

Bensoussan, Patrick. "Le mouvoir des mots: Essai d'approche transculturelle du passage à l'acte en pays créole." *Psychopathologie Africaine* 11, no. 1 (1986–1987): pp. 5–18.

Bercherie, Paul. *Les fondements de la clinique.* Paris: La Bibliothèque d'Ornicar, 1980.

Berchtold, Jacques, and Michel Porret, eds. *La peur au XVIIIe siècle, discours, représentations, pratiques.* Genève: Droz, Faculté de Genève, 1994.

Bergeron, Jules. "Rapport sur la répression de l'alcoolisme." *Annales d'hygiène publique et de médecine légale* 38 (1872).

Bergner, Gwen. "Who Is That Marked Woman? or, The Role of Gender in Fanon's *Black Skin, White Masks.*" *PMLA* 110, no. 1 (January 1995): pp. 75–88.

Bérillon, Dr. "Le problème psycho-biologique du métissage dans les races humaines." *Revue de Psychologie appliquée* (June 1926–April 1927).

——. "Le métissage: son rôle dans la production des enfants anormaux." *Revue de Psychologie appliquée* 1 (January 1927): pp. 3–5.

Bernabé, Jean, Patrick Chamoiseau, and Raphaël Confiant. *Éloge de la Créolité.* Paris: Gallimard, 1989. Trans. Mohamed B. Taleb Khyar as "In Praise of Creoleness." *Callaloo* 13 (1990): pp. 886–909.

Berthelier, Robert. "Tentative d'approche socio-culturelle de la psycho-pathologie nord-africaine." *Psychopathologie Africaine* 5, no. 2 (1969): pp. 171–222.

——. *L'Homme maghrébin dans la littérature psychiatrique.* Paris: L'Har-mattan, 1994.

Bertile, Wilfrid. *Le logement dans les départements d'Outre-Mer: Rapport au Premier Ministre.* Paris: La Documentation Française, 1984.

Bertile, Wilfrid, Alain Lorraine, and le Collectif Dourdan. *Une commu-nauté invisible: 175,000 Réunionnais en France métropolitaine.* Paris: l'Harmattan, 1996.

Bhabha, Homi. "Minority Maneuvers and Unsettled Negotiations." *Crit-ical Inquiry* 23 (spring 1997): pp. 341–459.

Biros, Bernard. "Essai sur l'identité créole." Ph.D. diss., Faculté de Méde-cine, Necker, 1979.

Blackburn, Robin. *The Making of New World Slavery from the Baroque to the Modern, 1492–1800.* London: Verso, 1997.

——. *The Overthrow of Colonial Slavery, 1776–1848.* London: Verso, 1997.

Blake, J. *Family Structure in Jamaica: The Social Context of Reproduction.* Glencoe: Free Press, 1961.

Blanchard, Pascal. "Nationalisme et Colonialisme: Idéologie Coloniale, Discours sur l'Afrique et les Africains de la Droite Nationaliste française des années 30 à la Révolution nationale." Ph.D. diss., University Paris I, 1994.

Blanchard, Pascal, Stéphane Blanchoin, Nicolas Bancel, Gilles Boëtsch, and Hubert Gerbeau. *L'autre et nous: "scènes et types."* Paris: Syros/ ACHAC, 1995.

Blanc, Louis. *Histoire de la Révolution de 1848.* Bruxelles, 1870.

Bloch, Françoise, and Monique Buisson. "Du don à la dette: la con-struction du lien social familial." *MAUSS* 11 (1991): pp. 54–71.

——. "La circulation du don entre générations, ou comment reçoit-on?" *Communications* 59 (1994): pp. 55–72.

Bloch, Maurice. New foreword to *Prospero and Caliban,* by Octave Man-noni. Ann Arbor: University of Michigan Press, 1990.

Bock, Gisela, and Pat Thane, eds. *Maternity and Gender Policies: Women and the Rise of the European Welfare States, 1880s–1950s.* New York: Routledge, 1994.

Boisvert, Georges. "Histoire de l'implantation de l'Assistance Psychi-atrique dans l'île de La Réunion." M.A. thesis, University of Caen, 1985.

Boiteau, Pierre. *Contribution à l'histoire de la nation malgache.* Paris: Édi-tions Sociales, 1958.

Boltanski, Luc. "America, America . . . le plan Marshall et l'importation du 'management.'" *Actes de la recherche en sciences sociales* 38 (1981): pp. 19–41.

Bonnetain, Paul. *Les Petites épouses*. Paris: Calmann Lévy, n.d.

Bonniol, Jean-Luc. *La couleur comme maléfice: Une illustration créole de la généalogie des Blancs et des Noirs*. Paris: Albin Michel, 1992.

Borreil, Jean. *La Raison nomade*. Paris: Payot, 1993.

Bouche, Denise. "Autrefois, notre pays s'appelait la Gaule . . . Remarques sur l'adaptation de l'enseignement au Sénégal de 1817 à 1960." *Cahiers d'Études Africaines* 8, no. 2 (1968): pp. 110–12.

Bouillon, Antoine. *Madagascar, Le colonisé et son âme: Essai sur le discours psychologique colonial*. Paris: Éditions l'Harmattan, 1981.

Boulard, Fabrice. "Le métissage, richesse et souffrance mêlées." *Quotidien*, 11 November 1992, p. 12.

Bouvier, Pierre. *Fanon*. Paris: Éditions Universitaires, 1971.

Boxer, Marilyn, and Jean H. Quataert, eds. *Socialist Women: European Socialist Women in the Nineteenth and Early Twentieth Centuries*. New York: Elsevier-Holland, 1978.

Boyer, Monique. *Métisse*. Paris: L'Harmattan, 1992.

Brantlinger, Patrick, and Donald Ulin. "Policing Nomads: Discourse and Social Control in Early Victorian England." *Cultural Critique* 25 (fall 1993): pp. 33–64.

Brocheux, Pierre, and Daniel Hémery. *Indochine, la colonisation ambiguë: 1858–1954*. Paris: Éditions La Découverte, 1995.

Brunet, Auguste. *Trois cent ans de colonisation: La Réunion*. Paris: Éditions de l'Empire Français, 1948.

Bulletin Officiel de l'île de La Réunion, decree of 24 October 1848.

Bulletins et Mémoires de la Société d'Anthropologie de Paris, December 1910.

Bulletin Officiel de l'île de La Réunion, 1865.

Burrows, Edgar, and Michael Wallace. "The American Revolution: The Ideology and Psychology of National Liberation." *Perspectives in American History* 6 (1972): pp. 167–306.

Burton, Richard D. E. " 'Maman-France doudou': Family Images in French West Indian Colonial Discourse." *Diacritics* 23, no. 3 (1993): pp. 69–90.

——. *La famille coloniale: La Martinique et la Mère-Patrie, 1789–1992*. Paris: L'Harmattan, 1994.

Bush, Barbara. *Slave Women in Caribbean Society, 1650–1838*. Bloomington: Indiana University Press, 1990.

Caillet, Emile. *Essai sur la psychologie du Hova*. Paris: PUF, 1926.

Caldwell, Gail. "Author Toni Morrison Discusses Her Latest Novel *Beloved*." In *Conversations with Toni Morrison*, ed. Danille Taylor-Guthrie, pp. 239–45. Jackson: University Press of Mississippi, 1994.

Casseville, Henry. *Thi-Nhi, autre fille d'Annam*. Paris: Figuière, 1922.

Caute, David. *Frantz Fanon*. Paris: Seghers, 1970.

Cellier, Pierre. "École et société: L'enseignement du français." *Cahiers de La Réunion et de l'Océan Indien* 4 (1974): pp. 21–25.

Cendrieus, Jehan. *François Phuoc, Métis*. Paris: Bibliothèque Charpentier, 1929.

Cercle Éliard Laude. *Réunion 1969: Une Colonie française*. Paris: François Maspéro, 1969.

CERM, eds. *La condition féminine*. Paris: Éditions Sociales, 1978.

Césaire, Aimé. "Victor Schoelcher et l'abolition de l'esclavage." In *Esclavage et colonisation*, pp. 1–28. Paris: PUF, 1948.

Chane-Kune, Sonia. *Aux origines de l'identité réunionnaise*. Paris: L'Harmattan, 1996.

——. *La Réunion n'est plus une île*. Paris: L'Harmattan, 1996.

Charbit, Catherine, Yves Charbit, and Catherine Bertrand. "La pluripaternité en Guadeloupe et en Martinique." *Nouvelles Questions Féministes* (spring 1985): pp. 9–10.

Chaudenson, Robert. "Mûlatres, Métis, Créoles." In *Métissages: Littérature-Histoire*. Vol. 1. Ed. Jean-Claude Carpanin Marimoutou and Jean-Michel Racault (Paris: L'Harmattan, 1992).

——. *Lexique du parler créole de la Réunion*. Paris: Champion, 1974.

Chaudenson, Robert, et al. *Encyclopédie de l'Île de La Réunion*. Vol. 7. Saint-Denis, Réunion: Livres Réunion, 1980.

Chauvac, M., C. Iglicki, N. Quelven, M. Raoul, M. Sebeille, and J. P. Herode. *Étude sur les registres d'affranchissement des esclaves à Saint-Denis*. Saint-Denis, Réunion: École Normale, 1973.

Cherubini, Bernard, ed. *Le Monde rural à La Réunion: Mutations foncières, mutations paysagères*. Paris: Université de La Réunion/L'Harmattan, 1996.

Chesneaux, Jean. *Contribution à l'histoire de la nation vietnamienne*. Paris: Éditions sociales, 1955.

Chivas Baron, Clotilde. *Trois femmes annamites*. Paris, 1922.

——. *Confidences de métisse*. Paris, 1927.

Clarke, Edith. *My Mother Who Fathered Me*. London: G. Allen and Unwin, 1966.

Clastres, Pierre. "On Ethnocide." Trans. Julian Pefanis and Bernadette Maher. *Art and Text* 28 (1980): pp. 51–58.

Clayton, A. *Contes Franco-Annamites: Livre de lecture pour les écoles du Tonkin*. Hanoi: Imprimerie F. H. Schneider, 1887.

Cochin, Auguste. *L'abolition de l'esclavage*. Vol. 1. Paris: Lecoffre, 1861.

Coetzee, J. M. "Blood, Taint, Flaw, Degeneration: The Novels of Gertrude Millin." In *White Writing: On the Culture of Letters in South Africa*, pp. 136–62. New Haven: Yale University Press, 1988.

Collectif des Chrétiens pour l'autodétermination des DOM-TOM. *Encore la France Coloniale*. Paris: L'Harmattan, 1976.

Collin, Paulette. "La psychiatrie à l'île de La Réunion en 1960." M.A. thesis, University of Lille, 1963.

Colmant, Laure. "Patrick Chamoiseau: Le système scolaire doit exalter la diversité." *Le Monde de l'Éducation,* September 1994, pp. 47–48.

Confiant, Raphäel. *Aimé Césaire: Une traversée paradoxale du siècle.* Paris: Stock, 1994.

"Comment l'aristocratie du sucre fit assassiner De Villeneuve: Interview du Docteur Raymond Vergès. Député de La Réunion." *La Défense,* 10 January 1947, p. 1.

Constant, Benjamin. *Écrits politiques.* Paris: Gallimard, 1997.

——. *Principes de politique.* Paris: Hachette, 1997.

Cook, Mercer. "The Life and Writings of Louis T. Houat." *Journal of Negro History* 30 (1945): pp. 185–98.

Couchard, Françoise. *Emprise et violence maternelles.* Paris: Dunod, 1991.

——. "On bat une fille." *Revue Française de Psychanalyse* 3 (1993): pp. 773–850.

Cravero, Jean-Philippe. "Contribution à l'étude de la sorcellerie réunionnaise." Unpublished CES de Psychiatrie, Faculté Kremlin Bicêtre, 1979.

Cravero, Jean-Philippe, and Thierry Dionot. "Modalités expressives des dépressions à l'Île de La Réunion." *Psychopathologie Africaine* 17, nos. 1–3 (1981): pp. 64–72.

Dagenais, Huguette, and Jean Poirier. "L'envers du mythe: la situation des femmes en Guadeloupe." *Nouvelles Questions Féministes* (spring 1985): pp. 9–10.

Daget, Serge. *La répression de la traite des Noirs au XIXe siècle.* Paris: Karthala, 1997.

David, Marcel. *Le printemps de la Fraternité: Genèse et vicissitudes, 1830–1851.* Paris: Aubier, 1992.

Davis, Angela. *Women, Race, and Class.* New York: Random House, 1982.

Dayot, Eugène. *Bourbon pittoresque.* 1848.

De Baecque, Antoine. "The Allegorical Image of France, 1750–1800: A Political Crisis of Representation." Trans. Marc Roudebush. *Representations* 47 (summer 1994): pp. 111–43.

——. "La Révolution française: Régénérer la culture?" In *Pour une histoire culturelle,* ed. Jean-Pierre Rioux and Jean-François Sirinelli. Paris: Seuil, 1997.

De Baleine, Philippe. *Les danseuses de la France.* Paris: Plon, 1979.

Debré, Michel. *Une politique pour La Réunion.* Paris: Plon, 1974.

——. *Trois républiques pour une France: Mémoires.* Vol. 1. Paris: Albin Michel, 1984.

——. *Gouverner Autrement: Mémoires.* Vol. 4. Paris: Albin Michel, 1993.

De Cecatti, René. "La Bicyclette créole ou la voiture française: Entretien avec Raphaël Confiant." *Le Monde: Carrefour des littératures européennes,* November 1992, p. 3.

De Certeau, Michel. *L'écriture de l'histoire.* Paris: Gallimard, 1975.

———. *The Practice of Everyday Life.* Berkeley: University of California Press, 1988.

———. *L'invention du quotidien, Arts de faire.* Paris: Folio, 1990.

Defos Du Rau, Jean. *L'Île de La Réunion: Étude de Géographie Humaine.* Bordeaux: Institut de Géographie, 1960.

De Gobineau, Arthur. *Essai sur l'inégalité des races humaines.* Paris: 1853. English translation: *The Moral and Intellectual Diversity of Races, with Particular Reference to Their Respective Influence in the Civil and Political History of Mankind.* Philadelphia: Lippincott, 1856.

De Godefroy, Frédéric. *Dictionnaire de l'ancienne langue française du Xle. au XVe. siècle.* Genève, Paris: Slatkine, 1982.

De La Brosse, M. P. *Une des grandes énergies françaises: Paul Bert.* Hanoi: 1925.

Delassus, J. M., and E. Verrière. "La santé mentale à La Réunion," *Bulletin d'information Cenaddom* 69 (1983): pp. 20–30.

De Lauretis, Teresa. *Technologies of Gender: Essays on Theory, Film, and Fiction.* Bloomington: Indiana University Press, 1987.

Delavignette, Robert. "Le Théatre de Gorée et la culture franco-africaine." *Afrique française* 10 (October 1937): pp. 471–72.

Deleuze, Gilles. *Pourparlers.* Paris: Éditions de Minuit, 1990.

Deming Lewis, Martin. "One Hundred Million Frenchmen: The Assimilation Theory in French Colonial Policy." *Comparative Studies in Society and History* 4, no. 2 (January 1962): pp. 129–53.

Denizet, Jacques. *Sarda Garriga: L'homme qui avait foi en l'homme.* Saint-Denis, Réunion: Editions CNH, 1990.

De Pourvouville, Albert. *Le mal d'argent.* Paris: 1926.

———. *Histoire populaire des colonies françaises.*

Derrida, Jacques. *Otobiographies: L'enseignement de Nietzsche et la politique du nom propre.* Paris: Galilée, 1984.

———. "The Laws of Reflection: Nelson Mandela, in Admiration." Trans. Mary Ann Laws and Isabelle Lorenz. In *For Nelson Mandela,* ed. Jacques Derrida and Mustapha Tlili, pp. 13–42. New York: Henry Holt, 1987.

———. *Politiques de l'amitié.* Paris: Galilée, 1994.

De Saussure, Léopold. *La psychologie de la colonisation française dans ses rapports avec les sociétés indigènes.* Paris: F. Alcan, 1899.

Deschamps, Hubert. *The French Union: History, Institutions, Economy, Countries, and Peoples—Social and Political Changes.* Paris: Éditions Berger-Levrault, 1956.

"Des droits politiques pour les indigènes." *Le Paria* 2 (1 May 1922): p. 1.

Desports, Jean-Marie. *De la servitude à la liberté: Bourbon des origines à 1848.* Saint-Denis, Réunion: Océan Éditions, 1989.

De Tocqueville, Alexis. *Souvenirs.* Vol. 12. Paris: Gallimard, 1964.

Devillers, Philippe. *Paris, Saigon, Hanoi: Les archives de la guerre 1944–1947.* Paris: Archives Gallimard, Julliard, 1988.

Dewitte, Philippe. *Les Mouvements nègres en France, 1919–1939.* Paris: L'Harmattan, 1985.

Diderot. "Le rêve d'Alembert." *Oeuvres Complètes.* Vol. 8.

Dirayson-Seylor, Olivier. *Amours d'Extrême-Orient.* Paris: Carrington, 1905.

———. *Demi-Blanc.* Paris: 1912.

Doerner, Klaus. *Madmen and the Bourgeoisie: A Social History of Insanity and Psychiatry.* Oxford: Blackwell, 1981.

Douglas, Mary. *Purity and Danger.* London: Routledge and Kegan, 1966.

Dr. Gaide. *L'Assistance Médicale et le Protection de la Santé Publique.* Exposition Coloniale Internationale. Indochine Française. Inspection des Services Sanitaires et Médicaux de l'Indochine. Hanoi: Imprimerie d'Extrême-Orient, 1931.

DuBois, W. E. B. *The Souls of Black Folk.* New York: Fawcett Publications, 1903.

Duchen, Claire. *Women's Rights and Women's Lives in France, 1944–1968.* New York: Routledge, 1994.

Duchet, Michèle. *Anthropologie et histoire au siècle des Lumières.* Paris: Maspéro, 1971.

Dumas, Alexandre. *Georges.* 1843.

D'un inconscient post-colonial, s'il existe. Paris: Association Freudienne Internationale, 1995.

Duval, Gilbert. "Suicides, tentatives de suicide, violences à la Réunion: Abord clinique, épidémiologique, sociologique, culturel." In *L'Espoir Transculturel: Des communautés d'origine aux nouvelles solidarités* (1988).

Enloe, Cynthia. *The Morning After: Sexual Politics at the End of the Cold War.* Berkeley: University of California Press, 1993.

Erau, Paul. *Trois siècles de Médecine Coloniale Française* [Year of the Colonial Exhibition in Paris]. Paris: Commissariat de l'Exposition Coloniale de Paris: 1931.

Étudiants Anticolonialistes, no. 1 (1949).

Eve, Prosper. *La religion populaire à La Réunion.* Université de La Réunion: Institut de Linguistique et d'Anthropologie, 1985.

———. *Tableau du Syndicalisme à la Réunion.* Saint-Denis, Réunion: Éditions CNH, 1991.

———. *Île à peur: La peur redoutée ou récupérée à La Réunion des origines à nos jours.* Saint-Denis, Réunion: Océan Éditions, 1992.

——. *La Première Guerre Mondiale vue par les poilus réunionnais.* Saint-Denis, Réunion: Éditions CNH, 1992.

——. *Le jeu politique à La Réunion de 1900 à 1939.* Paris: L'Harmattan, Université de La Réunion, 1994.

——. *De La Réunion coloniale au département. La concrétisation d'un désir.* Saint-Denis, Réunion: Association "Notre Département a 50 ans," 1996.

Fallope, Josette. *Esclaves et Citoyens: Les Noirs à la Guadeloupe au XIXe siècle.* Basse-Terre, Guadeloupe: Société d'Histoire de la Guadeloupe, 1992.

Fanon, Frantz. "Fondement réciproque de la culture nationale et des luttes de libération." *Présence Africaine,* nos. 24–25 (1959): pp. 82–89.

——. "Mr. Debré's Desperate Endeavors." Published originally in *El Moudjahid,* no. 37 (25 February 1959). Reprinted in Frantz Fanon, *Toward the African Revolution: Political Essays,* pp. 158–62. Trans. Haakon Chevalier. New York: Grove Press, 1967.

——. "Colonial War and Mental Disorders." In *The Wretched of the Earth.* New York: Grove Press, 1963.

——. *The Wretched of the Earth.* Trans. Constance Farrington. New York: Grove Press, 1963.

——. *Peaux noires et masques blancs.* Paris: Seuil, 1975.

——. "De l'impulsivité criminelle du Nord-Africain à la guerre de libération nationale." In *Les damnés de la terre,* pp. 215–28. Trans. Constance Farrington. Paris: François Maspéro, 1981.

——. *Black Skin, White Masks.* Trans. Constance Farrington. New York: Grove Press, 1967.

Farge, Arlette. "Michel Foucault et les archives de l'exclusion." In *Penser la folie, Essais sur Michel Foucault,* pp. 63–78. Paris: Galilée, 1992.

Farrère, Claude. *Les civilisés.* Paris: Librairie Paul Ollendorf, 1908.

Farroudh-Siefer, Léon. *Le mythe du négre et de l'Afrique Noire dans la littérature française de 1800 à la Deuxième Guerre Mondiale.* Dakar: Nouvelles Éditions Africaines, 1980.

Faugère, E. "Une plantation de canne à sucre à La Réunion: Logiques familiales et logiques en conflit." M.A. thesis, Marseille, 1993.

Favret, Jeanne, and Jean-Pierre Peter. "L'animal, le fou, la mort." In *Moi, Pierre Rivière, ayant égorgé ma mère, ma soeur, et mon frère . . . Un cas de parricide au XIXe. siècle,* ed. Michel Foucault. Paris: Julliard, 1984.

Femmes en Chiffre, Réunion. Saint-Denis, Réunion: Service Régional de L'INSEE, 1988.

Fenichel, Otto. *The Psychoanalytical Theory of Neurosis.* New York: W. W. Norton, 1972.

Ferrere, Jacky. "Au nom du père." *JIR,* 1 March 1993, p. 13.

——. "Paul Vergès: L'adversaire politique numéro un." *JIR,* 16 March 1993, p. 6.

——. "Union sacrée autour de J. F. Bosviel." *JIR*, 23 March 1993.

Finot, Jean. *Préjudice de la race*. English translation by Florence Wade-Evans. *Race Prejudice*. London: Archibald Constable, 1906.

Foccart, Jacques. *Tous les soirs avec De Gaulle: Journal de l'Elysée-I, 1965–1967*. Paris: Fayard, Jeune Afrique, 1997.

Fontaine, Brigitte. "Historique et point de vue sociologique de la presse écrite et audiovisuelle à l'île de La Réunion des origines à nos jours." M.A. thesis, University of Réunion, 1982.

Foucault, Michel. *The Archaeology of Knowledge and the Discourse on Language*. New York: Harper, 1972.

——. *Histoire de la sexualité: La volonté de savoir*. Paris: Gallimard, 1976.

——. *Discipline and Punish: The Birth of the Prison*. Trans. Alan Sheridan. New York: Vintage Books, 1979.

——. *Résumé des cours, 1970–1982*. Paris: Julliard, 1989.

——. *Il faut défendre la société*. Paris: Gallimard/Seuil, 1997.

Foucault, Michel, ed. *Moi, Pierre Rivière, ayant égorgé ma mère, ma soeur, et mon frère . . . Un cas de parricide au XIXe. siècle*. Paris: Julliard, Collection Archives, 1984.

Fournier, Christiane. *Homme jaune et femme blanche*. Paris: Flammarion, 1933.

Fraisse, Geneviève, and Michelle Perrot, eds. *Histoire des femmes: Le XIXe. siècle*. Paris: Plon, 1991.

Fremigacci, Jean. "L'État colonial français, du discours mythique aux réalités—1880–1940." *Matériaux pour l'histoire de notre temps*, nos. 32–33 (July–December 1993): pp. 27–35.

Freud, Sigmund. *Moses and Monotheism*. London: Hogarth Press, 1939.

——. "The Loss of Reality in Neurosis and Psychosis." In *Collected Papers*. Vol. 2. London: Hogarth Press, 1948.

——. "Thoughts for the Times on War and Death." In *Collected Papers*, ed. Joan Riviere. Vol. 4. London: Hogarth Press, 1948.

——. "Infantile Organization of the Libido." In *The Standard Edition of the Complete Works of Sigmund Freud*. Vol. 19. Trans. James Strachey et al. London: Hogarth Press, 1953.

——. "Some Psychical Consequences of the Anatomical Distinction between the Sexes." In *The Standard Edition of the Complete Psychological Works of Sigmund Freud*. vol. 19.

——. "Psychotherapy of Hysteria." In *Studies on Hysteria (1893–1895)*, by Josef Breuer and Sigmund Freud, pp. 253–306. Trans. James Strachey. New York: Basic Books, 1957.

——. "Family Romances (1909) [1908]." In *The Standard Edition of the Complete Works of Sigmund Freud*. Vol. 9 (1906–1908). London: Hogarth Press, 1959.

——. *Inhibitions, Symptoms, and Anxiety.* Trans. Alix Strachey. New York: W. W. Norton, 1959.

——. *Civilization and Its Discontents.* Trans. James Strachey. New York: W. W. Norton, 1961.

——. *The Interpretation of Dreams.* Vol. 6 of *The Standard Edition of the Complete Works of Sigmund Freud.* Trans. James Strachey. London: Hogarth Press, 1900.

——. "Letter to Romain Rolland, A Disturbance of Memory on the Acropolis." In *Standard Edition.* Vol. 22. London: Hogarth Press, 1936.

Fuma, Sudel. *Esclaves et citoyens, Le destin de 62,000 Réunionnais.* Saint-Denis, Réunion: Fondation pour la recherche et le développement dans l'Océan Indien, 1982.

——. *L'esclavagisme à La Réunion, 1794–1848.* Paris: L'Harmattan–Université de La Réunion, 1992.

——. *Chambre noire, Chants obscurs.* Saint-Denis, Réunion: Conseil Général, 1994.

Furstenberg, Frank F., Jr. "Women and Children Last." *New York Review of Books,* 16 October 1994.

Fuss, Diana. "Interior Colonies: Frantz Fanon and the Politics of Identification." *Diacritics* 24, nos. 2–3 (summer–fall 1994): pp. 20–42.

Gallissot, René. "Les thèses du 'Socialisme colonial' en Tunisie: Colonisation socialiste et formation d'une nouvelle patrie par le mélange des races. Le discours de J. Durel au Conseil National du Parti Socialiste S.F.I.O. de Juillet 1928." *Pluriel* 12 (1977): pp. 53–59.

Galton, Francis. *Hereditary Genius: An Inquiry into Its Laws and Consequences.* 1892. Reprint, Gloucester: Peter Smith, 1972.

Gamaleya, Clélie, *Filles d'Héva.* Saint-Denis, Réunion: UFR, 1984.

Garrigues, Jean. "Les images de la Révolution de 1830 à 1848: enjeux politiques d'une mémoire." In *Le XIXe siècle et la Révolution Française,* pp. 91–103. Paris: Éditions Créaphis, 1992.

Gauchet, Marcel. "La dette du sens et les racines de l'État." *Libre* 2 (1977): pp. 5–43.

Gauthier, Arlette. *Les soeurs de Solitude: La condition féminine dans l'esclavage aux Antilles du XVII au XIX siècle.* Paris: Éditions Caribéennes, 1985.

Gauvin, Axel. *Du créole opprimé au créole libéré.* Paris: L'Harmattan, 1977.

"Gayatry Spivak on the Politics of the Postcolonial Subject, Interview by Howard Winant." *Socialist Review* 3 (1990).

Geismar, Peter. *Fanon: The Revolutionary as Prophet.* New York: Grove Press, 1971.

Gendzier, Irene. *Frantz Fanon: A Critical Study.* London: Pantheon Books, 1973.

Gengembre, Gérard. "De Bug-Jargal à Toussaint Louverture: Le Romantisme et l'esclave révolté." In *Les abolitions de l'esclavage,* pp. 309–18. Ed. Marcel Dorigny. Paris: Presses Universitaires de Vincennes et Éditions UNESCO, 1995.

Georges, François. *Deux études sur Sartre.* Paris: Christian Bourgeois Éditeur, 1976.

Gilbert, Sandra. "Soldier's Heart: Literary Men, Literary Women, and the Great War." In *Behind the Lines: Gender and the Two World Wars.* Ed. Margaret Randolf Higonnet, Jane Jenson, Sonja Michel, and Margaret Collins Weitz. New Haven, Conn.: Yale University Press.

Gillet, François. "Le cercle des électeurs disparus." *Quotidien,* 23 March 1993, p. 9.

Gilman, Sander L. *Difference and Pathology: Stereotypes of Sexuality, Race, and Madness.* Ithaca: Cornell University Press, 1985.

——. *The Case of Sigmund Freud: Medicine and Identity at the Fin de Siècle.* Baltimore: Johns Hopkins University Press, 1993.

——. *Freud, Race, and Gender.* Princeton, N.J.: Princeton University Press, 1993.

Girard, Patrick. "Le mulâtre littéraire ou le passage au blanc." In *Le couple interdit,* ed. Léon Poliakov, pp. 191–214. Paris: Mouton, 1980.

Girardet, René. *L'Idée Coloniale de la France.* Paris: La Table Ronde, 1972.

Girault, Arthur. *Rapport sur un projet de décret concernant les métis.* Paris: 1928.

——. "La condition juridique des métis dans les colonies françaises." *Revue politique et parlementaire,* 10 April 1929, pp. 124–31.

——. *Principes de Colonisation et de Législation Coloniale.* Paris: 1895.

Gliozzi, Giuliano. "Le métissage et l'histoire de l'espèce humaine: De Maupertuis à Gobineau." In *Métissages,* vol. 1, pp. 51–58. Ed. Jean-Claude Carpanin Marimoutou and Jean-Michel Racault. Paris: L'Harmattan, 1992.

Glissant, Édouard. *Le discours antillais.* Paris: Seuil, 1981.

——. "Beyond Babel." *World Literature Today* 63, no. 4 (autumn 1989): pp. 561–63.

——. *Poétique de la relation.* Paris: Gallimard, 1990.

——. *Introduction à une poétique du divers.* Paris: Gallimard, 1996.

Godbout, Jacques, and Alain Caillé. *L'Esprit du don.* Paris: La Découverte, 1992.

Golden, Thelma, ed. *Black Male: Representations of Masculinity in Contemporary American Art.* New York: Whitney Museum of American Art, 1994.

Gooding-Williams, Robert, ed. *Reading Rodney King, Reading Urban Uprising.* New York: Routledge, 1993.

Gordon, Lewis R. *Fanon and the Crisis of European Man: An Essay on Philosophy and the Human Sciences.* New York: Routledge, 1995.

Gordon, Linda. *Pitied but Not Entitled: Single Mothers and the History of Welfare, 1890–1935.* New York: Free Press, 1994.

Gossett, Thomas F. *Race: The History of an Idea in America.* Dallas: Southern University Press, 1963.

Govindama, Yolande. "La fonction symbolique de la déesse Pétiaye dans la mentalité des femmes hindoues de La Réunion." In *Cultures: Exils et Folies dans l'Océan Indien,* ed. Jean-François Reverzy, pp. 157–62. Paris: INSERM, l'Harmattan, 1990.

Gracchus, Fritz. *Les lieux de la mère dans les sociétés afro-américaines.* Paris: Éditions Caribéennes, 1987.

Grall, Charles. *Hygiène coloniale appliquée. Hygiène de l'Indochine.* Paris: Librairie J. B. Baillière et Fils, 1908.

Grant, Joanne, ed. *Black Protest: 350 Years of History, Documents, and Analyses.* New York: Fawcett Columbine, 1968.

Grimal, Pierre. *Dictionnaire de la mythologie grecque et romaine.* Paris: PUF, 1958.

Guenin, Georges, ed. *L'épopée coloniale de la France racontée par les contemporains.* Paris: Larose, 1932.

Guex, Germaine. *Le syndrome d'abandon.* Paris: PUF, 1973.

Guillaumin, Colette. *L'Idéologie raciste, Genèse et language actuel.* Paris: Mouton, 1972.

Gullickson, Gay L. *Unruly Women of Paris: Images of the Commune.* Ithaca: Cornell University Press, 1997.

Haesler, Aldo. "La preuve par le don." *MAUSS,* 1993, pp. 174–93.

Halimi, Edith. "Renaître métisse et exorciser ses malaises," *JIR,* 12 December 1992, p. 15.

Halimi, Gisèle, with Simone de Beauvoir. *Pour Djamila Boupacha* (Paris: Gallimard, 1962).

Halimi, Serge. *Sisyphus Is Tired: The French Left and the Exercise of Power (1924–1986).* Ph.D. diss., University of California–Berkeley, 1990. Published as *Sysyphe est fatigué: Les Échecs de la Gauche au pouvoir.* Paris: Robert Laffont, 1993.

Hall, Richard. *Empires of the Monsoon: A History of the Indian Ocean and Its Invaders.* London: Harper Collins, 1996.

Haller, John S., Jr. *Outcasts from Evolution: Scientific Attitudes of Racial Inferiority, 1859–1900.* Chicago: University of Illinois Press, 1971.

Haller, Mark. *Eugenics: Hereditarian Attitudes in American Thought.* New Brunswick: Rutgers University Press, 1963.

Harding, Sandra, ed. *The "Racial" Economy of Science: Toward a Democratic Future.* Bloomington: Indiana University Press, 1993.

Hardy, Georges. *Histoire coloniale et psychologie ethnique.* Paris: Revue de l'Histoire des Colonies Françaises, 1925.

——. *Histoire de la colonisation française.* Paris: Librairie Larose, 1928.

——. *La pénétration saharienne et la psychologie du nomade saharien.* Paris: Revue de l'Histoire des Colonies Françaises, 1929.

——. *Psychologie et Colonization.* Paris: Le Monde Nouveau, 1929.

——. *Sur la psychologie de quelques métiers marocains.* Paris: Outre-Mer, 1929.

——. *De la gaieté chez les Noirs d'Afrique.* Paris: Outre-Mer, 1930.

——. *Psychologie avant-tout.* Paris: Outre-Mer, 1934.

——. *Pour une étude de la mimique.* Alger: Revue Africaine, 1936.

——. *La géographie psychologique.* Paris: Gallimard, 1939.

——. "La psychologie des populations coloniales." *Revue de Psychologie des Peuples* 3 (1947): pp. 233–61.

Harman, Jules. *Domination et colonisation.* Paris: Ernest Flammarion, 1910.

Hassoun, Jacques. *Les contrebandiers de la mémoire.* Paris: Syros, 1994.

——. *La Cruauté mélancolique.* Paris: Aubier, 1995.

Hecht, Gunther. *Die Bedeutung des Rassengedankens in der Kolonialpolitik.* Berlin, 1937.

Hein, Catherine. "Jobs for the Girls: Export Manufacturing in Mauritius." *International Labour Review* 123, no. 2 (1984): pp. 251–65.

——. *Multinational Enterprises and Employment in the Mauritian Export Processing Zone.* Geneva: International Labour Office, 1988.

Historical Relations across the Indian Ocean. UNESCO, 1980.

hooks, bell. "Feminism as a Persistent Critique of History: What's Love Got to Do with It?" In *The Fact of Blackness: Frantz Fanon and Representation,* ed. Alan Read, pp. 76–85. London: ICA, 1996.

Houat, Louis-Timagène. *Mémoire pour Louis Timagène Houat et pour ses compagnons d'infortune, tous hommes de couleur illégalement déportés de l'île Bourbon au mépris de l'amnistie royale de 1837.* Paris: 1837. Centre des Archives d'Outre-Mer (CAOM), Aix-en-Provence. Service Geog. C. 102. d. 726.

——. *Un proscrit de l'île de Bourbon à Paris.* Paris: Imp. Félix Malteste, 1838.

——. *Les Marrons.* Saint-Denis, Réunion: CRI, 1989.

Hugo, Victor. *Bug Jargal.* 1832.

Hunt, Lynn. *Politics, Culture, and Class in the French Revolution.* Berkeley: University of California Press, 1984.

——. *The Family Romance of the French Revolution.* Berkeley: University of California Press, 1992.

Hurstel, Françoise. "La fonction paternelle, questions de théorie ou: des lois à la Loi." In *Le Père. Métaphore paternelle et fonctions du père: L'Interdit, la Filiation, la Transmission,* pp. 235–62. Paris: Denoël, 1993.

Idelson, Bernard. "De la RTF à RFO: La Télévision réunionnaise à travers

le récit d'un acteur-pionnier, JVD." M.A. thesis, University of La Réunion, 1995.

"Identities in Search of a Strategy." *Socialist Review* 21, nos. 3–4 (1991).

"Imaginaire Colonial, Figures de l'immigré." *Hommes et Migrations,*
May–June 1997.

Irigaray, Luce. *Speculum of the Other Woman.* Trans. Gillian C. Gill.
Ithaca: Cornell University Press, 1985.

Ismael-Daoudjee, Amode. "Quelques aspects du vécu culturel et sociologique de l'alcoolisme à La Réunion." *Alcoolisation et Suralcoolisation à
La Réunion.* Région Réunion: Comité de la Culture, de l'Éducation, et
de l'Environnement, 10–11 July 1987.

"Itinéraires et Contacts de Cultures." In *Le Roman Colonial,* p. 217. Paris:
L'Harmattan, 1987.

Jay, Martin. "Sartre, Merleau-Ponty, and the Search for a New Ontology
of Sight." In *Modernity and the Hegemony of Vision,* ed. David Michael
Levin, pp. 143–85. Berkeley: University of California Press, 1993.

Jay, Maurice. "L'état actuel et les besoins futurs de l'assistance psychiatrique dans le département de la Réunion." *L'Information psychiatrique*
6 (June 1963): pp. 335–62.

———. *L'assistance psychiatrique à La Réunion. Histoire.* n.d.

Jeffords, Susan. *The Remasculinization of America: Gender and the Vietnam
War.* Bloomington: Indiana University Press, 1989.

Jones, Kathleen, and Françoise Vergès. "Aux Citoyennes! Women, Politics, and the Paris Commune of 1871." *History of European Ideas* 13, no. 6
(1991): pp. 711–32.

———. "Women of the Paris Commune." *Women's Studies International
Forum* 14, no. 5 (1991): pp. 491–503.

Joubert, Jean-Louis. "Pour une exploration de la Lémurie: Une mythologie littéraire de l'Océan Indien." *Annuaire des Pays de l'Océan Indien* 3
(1976): pp. 51–63.

Jourda, Pierre. *L'Exotisme dans la littérature française depuis Chateaubriand.* Paris: Boivin-Université de Montpellier, 1956.

Kaeppelin, Paul. *Les Escales françaises sur la Route de l'Inde, 1638–1731.*
Paris: A. Challamel, 1908.

Kakar, Sudhir. *The Colors of Violence: Cultural Identities, Religion, and
Conflict.* Chicago: University of Chicago Press, 1996.

Kincaid, Jamaica. *A Small Place.* New York: Plume Book, 1988.

Klein, Melanie. "A Contribution to the Psychogenesis of Manic-Depressive States." *International Journal of Psycho-Analysis* 16 (1935): pp. 145–
74.

Klejman, Laurence, and Florence Rochefort. *L'égalité en marche: Le féminisme sous la Troisième République.* Paris: des femmes, 1989.

Knibiehler, Yvonne, and Régine Goutalier. *Femmes et Colonisation: Rap-*

port *Terminal au Ministère des Relations Extérieures et de la Coopération.*
Aix-en-Provence: Université de Provence. Institut d'Histoire des Pays
d'Outre Mer, 1986.

Kofman, Sarah. *The Enigma of Woman: Woman in Freud's Writings.* Trans.
Catherine Porter. Ithaca: Cornell University Press, 1986.

Koven, Seth, and Sonya Michel. *Mothers of a New World: Maternalist
Politics and the Origins of Welfare States.* New York: Routledge, 1992.

Krüll, Marianne. *Freud and His Father.* Trans. Arnold J. Pomerans. New
York: W. W. Norton, 1986.

Kutzinski, Vera M. *Sugar's Secrets: Race and the Erotics of Cuban Nationalism.* Charlottesville: University Press of Virginia, 1993.

Lacan, Jacques. "Motifs du crime paranoïaque: Le crime des soeurs Papin." *Le Minotaure,* nos. 3–4 (1933): pp. 25–28.

———. "La famille." In *Encyclopédie Française.* Vol. 8. Paris: Librairie Larousse, 1938.

———. "Le stade du mirroir comme formateur de la fonction du Je telle
qu'elle nous est révélée dans l'expérience psychanalytique. Communication faite au XVIe. Congrès International de Psychanalyse." In *Ecrits,*
pp. 93–100. Paris: Seuil, 1966. English translation by Alan Sheridan:
"The Mirror Stage as Formative of the Function of the I as Revealed in
Psychoanalytic Experience." in *Écrits: A Selection,* pp. 1–7. New York:
W. W. Norton, 1977.

Laclau, Ernesto. "Universalism, Particularism, and the Question of Identity." *October* 61 (summer 1992): pp. 83–90.

Lacpatia, Firmin. *Boadour.* Saint-Denis, Réunion: AGM, 1978.

*La Gauche au pouvoir dans 9 mois? Ce que proposent les organisations démo-
cratiques pour la Réunion. Supplément au Journal* Témoignages *du 4 Juin
1977.* Saint-Denis, Réunion: Juillet, 1977.

Lamartine. *Histoire de la Révolution de 1848.* 1850. Paris: Vent du Large,
1948.

Lambert, Michael C. "From Citizenship to Négritude: 'Making a Difference' in Elite Ideologies of Colonized Francophone West Africa." *Society for Comparative Study of Society and History* 35, no. 2 (April 1993):
pp. 239–62.

Laplanche, Jean, and Jean-Baptiste Pontalis. *The Language of Psychoanalysis.* Trans. Donald Nicholson-Smith. New York: W. W. Norton,
1973.

———. *Fantasme originaire. Fantasmes des origines. Origines du fantasme.*
Paris: Hachette, 1985.

Laplantine, François. "Ethnopsychiatrie et ethnoscience. Les problèmes
posés par l'étude des savoirs étiologiques et des savoir-faire thérapeutiques concernant les maladies mentales." *Confrontations psychiatriques*
21 (1982): pp. 11–27.

——. *L'Ethnopsychiatrie*. Paris: PUF, Que Sais-Je?, 1988.

La Réunion, Égalité et Développement. October 1990.

Laroche, Benjamin. *Histoire de l'abolition de l'esclavage dans les colonies*, vol. 1, *La Réunion*. Paris: Firmin Didot, 1851.

Lauret, Daniel. *Le créole de la réussite*. Saint-Denis, Réunion: Éditions du Tramail, 1991.

Lauret, Jocelyne. "Un siècle de fraudes électorales à La Réunion." M.A. thesis, University of Réunion, 1990.

Lauriol, L. "Quelques remarques sur les maladies mentales aux colonies." Unpublished thesis in Medicine, Paris, 1938.

Lauvernier, Chantal. *Ban-Baï, Raymond Vergès, 1882–1957*. Paris: Imprimerie de Montlijeon, 1994.

Laval, Jean-Claude. *La justice répressive à La Réunion de 1848 à 1870*. Saint-Benoît, Réunion: Université Populaire, 1986.

Leblond, Marius. *Après l'exotisme de Loti, le Roman Colonial*. Paris: Buissière, 1926.

Leblond, Marius-Ary. *La Grande Île de Madagascar*. Paris: Ch. Delagrave, 1907.

——. "L'île de La Réunion." In *L'île de la Réunion*, ed. Raphaël Barquissau, Hippolyte Foucque, and Hubert Jacob de Cordemoy. Paris: Émile Larose, 1925.

Le Bon, Gustave. *Les lois psychologiques de l'évolution des peuples*. Paris: Félix Alcan, 1894.

Leconte De Lisle. *Catéchisme Populaire Républicain*. Paris: Alphonse Lemerre, 1870.

Legendre, Pierre. *L'Inestimable objet de la transmission: Étude sur le principe généalogique en Occident. Leçons IV.* Paris: Fayard, 1985.

Leguat, François. *Aventures aux Mascareignes. Voyage et aventures de François Leguat et de ses compagnons en deux îles désertes des Indes Orientales, 1707, suivi du Recueil de quelques mémoires servant d'instruction pour l'établissement de l'île d'Eden par Henri Duquesne, 1689*. Paris: Éditions de La Découverte, 1984.

Leguen, Marcel. *Histoire de l'Île de La Réunion*. Paris: L'Harmattan, 1979.

Le Huu Khoa, *L'Interculturel et l'Eurasien*. Paris: L'Harmattan, 1993.

Leloutre, Jean-Claude. *La Réunion, département français*. Cahiers Libres 134. Paris: François Maspéro, 1968.

Le Mappian. "La psychiatrie à l'Île de La Réunion." *L'Information psychiatrique*, January 1955, pp. 38–49.

Les Cahiers de L'île de La Réunion et de l'Océan Indien. 1972–1976 and 1979.

Les Cahiers de La Réunion et de l'Océan Indien. November 1972.

Lesel, Livia. *Le Père oblitéré: Chronique antillaise d'une illusion*. Paris: L'Harmattan, 1995.

Les Indiens de la Réunion. 2 vols. Saint-Denis, Réunion: NID, 1982.

Lesne, Christian. *Cinq essais d'ethnopsychiatrie antillaise.* Paris: L'Harmattan, 1990.

Les problèmes des Antilles et de La Réunion. 22 July 1948.

Lê Thanh Khôi. *Le Vietnam.* Paris: Éditions de Minuit, 1955.

Letoublon, Françoise. "Un cercle d'ébène sur son bras d'ivoire. L'antiquité grecque face au métissage." In *Métissages,* vol. 1, pp. 83–98. Ed. Jean-Claude Carpanin Marimoutou and Jean-Michel Racault. Paris: L'Harmattan, 1992.

Lionnet, Françoise. *Autobiographical Voices: Race, Gender, Self-Portraiture.* Ithaca: Cornell University Press, 1989.

———. *Postcolonial Representations: Women, Literature, Identity.* Ithaca: Cornell University Press, 1995.

Lionnet, Françoise, and Ronnie Scharfman, eds. "Post-Colonial Conditions: Exiles, Migrations, and Nomadisms." *Yale French Studies,* nos. 82–83 (1993).

Lombard, Denys, Catherine Champion, and Henri Chambert-Loir. *Rêver l'Asie: Exotisme et littérature coloniale aux Indes, en Indochine et en Insulinde.* Paris: Editions de l'Ecole des Hautes Etudes en Sciences Sociales, 1993.

Lowe, Lisa. *Critical Terrains: French and British Orientalisms.* Ithaca: Cornell University Press, 1991.

Lubiano, Wahneema. "Black Ladies, Welfare Queens, and State Minstrels: Ideological War by Narrative Means." In *Race-ing, Justice, Engendering Power: Essays on Anita Hill, Clarence Thomas, and the Construction of Social Reality,* ed. Toni Morrison, pp. 323–64. New York: Pantheon Books, 1992.

Ludmerer, Kenneth. *Genetics and American Society: A Historical Approach.* Baltimore: Johns Hopkins University Press, 1972.

Lucas, Raoul, *L'Engagisme indien à La Réunion.* Sainte-Clotilde, Réunion: Les Cahiers du CRI, 1986.

Lüsebrink, Hans-Jürgen. "Métissage, Contours et enjeux d'un concept carrefour dans l'aire francophone." *Études Littéraires: Analyses et Débats* 25, no. 3 (winter 1992–1993): pp. 93–106.

———. "Métissage culturel et société coloniale: Émergence et enjeux d'un débat, de la presse coloniale aux premiers écrivains africains (1935–1947)." In *Métissages,* vol. 1, pp. 109–18. Ed. Jean-Claude Carpanin Marimoutou and Jean-Michel Racault. Paris: L'Harmattan, 1992.

Lyotard, Jean-François. "Notes on Legitimation." *Oxford Literary Review* 9, nos. 1–2 (1987): pp. 106–18.

———. *The Differend: Phrases in Dispute.* Trans. Georges Van Den Abbeele. Theory and History of Literature, vol. 46. Minneapolis: University of Minnesota Press, 1988.

Ly-Tio-Fane Pineo, Huguette. *La Diaspora chinoise dans l'Océan Indien occidental.* Aix en Provence: IHPOM, 1981.

MacCannell, Juliet Flower. *The Regime of the Brother after the Patriarchy.* London: Routledge, 1991.

Makolkin, Anna. *Name, Hero, Icon: Semiotics of Nationalism through Heroic Biography.* New York: Mouton de Gruyter, 1992.

Malleret, Louis. *L'Exotisme indochinois dans la littérature française depuis 1860.* Paris: Larose, 1934.

Manganyi, Chabani. *Being-Black-in-World.* Johannesburg: Spro-Cas/Ravan, 1973.

——. *Treachery and Innocence: Psychology and Racial Differences.* Johannesburg: Ravan, 1991.

Mannoni, Octave. "Ébauche d'une psychologie coloniale: Le complexe de dépendance et la structure de la personnalité." *Psyché* 12 (October 1947): pp. 1229–42, and 13–14 (November–December 1947): pp. 1453–79.

——. "La personalité malgache, Ébauche d'une analyse des structures." *Revue de Psychologie des Peuples* 3 (July 1948): pp. 263–81.

——. "Colonisation et Psychanalyse." *Chemins du Monde,* October 1948, pp. 89–96.

——. *Prospéro et Caliban: Psychologie de la Colonization.* 1949. Paris: Éditions Universitaires, 1984. Trans. Pamela Powesland as *Prospero and Caliban: The Psychology of Colonization.* Ann Arbor: University of Michigan Press, 1990.

——. "The Decolonization of Myself." *Race,* April 1966.

——. "Administration de la folie, folie de l'administration." In *Un commencement qui n'en finit pas: Transfert, interprétation, théorie,* pp. 137–57. Paris: Éditions du Seuil, Champ Freudien, 1980.

Marbeau-Cleirens, Béatrice. *Les mères imaginées: Horreur et vénération.* Paris: Les Belles Lettres, 1988.

Marchat, Jean-Jacques. "Le PCR incontournable aux sénatoriales." *L'Écho,* 24 September 1992, p. 9.

Marimoutou, Jean-Claude Carpanin. "Écrire Métis." In Cahiers CRLH-CIRAOI. *Métissages.* Vol. 1, pp. 247–60. Paris: L'Harmattan, 1991.

——. "Le triste fardeau de l'homme blanc, les colonies désenchantées: Raymond Vergès et le roman colonial." Postface to *Boscot, sous-off. et . . . assassin?* by Jean-Paul Skler, pp. 189–211. Saint-Denis, Réunion: Grand Océan, 1996.

Marimoutou, Michèle. *Les engagés du sucre.* Saint-Denis: Éditions du Tramail, 1989.

Marquet, Jeanne. *Le jaune et le blanc.* Paris: 1927.

Martial, René. "L'immigration et les fous." *Bulletin de l'Académie des Sciences Morales et Politiques* (1932).

———. "Étude de l'aliénation mentale dans ses rapports avec l'immigration." *Hygiène Mentale*, nos. 2–3 (1933).

———. *La race française*. Paris: Mercure de France, 1935.

———. "Race, groupements sanguins et hygiène mentale." *Hygiène Mentale*, no. 8 (1935).

———. "Race et Immigration." *Bulletin de l'Académie des Sciences Morales et Politiques* (1936).

———. "Métissage et Immigration." Paper delivered at the Première réunion des Eugénistes de l'Amérique Latine, 1937.

———. *Race, Hérédité, Folie: Étude d'anthroposociologie appliquée à l'immigration* [Race, Heredity, Madness: Anthroposociological Study Applied to Immigration]. Paris: Mercure de France, 1938.

———. *Les Métis*. Paris: Flammarion, 1942.

Martin, Marie-Madeleine. *Histoire de l'unité française: L'idée de Patrie en France des origines à nos jours*. Paris: PUF, 1982.

Martin, Michel L., and Alain Yacou, eds. *Mourir pour les Antilles. Indépendance Nègre ou esclavage, 1802–1804*. Paris: Éditions Caribbéennes, 1991.

Martinkus-Zemp, Ada. *Le Blanc et Le Noir: Essai d'une description de la vision du Noir par le Blanc dans la littérature française de l'entre-deux guerres*. Paris: A. G. Nizet, 1975.

Marx, Karl. "The Eighteenth Brumaire of Louis Bonaparte." In *Surveys from Exile*, pp. 143–249. New York: Vintage Books, 1974.

———. *Critique of Hegel's Doctrine of the State: Early Writings*. Trans. Rodney Livingstone and Gregor Benton. New York: Vintage Books, 1975.

———. "On the Jewish Question." In *Early Writings*, pp. 212–42. New York: Vintage Books, 1975.

Mathieu, Martine. "Créolisation et Histoire de Famille: Remarques sur les conceptions littéraires réunionnaises." *Études Créoles* 10, no. 1 (1987): pp. 62–71.

Maunier, René. *Sociologie Coloniale: Introduction à l'étude du contact des races*. Paris: Éditions Domat-Montchrestien, 1932. English translation by E. O. Lorimer. *The Sociology of Colonies: An Introduction to the Study of Race Contact*. London: Routledge and Kegan Paul, 1949.

———. *Sociologie Coloniale: Psychologie des expansions*. Paris: Éditions Domat-Montchrestien, 1936.

Maurin, Henri, and Jacques Lentge, eds. *Le Mémorial de La Réunion: La Réunion d'aujourd'hui, 1964–1979*. Vol. 7. Saint-Denis, Réunion: Éditions Australe, 1989.

Mazet, Jacques. *La condition juridique des Métis*. Paris: Domat-Montchrestien, 1932.

M'Bodj, Mamadou. "Aspects de la psychiatrie dans le monde." *Psychopathologie Africaine* 14 (1978).

McClintock, Anne. "The Angels of Progress: Pitfalls of the Term 'Post-Colonialism.'" *Social Text* 10, nos. 2–3 (1992): pp. 84–98.

McCullogh, Jock. *Black Soul, White Artifact: Fanon's Clinical Psychology and Social Theory.* Cambridge: Cambridge University Press, 1983.

——. *Colonial Psychiatry and the "African Mind."* Cambridge: Cambridge University Press, 1995.

Mekhaled, Boucif. *Chroniques d'un massacre: 8 mai 1945. Sétif, Guelma, Kherrata.* Paris: Syros, 1995.

Memmi, Albert. *The Colonizer and the Colonized.* New York: Orion Press, 1965. Originally, *Portrait du Colonisé précédé du Portrait du Colonisateur.* Paris: Buchet-Chastel, 1957.

——. "La vie impossible de Frantz Fanon." *Esprit,* September 1971, pp. 248–73. Translated as "The Impossible Life of Frantz Fanon." *Massachusetts Review* 14, no. 1 (winter 1973): pp. 9–39.

——. *La statue de sel.* 1972. Paris: Folio, 1993.

Mémorial de La Réunion. Vol. 6, pp. 426–27.

Mercer, Kobena. "'Decolonisation and Disappointment: Reading Fanon's Sexual Politics." In *The Fact of Blackness,* ed. Alan Read, pp. 114–65. London: ICA, 1996.

Mesnard, Eric. "Les mouvements de résistance dans les colonies françaises: L'affaire Bissette (1823–1827)." In *Les abolitions de l'esclavage de L. F. Sonthonax à V. Schoelcher, 1793, 1794, 1848,* ed. Marcel Dorigny, pp. 293–97. Paris: Presses Universitaires de Vincennes/Editions UNESCO, 1995.

Meyer, Charles. *Des Français en Indochine, 1860–1900.* Paris: Hachette, 1985.

Meyer, Jean, Jean Tanade, Annie Rey-Goldzeiguer, and Jacques Thobie. *Histoire de la France Coloniale: Des Origines à 1914.* Paris: Armand Colin, 1991.

Miège, Jean-Louis. *Expansion européenne et décolonisation de 1870 à nos jours.* Paris: PUF–Nouvelle Clio, 1973.

Mink, Gwendolyn. *The Wages of Motherhood: Inequality in the Welfare State, 1917–1942.* Ithaca: Cornell University Press, 1995.

Moi, Toril. *Simone de Beauvoir: The Making of an Intellectual Woman.* Cambridge, Mass.: Blackwell, 1994.

Mongia, Padmini. Introduction to *Contemporary Postcolonial Theory.* London: Arnold, 1996.

Montaigne, *Essais* 2.1.3.

Morejón, Nancy. *Nacion y mestizaje en Nicolás Guillen.* Havana: Union, 1982.

Morel, Benedict Augustin. *Traité des Dégénérescences Physiques, Intellectuelles et Morales de l'Espèce Humaine et des Causes qui produisent ces variétés maladives.* Paris: J. B. Baillère, 1857.

Mörner, Magnus. *Le métissage dans l'histoire de l'Amérique Latine.* Paris: Fayard, 1971.

Morrison, Toni. *Playing in the Dark: Whiteness and the Literary Imagination.* Cambridge: Harvard University Press, 1992.

Morrissey, Marietta. *Slave Women in the New World: Gender Stratification in the Caribbean.* Lawrence: University Press of Kansas, 1989.

Moses, Claire. *French Feminism in the Nineteenth Century.* Albany: New York State University Press, 1984.

Mouffe, Chantal. "Feminism, Citizenship, and Radical Democratic Politics." In *Feminists Theorize the Political,* ed. Judith Butler and Joan W. Scott, pp. 369–84. New York: Routledge, 1992.

Mouls, Gérard. "Histoire de l'asile des aliénés de Saint-Paul." M.A. thesis, University of Medicine, Cochin-Port-Royal, 1974.

——. *Études sur la sorcellerie à La Réunion.* Saint-Denis, Réunion: Éditions UDIR, 1982.

Murad, Lion, and Patrick Zylberman. *L'hygiène dans la République: La santé publique en France ou l'utopie contrariée, 1870–1918.* Paris: Fayard, 1996.

Nandy, Ashis. *The Intimate Enemy: Loss and Recovery of Self under Colonialism.* Delhi: Oxford University Press, 1983.

——. *The Savage Freud and Other Essays on Possible and Retrievable Selves.* Princeton: Princeton University Press, 1995.

N'Dumbe III, Alexandre Kum'a. *Hitler voulait l'Afrique: Le projet du 3e. Reich sur le continent africain.* Paris: L'Harmattan, 1980.

——. *Négritude et Germanité: L'Afrique Noire dans la littérature d'expression allemande.* Dakar: Nouvelles Éditions Africaines, 1983.

Nemo, Jacques. *Musulmans de La Réunion.* Saint-Denis, Réunion: ILA, 1983.

Nguyên Xuân Tué. "*Congaï,* une race de femmes annamites, produit de la colonisation." *Reflets Littéraires: Indochine* (1992): pp. 69–77.

Nicholas, Lionel J., and Saths Cooper, eds. *Psychology and Apartheid: Essays on the Struggle for Psychology and the Mind in South Africa.* Johannesburg: Vision/Madiba Publication, 1990.

Nicole, Rose-May. "1838: Louis Timagène Houat: Un proscrit de l'île Bourbon à Paris." *Expressions* 3 (August 1989).

——. "Quelques facettes de la représentation du Noir (1822–1840)." In *Iles et fables. Psychanalyse, Langues et Littérature,* ed. Jean-François Reverzy and Jean-Claude Carpanin Marimoutou, pp. 147–54. Paris: L'Harmattan, 1990.

——. "La partenaire blanche des couples mixtes dans Les Marrons (1844) et dans Eudora (1955)." In *Métissages: Littérature, histoire,* vol. 1, pp. 161–68. Ed. Jean-Claude Carpanin Marimoutou and Jean-Michel Racault. Paris: L'Harmattan, 1992.

——. *Noirs, Cafres, et Créoles. Étude de la représentation du Non-Blanc Réunionnais. Documents et Littératures Réunionnaises, 1710–1980.* Paris: L'Harmattan, 1996.

—— *Laetitia.* Peuples Noirs, peuples africains, n.d.

Norindr, Panivong. *Phantasmatic Indochina: French Colonial Ideology in Architecture, Film, and Literature.* Durham: Duke University Press, 1997.

North-Coombes, Alfred. *La Découverte des Mascareignes par les Arabes et les Portuguais.* Port-Louis, Mauritius: Service Bureau, 1979.

Nunes, Zita. "Anthropology and Race in Brazilian Modernism." In *Colonial Discourse/Postcolonial Theory,* ed. Francis Barker, Peter Hulme, and Margaret Iversen, pp. 115–25. Manchester: Manchester University Press, 1994.

Nye, Robert A. *Crime, Madness, and Politics in Modern France: The Medical Concept of National Decline.* Princeton: Princeton University Press, 1984.

Oeuvres d'Évariste Parny. Vol. 1. 5th song. Paris: Debray, 1838.

Omi, Michael, and Howard Winant. "The Los Angeles 'Race Riot' and Contemporary U.S. Politics." In *Reading Rodney King: Reading Urban Uprising,* pp. 97–114. ed. Robert Gooding-Williams. New York: Routledge, 1993.

Oraison, Marc. *Le Parti Communiste Réunionnais et l'Autonomie Démocratique et Populaire.* Saint-Denis, Réunion: Université de La Réunion, 1978.

Ortigues, Marie-Cécile, and Edmond Ortigues. *Oedipe Africain.* Paris: L'Harmattan, 1984.

Ostheimer, John M. *The Politics of Western Indian Ocean Islands.* New York: Praeger, 1975.

Oswald, Martin. *Autonomia: Its Genesis and Early History.* American Philological Association: Scholars Press, 1982.

Oudin-Bastide, Caroline. "L'assimilation, La stratégie du pouvoir: la lutte des colonies," CARÉ 7 (February 1981): pp. 89–119.

Ozouf, Mona. "Liberté, Égalité, Fraternité." In *Les Lieux de mémoire. III: Les France. 3: De l'archive à l'emblème,* ed. Pierre Nora, pp. 583–629. Paris: Gallimard, 1992.

Parole and Société. *Les oubliés de la décolonisation française,* no. 2 (1973): pp. 204–8.

Parry, Benita. "Problems in Current Theories of Colonial Discourse." *Oxford Literary Review* 9, nos. 1–2 (1987). Reprinted in *The Post-Colonial Studies Reader,* ed. Bill Ashcroft, Gareth Griffiths, and Helen Tiffin, pp. 36–44. London: Routledge, 1995.

Pasquet, Catherine, and René Squarzoni. "Les femmes à La Réunion: Une évolution impressionnante, une situation ambigüe." *Études et synthèses,* no. 1 (1988): p. 35. Observatoire Départemental de La Réunion.

Pastoureau, Michel. "Le coq gaulois." In *Les lieux de mémoire. Les France. De l'archive à l'emblème,* ed. Pierre Nora, pp. 507–39. Paris: Gallimard, 1992.

Pateman, Carole. *The Sexual Contract.* Stanford: Stanford University Press, 1988.

Payet, J. V. *Histoire de l'esclavage à l'île Bourbon.* Paris: L'Harmattan, 1990.

Payet, Monique. "La femme mise en chansons: L'image des femmes à travers quelques ségas réunionnais." In *Figures et Paroles de Femmes, Recueil d'articles parus dans* Témoignages, pp. 15–17. N.d.

Pelletier, Jacques. "La Chaloupe, Ile de La Réunion, une société créole. Stratégies individuelles et hiérarchies des réseaux." Ph.D. diss., École des Hautes Études en Sciences Sociales, Paris, 1983.

Perinbam, B. Marie. "Parrot or Phoenix? Frantz Fanon's View of the West Indian and Algerian Woman." *Journal of Ethnic Studies* 1, no. 2 (summer 1973): pp. 45–55.

——. *Holy Violence. The Revolutionary Thought of Frantz Fanon.* Washington, D.C.: Three Continent Press, 1982.

Perotin, Yves. "Comment on s'habillait au temps de Sarda-Garriga." In *Chroniques de Bourbon,* pp. 197–203. Nerac: Couderc, 1957.

Perrot, Michelle, ed. *L'Impossible prison: Recherches sur le système pénitentiaire au XIXe. siècle.* Paris: Éditions du Seuil, 1980.

Peyras, Jean. "Identités culturelles et métissages ethniques dans l'antiquité." In *Métissages: Littérature, Histoire,* vol. 1, pp. 183–98. Ed. Jean-Claude Carpanin Marimoutou and Jean-Michel Racault. Paris: L'Harmattan, 1992.

Philonenko, Alexis. *La théorie kantienne de l'histoire.* Paris: Vrin, 1986.

Pick, Daniel. *Faces of Degeneration: A European Disorder, c. 1848–c. 1918.* Cambridge: Cambridge University Press, 1989.

Pitkin, Hanna Fenichel. *Fortune Is a Woman: Gender and Politics in the Thought of Niccolò Machiavelli.* Berkeley: University of California Press, 1984.

Poliakov, Léon. *Le Mythe aryen.* Paris: Éditions Complexes, 1987.

Porot, Adolphe. "Notes de psychiatrie musulmane." *Annales Médico-Psychologiques* 1 (1918).

——. "Quelques aspects de l'âme indigène." Paper delivered at Conférence à la Ligue de l'enseignement à Oran, March 1922.

"Postcolonialisme: Décentrement, Déplacement, Dissémination." *Dedale* 5–6 (spring 1997).

Postel, Jacques, *Genèse de la psychiatrie.* Paris: Le Sycomore, 1981.

Potier, Josyane, and René Potier. *Étude anthropologique d'une zone sucrière à La Réunion.* Saint-Denis, Réunion: Université de La Réunion, 1973.

Pratt, Mary Louise. *Imperial Eyes: Travel Writing and Transculturation.* New York: Routledge, 1992.

Price, Richard, ed. *Maroon Societies: Rebel Slave Communities in the Americas.* 3d ed. Baltimore: Johns Hopkins University Press, 1996.

Prudhomme, Claude. *Histoire religieuse de La Réunion.* Paris: Éditions Karthala, 1984.

Psychopathologie Africaine. Sciences Sociales et Psychiatrie en Afrique 25, no. 2 (1993).

Puget, Janine. "État de menace et psychanalyse: De l'étrange structurant à l'étrange aliénant." In *Violence d'État et Psychanalyse,* by Janine Puget et al., pp. 1–40. Paris: Dunod, 1989.

Pujarniscle, Eugène. *Philoxène ou de la littérature coloniale.* Paris: Firmin Didot, 1931.

Rabou, Jean-Louis. "Question de sincérité." *Quotidien,* 3 March 1993, p. 1.

——. "Des méthodes de voyou." *Quotidien de l'Île de La Réunion,* 5 April 1993, p. 3.

Racamier, Paul-Claude. *Le génie des origines: Psychanalyse et psychoses.* Paris: Bibliothèque Scientifique Payot, 1992.

Racault, Jean-Michel. "Pastorale ou 'Dégénération': L'image des populations créoles des Mascareignes à travers les récits de voyages dans la seconde moitié du XVIIIe siècle." In *Révolution française et Océan Indien,* ed. Claude Wanquet and François Julien, pp. 71–81. Paris: L'Harmattan–Université de La Réunion, 1994.

Rainwater, Lee, and William L. Yancey, eds. *The Moynihan Report and the Politics of Controversy.* Cambridge: MIT Press, 1967.

Ramassamy, Albert. "Une décision politique, sage et juste." *JIR,* 22 December 1992, p. 2.

Ramassamy, Ginette. "Syntaxe du Créole Réunionnais: Analyse de corpus d'unilingues créolophones." Ph.D. diss., University of Sorbonne, Paris, 1985.

Rancière, Jacques. "The Image of Brotherhood." *Edinburgh Magazine* 2 (1977). Trans. Kari Hanet.

——. *La nuit des prolétaires.* Paris: Fayard, 1981. English translation by John Driery. Philadelphia: Temple University Press, 1989.

——. *Les mots de l'histoire: Essai de poétique du savoir.* Paris: Seuil, 1992.

——. "Politics, Identification, and Subjectivization." *October* 61 (summer 1992): pp. 58–64.

Randau, Robert. *Le chef des porte-plumes: Roman de la vie coloniale.* Paris: Éditions du monde nouveau, 1922.

Randolph, R. R. "The 'Matrifocal Family' as a Comparative Category." *American Anthropologist* 66, no. 3 (1964): pp. 628–31.

Rank, Otto. *Le mythe de la naissance du héro.* Paris: Payot, 1983.

Régis, Emmanuel, and Henri Reboul, "L'assistance aux aliénés aux colonies." In *Rapport au XXII Congrès des Médecins aliénistes et neurologistes de langue française, Tunis 1–7 avril 1912* (Paris: Masson, 1912).

Renouvier, Charles. *Manuel Républicain de l'Homme et du Citoyen*. Paris: Éditions Garnier Frères, 1981.

Retamar, Roberto Fernández. *Caliban and Other Essays*. Trans. Edward Baker. Minneapolis: University of Minnesota Press, 1989.

Reverzy, Jean-François. "Chronique des transferts insulaires: Esquisse des figures du double dans le monde indoocéanique." *Nouvelle Revue d'Ethnopsychiatrie* 11 (1988): pp. 107–16.

——. "L'Envers du volcan: Études d'anthropologie psychanalytique des positions et des registres du symptome-suicide à l'île de La Réunion." In *L'Espoir Transculturel: Des communautés d'origine aux nouvelles solidarités*. 1988.

Reverzy, Jean-François, ed. *Cultures, Exils et Folies dans l'Océan Indien*. Paris: INSERM, L'Harmattan, 1990.

Reverzy, Jean François, et al. "Suicide et insularité: la réalité réunionnaise." *Psychologie médicale* 19, no. 5 (1987): pp. 623–28.·

——. *Suicide et tentatives de suicide à La Réunion*. Saint-Denis, Réunion: CORI, INSERM, 1989.

Ricón, Lia. "L'autoritarisme dans la société argentine et son rôle dans l'apparition de pathologies graves." In *Violence d'État et Psychanalyse*, ed. Janine Puget et al., pp. 67–85. Paris: Dunod, 1989.

Rivière, Max. "L'île de la Réunion contre le colonialisme." *Étudiants Anticolonialistes,* no. 6 (June 1950).

Robert, Marthe. *Roman des origines et origine du roman*. Paris: Gallimard, 1972.

Robert, Michel. *La Réunion: Combats pour l'Autonomie*. Paris: L'Harmattan, 1976.

Rogin, Michael Paul. *Fathers and Children: Andrew Jackson and the Subjugation of the American Indian*. New York: Vintage Books, 1975.

——. *Subversive Genealogy: The Politics and Art of Herman Melville*. New York: Alfred A. Knopf, 1983.

——. *"Ronald Reagan," the Movie: and Other Episodes in Political Demonology*. Berkeley: University of California Press, 1987.

——. *Blackface, White Noise: Jewish Immigrants in the Hollywood Melting Pot*. Berkeley: University of California Press, 1996.

Róheim, Geza. *Psychanalyse et Anthropology*. Paris: Gallimard, 1967.

——. *Origine et fonction de la culture*. Paris: Gallimard, 1972.

——. *Les portes du rêve*. Paris: Payot, 1973.

——. *La panique des dieux*. Paris: Payot, 1974.

Rohrbach, Julius. *Das neue Deutsche Kolonialreich: Umfang, Aufgaben und Leistungmöglichkeiten*. Berlin: 1940.

Roques, P. L. "1815–1848. La vie politique à Bourbon. Les institutions et les hommes." M.A. thesis, University of Provence, 1972.

Rosenblum, Mort. *Mission to Civilize: The French Way.* San Diego: Harcourt Brace, Jovanovich, 1986.

Ross, Kristin. *The Emergence of Social Space: Rimbaud and the Paris Commune.* Minneapolis: University of Minnesota Press, 1988.

——. *Fast Cars, Clean Bodies, Decolonization and the Reordering of French Culture.* Cambridge, Mass.: MIT Press, 1995.

Roudinesco, Elisabeth. *Histoire de la psychanalyse française, 2. 1925–1985.* Paris: Fayard, 1986.

——. *Jacques Lacan: Esquisse d'une vie, histoire d'un système de pensée.* Paris: Fayard, 1993.

——. "Lectures de *l'Histoire de la folie* (1961–1986)." In *Penser la folie, Essais sur Michel Foucault,* pp. 11–35. Paris: Éditions Galilée, 1992.

Roumeguere, J. Y. *La migration des ressortissants des départements d'outre-mer: Aspect médicaux et psycho-sociologiques.* Nice: IDERIC, 1972.

Rousse, Eugène. "Le bilan de 25 années de Michel Debré à La Réunion dans le domaine des libertés." *Témoignages,* 1989.

——. *Combat des Réunionnais pour la liberté.* Vol. 3. Saint-Denis, Réunion: Éditions CNH, 1994.

Roy, Arundhati. *The God of Small Things.* London: Flamingo, 1997.

Royer, Clémence. *Du groupement des peuples et de l'hégémonie universelle.* Paris, 1877.

Rubin, Gabrielle. *Les sources inconscientes de la misogynie.* Paris: Robert Laffont, 1977.

Russier, Henri, and Henri Brenier. *L'Indochine française.* Paris: Armand Colin, 1911.

Said, Edward. *Orientalism.* London: Routledge and Kegan Paul, 1978.

——. *Culture and Imperialism.* New York: Alfred A. Knopf, 1993.

Saintoyant, J. *La colonisation française pendant la Révolution, 1789–1799.* Paris: 1930.

Sala-Molins, Louis. *Le Code Noir, ou le calvaire de Canaan.* Paris: PUF, 1987.

Salmoral, Manuel Lucena. *Los Códigos Negros de la América Espanola.* Paris: Universidad de Alcalá/Ediciones UNESCO, 1996.

Sambuc, Henri. "Enquête sur la question des métis." *La Revue du Pacifique,* May 1931, pp. 256–72.

——. "Les Métis franco-annamites en Indochine." *La Revue du Pacifique,* April 1931, pp. 194–209.

Sam-Long, Jean-François. *Sorcellerie à La Réunion.* Saint-Denis, Réunion: Anchaing, 1979.

——. *Le roman du marronnage.* Saint-Denis, Réunion: Éditions UDIR, 1990.

——. *Le défi d'un volcan: Faut-il abandonner la France?* Paris: Stock, 1993.

Sarraut, Albert. *La Mise en valeur des colonies françaises.* Paris: Payot, 1923.

Sartre, Jean-Paul. *Réflexions sur la question juive.* Paris: Folio, 1954.

Scherer, André. *Histoire de La Réunion.* Paris: PUF, Que Sais-Je?, 1966.

Schmidt, Nelly. "Aspects des répercussions de la Révolution aux Caraïbes au XIXe siècle: Histoire et mythes en situation coloniale." In *Le XIXe siècle et la Révolution Française,* pp. 281–95. Paris: Éditions Créaphis, 1992.

——. *Victor Schoelcher et l'abolition de l'esclavage.* Paris: Fayard, 1994.

——. *L'engrenage de la Liberté: Caraïbes-XIXe siècle.* Aix en Provence: Publications de l'Université de Provence, 1995.

Schneider, Monique. "Freud entre le mythe et le roman." In Groupe de recherches sur la critique littéraire et les Sciences Humaines, "Le roman familial." *Cahiers de l'Université* 5 (1985): pp. 146–55.

Scott, Joan W. "Experience." In *Feminists Theorize the Political,* ed. Judith Butler and Joan W. Scott, pp. 22–40. New York: Routledge, 1992.

"Secrets de famille et pensée perverse." *Gruppo: Revue de psychanalyse familiale et groupale* 8 (1992).

Senghor, Léopold Sedar. "Le problème culturel en A.O.F." *Le Périscope Africain,* no. 382 (18 September 1937): pp. 1–3, and no. 3 (2 October 1937): p. 3.

Sibony, Daniel. *Écrits sur le racisme.* Paris: Christian Bourgeois Éditeur, 1987.

Simon, Thierry. "La santé à La Réunion de 1900 à nos jours: D'une colonie cachectique à un département presque comblé." Thesis in Medicine, University of Tours, 1990.

Simon-Barouh, Ida. "Identités eurasiennes." *Pluriel* 21 (1980): pp. 69–80.

Simon, Pierre-Jean. "Un village franco-indochinois en Bourbonnais: Aspects de la colonization et de la décolonisation de l'Indochine orientale." Ph.D. diss., University of Lille, France, 1974.

——. "Portraits coloniaux des Vietnamiens (1858–1914)." *Pluriel* 1 (1977): pp. 29–54.

Sissoko, Fily Dabo. "Les noirs et la culture." *Congrès International de l'Évolution culturelle des peuples coloniaux.* Exposition Internationale de Paris, 1937. Rapport et compte-rendus, Paris, 1938, pp. 108–22.

——. "À propos du Congrès de l'Évolution culturelle des peuples coloniaux: Réponse à Ousmane Socé." *Paris-Dakar,* 27 January 1939, pp. 1, 5.

Sker, Jean-Paul. *Boscot, sous-off. et . . . assassin?* Saigon: Imprimerie C. Ardin, 1930. Rept. Saint-Denis, Réunion: Grand Océan, 1996.

Slotkin, Richard. *Regeneration through Violence: The Mythology of the American Frontier, 1600–1860.* Middletown, Conn.: Wesleyan University Press, 1973.

———. *The Fatal Environment: The Myth of the Frontier in the Age of Industrialization, 1800–1890.* Middletown, Conn.: Wesleyan University Press, 1985.

Smith, John David, ed. *Anti-Black Thought, 1863–1925: Racial Determinism and the Fear of Miscegenation.* New York: Garland Publishing, 1993.

Socé, Ousmane. *Mirages de Paris.* 1937. Paris: Nouvelles Latines, 1964.

Solien Gonzalez, N. L. "Toward a Definition of Matrifocality." In *Afro-American Anthropology: Contemporary Perspectives.*

Spillers, Hortense J. "Mama's Baby, Papa's Maybe: An American Grammar Book." *Diacritics* (summer 1987): pp. 65–81.

Spillers, Hortense, ed. *Comparative American Identities: Race, Sex, and Nationality in the Modern Text.* New York: Routledge, 1991.

Stoddard, Lothrop. *The Rising Tide of Color against White World-Supremacy.* New York: Charles Scribner's Sons, 1920.

Stoler, Ann Laura. "Carnal Knowledge and Imperial Power: Gender, Race, and Morality in Colonial Asia." In *Gender at the Crossroads of Knowledge: Feminist Anthropology in the Postmodern Era,* ed. Micaela di Leonardo. Berkeley: University of California Press, 1991.

———. *Race and the Education of Desire: Foucault's History of Sexuality and the Colonial Order of Things.* Durham: Duke University Press, 1995.

Stora, Benjamin. "Passé colonial et représentations françaises de la guerre d'Algérie: le masque de l'universalisme républicain." Communication at the 16th Congress of IPSA, Berlin, August 1994.

Storper-Perez, Danielle. *La folie colonisée.* Paris: François Maspéro, 1974.

Swain, Gladys. *Le Sujet de la folie: Naissance de la psychiatrie.* Toulouse: Privat, 1977.

———. *Dialogue avec l'insensé.* Paris: Gallimard, 1994.

Szasz, Thomas S. "The Negro in Psychiatry: An Historical Note on Psychiatric Rhetoric." *American Journal of Psychotherapy* 25, no. 2 (1971): pp. 469–71.

———. "The Sane Slave: An Historical Note on the Use of Medical Diagnosis as Justificatory Rhetoric." *American Journal of Psychotherapy* 25, no. 2 (1971): pp. 469–71.

Tableau Économique de La Réunion: Édition 93/94. Saint-Denis, Réunion: INSEE, Région Réunion, 1994.

Taboulet, Georges. *La Geste française en Indochine: Histoire par les textes de la France en Indochine des origines à 1914.* Vol. 1. Paris: Adrien Maisonneuve, 1955.

Taguieff, Pierre-André. "Doctrines de la race et hantise du métissage." *Nouvelle Revue d'Ethnopsychiatrie* 17 (1991): pp. 53–100.

Tal, Isabelle. *Les Réunionnais en France.* Paris: Éditions Entente, 1975.

Tardieu, Jean. *Lettre de Hanoï.* Paris: Gallimard, 1997.

Técher, Karine, and Mario Serviable. *Histoire de la presse à La Réunion.* Saint-Denis: ARS Terres Créoles/URAD, 1991.

Thetiot, Gabrielle. "'Dangereux pour l'ordre public,' Les malades mentaux à La Réunion, 1849–1912." M.A. thesis, University of Réunion, 1987.

Theweleit, Klaus. *Male Fantasies: Women, Floods, Bodies, History.* Trans. Stephen Conway. Minneapolis: University of Minnesota Press, 1987.

Thiebaut, Evelyne, and Frank Waserhole. "La Violence à l'île de La Réunion: Criminalité et interculture créole." CES of psychiatry, University of Grenoble, 1982.

Thomas, Alexander, and Samuel Sillen. *Racism and Psychiatry.* New York: Brunner/Mazel, 1972.

Thompson, Virginia. *French Indo-China.* New York: Macmillan, 1942.

Thornton, Russell. *American Indian Holocaust and Survival: A Population History since 1492.* Norman: University of Oklahoma Press, 1987.

Thoung Vuong-Riddick. "La Découverte de l'Indochine et des Indochinois." In *Reflets Littéraires: Indochine,* pp. 27–33. 1992.

Todorov, Tzvetan. *On Human Diversity, Nationalism, Racism, and Exoticism in French Thought.* Trans. Catherine Porter. Cambridge: Harvard University Press, 1993. Originally *Nous et les autres.* Paris: Éditions du Seuil, 1989.

——. *Benjamin Constant, la passion démocratique.* Paris: Hachette, 1997.

Torok, Maria, and Nicholas Rand. "Reading *The Sandman.*" In *Speculations after Freud: Psychoanalysis, Philosophy, and Culture,* ed. Sony Shamdasani and Michael Münchow. London: Routledge, 1994.

Toumson, Roger, and Simonne Henry-Valmore. *Aimé Césaire, le nègre inconsolé.* Paris: Syros, 1994.

Toussaint, Auguste. *Histoire des Îles Mascareignes.* Paris: Berger-Levraut, 1972.

"Une visite à René Maran." *Le Paria* (20 November 1923): p. 2.

Vacher de Lapouge, Georges. *Race et milieu social.* Paris: Marcel Rivière, 1909.

Vergès, Françoise. "Merveilles de la prise de possession." In *L'Insularité: Thématiques et Représentations,* ed. Jean-Claude Marimoutou and Jean-Michel Racault, pp. 213–22. Paris: Université de La Réunion/L'Harmattan, 1995.

——. "Chains of Madness, Chains of Colonialism: Fanon and Freedom." In *The Fact of Blackness: Frantz Fanon and Visual Representation,* ed. Alan Read, pp. 46–75. London: ICA, 1996.

——. "To Cure and to Free: The Fanonian Project of Decolonized Psychiatry." In *Fanon: A Critical Reader,* ed. Lewis R. Gordon, T. Denean Sharpley-Whiting, and Renée T. White, pp. 85–99. Oxford, U.K.: Blackwell, 1996.

——. "Creole Skin, Black Mask: Fanon and Disavowal." *Critical Inquiry* 23, no. 3 (spring 1997): pp. 578–95.

——. "Une citoyenneté paradoxale: Affranchis, Colonisés et citoyens des Vieilles Colonies." In *L'abolition de l'esclavage,* pp. 17–44. Brussels: Éditions Complexe, 1998.

——. "I Am Not the Slave of Slavery: The Politics of Reparation in (French) Postcolonies." In *Frantz Fanon: Critical Perspectives,* ed. Anthony Alessandrini. New York, Routledge, forthcoming.

Vergès, Jacques. "La lutte des étudiants créoles." *Étudiants Anticolonialistes,* no. 6 (June 1950).

——. *De la Stratégie judiciaire.* 3d ed. Paris: Éditions de Minuit, 1981.

Vergès, Paul. *Les départements d'Outre-Mer face au choc de 1992: Débat au Parlement Européen et annexes.* Parlement Européen, 1992.

——. *D'une île au monde: Entretiens avec Brigitte Croisier.* Paris: L'Harmattan, 1993.

Vergès, Raymond. "Les Grands Jours de la Révolution Chinoise." *La Vie* 1 (February 1912): p. 24.

——. "Le caoutchouc en Cochinchine." *La Vie* 3 (March 1912): p. 87.

——. "Le choc des races de Charles Géniaux." *La Vie* 4 (March 1912): pp. 120–21.

——. "La matinée des Sciences et des Arts." *Le Peuple,* 1 October 1928, p. 1.

——. "Causerie faite par le Citoyen le 16 Octobre 1932 à la Section de Saint-Denis." Ligue des Droits de l'Homme et du Citoyen. Saint-Denis, Réunion: Imprimerie Industrielle, H. Vavasseur, 1932.

——. "L'action médicale de la France aux Colonies." In *La Réunion vous parle: Semaine de la France d'Outre-Mer à l'Île de la Réunion, 15–21 Juillet 1941,* pp. 136–51. Saint-Denis, Réunion: 1941.

Vigier, Philippe. "La recomposition du mouvement abolitioniste français sous la monarchie de Juillet." In *Les abolitions de l'esclavage,* ed. Marcel Dorigny, pp. 285–91. Paris: Presses Universitaires de Vincennes et Éditions UNESCO, 1995.

Vignar, Marcelo N. "Violence sociale et réalité dans l'analyse." In *Violence d'État et Psychanalyse,* by Janine Puget et al., pp. 41–66. Paris: Dunod, 1989.

Vigouroux, François. *Le secret de famille.* Paris: PUF, 1993.

Virapoullé, Jean-Paul. "Le PCR a manipulé les jeunes!" *Quotidien de l'île de La Réunion,* 1 March 1993, p. 7.

Volsy Focard. *Dix-huit mois de République à l'île Bourbon, 1848–1849.* Saint-Denis, Réunion: 1863.

Vovelle, Michel, ed. *La Révolution Française: Images et Récits.* Vol. 2, *Octobre 1789–Septembre 1791.* Paris: Messidor, 1986.

——. *Les Images de la Révolution française.* Paris: Publications de la Sorbonne, 1988.

Voyages de Vasco da Gama: Relations des expéditions de 1497–1499 et 1502–1503. Paris: Editions Chandeigne, 1995.

Vu Trong Phung. *Ky nghê lây Tây* [Job: Marrying a European]. Hanoi: Édition Phuong Dông, 1936. Reedited, Hanoi: Nhà xuât ban, 1989.

Wahnich, Sophie. *L'impossible citoyen: L'étranger dans le discours de la Révolution française.* Paris: Albin Michel, 1997.

Walker Bynum, Caroline. "'The Body of Christ in the Later Middle Ages': A Reply to Leo Steinberg." *Renaissance Quarterly,* 39 (1986): pp. 399–439.

Walter, Richard D. "What Became of the Degenerate? A Brief History of a Concept." *Journal of the History of Medicine and the Allied Sciences* 2 (1956): pp. 422–29.

Wanquet, Claude. "Les débuts de la Franc-Maçonnerie à La Réunion." In *Problèmes religieux et minorités en Océan Indien,* pp. 30–44. Aix-en-Provence: IHPOM, 1981.

——. *Histoire d'une révolution: La Réunion, 1789–1803.* 4 vols. Marseille: Jeanne Laffitte, 1984.

——. "Révolution Française et Identité Réunionnaise." *Revue française d'histoire d'outre-mer* 282–83 (1989): pp. 35–74.

——. *La France et la première abolition de l'esclavage, 1794–1802.* Paris: Karthala, 1998.

Wanquet, Claude, ed. *Fragments pour une histoire des économies et sociétés de plantation à La Réunion.* Saint-Denis, Réunion: Publications de l'Université de La Réunion, 1989.

Wanquet, Claude, and François Julien, eds. *Révolution française et Océan Indien: Prémices, paroxysmes, héritages et déviances.* Paris: Université de La Réunion/L'Harmattan, 1994.

Washington, Elsie B. "Talk with Toni Morrison." In *Conversations with Toni Morrison,* ed. by Danille Taylor-Guthrie, Jackson: University Press of Mississippi, 1994. pp. 234–38.

Weber, Albert. *L'Émigration réunionnaise en France.* Paris: L'Harmattan, 1994.

Weber, Eugen. *Peasants into Frenchmen: The Modernization of Rural France, 1870–1914.* Stanford, Calif.: Stanford University Press, 1976.

Weber, Jacques. "L'Émigration indienne des comptoirs, 1828–1861." In *Migrations, minorités et échanges en Océan Indien, XIXe–XXe siècles.* Aix-en-Provence: IHPOM, 1979.

Werth, Léon. *Cochinchine: Voyage.* Paris: Viviane Hamy, 1997.

Wild, Herbert. *L'autre race.* Paris: Albin Michel, 1930.

Winnicott, Donald W. "The Capacity to Be Alone." In *Collected Papers: Through Pediatrics to Psycho-Analysis.* London: Tavistock, 1971.

——. "Discussions of War Aims." In *Home Is Where We Start From: Essays by a Psychoanalyst,* ed. Clare Winnicott, Ray Shepherd, and Madelaine Davies, pp. 210–20. New York: W. W. Norton, 1986.

——. "Psychoanalysis and Science: Friends or Relations?" In *Home Is Where We Start From,* pp. 13–18.

Wolf, Eliane. *Quartiers de Vie: Approche ethnologique des populations défavorisées de l'île de La Réunion.* Saint-Denis, Réunion: CIIRF, ARCA, 1989.

Wong-Hee-Kam, Edith. *La diaspora chinoise aux Mascareignes: Le cas de La Réunion.* Paris: Université de La Réunion, L'Harmattan, 1996.

Woodhull, Winifred. *Transfigurations of the Maghred: Feminism, Decolonization, and Literatures.* Minneapolis: University of Minnesota Press, 1993.

Xiaomei Chen. *Occidentalism: A Theory of Counter-Discourse in Post-Mao China.* New York: Oxford University Press, 1995.

Xiberras, Georges. "La mère et l'enfant." In *L'enfant réunionnais et son milieu.* Saint-Denis, Réunion: CDDP-CREAI, 1979.

Young, Lola. "Missing Persons: Fantasizing Black Women in *Black Skin, White Masks.*" In *The Fact of Blackness,* pp. 102–13.

Zimra, Clarisse. "A Woman's Place: Cross-Sexual Perceptions in Race Relations: The Case of Mayotte Capecia and Abdoulaye Sadji." *Folio,* August 1978, pp. 174–92.

Index

Françoise Vergès is a Lecturer at the University of Sussex, United Kingdom. She has written for a number of publications on issues of colonial and postcolonial psychiatry, slavery, techniques of discipline in the colony, and discourses of emancipation.

Library of Congress Cataloging-in-Publication Data

Vergès, Françoise.
Monsters and revolutionaries : colonial family romance and métissage / Françoise Vergès.
p.   cm.
Includes bibliographical references and index.
ISBN 0-8223-2262-5 (cloth : alk. paper). —
ISBN 0-8223-2294-3 (paper : alk. paper)
1. Réunion—History—1764–1946.   2. Réunion—Race relations.
3. Ethnopsychology—Réunion—History.   4. Acculturation—Réunion—
History.   5. Racially mixed people—Réunion—History.   6. France—
Colonies—Administration.   7. France—Colonies—Race relations.
8. Ethnopsychology—France—History.   I. Title.
DI469.R45V47   1999
969'.8102—dc21   98-39781